New Directions in Jewish American and Holocaust Literatures

SUNY SERIES IN CONTEMPORARY JEWISH LITERATURE AND CULTURE

Ezra Cappell, editor

Dan Shiffman, *College Bound:
The Pursuit of Education in Jewish American Literature, 1896–1944*

Eric J. Sundquist, editor, *Writing in Witness: A Holocaust Reader*

Noam Pines, *The Infrahuman: Animality in Modern Jewish Literature*

Oded Nir, *Signatures of Struggle:
The Figuration of Collectivity in Israeli Fiction*

Zohar Weiman-Kelman, *Queer Expectations:
A Genealogy of Jewish Women's Poetry*

Richard J. Fein, translator, *The Full Pomegranate:
Poems of Avrom Sutzkever*

Victoria Aarons and Holli Levitsky, *New Directions in Jewish American
and Holocaust Literatures: Reading and Teaching*

New Directions in Jewish American and Holocaust Literatures
Reading and Teaching

Edited by

Victoria Aarons and Holli Levitsky

Published by State University of New York Press, Albany

© 2019 State University of New York

All rights reserved

No part of this book may be used or reproduced in any manner whatsoever without written permission. No part of this book may be stored in a retrieval system or transmitted in any form or by any means including electronic, electrostatic, magnetic tape, mechanical, photocopying, recording, or otherwise without the prior permission in writing of the publisher.

For information, contact State University of New York Press, Albany, NY
www.sunypress.edu

Library of Congress Cataloging-in-Publication Data

Names: Aarons, Victoria, editor. | Levitsky, Holli, editor.
Title: New directions in Jewish American and Holocaust literatures : reading and teaching / edited by Victoria Aarons and Holli Levitsky.
Description: Albany : State University of New York Press, [2019] | Series: SUNY series in contemporary Jewish literature and culture | Includes bibliographical references and index.
Identifiers: LCCN 2018017080 | ISBN 9781438473192 (hardcover) | ISBN 9781438473185 (pbk.) | ISBN 9781438473208 (ebook)
Subjects: LCSH: American literature—Jewish authors—History and criticism. | Holocaust, Jewish (1939–1945), in literature.
Classification: LCC PS153.J4 N497 2019 | DDC 810.9/8924—dc23
LC record available at https://lccn.loc.gov/2018017080

10 9 8 7 6 5 4 3 2 1

*For Deborah Plutzik Briggs and Jonathan Plutzik
and in memory of Hyam Plutzik (1911–1962)*

Contents

INTRODUCTION   1
    Holli Levitsky

PART I
READING

CHAPTER 1
Black Milk: A Holocaust Metaphor   21
    Eric J. Sundquist

CHAPTER 2
The American Voices of Hidden Child Survivors: Coming of
Age Out of Time and Place   47
    Phyllis Lassner

CHAPTER 3
Reimagining History: Joe Kubert's Graphic Novel of the
Warsaw Ghetto Uprising   69
    Victoria Aarons

CHAPTER 4
Alternate Jewish History: Philip Roth's *The Plot Against America*
and Michael Chabon's *The Yiddish Policemen's Union*   85
    Andrew M. Gordon

CHAPTER 5
Reading the Shema: Jewish Literature as World Literature   103
    Naomi B. Sokoloff

CHAPTER 6
The "Story Without an Ending": Art, Midrash, and History in
Dara Horn's *The World to Come*   119
    Sandor Goodhart

CHAPTER 7
Midrash and Social Justice   139
    Sol Neely

PART II
TEACHING

CHAPTER 8
The Midrashic Legacy   167
    Monica Osborne

CHAPTER 9
Anne Frank, Figuration, and the Ethical Imperative   183
    Aimee Pozorski

CHAPTER 10
Nathan Englander's "Anne Frank" and the Future of Jewish America   205
    Hilene Flanzbaum

CHAPTER 11
Narrating the Past in a Different Language: Teaching the Holocaust through Third-Generation Fiction   223
    Jessica Lang

CHAPTER 12
A Complicated Curriculum: Teaching Holocaust Empathy and Distance to Nontraditional Students   241
    Jeffrey Scott Demsky and N. Ann Rider

CHAPTER 13
Teaching Jewish American Literature in a Spanish Context   267
    Gustavo Sánchez Canales

CHAPTER 14
Teaching William Styron's *Sophie's Choice*: Understanding the
Holocaust   285
    Zygmunt Mazur

CHAPTER 15
"A novel that dare not speak its name": Biographical Approaches
to Saul Bellow   301
    Judie Newman

CONTRIBUTORS   321

INDEX   327

Introduction

Holli Levitsky

What does it mean to read, and to teach, Jewish American and Holocaust literatures in the early twenty-first century? Have the post-millennium decades revealed new creative and critical directions toward these related fields? These are questions to which the editors of and contributors to this volume have given considerable thought, and which were first given shape in the 2004 collection that preceded this volume, *Jewish American and Holocaust Literature: Representation in the Postmodern World*, edited by Alan L. Berger and Gloria L. Cronin. Their project was to identify the nature of Jewish American and Holocaust literatures at the turning point of the new millennium. "New beginnings always occasion reflection on the past," the editors write, and, indeed, their collection examines recurring tensions between modernity and tradition, secularity and religion, formlessness and formality. The chapters look back on the twentieth century, chronicling the shifting moments in the development of Jewish American literature at a critical juncture in history.

What our book shares with the earlier volume is that Jewish American literature continues to reshape itself as it responds to the cultural, social, and political climate of a mutating American ethos. So, too, this current volume shares the premise that Jewish American writing, as we move further away from the catastrophic rupture of the Second World War, is returning to the Holocaust. How do the genres of Jewish American and Holocaust literatures intersect? How do we talk about the Holocaust in the twenty-first century? What are the forms of Holocaust expression at this moment in history? The distinguished scholars included in this volume, writing in a wide range of areas of scholarly interest, have implicitly and explicitly engaged these and other pertinent questions in the field.

Those elements linking Jewish American and Holocaust literatures that were identified in the 2004 collection have become increasingly emphatic in 2018, a time that will witness the coming end of survivor testimony. The sheer number of published young Jewish American writers who are returning to the subject of the Holocaust speaks to the renewed energy in this field as well as to innovative genres and forms of representation. Jewish American and Holocaust literatures are experiencing a renewal, as was predicted in 2004. Authors are producing novels and story collections that reflect a powerful blending of deeply human, national, and historical concerns resulting from this late post-Holocaust state. Jewish American and Holocaust literatures have become increasingly intertwined. The result of our current cultural and historical context is the blending and blurring of distinctions among genres.

With the prominence of Jewish American authors writing about the Holocaust—such as Nathan Englander, Michael Chabon, Jonathan Safran Foer, Nicole Krauss, Julie Orringer, Dara Horn, and others—nontraditional forms such as the testimonial, diary, midrash, and graphic memoir are blurred in an attempt to express the traumatic impact of the past. We identify Jewish American writing as emerging both from writers who write *in* the United States and writers who write *of* the United States. Holocaust literature has become transnational—or perhaps it always was. These ways of talking about Jewish American and Holocaust literatures reflect the state of literature generally, where disciplinary fields now appear to move across continents, oceans, and regions, rather than being defined singularly by national and other categorical boundaries.

Our current thinking and discussions have been reshaped even more recently by emerging third-generation novelists and writers who focus increasingly on the Holocaust in terms of Jewish American identity. This volume uniquely emphasizes those third-generation voices, whose increased distance from the events perhaps accounts for not just their renewed interest in the subject, but also the possible pervasiveness of the topic of the Holocaust across contemporary literary works.

We have loosely divided this volume into two sections: "Reading" and "Teaching." We have done so to indicate the focus on the direction of the field as it reflects on the range of possibilities for thinking about American Jewish and Holocaust literatures. Of course, these directions overlap. Reflection on the teaching and reading practices in Jewish American and Holocaust literatures in the early decades of the twenty-first century offers us an opportunity to step back to an earlier time. How do we account for the continued popularity of both genres? What do we take with us into the twenty-first-century classroom? What do we create anew? This current volume speaks to a renewed interest in the direction that Jewish American and Holocaust literary expression has taken—its range, its focus, and its emphasis—which stems in part from the evolution of our own scholarship and teaching over the past several decades, but, also and even more relevant to the chapters contained in this volume, from specific concerns presented in the twenty-first-century classroom.

Discussions—scholarly and imaginative—concerning Jewish American and Holocaust literatures have, during the course of the past century, moved in largely unanticipated ways. Arguably, Jewish American literature, and thus the scholarly imprint on, might be said to reflect, if not distinct, then markedly recognizable, movements: the urban literature and landscape of the immigrant and the antinomies of loss and gain, present and past, hope and regret (the study of writers such as Anzia Yezierska, Mary Antin, Abraham Cahan, et al.); the influence of Yiddish on American culture (I. B. Singer as Yiddish literary "spokesperson"); the rise of a postwar Jewish American voice shaped by its ironic self-assessment as well as its critical gaze on a developing American ethos against the weight of Jewish history (most notably the hegemonic trio of Saul Bellow, Bernard Malamud, and Philip Roth, despite the obvious differences in their signature authorial styles); the evolving response to the Holocaust in the decades following the aftermath of genocide (what might be considered the "first" American Jewish Holocaust novel, *The Pawnbroker*, by Edward Lewis Wallant, for example); a scholarly move toward and awareness of a gendered Jewish American presence, and its attention to and "rediscovery" of women writers (for example, Grace Paley, Tillie Olsen, Hortense Calisher, and others); and, to be sure, periods reflecting responses to political, historical, cultural, and ideological movements and preoccupations, such as psychoanalysis, Marxism, and modernism, defining periods and points of departure and change. And while Jewish American and Holocaust writing might be said to morph from distinct periods, certainly in the later decades of the twentieth century and early decades of the twenty-first, such defining markers no longer distinguish contemporary Jewish American writing. Rather, the lack of such defining markers has itself become a marker. In an era of massive global immigration and the ability to hybridize (or "hyphenate") identity, a Jewish American writer can be also Guatemalan or French; write in English and Russian; and identify racial, social, sexual, or other identity markers along with his or her Jewish identity.

The years surrounding the twenty-first century have seen new directions and new forms of expression in Jewish American literature, both in the invention of narratives and in the methodologies and discursive approaches taken toward these texts. The variations in and transformations of Jewish American and Holocaust literatures should be considered anew, especially as a measure of what has transpired in the four decades since Irving Howe's oft-recited and disquieting prediction in the 1977 introduction to his edited collection *Jewish American Stories* of the "end" of Jewish American writing. Howe's concern, shared, we suspect, by other literary critics of his generation, was that an identifiable body of literature shaped by "a distinctive sensibility and style derived from the Jewish experience in this country" was no longer viable, especially given the distance—geographical, emotional, familial, conceptual—between a Jewish past and contemporary American life (16). New generations of American Jews, Howe thus proposed, necessarily "must suffer a depletion of resources, a thinning-out of materials and memories," resulting in the absence of a consanguineous "felt life," the kind of "shared experience" that might, but for the accidents of birth, have "enable[d] a new outburst of writing about American Jews" (16). Howe's concern, all these many years later, might be thought of as parochial, insular in its limiting definition of identity, caught up, too, in diasporic fears of attenuation, of diminishing returns.

While Howe's forewarning has proven mistaken, such anxieties, however, are not to be taken lightly; contemporary Jewish American writing engages issues of Jewish history and culture. The signifier "Jewish American" has taken on an extended definition, including writers whose origins of birth were, in many instances, elsewhere. In some ways, perhaps, we are witnessing once again a literature born from the intersection of cultures, not entirely unlike the writing produced by the early twentieth-century immigrants. The early decades of the twenty-first century feature Jewish writers from around the globe who find themselves relocated in the United States, writers (from places as diverse as Israel, Canada, Russia, Latvia, South Africa, and South America) who reside in North America, one of the epicenters of Jewish literary expression. As the editors of *The New Diaspora: The Changing Landscape of American Jewish Fiction* suggest, these writers "are part of a larger global movement, and their literature reflects both their commonality with other cultures and their distinctive history" (11). Set against this diasporic influx of voices, it is not surprising to find writers who come from both religious and secular backgrounds returning to ancient texts whose landscapes define new and often unpredictable possibilities. As Morris Dickstein puts it, "The vigorous renewal of Jewish-American writing today remains a genuine surprise. The very assimilation that was thought to have thinned out its material and toned down its voice has instead given impetus to new ways of being Jewish and of writing about it." For Dickstein, new generations of Jewish American writers "work out of an embarrassment of choice" (5).

Thus, the individual chapters that follow hope to suggest the ways in which our thinking and discussions have been shaped and reshaped by the literature of Jewish cultural thought and life. As creative writers have reimagined Jewish history and culture through a contemporary lens, the mingling of Jewish American and Holocaust literature emerged as a necessary reflection—or refraction—of the continued specter of the Holocaust. As suggested earlier, we are nearing a time in which survivor testimony will come to an end. Still, the Holocaust continues to surface as the persistent phantasm of Jewish history, agitating the imagination of the creative writer in new and unexpected ways. In this way, the evaluative measures, methods, and directions that have emerged provide a disciplinary barometer, gauging the value and perspectives of both new and seasoned authors and their works, as well as forecasting the interest of students, teachers, and scholars. Many of the approaches taken in these chapters originated in presentations, nascent ideas, and ruminations over the past several years at the annual disciplinary Jewish American and Holocaust Literature Symposium. Over two decades since its founding as a subsection of the American Literature Association, the symposium's participants have helped to build a scholarly field while providing the foundation for the dissemination of its most important new thinking. In its maturity, this field has much to offer to students; the insights and strategies collected over the years have given us numerous opportunities to enhance existing courses, create new courses, and develop new classroom practices. As a result, we offer here some of the shared pedagogical practices developed by scholars and teachers in the field of American Jewish and Holocaust studies.

The individual chapters included in this volume examine varied and overlapping approaches to reading and teaching and suggest ways of engaging students in the classroom with cultural, religious, historical, and other aspects of Jewish American and Holocaust literatures. This rich and complex body of literature requires a diversity of views, points of departure, and points of return. These include a focus on individual authors' works, on the application of theoretically based methods for reading, on evolving patterns in Jewish American literature, and on historical and contemporary approaches to the Holocaust. The chapters contained herein present a close look at how religion, culture, history, and pedagogy interact in the classroom to help students better understand the complexity of works by the cultural groups who write them and whose lives are depicted within them. Given the space limitations, the editors of this volume were faced with many difficulties in narrowing and selecting topics and scholars to be included, not in the least because of the number of thought-provoking, challenging, and inspiring presentations given at the symposium over the course of its history. We have attempted to gather a sampling of topics that both demonstrate distinctive emphases and show their intersection, ever conscious of including topics that we thought might be of interest to those of us in the field, but also those that reflect a range of contemporary approaches to teaching Jewish American and Holocaust literatures in order to demonstrate the place of this body of literature in the twenty-first century.

Reluctantly, then, we were forced to leave out some of the important work that has enriched our field, but we hope that the chapters in this volume might themselves spark openings for further deliberation, discussion, and lively disputation. We hope, too, that this collection, in drawing on a variety of approaches, disciplines, and perspectives, will suggest the range of expression through which narratives of Jewish life in the United States as well as the complexities surrounding discussions of the Holocaust might be transmitted not only to a contemporary generation of college-aged students who are coming to this literature for the first time, but also to those for whom such familiar texts might be opened up in new and exciting ways.

In shaping the volume, two kinds of essays emerged, and we grouped them accordingly: those that address texts and issues relevant to the field of Jewish studies and those that offer approaches to teaching individual texts. Thus we move from more general studies to more direct pedagogical methods. We intentionally asked our contributors, leaders in the field of Jewish studies, to define the directions they find most relevant to contemporary perspectives in Jewish American and Holocaust literatures. So, too, we hoped that we could draw on the expertise of our contributors in developing new work that might be suggestive of the future direction for the field. One of the first trends we noticed in many of our contributors' chapters was a focus on the value of teaching third-generation Holocaust literature. All the while cognizant of the complexities in teaching such challenging material, especially for an audience increasingly distanced—emotionally, intellectually, geographically, and temporally—from the Holocaust, the chapters that take on the challenge of this subject present here a wealth of possible directions in terms of genre and approach.

Unlike the earlier volume, this collection brings more recent critical approaches to the field. While many of the essays draw on cultural studies generally, the volume includes chapters that cross the terrains of literary formalism, historicism, and exegetical reading. They expose an increased emphasis on Holocaust aesthetics, a broadening of the geographical boundaries for the field, and the value of a pedagogy of "conversations" among literary works both near and disparate for twenty-first-century students. No one particular focus overrides the volume, as is the case with the discipline at large.

As a way of introducing our twin foci on Jewish American and Holocaust literatures as well as on critical approaches to such writing, we have grouped the chapters in pairs and clusters. We begin our collection with the section on reading. Chapters 1 and 2 share an emphasis on both aesthetics and history, and in their introductions to differing genre, contextual background, and approach thus lay the groundwork for the chapters that follow. We open with Eric Sundquist's important essay on Holocaust tropes, "Black Milk: A Holocaust Metaphor." Here Sundquist shows that the literary expression of the Holocaust is pervaded by figures of speech that reenact silence. In a close reading of representative texts such as Cynthia Ozick's short story "The Shawl" and Paul Celan's poem "Todesfuge" ("Deathfugue"), Sundquist makes claims for a genre of Holocaust writing in which silence is invoked through the language of trauma. Set against the backdrop of the Final Solution, Sundquist's argument shows "that only language stretched to the boundaries of meaning may be capable of rendering experiences that are themselves at the limits of existence." Significantly, this chapter raises the terms and structures for our further discussion of Holocaust representation in showing the articulation of a collective voice of despair. Similarly, in chapter 2, Phyllis Lassner examines both historical and aesthetic limits in the narratives of children who survived the Holocaust. In "The American Voices of Hidden Child Survivors: Coming of Age Out of Time and Place," Lassner introduces autobiographical stories of hidden children who ultimately immigrated to the United States. Lassner suggests the ways in which such narratives of loss and survival "express the displacement from identity, language, and home" experienced by child survivors and the persistence of such anxieties and defining markers long after their relocation and reinvented lives. In framing her chapter, Lassner raises the following question crucial to the study of hidden children during the Holocaust: "How do we situate, analyze, and teach the thematic and narrative contributions of hidden child writing and art to American Jewish culture?"

The twentieth century was monumental for Jewish history, with the massive immigration from Eastern Europe and the rise of American Jewry, the European Holocaust, and the creation of the State of Israel. In the course of that century, as the Jews struggled to survive and prosper, they repeatedly had to reinvent themselves. With memory as the controlling trope, graphic novelists and illustrators, through the juxtaposition of text and image, extend the narrative of the Holocaust into the present. In re-creating moments of traumatic rupture, dislocation, and disequilibrium—the primary tropes of Holocaust representation—such graphic narratives contribute to the evolving field of Holocaust representation by establishing a visual testimony to memory. As we find in chapter 3, "Reimagining History: Joe Kubert's Graphic Novel of the Warsaw Ghetto Uprising," the interplay of text and image lends itself to the midrashic imperative of Holocaust testimony, giving voice to unrecoverable loss. Victoria Aarons's examination of Joe Kubert's 2003 graphic narrative of the Warsaw Ghetto Uprising, *Yossel, April 19, 1943*, reveals the ways in which the intersection of text and image hope to reenact the trauma of the particular historical rupture. In her chapter, Aarons shows the blurring of genres characteristic of Holocaust literature. History here, Aarons suggests, becomes narrative, an extension of the traumatic moment, thus bridging the gap between distance and proximity. Against the backdrop of the Warsaw Ghetto Uprising, Kubert creates an alternate history, constructing a "might have been" narrative in which he imagines himself as someone he might have become save for the accidents of history. The graphic novel becomes, in this instance, as Aarons shows, a meditation on loss.

As Philip Roth writes, the Jews were "created and undone a hundred times over" in the twentieth century ("Imagining Jews" 246). In chapter 4, "Alternate Jewish History: Philip Roth's *The Plot Against America* and Michael Chabon's *The Yiddish Policemen's Union*," Andrew Gordon examines the counterfactual novel or alternate history as a subgenre of fantasy and science fiction, a means of speculating on and reconceiving history. Both novels reimagine twentieth-century Jewish history, showing both the imaginative power of fiction and the contingent nature of history. In *The Plot Against America* (2004), Roth, imitating a memoir, tweaks the American involvement in World War II to imagine a United States sliding toward fascism and a potential American holocaust for the Jews. In *The Yiddish Policemen's Union* (2007), Chabon, imitating the hard-boiled detective novel, invents a post-Holocaust Jewish state, not in Israel but in Alaska. In their form and content, they offer profound commentaries on the fluidity of history while highlighting the special relationship of the Jews to history, past, present, and future. "Strange times to be a Jew" is the repeated refrain of the characters in *The Yiddish Policemen's Union*; the implication of both novels is that, throughout history, it has always been, and continues to be, strange times to be a Jew.

How do we extend our understanding of Jewish history, identity, and thought beyond the notion that Jews have a special relationship with history? Chapters 5, 6, and 7 all share roots in religious Judaic hermeneutic practices, returning our focus to the text. In chapter 5, "Reading the Shema through Modern Poetry: Jewish Literature as World Literature," Naomi Sokoloff engages the focus of this volume by examining the ways in which the Shema, Judaism's basic declaration of monotheistic belief, can be used as a bridge connecting ancient Jewish writing with contemporary world writing. By examining modern poems that draw on and respond to the Shema, students can learn how recent literary works revisit and reconsider traditional sources and how, in the process, writers across languages and geographical boundaries enter into a kind of conversation with one another. Sokoloff reminds us that reinterpretation has always been an integral part of Jewish thinking. In that same vein, she argues, teachers can engage students with poetry to encourage close reading, strengthen understanding of Jewish literature, and explore ways in which Jewish literature fits into the study of world literature. Jewish literature is a global phenomenon, and this poetry focuses on the kind of universal themes that have an important role to fill in undergraduate education.

As a tradition of interpreting biblical narratives, midrash forms the basis of a specifically Jewish hermeneutics, one that extends the understanding of Jewish history, identity, and thought. In chapter 6, "'The Story Without an Ending': Art, Midrash and History in Dara Horn's *The World To Come*," Sandor Goodhart exposes Horn's novel as revelatory, conflating the present world and the world to come, revealing historical time as an illusion. In its coverage of five generations of characters—including the unborn—and countless narrative forms that detail their histories, Goodhart notes the book as one of the most complex and exciting on the contemporary Jewish American scene. He writes: "If the world to come is the future, then from the point of view of the past, the 'world to come' is the present." For Goodhart, Horn's novel is that world to come. Her title thus reorients readerly attention to whatever present world in which the characters function, and her book works as a midrash does: responding to a fundamental gap in a prior text in such a way that constitutes a material extension of it.

Similarly, in chapter 7, Sol Neely shows the applicability and contribution of midrashic values to his own courses on social justice. In "Midrash and Social Justice," Neely outlines midrash as a contemporary hermeneutic that extends literary, philosophic, and religious study. In discussing the course he developed at his rural institution, he shows how such an extension furthers the reach of midrash beyond exegesis, that midrashic methods "interrogate the sources of human misery in order that we might repair them and transform the world."

Goodhart and Neely share a deep interest in the ways in which the ancient rabbinic interpretive mode of midrash can be thought of as a methodology for reading contemporary Holocaust literature. When we read midrashically, we are engaging in the work of memory, accounting for the "secondariness of every text." The second part of the volume focuses on teaching, and we purposely bridge the volume through chapters on midrash as a reading, and teaching, practice. In the rabbinical tradition, midrash offers the methodological means to open up a text to deeper reading, resulting in multilayered lessons that engage with cultural and historical contexts. It also extends the practice of teaching such trauma-laden texts. In chapter 8, "The Midrashic Legacy," Monica Osborne establishes a working definition of midrash that moves beyond its scriptural and rabbinic tradition. In drawing on the teachings of Goodhart, Geoffrey Hartman, and others, Osborne asks us to look at midrash not simply as an interpretive mode that fills in the gaps in our understanding, but one that extends and deepens knowledge of a prior text. Here Osborne shows midrash to be "a powerful pedagogical tool because it has the capacity to deepen students' understanding of any text and, perhaps most importantly, it allows them to begin to consider their own sense of ethical responsibility in our world."

As noted earlier, a developing trend in Holocaust studies has been the introduction of third-generation writing. The focus here on third-generation writers—recognized as the grandchildren of Holocaust survivors or those writing from a third-generation perspective that returns us to the events of the Shoah—distinguishes this volume from the earlier one. The new novelists and writers discussed in these chapters bring a renewed attention to the Holocaust through a third-generation lens, reflecting as much about the past as it does about this generation's particular understanding of the place of the Holocaust for an understanding of Jewish identity, other culturally and politically marginalized figures, and current cultural and historical contexts.

As with second-generation Holocaust writing, particular stories from third-generation writers have emerged as exemplary in terms of shaping the contours of the genre and probing the most poignant questions about the distance of memory. In chapters 9, 10, and 11, contributors Aimee Pozorski, Hilene Flanzbaum, and Jessica Lang examine such third-generation narratives that open themselves to current patterns in Holocaust literary representation. As such, these chapters offer useful dialogue with one another. Both Pozorski, in "Anne Frank, Figuration, and the Ethical Imperative," and Flanzbaum, in "Nathan Englander's 'Anne Frank' and the Future of Jewish America," return to Englander's short story as the structure for making larger claims about twenty-first-century attitudes toward Holocaust memory and the place of the Holocaust in contemporary society. Pozorski looks specifically at the ways in which the image of Anne Frank has been invoked and, like Osborne, for the ethical considerations of such literary invocations. In her discussion of Philip Roth's novel *The Ghost Writer* and Nathan Englander's short story "What We Talk About When We Talk About Anne Frank," she focuses on the ways these authors have used the image of a historical (albeit iconic) figure to represent the Holocaust. What does Anne Frank as a metaphor mean in terms of understanding the Holocaust? Roth's novel might be considered one of the first to reimagine the historical figure of Anne Frank, but Englander's construction of the image of Anne Frank as a "poster child" of the Holocaust shows the continuing preoccupation with her historical figuration. Pozorski's analysis of Englander's short story exposes the figure of Anne Frank as yet another Holocaust trope, but one that signals a writerly insecurity about the enterprise of writing about the Holocaust. The ongoing figuration of Anne Frank forces us to examine anew Adorno's now well-known injunction against poetry after Auschwitz. Does the replacement of Anne Frank from historical person to literary trope somehow dilute the singular tragedy of her life? What is lost and what is gained in terms of understanding the Holocaust when we turn a person into a metaphor? Finally, she ponders "the ethical imperative," noting that authors like Roth and Englander have used Anne Frank as a trope "in order to emphasize the ways in which we are responsible for the well-being of one another."

Flanzbaum, in chapter 10, approaches Englander's humorously ironic and cautionary story multidirectionally in an attempt both to stimulate broader conversations in the literature classroom and to address the kinds of controversial questions within Judaism that literature courses often neglect. Such intersections or tensions among literature, the act of writing, and Judaism provide the stage on which students might connect such issues as Jewish identity, intermarriage, secularism, and remembrance within the experiential context of their own lives, including such complexities as hyphenate identity, voyeurism, fundamentalism, and moral responsibility. Ultimately, this multidirectionality can have the function of breathing new life into what might be perceived as a tired subject. The narrative crisis at the center of the story raises the stakes for the characters who experience it, but the reader is similarly exposed to the question at its heart: "Would you have had the courage to hide Anne Frank?"

Jessica Lang opens her chapter with a related cautionary tale. In "Narrating the Past in a Different Language: Teaching the Holocaust through Third-Generation Fiction," Lang wonders why the clear abundance of and access to material testimony and Holocaust resources has not made it easier to teach the Holocaust. Is it that the canonical texts may no longer serve their original purpose? Have the increasing accessibility and approachability of these texts moved us away from, rather than revealed, the hard truths they attempt to teach? Even as the crises that precipitated the Holocaust are still with us in the form of racism, genocide, and anti-Semitism, for Lang, it is not enough to approach it through contemporary catastrophes. Stories by third-generation writers, on the other hand, are determined to teach the inevitable direction toward which all Holocaust pedagogy must turn—its very inaccessibility. Lang illustrates a productive method for interpreting this growing and deeply complex body of writing: recognize its distance from those originary texts that bear witness while valuing the limitations of the third-generation subject-position.

Pozorski, Flanzbaum, and Lang share a third-generation focus and thus offer a "cluster" of thinking about this generational turn. The increased distance of the writers from the events accounts for not only their renewed interest in the subject, but also the possible pervasiveness of the topic of the Holocaust across contemporary literary works. Lang also emphasizes a need to identify and seek to grasp the "hard truths" of the Holocaust, even as their very inaccessibility (necessarily) eludes success. The inaccessibility is addressed differently in chapter 12, "A Complicated Curriculum: Teaching Holocaust Empathy and Distance to Nontraditional Students." Jeffrey Demsky and N. Ann Rider want to move the discussion away from a primary focus on empathic readings. Their concern is that "traditional empathy-arousing renderings" are no longer effective for the twenty-first-century learner, who has become accustomed to a complex system of pedagogical methods. As teachers, they want the contemporary classroom to provide students with a fully engaged learning experience, beyond just affective response, in order to engage them in a deeper, more thoughtful reading experience, one that draws on "authorial goals and techniques." Juxtaposing such traditional Holocaust texts as Elie Wiesel's *Night* alongside a more recent text, such as Imre Kertés's *Fatelessness*, creates a cognitive distance—rather than intimacy—that engages students more fully and becomes a forceful pedagogical tool. Such an exercise reveals the value of a pedagogy of "conversations" among literary works both contemporary and older for twenty-first-century students.

The final three chapters, considered together, forcefully highlight the broadening of geographical boundaries for the field. They make clear that the issues within Jewish American and Holocaust literatures continue to passionately inform the pedagogy of teachers in such distant places as Spain, Poland and the UK. The value in teaching the intersection of cultures becomes for each teacher a way to expose their students to the ways in which stories from one world can help them understand another. In chapter 13, "Teaching Jewish American Literature in a Spanish Context," Gustavo Sánchez Canales orients the place of Jewish American literary studies in a contemporary Spanish context. How, he asks, might students be motivated to read challenging international works while maintaining the necessary and specific sort of academic rigor demanded at his university? In his investigation, Sánchez Canales draws on his own experiences in "integrating Jewish-American fiction into general courses on US literature" by introducing connections through the fiction of writers such as Saul Bellow, Chaim Potok, and Philip Roth. Drawing connections between Jewish American writers and Spanish writers, he can "facilitate a comparative analysis, thus exposing students to other writers about whom they had read little or nothing in the course of their university studies." In arguing for such a comparative study between Jewish American writers and novelists more familiar to a contemporary Spanish undergraduate audience, Sánchez Canales makes wider claims for the effectiveness of the "student-centered classroom" in general and for the value in teaching the intersection of cultures.

In chapter 14, "Teaching William Styron's *Sophie's Choice*: Understanding the Holocaust," Zygmunt Mazur explores the ways in which Styron's novel acts as a guide for teaching a number of different structural and substantive issues both in Holocaust studies and literary studies, such as emerging debates and general problems of narrative strategy. Pointing first to its controversy as a Holocaust novel written by a non-Jewish Southern American author, Mazur argues that understanding the debates about authorial identity helps students understand the ethical complexities surrounding the study of ethnic literatures. The novel can be approached by following the narrator's journey of discovery, which involves his realization of his own prejudice against Jews. Teaching this novel in a Polish university highlights the value of exposing students to the ways in which new contexts for reading and teaching broaden understanding of complex topics and enliven classroom discussion.

Finally, in chapter 15, "'A novel that dare not speak its name': Biographical Approaches to Saul Bellow," Judie Newman complicates the central questions raised by a biographical approach to literature in general and, more specifically, to Jewish studies through the instructive case of Saul Bellow. How do we locate Saul Bellow the writer, a man who emerges through biographical accounts in a variety of competing and paradoxical guises: son, father, husband, lover, playwright, novelist, essayist, thinker, political radical, conservative, analysand,

Jew and American? Further, how do we use such biographical details when teaching Jewish American writing? What constrains a biographical undertaking? What challenges its reliability? Newman's study of the place of biography in Jewish American literature penetrates these questions. Bellow as a character in the biographies of him complicates the reliability of biographical accounts, resisting, as Newman suggests, easy definition. This closing chapter poses broader interpretive questions that emerge out of the more focused study of Bellow. But it also offers new ways of engaging Bellow's work. Conventionally approached as a novelist of ideas, whose characters are defined, in large part, by their habitual meditative soliloquies and contemplative, existential anxieties, Bellow in Newman's reading emerges as a writer whose "intertextuality is creative, multifarious and something of a challenge to most of his readers." If, as Newman suggests, Bellow's biography is "a novel that dare not speak its name, it is a novel with a large cast." In Newman's hands, biography emerges as a means to complicate and enhance even the most thoroughly investigated text.

Before drawing to a close, I want to take a moment to return to the annual Jewish American and Holocaust Literature Symposium, whose origin and history uniquely connect this volume to the earlier collection *Jewish American and Holocaust Literature: Representation in the Postmodern World*. A gathering of scholars, writers, and artists invested in the study of these rich and vital fields, the annual symposium, now in its twenty-fourth year, began as a forum to bring together those who were committed to researching and teaching literature by and about American Jews as well as the American Jewish experience and the literary expression of the Shoah. This deeply invested group of scholars and writers, through our shared enthusiasm, formed a kind of *chavruta*, an occasion for learning together, for drawing on our collective strengths, knowledge, and experiences in what has become—over many years of lively debate, exegesis, and midrashic commentary—an extension of our individual reading, thinking, and teaching. First founded by Alan Berger, Gloria Cronin, and Dan Walden—major voices in the field of Jewish American literature—these gatherings have created open-ended occasions for inquiry and for the exploration and exchange of texts and possibilities for understanding and expanding the long tradition of Jewish literary expression. Collectively, our self-styled *chavrutot* have provided the stage for scholars of American Jewish and Holocaust literatures to enact an array of possibilities for understanding and interpreting the complex histories, mythologies, and traditions that have shaped Jewish life and thought. These occasions have brought us together in the shared project of our long-standing preoccupation with the interpretive possibilities of Jewish literature both past and contemporary, its return to ancient and enduring texts and traditions, but also its mutating dialogic openings. We have discovered that our approach to teaching this extensive and engaging body of literature is fluid, wide-ranging, and unconstrained by historical period, geographies, or ideological, political, or academic fashions.

Our ongoing dialogue has taken place in recent years in the fortuitous if unlikely location overlooking the Atlantic in South Beach, Florida. Fortunately for our collective group, the historic Betsy Hotel, home base of our *beit midrash* and made available to us by the descendants of the American Jewish poet Hyam Plutzik (1911–1962), has graciously embraced our shared project and made such uninterrupted conversations possible. Our *chavruta* has flourished at the Betsy, a result of many related factors: the hospitality and vision of Deborah Plutzik Briggs, executive director of the Plutzik Goldwasser Family Foundation and vice president for philanthropy; and Jonathan Plutzik, co-president of the Plutzik Goldwasser Family Foundation and chairman and owner of the Betsy Hotel. Both have supported our extending invitations to scholars, writers, filmmakers, and artists from around the globe to promote a rich "salon" ethos through community-conference partnerships. In the hotel's "Writer's Room," the Betsy houses Hyam Plutzik's original desk, some of his books, and broadsides of his poetry—an homage to a Jewish American poet whose life was cut short on the cusp of international prominence. Visiting writers are invited to use the room as a retreat so that the spirit of this remarkably nuanced American Jewish poet continues to infuse present literary production.

Reading Thane Rosenbaum's *How Sweet It Is!*, his bittersweet novel about a family—a survivor couple and their son, Adam, in 1972 Miami Beach—reminds us of the city as a de facto landscape of Jewish literature. Rosenbaum's evocation of I. B. Singer's walks along Miami's spirited beachfront calls to mind the twentieth-century Jewish Diaspora, which brought Jews from Europe, first to New York, and then in a migration south to Florida. Indeed, the book's closing line all but predicts the work of our contemporary pilgrimage to Miami Beach—in particular those scholars who seek a kind of literary salvation in Jewish American literature. He writes: "All forsaken refugees surrender to this magical city and await the arrival of the Miami Messiah, who, of course, never comes" (194). According to Deborah Dash Moore, in *To the Golden Cities: Pursuing the American Jewish Dream in Miami and L.A.*, "By 1960 observers estimated that roughly 80 percent of the Beach's population was Jewish" (63). In supplementing the annual symposium's academic talks with visits to exhibitions and exhibits at the Wolfson Jewish Museum, the Miami Holocaust Memorial, and other Jewish cultural sites, we have brought history and tradition in contact with our contemporary work. The triangulation of civic, social, and intellectual spaces has animated and revitalized the study of this rich body of ever-growing literature. After many years of study and a body of scholarly writing growing out of our discussions, it seemed right that we started once again to ask questions about how to use such jointly gained and mutually produced knowledge to read and teach the literature that has enriched our own lives. Some of the scholarship that has—either directly or indirectly—benefited from our gathering suggests the breadth of the field.

This volume was compiled to produce a conversation among scholars of Jewish studies about how to approach the challenges inherent in reading and teaching Jewish American and Holocaust literatures in the twenty-first-century classroom. We hope that readers might come to these essays as prompts for their own teaching as openings for further discussions. As we move through this book, we hope that it is clear how each chapter speaks to and extends both previous and subsequent chapters. If midrashic extensions are openings for moments of continuity and amplification, then this book has been an experience in midrash, in the interpretation and reinterpretation of possibilities for understanding and carrying over time the legacy of Jewish thought. The direction for Jewish studies is fluid and open to interpretive possibilities, elastic in a way that Jewish exegesis and midrash perhaps always have been. After all, the project of carrying texts into the future might be seen as a response to *zachor*, the call to remember. Thus these chapters might be seen as memory pieces, extending the text of the past, stories, as Israeli novelist David Grossman puts it, that are "filtered through the prisms of time and memory, to be refracted into the entire spectrum of colors and shades" (69). Finally, then, this volume of essays is intended to further enrich our reading, our teaching, our discussions, and ultimately our understanding of the continuing legacy of Jewish American and Holocaust literatures.

References

Aarons, Victoria, Avinoam J. Patt, and Mark Shechner. *The New Diaspora: The Changing Landscape of American Jewish Fiction*. Detroit: Wayne State University Press, 2015.

Dickstein, Morris. "Promised Lands: The Boldness of Jewish-American Writing in the Post-war Years—and Its Vigorous Renewal Today." *Times Literary Supplement*, April 15, 2016, 3–5.

Grossman, David. *Writing in the Dark: Essays on Literature and Politics*. Translated by Jessica Cohen. New York: Farrar, Straus and Giroux, 2008.

Howe, Irving. "Introduction." In *Jewish-American Stories*, edited by Irving Howe. New York: New American Library, 1977.

Moore, Deborah Dash. *To the Golden Cities: Pursuing the American Jewish Dream in Miami and L.A.* Boston: Harvard University Press, 1996.

Rosenbaum, Thane. *How Sweet It Is!* Simsbury, CT: Mandel Vilar Press, 2015.

Part I
READING

1

Black Milk

A Holocaust Metaphor

Eric J. Sundquist

This is the reason why three-year-old Emilia died: the historical necessity of killing the children of Jews was self-demonstrative to the Germans.

—Primo Levi, *Survival in Auschwitz*

Not quite a year after her liberation from Auschwitz, Seweryna Szmaglewska returned to the scene of her backbreaking labor in the empty ponds from which hard clay was extracted with picks and spades for roadway construction. She could still hear the sorrowful song of motherhood sung by a fifteen-year-old Greek Jew named Alegri in 1943. The song's first word, "Mamma," which had the same connotation in Polish as in Greek, was the only way in which Alegri, "tossed into the multi-tongued mob like a deaf-mute," could speak to the other women. Now, in 1945, Alegri was gone, along with the vast majority of Greek Jews who entered Auschwitz. The cloud of smoke from the crematory had vanished, but footprints still ran along the floor of the ponds:

> Past are the days of shrieks, curses, and moans; no echo is left behind. Only, sometimes, as you stand on the dikes between the ponds, listening to the deep whistling of the wind in the reeds, you may hear that sad song sung in an alien tongue, exotic and incomprehensible, you may hear the "mamma" echoing from time to time in that cry of despair.[1]

The world of the Holocaust is pervaded by many such cries of despair—strangled, choking voices; shrieks and murmurs; stillness and muteness. No single manifestation of speech or silence is foundational, and yet the silencing of the human voice by murder surely has priority, and perhaps no human voice has greater priority than that of a child or infant on the verge of language, calling to its mother. Cynthia Ozick dramatized this searingly in her short story "The Shawl" when the infant Magda cries out for her missing shawl:

> Ever since the drying up of Rosa's nipples, ever since Magda's last scream on the road, Magda had been devoid of any syllable; Magda had been mute. . . . Even the laugh that came when the ash-stippled wind made a clown out of Magda's shawl was only the air-blown showing of her teeth. . . . But now Magda's mouth was spilling a long viscous rope of clamor.
> "Maaaa—"
> It was the first noise Magda had ever sent out from her throat since the drying up of Rosa's nipples.
> "Maaaa . . . aaa!"

By the time Rosa retrieves the shawl from the barracks, Magda has been thrown by a guard against the electrified fence, which itself speaks the word she had started to scream: "The electric voices began to chatter wildly. 'Maamaa, maaamaaa,' they hummed altogether."[2]

The lost shawl, summoned by Magda's cry, has taken the place of Rosa's empty breast: "The duct-crevice extinct, a dead volcano, blind eye, chill hole, so Madga took the corner of the shawl and milked it instead." Such elaborate metaphors, which fly straight in the face of Theodor Adorno's notorious proscription of poetry in the wake of the Holocaust, appear to strip the story's action of historical specificity. "Rosa," the companion piece to which "The Shawl" was joined in the 1989 novella *The Shawl*, forces a return to the historical, not only through its setting in 1977 Miami but also through its creation of a complex, allusive web of intertextual clues to what is missing in the first story. On the basis of the second story we are able, for example, to reconstruct a family, Rosa and her niece Stella being its only survivors, and find a possible explanation of Magda's Aryan features—"eyes blue as air, smooth feathers of hair nearly as yellow as the Star sewn into Rosa's coat—which "The Shawl" only hints at.[3] When she brought the two short stories together in the novella, Ozick dramatically enlarged the issue of Magda's identity by prefacing her book with one such clue, an epigraph from the concluding lines of Paul Celan's poem "Todesfuge" ("Deathfugue"):

> dein goldenes Haar Margarete
> dein aschenes Haar Sulamith
> [your golden hair Margarete
> your ashen hair Shulamith]

Though she quoted only two lines from Celan's famous poem, Ozick expected her readers to remember the poem's relentless cyclicality, enforced by the fugue-like repetitions and lack of punctuation, which carries us back, over and over, to its stunning opening lines:

> Black milk of daybreak we drink it at evening
> we drink it at midday and morning we drink it at night
> we drink and we drink
> we shovel a grave in the air there you won't lie too
>   cramped . . .[4]

Spoken in the collective voice of perishing Jews, the "black milk" drunk day and night of the opening lines refers first of all to the death sentence passed on all Jewish life. "Terrible nursemaids / Have usurped the place of mothers," as Nelly Sachs, later Celan's longtime correspondent, wrote in "O the night of the weeping children!," a poem published the same year as "Todesfuge." "Instead of mother's milk, panic suckles those little ones."[5] In Celan's lines, Ozick thus provided an additional perspective on Magda's short, cruel life. Magda has the golden hair of Margarete, the idealized embodiment of German romantic love in Goethe's *Faust*, rather than the black hair of Shulamith, the embodiment of Israel's eroticized relationship with God in the Song of Songs.

But like other blond-haired, blue-eyed Jews, who, according to a 1938 study at odds with the Nazi racial paradigm, constituted 11 percent of the population of German schoolchildren,[6] she belongs to the people of Shulamith and must die accordingly.

Lyrically enacting the end of Jewish reproduction envisioned in the Final Solution, the poem's fugue-like rhythms, running from beginning to end, join "black milk" to the "ashen hair" of Jewish women, whose hair was often harvested for industrial use in the Reich before the remainder of the body was burned. Magda's eclipsed cry is the vocal signal that Jewish women's breasts have dried up, their wombs have been burned out—whether by starvation or, as in some instances, by chemical sterilization—and the decision has been reached to bring an end to Jewish regeneration once and for all. Magda has already drunk black milk; soon she will be turned to ash. "Black milk" therefore also directs us to the atmosphere of smoke and ash enveloping the death camps and killing fields in the East. Rain laden with crematoria soot and the "odor of burning flesh" fell in Auschwitz, recalled Charlotte Delbo. "We were steeped in it."[7] "I am an incarnation of the body-burners of Ponar," wrote Abraham Sutzkever, speaking in the voice of a Jew forced to burn excavated corpses outside Vilna. "My bread is baked of ash. Every loaf—a face."[8]

The figures and actions of "Todesfuge" take us across a range of Holocaust experiences, but the enormity of the Final Solution is captured in Celan's two opening words, and the indelible terror of their paradoxical juxtaposition has served many purposes. Speaking in a recent memoir of the vitality of Czernovitz, his own birthplace, as well as that of Celan and many other distinguished writers, Aharon Appelfeld reflected on the great flowering of Eastern European literature cut off by the Holocaust:

> Czernovitz expelled its Jews, and so did Vienna, Prague, Budapest, and Lemberg. Now these cities live without Jews, and their few descendants, scattered through the world, carry memory like a wonderful gift and a relentless curse. For me, too, the childhood home is that "black milk" . . . which nourishes me morning and evening while at the same time it drugs me.[9]

Appelfeld's longing for a homeland that can never be reclaimed—more specifically for a place where both his mother and grandmother were slain—is by no means unique. Of those Jews who survived the

Holocaust, few could imagine a postwar life in Germany or Eastern Europe. Whether she borrowed Celan's central metaphors or came upon them by inspiration, the memoirist Fanya Hiller demonstrated that they cast a long shadow. In the Polish Displaced Persons camp in Bytom at war's end, Hiller carried on a short correspondence with Jan, a courageous young gentile Ukrainian who had become both her savior and her lover, each of them swinging back and forth in their commitments to the other as he searched in vain for the false papers he would need if he accompanied her to Paris, where she hoped to study medicine, and she contemplated life instead as a Ukrainian housewife in a graveyard for Jews. Their baby, she imagined, would have the face of her Jewish father—but with a cross hanging around his neck:

> No, not a graveyard, for there were no graves. The Jews had been burned to ashes, and the ashes had been turned to dust which was in the air we breathed and the water we drank. . . .
>
> I saw myself holding a baby to my breast, and my breast and the baby were black with the ashes of their murdered relatives. Black milk came out of my breast. My baby coughing . . . [and then] Jan holding the baby and crying as the child turned stiff in his arms and broke in two like a dry twig, then turned to dust and became part of the dust in the air and the water.[10]

For Hiller, the principal figures of "Todesfuge"—black milk, ash, graves in the air—come together in a vision of Eastern Europe in which Jews, the people of Shulamith, have no future.

In *The Deputy*, his 1963 play about the complicity in the Holocaust of Pope Pius XII, Rolf Hochhuth invoked Celan's metaphors in arguing *against* metaphor. He first quoted a scene from Rudolf Höss's confessional memoir, *Commandant of Auschwitz*, in which a young Jewish woman soothingly prepares her children for the gas chamber and then, before stepping in, tells Höss: "I avoided being selected as one of those fit for work. I wanted to experience the whole procedure consciously and exactly." Here, presumably, was the experience itself, unmediated. In Celan's poem, by contrast, Hochhuth comments, "the gassing of the Jews is entirely translated into metaphors" such as "black milk," which, notwithstanding their tremendous force of suggestion, "still screen the infernal cynicism of what really took place . . . [that] this gigantic plant with scheduled railroad connections was built especially in order that normal people . . . might kill other people."[11] And yet, of course, the condemned woman's testimony to what really takes place is cut off the moment she enters the gas chamber. Like one of Primo Levi's "true witnesses," those "who saw the Gorgon, [but] have not returned to tell about it or have returned mute,"[12] she can tell us nothing more.

There are many reasons to question this mystification of the gas chamber, from which, like a black hole in existential space, nothing can emerge and about which no words can be ventured. There are numerous eyewitness descriptions of what transpired in the gassing procedure to which the words of someone miraculously returned from the dead would add very little. Just as important, Hochhuth obscures the important function of Celan's metaphoric language. Omer Bartov has spoken of the difficulty in finding an acceptable imaginary mold in which to cast the atrocity of the Holocaust—"elusive precisely because it is ubiquitous, inconceivable because it is fantastic, faceless because it is protean."[13] The frequency with which eyewitnesses described their experiences as "unspeakable" or "beyond words" attests to the fact that only language stretched to the boundaries of meaning may be capable of rendering experiences that are themselves at the limits of existence. But the urgency of Fanya Hiller's metaphors lies in the fact that, like Celan's in "Todesfuge," Ozick's in "The Shawl," and Sachs's in "O the night of the weeping children!," they are but a hairsbreadth away from the literal. "Black milk" was literalized in what Szalma Winer, in his singular testimony about the gas van murders at Chełmno, witnessed: "From one of the vans a young woman with an infant at her breast was thrown out. The child had died while drinking its mother's milk."[14] Notwithstanding its scale and seeming inexplicability, the Holocaust was not an abstraction but a multitude of individual atrocities that had one underlying purpose. Figures such as "black milk," "terrible nursemaids," and the cry of "Mamma" refer us directly to this foundational intention—the Nazis' determination to bring an end to Jewish life, a fact so basic that it often goes unstated. In the testimony and literature of the Holocaust, few things are as difficult to confront as the murder—frequently the sadistic, brutal murder—of children, and yet nothing was more integral to the Final Solution, which took the lives of 1.5 million children, more than a million of them Jewish. Canonical works such as *The Shawl* and "Todesfuge" that dramatize this fact have been the subject of much critical commentary. Rather than adding to this commentary, my hope here is to consider some of the historical and literary contexts to which their principal maternal metaphors give us access.

∼

Who drinks "black milk"?—Jews, surely, the people of Shulamith who do not have blond hair and blue eyes, or whose Jewishness, like Magda's, is masked by a deceptive appearance, one of the great fears of Nazism. But Celan's metaphor applies also to those who became enraptured with the idea of a world free of Jews, one in which other "inferior" races would be subjugated and Aryan reproduction would be magnified. Such delusions of racial purity can take hold when a figurative language—in which Jews are vermin, syphilitic predators, incarnations of the devil, and parasites feeding on the body of the German people, to cite a few of the common accusations popularized by Hitler and his followers—is turned first into an ethical code and then into law. The Third Reich, by one count, promulgated 1,448 anti-Jewish legal measures between 1933 and 1939, with more and far worse to follow,[15] in the process inventing a lexicon of euphemisms and prevaricating bureaucratic phrases—"Final Solution," "special treatment," "migration," and the like—in which genocide could be shrouded.

What happens when a nation's cultivated language "is made up of poisonous elements or has been made the bearer of poisons?" asked Victor Klemperer in his masterful study of the language of the Third Reich. "Words can be like tiny doses of arsenic: they are swallowed unnoticed, appear to have no effect, and then after a little time the toxic reaction sets in."[16] Although this perversion of everyday language lies outside the internal dynamics of "Todesfuge," it is the poem's precondition. "Black milk" may thus also be seen to refer to the poison swallowed daily by the German people during the Hitler years—a poison consonant with the poisonous image of the Jew it publicized. Portraying Jews as mortal enemies, the carriers of disease and damaging genes, Nazi propaganda dwelled relentlessly on the danger posed by the *Fremdkörper* (the foreign body) of the Jew to the *Volkskörper* (the national body) of the German people. Five months after the Nazi invasion of Poland, for example, a Łódź magazine addressed the matter: "The Jew, who crawled forth from the dark quarters of the ghetto into the surrounding neighborhoods of the Germans, who ate his way into the other *Volkskörper* like the maggot into liver, has been subdued and controlled."[17] More specifically, then, we may see in "black milk" an allusion to the Nazi accusation, a product of widespread pseudomedical fantasies, that Jewish blood was contaminating to Aryan purity. The intensity of this belief is best appreciated in the context of the Nazi obsession with blood purity and reproduction, especially among the military elite. Members of the SS and their potential mates were subjected to rigorous ancestral screening. A representative wedding ceremony, for example, included the admonition that the betrothed couple was the blood link across generations—from an "endless chain of ancestors" who "hold out their hands to those who are not yet born."[18] Under the *Lebensborn* initiative, which sprang from Reichsführer SS Heinrich Himmler's racial fantasies, children deemed racially suitable in territories occupied during the war were kidnapped and sent to be raised in foster homes in the Reich. Among the many ways women expressed their devotion to Hitler, frequently fanatical and sometimes erotic, some pregnant women reflexively called out his name during the pains of childbirth,[19] and German women were awarded the Honor Cross of German Motherhood according to the number of children they bore—bronze for four, silver for six, gold for eight.

In this worldview, the most vital threat of the Jewish enemy lay in the specter of biological subversion. The sexual menace of the Jew, historically a minor aspect of anti-Semitism, became pronounced in Nazi propaganda. Combining the Jew as rapist with the blood libel—the accusation that Jews used the blood of slain Christians, children in particular, in making Passover matzos or for other ritual purposes—one Nazi illustration depicted a naked Aryan woman crucified by a crouching, diabolically drawn Jew who had, according to the caption, raped her while blood flowed from her wounds.[20] "With satanic joy in his face," Hitler wrote in *Mein Kampf*, "the black-haired Jewish youth lurks in wait for the unsuspecting girl whom he defiles with his blood, thus stealing her from her people."[21] Not just in Hitler's imagination but elsewhere as well, the greatest offense of sexual assault lay in the danger of genetic contamination. "One single cohabitation of a Jew with an Aryan is sufficient to poison her blood forever," wrote Julius Streicher in an article indebted to Hitler, as well as to Artur Dinter's bestselling 1919 novel *Sin against Blood*, and published in his periodical *German People's Health through Blood and Soil*. "Together with the 'alien albumen' [the Jewish man's sperm] she has absorbed the alien soul. Never again will she be able to bear purely Aryan children, even when married to an Aryan." The Jew "has been aware of the secrets of the race question for centuries,"

Streicher continued, and ravishes German women in order to impregnate them with "an alien species" and thus bring about "the annihilation of the nations which are superior to him."[22] Streicher's version of the Jew's threat to racial purity was extreme but hardly unusual. The centerpiece of the 1935 Nuremberg Laws, the Law for the Protection of German Blood and German Honor, outlawed marriage and sexual relations "between Jews and subjects of the state of German or related blood," but interpretation of the law proved to be capacious. In 1939 Frankfurt, a Jewish man was jailed for assault simply for having looked at a fifteen-year-old German girl, behavior deemed to have "a clearly erotic basis."[23] Equally dangerous was the sale of contaminated mother's milk. The case of a "pure-blooded Jewess" selling her milk to a pediatrician prompted the Ministry of Justice to inform Hitler that the woman would be put on trial: "Babies of German blood [who] were nourished on this milk in a maternity hospital. . . . have been wronged, for the milk of a Jewish woman cannot be considered nourishment for German children."[24] The Jew's milk was black; German offspring would be poisoned.

∾

With the onset of war, creating a world without Jews was a defining feature of Third Reich ideology, eventually becoming the only war the Nazis sought to win amid calamitous losses on the battlefield. The defining instance of this worldview was Heinrich Himmler's infamous 1943 speech to senior SS officers in which he addressed the moral duty to exterminate the Jews, children included:

> I ask of you that what I say in this circle you really only hear and never speak of. We come to the question: how is it with the women and children? I have resolved even here on a completely clear solution. That is to say I do not consider myself justified in eradicating men . . . and allowing the avengers in the shape of the children to grow up for our sons and grandsons [to contend with]. The difficult decision had to be taken, to cause this *Volk* to disappear from the face of the earth. To organize the execution of this mission was the most difficult task we had hitherto. It was accomplished without—as I believe I am able to say—our men or our officers suffering injury to spirit or soul.[25]

What did Himmler's words mean in practice? Magda, like the real-life infant Ozick said she read about in William Shirer's bestselling book *The Rise and Fall of the Third Reich*,[26] is thrown against an electrified fence, from the guard's point of view a necessary and utterly routine act. Had Magda been discovered upon arrival in the camp, she would have gone straight to the gas. Such a death might be counted as merciful. As a matter of efficiency, children were often simply burned, sometimes dead, sometimes alive, as Elie Wiesel found upon arriving in Auschwitz: "A truck drew close and unloaded its hold: small children. Babies! Yes, I did see this, with my own eyes . . . children thrown into the flames."[27] In the summer of 1944, as Hungary's Jews, Wiesel among them, were processed sometimes at the rate of twenty thousand a day, Sara Nomberg-Przytyk recalled the stillness suddenly broken by the screaming of children being burned alive in ditches, "as if a single scream had been torn out of hundreds of mouths . . . a scream repeated a thousand times in the single word, 'Mama,' a scream that increased in intensity every second, enveloping the whole camp and every inmate."[28] But efficiency was not always the motive. Mothers who had participated in the Warsaw Uprising in 1943, according to Vassili Grossman, were forced at Treblinka "to lead their children between the red-hot bars on which thousands of dead bodies writhed and squirmed . . . where the bellies of dead women with child burst open from the heat and still-born infants burned up inside their rent wombs," all the while the children shrieked, "Mama, mama, what are they going to do to us? Will they burn us?"[29] In Treblinka, Jewish children—in particular, the corpses of children—were referred to as "trinkets."[30]

The sadistic will to treat Jewish children as objects of abhorrence at times amounted to sport. One SS man made a bet that he could cleave a ten-year-old Jewish boy with one stroke of his ax, a bet he easily won.[31] Other soldiers held a contest to see who could throw Jewish children the farthest, while others were challenged to toss them, from a distance of twelve meters, in such a way that their heads would strike the trunk of a tree. For every cracked skull they would receive a glass of schnapps.[32] A Wehrmacht soldier writing home to his wife reported shooting babies like skeet: they "flew in great arcs and we shot them to pieces in the air before they fell into the ditch and the water."[33] In the September 1942 *Aktion* at the Łódź Ghetto hospital, when infants were thrown from upper floors into trucks waiting below, a young SS man asked permission from his superior to catch those "little Jews" on his bayonet. After several successes and then a miss, he quit the game, complaining that it was too "messy."[34]

The reports of young children smashed against trees, rocks, or walls, or torn to pieces by hand, are literally too numerous to mention. Mieczyslaw Sekiewicz testified to a scene he witnessed in 1941 outside Konin, where two large groups of Jews were killed in a mid-November operation. One SS officer smashed a child's head on his car, according to a local veterinary surgeon, and when the mother screamed, he "lashed out with the body of the child so that the head hit her on the mouth and the brain stuck to it. Then he took something from his car—lime or plaster of Paris—and stopped her mouth."[35] The attack on children was by definition, and frequently by design, an explicit attack on Jewish motherhood as well. According to testimony at her postwar trial, Irma Grese, an Auschwitz supervisor notorious for her sexual sadism, waited until a pregnant woman was ready to give birth and then tied her legs together and watched her suffer.[36] Olga Lengyel, a Jewish physician in Auschwitz, recalled another variation on this assault on Jewish reproduction that showed ideology taken to its vicious limits: a mother was forced to undress her daughter and look on while the girl's genitals were mutilated by specially trained dogs.[37] Robert Krell, a Hungarian survivor, later insisted that in Maidanek, fifty pregnant women were lined up and bayoneted in the stomach, while any men who came to their aid were shot. The number may not be credible, but there is little reason to doubt that such an assault took place.[38] In a 1941 action near Slonim, in Belarus, pregnant women were shot in the belly for fun, according to the testimony of Alfred Metzner, and then thrown into pits on top of children, who had been beaten to death and dumped in first.[39] Perhaps this was the source of the memory of a former Wehrmacht soldier, identified in his 1962 testimony only as Karl M., who guarded the site. From somewhere within the mass of bodies lying in still-exposed graves, Karl heard a child cry out "mama" several times, a voice "buried, crying out of the depths," before falling silent.[40]

Karl M. was haunted by his memories. Some members of a police battalion studied by Christopher Browning claimed that they were only willing to shoot children to save them from potentially worse abuse,[41] and there were surely many expressions of remorse and conscience, especially after the war. But mercy was not on the minds of those who took two hundred children from Warsaw's Gęsia Prison into the woods and chopped off their heads with axes,[42] or those who seized all children under age fourteen in the Kielce Ghetto, on the pretext that they were being relocated to Germany, and instead took them to the local cemetery, trapped them where two walls formed a corner, and blew them up with hand grenades.[43] Nor was it foremost in the thoughts of those who marched the children of the Jewish Children's Home in Minsk, along with the home's director, to a freshly dug ditch, where they were buried alive in sand: "The screams and cries could be heard far into the ghetto," said Hersh Smolar. "Children stretched out their hands, pleading for their lives. [Gauleiter Wilhelm] Kube walked alongside the ditch, tossing pieces of candy into it."[44] Treblinka survivor Oskar Strawczynski remembered the pleasure one guard took in beating young boys: "With the first few lashes on their naked flesh, these children's screams and cries, their shrieks of 'Mama,' would reach to heaven. . . . Kiewe [presumably Kurt Küttner, nicknamed "Kiwi"], however, was not affected. On the contrary, the more heartbreaking the screams, the more he enjoyed his job."[45]

German women were by no means exempt from the appetite for cruelty against Jewish children. Lidia Maximovna Slipchenko, a doctor who escaped occupied Odessa in October 1941, recalled a German woman who arrived to take up residence in an area to be cleansed of Jews: "as if she were drunk on cruelty, with wild cries she took hold of children and smashed a rifle butt into their heads with such force that their brains were spattered for some distance around."[46] Johanna Altvater, a former business secretary detailed to the local commandant in the Ukrainian border town of Volodymyr-Volynsky, made a specialty of killing children. She smashed a child's head against a wall and tossed the body at its father's feet; she threw children off a balcony in the children's ward in the hospital; and she lured children with candy: when they came to her ready for a treat, she shot them in the mouth with a small silver pistol.[47] Nor was the presence of German children any bar to anti-Jewish atrocities. A diarist in the occupied Soviet territory observed Commandant Ernest Epple hang a dying prisoner from a tree for the sport of his dogs: "The dogs attacked the victim, they growled, ripped his skin, tore his flesh to pieces. The miserable man screamed, writhed, pleaded for rescue. . . . Meanwhile, Epple's children were running around the gallows, yelling to the dogs and laughing gleefully."[48] In Janowska camp outside Lvov, the commandant, Gustav Wilhaus, often took target practice from the balcony of his villa. For the birthday of his daughter Heike, wrote diarist David Kahane, Wilhaus led her to the balcony and one by one picked off members of the "cripples brigade," those more dead than alive: "Heike was beside herself with enthusiasm and joy, and kept clapping her hands. She seemed to take enormous pleasure in her father's skill."[49] It is no surprise, then, that Charlotte Delbo remembered seeing the two blond, blue-eyed sons of Rudolf Höss playing a game of commandant and prisoner that must have seemed completely normal to them, the one pretending to beat and kick the other, who lay lifeless on the ground "like a limp bundle." His fury spent and filled with disgust for his imaginary Jew, "the big boy, pointing his switch at the invisible prisoners around him, orders, 'Zum Krematorium' [To the crematorium], and walks off, stiff, satisfied and repelled."[50]

Caught up in Nazi Germany's war against Jewish life and Jewish reproduction, Jewish writers needed a language in which to particularize a mass depravity seemingly without precedent and beyond representation. Children murdered in the Holocaust, wrote Abraham Sutzkever, become

> . . . puffs of living smoke.
> They call: Mama, Mama! from the smoke.
> The whole panorama is in smoke.
> The dolls and their worlds are smoke.
> And over them the birds are smoke.[51]

"Smoke of Jewish Children" is a poem of 1957, but Sutzkever had publicly confronted the more terrible, because intimately personal, murder of children much earlier, in his 1946 testimony at Nuremburg. At the end of December 1941, he recalled in response to questioning by the Soviet deputy prosecutor, the Germans had issued the notorious Vilna decree that Jewish women could no longer bear children. Sutzkever's wife gave birth in the ghetto hospital soon thereafter, and doctors attempted to hide the baby along with other newborn children. When Sutzkever was able to make his way to the hospital after escaping an *Aktion*, he heard from his wife how the edict against Jewish births had been put into effect: "She saw one German holding the baby and smearing something under its nose. Afterwards he threw it on the bed and laughed. When my wife picked up the child, there was something black under his nose. When I arrived at the hospital, I saw that my baby was dead. He was still warm."[52]

Sutzkever's flat cadences befit the courtroom. In the contemporaneous poem he had devoted to the murder fourteen years earlier, Sutzkever made the murder of one child stand for the destruction of a people and their world:

> Let the sun crumble like glass
> since you never beheld its light.
> That drop of poison extinguished your faith—
> you thought
> it was warm sweet milk.[53]

Celan is not likely to have known Sutzkever's poem at the time he wrote "Todesfuge," but Ozick, who has translated many of Sutzekever's poems, surely did when she wrote "The Shawl." She may also have had in mind Josef Zelkowicz, an archivist in the Łódź Ghetto who kept one of the most detailed and impassioned diaries to have survived. A section of his diary to which he gave the title "In Those Nightmarish Days" includes an account of the deportations that commenced on September 1, 1942, prefaced by Chaim Rumkowski's infamous speech demanding that parents turn over their children under age ten to be deported along with those over sixty-five. Rumkowski's speech itself is the most harrowing expression of his tragic reign. Invoking the *akedah*—"I never imagined that my own hand would be the one to bring them [children] to the sacrificial altar"—but one in which no ram is substituted for Isaac, Rumkowski, without offering solace, delivered the news to mothers and fathers: "I must carry out this difficult and bloody operation—must cut off limbs in order to save the body. . . . I have not come to calm you down today but to uncover the fullness of your sorrow and woe."[54]

In the *Aktion* that unfolded in the coming weeks, hundreds of Jews were murdered in the ghetto, and more than 15,000, most of them children and the elderly, were taken to Chełmno and killed. The scenes of parents' compliance and children's terror depicted by Zelkowicz are among the most fearsome of any ghetto diarist:

> Who could describe, who could paint a picture, of the insane, wild rush that follows: half dead human beings, barely able to move, throwing themselves down several stories of stairs, hurrying to carry out the order in time. . . . Woe be unto those who stumble and trip as they make their way—they'll never

get their footing again and will slip and fall on their own blood. Woe be unto the terrified child who wants to scream out one single word—"Mama!." He'll only manage to get the "Ma—" out of his mouth and will never be able to reach the "ma." A revolver shot will slice the word in two right in his throat. "Ma—" will emerge, while "ma" will curl up and fall back into his heart, like a bird shot down on the wing.[55]

If she did not read this passage from Zelkowicz's diary in the Yiddish original in the YIVO archives, Cynthia Ozick could have found a source for Magda's severed cry in the slightly different translation that appeared in Lucy Dawidowicz's *Holocaust Reader* in 1976. Zelkowicz's reportage is no less riveting for being indebted to lines from Ozick's more likely source, Chaim Nachman Bialik's famous poem "The City of Slaughter," in which the many brutalities of the 1903 Kishinev pogrom include the tale

> . . . of a babe beside its mother flung,
> Its mother speared, the poor chick finding rest
> Upon its mother's cold and milkless breast;
> Of how a dagger halved an infant's word,
> Its *ma* was heard, its *mama* never heard.[56]

Striking for its condemnation of Jewish cowardice and spoken in the voice of God, who laments his own capitulation, "The City of Slaughter" subsequently became a rallying cry for Jewish self-defense and provided a template for Jewish writers, during and after the Holocaust, attempting to fathom a slaughter of Jews and their children without precedent in scale and purpose.[57]

Even if they were spoken in the voice of a broken, powerless God, Bialik's allusive cadences place him within a narrative tradition that reaches back to the Bible. Heirs of this tradition, Celan and Ozick wrote with an equally strong sense of biblical and liturgical tradition. One can thus take the pursuit of "black milk" in another direction by following up the suggestion of John Felstiner that it may have a source in Lamentations, which says of Israel's agony after the Babylonian destruction of Jerusalem and its Temple: "Her elect were purer than snow, / Whiter than milk . . . / Now their faces are blacker than soot" (Lamentations 4: 7–8).[58] This is as far as Felstiner ventures, but just a slightly wider notice of the scenes portrayed in this chapter of Lamentations, whether or not it was Celan's conscious inspiration, makes the resonance stronger. Portraying devastation that includes starvation ("Their skin has shriveled on their bones") and cannibalistic infanticide ("With their own hands, tenderhearted women / Have cooked their children"), the speaker decries the end of Israel's capacity for nurture:

> Even jackals offer the breast
> And suckle their young;
> But my poor people has turned cruel,
> Like ostriches of the desert.
> The tongue of the suckling cleaves
> To its palate for thirst.

Lamentations depicts the failure of nurture—God's nurture of his people, His people's nurture of their own children. As the text read on Tisha B'av (the Ninth of Av), Lamentations has been central to the commemoration of Jewish persecution, reaching from the destruction of the First and Second Temples through the Holocaust. The brutality directed toward one's own children in the scripture calls our attention to the continuity between the biblical lament, the cases of infanticide recorded in medieval Jewish chronicles, and modern-day cases in which Jews not only turned over their children but even elected to take their lives.

Rosa saves herself by stuffing the shawl into her mouth when Magda is murdered: "if she let the wolf's screech ascending now through the ladder of her skeleton break out, they would shoot."[59] She would not have been able to save Magda by sacrificing herself, but parents frequently confronted more terrible choices. Felstiner believes that Celan, who lost his mother in the Holocaust, would have winced at Bruno Bettelheim's supposition that the opening of "Todesfuge" evokes the image of "a mother destroying her infant," an act meant to convey "the ultimate desperation" of the death camps.[60] Perhaps Celan would have winced, but the power of his metaphor reaches well beyond the poet's personal experience. Under genocidal assault, mothers and fathers may produce their own black milk in forms ranging from abandonment to outright murder.

Countless parents were willing to die with their children, whether in the gas chamber or elsewhere, rather than permit them to die alone, but some chose otherwise, either helplessly or willingly. Sara Selver-Urbach recalled her aunt bursting into their home in the Łódź Ghetto and admitting that she had given her children away during the September roundup, even as her son pleaded not to be taken: "Why didn't I pounce on them, why didn't I scratch their eyes out? What happened to me, how could I have given them my children, what made me stand there watching, while they took the children and put them on a cart?"[61] Having let his young daughter go during the same roundup, one father confessed, in Polish, "I am a murderer and I must atone," and then, shifting to Hebrew, asked for God's protection, reciting his own version of Yizkor, the prayer for the dead.[62] The duress of arrival in the death camp could produce even more wrenching responses. Ruth Cyprys recalled that, at the moment of selection when their transport train arrived in Auschwitz, some mothers "tore away the little hands clutching at their skirts." One of them, standing with those saved but "facing her child in the condemned crowd," covered her eyes so as not to see the child and plugged her ears so as not to hear her cries.[63] In Maidanek, Alexander Donat witnessed a more heartrending scene:

> A young woman was pushing her way through the crowd near us and a little girl ran after her, weeping and sobbing, "Mama! Mama!" The woman did not look back but pushed ahead and the little girl screamed louder. Suddenly a [guard] . . . grabbed the woman by her shoulder with his left hand, and slapped her with his right hand, yelling, "You Jewish bitch, are you running away from your own child?"
>
> She reeled under the blow. Then, her face distorted with pain and anger, she shouted, "Let me go, you beast! That isn't my child. I have no children. You mind your own business! How dare you hit me!"

The child said the woman was her mother, the beating continued, and the woman persisted in her denials. "'She isn't mine. I'm twenty-two. I want to live,' the woman tried to argue, but she weakened under the blows. In the end, she broke down, grabbed the child in her arms, and pressed it to her breast. She was whimpering now, and stood like a statue of suffering, resigned to her fate."[64]

In the face of hopeless odds, parents might even choose instead to preempt fate. During the Warsaw Ghetto uprising, as the Nazis set fire to building after building, mothers and fathers sometimes leapt with their children from the upper floors rather than be burned alive. Others in Warsaw and elsewhere poisoned their children and themselves. During their imprisonment in Auschwitz, Ruth Kluger recalled, her mother, despondent over their chances for survival, at one time proposed that they kill themselves by walking into the electrified fence. Although the proposal was not repeated and never discussed in their later lives, Kluger realized in maturity, when she had children of her own, that "one might well decide to kill them in Auschwitz rather than wait."[65] Such was the case when Jewish medical personnel took the lives of newborn children destined for a more brutal death. Newborns in the Warsaw Ghetto were poisoned with cyanide or smothered with pillows by doctors, women and men alike, who deemed their death at the hands of Jews preferable to what awaited them.[66] Because mothers and their newborns were routinely gassed in Auschwitz (unless one or both were temporarily preserved for medical experiments), Jewish doctors and nurses, usually without the mother's knowledge, often killed the infants by injection, by poison, or by drowning, and recorded the baby as stillborn. As Olga Lengyel remembered: "And so, the Germans succeeded in making murderers of even us. . . . Our only consolation is that by these murders we saved the mothers."[67]

More dreadful than abandonment or mutual suicide or mercy killing were those cases where parents chose to take the lives of their own children in states of hysteria or to save the lives of those around them. Lyusya Gekhman described the German assault on the Jews driven into the public square in the Ukrainian village of Radzivillov: "The Germans lifted children up in the air with their bayonets . . . The older children were beaten into unconsciousness. Many of the women lost their minds: they were screaming, singing, laughing insanely. Some started strangling their own children."[68] Byrna Bar Oni, who along with her sister joined a group of women partisans in the forest outside the Polish *shtetl* of Byten, recalled that women with young children were asked to spend the night in a more secluded spot lest the children's crying give the partisans away. Next morning came a harrowing report:

> We couldn't keep the children quiet. They felt our fear and restlessness. . . . We were sure the enemy had found us. Suddenly Golda, who was sick and distraught over losing her husband, began wrapping her child with her shawl. With a

terrible black look on her face, she choked her baby to death. The rest of the mothers tried to stop her, but then something happened: they, too, became engulfed in some inexplicable madness—a kind of mass hysteria—and began to choke their babies to death.[69]

Presented with the case of an infant inadvertently smothered to keep it quiet in the Warsaw Ghetto, Rabbi Shimon Efrati determined after the war that such a death did not require penance, because the act saved Jewish lives and, had those in hiding been discovered, the infant would have been killed along with everyone else.[70] In the heat of the moment, of course, no such consultation was possible. As a young boy in Bialystock, Samuel Pisar was hiding with his mother and sister, along with some thirty others, in an underground bunker when the ghetto was liquidated. Samuel's Latin teacher, Professor Bergman, was rocking his baby son, trying to stop his coughing:

> On the other side of the trapdoor above us came the shouts of German search parties and the barking of dogs. We all fell silent; only the baby's coughing continued. "Shhh," hissed a burly man near the door. The coughing did not stop. The man crawled over and placed a hand over the baby's mouth. The coughing ceased. Minutes passed. The child sank limply to the ground. All the while, Professor Bergman sat petrified. I knew he was not a coward. Even then, I knew that if he could think or feel anything at all, he was weighing one life against thirty, even if that life was his own son's.[71]

The Nazis' most demonic crime, concluded Primo Levi, was the creation of the *Sonderkommando*, the Jewish squads tasked with helping to deliver fellow Jews to the gas chambers and processing their corpses at Auschwitz and other death camps. In doing so, Levi remarks, the Nazis attempted to shift the burden of guilt onto others, as though to say, "you, too, like us and like Cain, have killed the brother."[72] Many other circumstances, as we have seen, conspired to place Jews in Levi's "gray zone" of complicity, entangled in the deaths of other Jews—even their own children. But Levi also warned us not to confuse victims with murderers, and so we must not forget who the real killers were.

In late June 1944, at the height of the annihilation of Hungarian Jews in Auschwitz, Kazimierz Wolff-Zdzienicki witnessed something unusual coming into view while the orchestra, made up of camp prisoners playing instruments confiscated from those on their way to death, played a diverting Sunday program. He strained to see what was approaching—perhaps a group of cyclists or prisoners carrying some new kind of shovel? No, a column never before seen was approaching from the direction of the crematoria and the warehouses where the victims' possessions were collected and sorted:

> Several hundred female prisoners were walking in orderly ranks of five, each pushing an empty pram. The head of the column was gradually approaching the gate of our camp. In the vanguard marched a tall SS woman with a beautiful Alsatian. Other SS women surrounded the column.
>
> The orchestra was playing a waltz. The tall concertmaster, a grey-haired Frenchman, swayed to the melody. The women had scarves around their heads, and their heads hung low. Many could not hold back the tears, and their sobs carried over the sound of the music.
>
> The prams were varied. Some glistened with chrome and enamel, while others were old and scratched. There were new limousine models and old-fashioned ones on high wheels, there were prams for newborns and toddlers' strollers. The prams rolled along in rows of five, empty prams. . . .
>
> Prisoners who had been sitting on the ground stood up. One by one, they began removing their caps. The concertmaster glanced at the orchestra, then at the SS men standing at the gate, and raised his baton. He brought it down twice in a slow, measured movement. When he brought it down a third time, Chopin's funeral march began.
>
> The parade of empty prams passed through the gate of the Birkenau Men's Camp to the strains of the march. The head of the column turned towards the camp. The prams were being sent to Germany.
>
> When the backs of the last of the women pushing the prams were out of sight, an SS man began screaming at the concert-master. He cursed him and ordered the orchestra back to their barracks.
>
> The Sunday concert had been uncharacteristically brief.[73]

Virtually no item of value seized from Jews—money, jewels, clothing, shoes, suitcases, eyeglasses, watches, razors, artificial limbs, hair, gold teeth—went to waste in the death camps, so why should baby carriages not also enrich the Third Reich? And let them be paraded, silent and emptied of life, as if in military formation. They were, after all, a fitting representation of Hitler's prophesied victory over the Jews. They were black milk personified.

Notes

1. Seweryna Szmaglewska, *Smoke over Birkenau*, trans. Jadwiga Rynas (New York: Henry Holt, 1947), 225.
2. Cynthia Ozick, *The Shawl* (1989; repr., New York: Vintage, 1990), 7, 9.
3. Ozick, *The Shawl*, 4.
4. Paul Celan, "Todesfuge," trans. John Felstiner, in Felstiner, *Paul Celan: Poet, Survivor, Jew* (New Haven: Yale University Press, 1995), 31–32.
5. Nelly Sachs, "O the night of the weeping children!," trans. Michael Hamburger, in *O the Chimneys*, by Nelly Sachs, trans. Michael Hamburger, Christopher Holme, Ruth and Matthew Mead, and Michael Roloff (New York: Farrar, Straus and Giroux, 1967), 7.
6. Heather Pringle, *The Master Plan: Himmler's Scholars and the Holocaust* (New York: Hyperion, 2006), 240.
7. Charlotte Delbo, *Days and Memory*, trans. Rosette Lamont (1990; repr., Evanston: Marlboro Press/Northwestern University Press, 2001), 1.
8. A. Sutskever, "Fragment," in *Selected Poetry and Prose*, trans. Barbara and Benjamin Harshav (Berkeley: University of California Press, 1991), 332.
9. Aharon Appelfeld, "Buried Homeland," *The New Yorker*, November 23, 1998, 61.
10. Fanya Gottesfeld Heller, *Strange and Unexpected Love: A Teenage Girl's Holocaust Memoirs* (Hoboken, NJ: KTAV Publishing House, 1993), 274–75.
11. Rolf Hochhuth, *The Deputy*, trans. Richard and Clara Watson (New York: Grove Press, 1964), 222–23.
12. Primo Levi, *The Drowned and the Saved*, trans. Raymond Rosenthal (1988; New York: Vintage, 1989), 83–84.
13. Omer Bartov, *Mirrors of Destruction: War, Genocide, and Modern Identity* (New York: Oxford University Press, 2000), 124.
14. Szlama Winer quoted in Patrick Montague, *Chełmno and the Holocaust: The History of Hitler's First Death Camp* (Chapel Hill: University of North Carolina Press, 2012), 109.
15. Alon Confino, *A World without Jews: The Nazi Imagination from Persecution to Genocide* (New Haven: Yale University Press, 2014), 50.

16. Victor Klemperer, *The Language of the Third Reich: A Philologist's Notebook*, trans. Martin Brady (2000; repr., New York: Continuum, 2006), 14.

17. *Lodzer Zeitung*, February 1940, quoted in Boaz Neumann, "The Phenomenology of the German People's Body (Volkskörper) and the Extermination of the Jewish Body," *New German Critique* 36 (winter 2009): 173.

18. Christian Ingrao, *Believe and Destroy: Intellectuals in the SS War Machine*, trans. Andrew Brown (Malden, MA: Polity Press, 2013), 60–61.

19. Richard Grunberger, *A Social History of the Third Reich* (1971; repr., New York: Penguin, 1974), 118.

20. See Shmuel Almog, ed., *Antisemitism through the Ages*, trans. Nathan H. Reisner (New York: Pergamon Press, 1988), plate 23.

21. Adolf Hitler, *Mein Kampf*, trans. Ralph Mannheim (Boston: Houghton Mifflin, 1971), 324.

22. Julius Streicher, "German People's Health from Blood and Soil," in *Nazi Conspiracy and Aggression*, vol. 8 (Washington, DC: United States Government Printing, 1946, 12 [International Military Tribunal at Nuremberg, "Red Series"]. As dramatized in *Sin against Blood*, a Nordic woman thus infected through a previous relationship with a Jew gives birth, with her Nordic husband, to a child who is, nevertheless, depicted to be obviously Jewish; the husband murders the Jew and defends himself at trial as having struck a blow against "the Jewish vampire." Artur Dinter, *Sin against Blood*, quoted in Maria Tartar, *Lustmord: Sexual Murder in Weimar Germany* (Princeton: Princeton University Press, 1995), 61.

23. Michael Burleigh, *The Third Reich: A New History* (New York: Hill and Wang, 2000), 296.

24. Léon Poliakov, *Harvests of Hate: The Nazi Program for the Destruction of the Jews of Europe* (1954; repr., New York: Holocaust Library, 1974), 59.

25. Heinrich Himmler quoted in Peter Padfield, *Himmler: Reichsführer SS* (1990; repr., London: Papermac, 1995), 469–70.

26. See http://www.nytimes.com/books/98/12/06/specials/ozick-shawl.html. I have not been able to locate such a scene in Shirer's book.

27. Elie Wiesel, *Night*, trans. Marion Wiesel (New York: Hill and Wang, 2006), 32.

28. Sara Nomberg-Przytyk, *Auschwitz: True Tales from a Grotesque Land*, trans. Roslyn Hirsch, ed. Eli Pfefferkorn and David H. Hirsch (Chapel Hill: University of North Carolina Press, 1985), 81.

29. Vassili Grossman, *The Years of War (1941–1945)*, trans. Elizabeth Donnelly and Rose Prokofiev (Moscow: Foreign Languages Publishing House, 1946), 398–99.

30. Chil Raichman, *The Last Jew of Treblinka: A Survivor's Memory 1942–1943*, trans. Solon Beinfeld (New York: Pegasus Books, 2011), 106.

31. Michael Hanusiak, *Lest We Forget* (Toronto: Progress Books, 1976), 98.

32. *The Black Book: The Nazi Crime against the Jewish People* (New York: The Jewish Black Book Committee, 1946), 365.

33. Ingrao, *Believe and Destroy*, 159.

34. Ben Edelbaum, *Growing Up in the Holocaust* (Kansas City, MO: n.p., 1980), 92.

35. Theo Richmond, *Konin: One Man's Quest for a Vanished Jewish Community* (1995; repr., New York: Vintage 1996), 482.

36. Daniel Patrick Brown, *The Beautiful Beast: The Life and Crimes of SS Aufseherin Irma Grese*, 2nd ed. (Ventura, CA: Golden West Historical Publications, 2004), 51.

37. Olga Lengyel, *Five Chimneys: A Woman Survivor's True Story of Auschwitz* (1947; repr., Chicago: Academy Chicago Publishers, 1995), 199.

38. Robert Krell quoted in Isidore Gold, *No More Silence: Testimony and Perspectives of a Holocaust Survivor*, ed. Marc DeWitt and Gene Krug (New York: Shengold Publishers, 1999), 128–29.

39. Ernest Klee, Willi Dresden, and Volker Riess, eds., *"The Good Old Days": The Holocaust as Seen by Its Perpetrators and Bystanders*, trans. Deborah Burnstone (Old Saybrook, CT: Konecky & Konecky, 1991), 179.

40. Waitman Wade Beorn, *Marching into Darkness: The Wehrmacht and the Holocaust in Belarus* (Cambridge: Harvard University Press, 2014), 135.

41. Christopher R. Browning, *Ordinary Men: Reserve Battalion 101 and the Final Solution in Poland* (1992; repr., New York: HarperPerennial, 1998), 73.

42. Israel Cymlich, "My War Experiences," in *Escaping the Hell of Treblinka*, by Israel Cymlich and Oskar Strawczynski (Jerusalem: Yad Vashem, 2007), 39.

43. "M. L," "Eyewitness Testimony 14: Infanticide," trans. Gabriel Trunk, in *Jewish Responses to Nazi Persecution: Collective and Individual Behavior*, ed. Isaiah Trunk (New York: Stein and Day, 1979), 125.

44. Hersh Smolar, *The Minsk Ghetto: Soviet-Jewish Partisans against the Nazis* (New York: Holocaust Library 1989), 73.

45. Oskar Strawczynski, "Ten Months in Treblinka," in Cymlich and Strawczynski, *Escaping the Hell of Treblinka*, 158.

46. Lidia Maximova Slipchenko, "Why Did It Happen to Us?," in *The Unknown Black Book: The Holocaust in the German-Occupied Soviet Territories*, ed. Joshua Rubenstein and Ilya Altman, trans. Christopher Morris and Joshua Rubenstein (Bloomington: Indiana University Press, 2008), 115.

47. Wendy Lower, *Hitler's Furies: German Women in the Nazi Killing Fields* (Boston: Houghton Mifflin, 2013), 126–27.

48. Samuel Golfard, *Diary, January to April 1943*, trans. Jacob Littman et al., in Wendy Lower, *The Diary of Samuel Golfard and the Holocaust in Galacia* (Lanham, MD: AltaMira Press, 2011), 113–14.

49. David Kahane, *Lvov Ghetto Diary*, trans. Jerzy Michalowicz (Amherst: University of Massachusetts Press, 1990), 89–90.

50. Charlotte Delbo, *None of Us Will Return*, in *Auschwitz and After*, trans. Rosette C. Lamont (New Haven: Yale University Press, 1995), 100.

51. Sutzkever, "Smoke of Jewish Children," *Selected Poetry and Prose*, 283.

52. Abraham Sutzkever, *Trial of the Major War Criminals* (Nuremberg, Germany: International Military Tribunal, 1947 ["Blue Series"], vol. 8, 306–7.

53. Abraham Sutzkever, "For My Child," in *Burnt Pearls: Ghetto Poems of Abraham Sutzkever*, trans. Ruth Wisse (Oakville, Ontario: Mosaic Press, 1981), 33.

54. Chaim Rumkowski speech quoted in Josef Zelkowicz, "In Those Nightmarish Days," in *In Those Nightmarish Days: The Ghetto Reportage of Peretz Opoczynski and Josef Zelkowicz*, ed. Samuel D. Kassow, trans. David Suchoff (New Haven: Yale University Press, 2015), 215–16.

55. Zelkowicz, "In Those Nightmarish Days," 251.

56. Chaim Nachman Bialik, "The City of Slaughter," trans. Abraham M. Klein, in *Selected Poems of Hayim Nahman [Chaim Nachman] Bialik*, ed. Israel Efros (New York: Bloch Publishing, 1948), 117.

57. See David G. Roskies, *Against the Apocalypse: Response to Catastrophe in Modern Jewish Culture* (Cambridge: Harvard University Press, 1984), 91.

58. Felstiner, *Paul Celan*, 34.

59. Ozick, *The Shawl*, 10.

60. Felstiner, *Paul Celan*, 34; Bruno Bettelheim, "Owners of Their Faces," in *Surviving and Other Essays* (New York: Vintage Books, 1980), 110.

61. Sara Selver-Urbach, *Through the Window of My Home: Memories from Ghetto Lodz*, trans. Siona Bodansky (Jerusalem: Yad Vashem, 1986), 96–97.

62. Anonymous, "A Father's Lament," in *Lodz Ghetto: Inside a Community Under Siege*, ed. Alan Adelson and Robert Lapides (New York: Viking, 1989), 349.

63. Ruth Altbecker Cyprys, *A Jump for Life: A Survivor's Journal from Nazi-Occupied Poland*, ed. Elaine Potter (1997; repr., New York: Continuum, 1999), 56–57.

64. Alexander Donat, *The Holocaust Kingdom: A Memoir* (1965; repr., Washington, DC: The Holocaust Library, 1999), 139.

65. Ruth Kluger, *Still Alive: A Holocaust Girlhood Remembered* (New York: The Feminist Press, 2001), 96–97.

66. Hannah Krall, *Shielding the Flame: An Intimate Conversation with Dr. Marek Edelman, the Last Surviving Leader of the Warsaw Ghetto Uprising*, trans. Joanna Staniska and Lawrence Weschler (New York: Henry Holt, 1986), 9, 47.

67. Judith Sternberg-Newman, *In the Hell of Auschwitz: The Wartime Memoirs of Judith Sternberg Newman* (West Kingston, RI: n.p., 1963), 43; Lengyel, *Five Chimneys*, 11.

68. Lyusya Gekhman, "The Germans in Radzivillov," in *The Complete Black Book of Russian Jewry*, by Ilya Ehrenberg and Vasily Grossman, trans. and ed. David Patterson (New Brunswick, NJ: Transaction Publishers, 2002), 94–95.

69. Byrna Bar Oni, *The Vapor* (Chicago: Visual Impact, 1976), 68.

70. Shimon Effrati, "Responsum 6," in *Rabbinic Responsa of the Holocaust Era*, trans. Robert Kirschner (New York: Schocken Books, 1985), 67–68, 79, 81–82.

71. Samuel Pisar, *Of Blood and Hope* (Boston: Little, Brown, 1980), 41.

72. Levi, *The Drowned and the Saved*, 53, 55.

73. Kazimierz Wolff-Zdzienicki, "The Prams," in *Polish Witnesses to the Shoah*, ed. Marian Tuski (London: Valentine Mitchell, 2010), 203–4.

2

The American Voices of Hidden Child Survivors

"Coming of Age Out of Time and Place"

Phyllis Lassner

For children who survived in hiding during the Holocaust, memories of the displacement from identity, language, and home haunt their memories and their writing. Wherever and however they built their lives in the aftermath, they continued to experience tensions between identities and languages they lost and those they acquired in the aftermath, between loyalties to their new worlds and to the families and communities they left behind, and between the silences these conditions produced and the desire to share only partially remembered stories. Robert Krell, a hidden child survivor and psychiatrist, attests that

> The child or adolescent survivor frequently has only fragments of memory. Some know little of their past, a few not even their first language. There are enormous problems of identity, having been clearly labelled a Jew but not with the attendant knowledge of tradition . . . It is no wonder that we feel at home in many places, for no place is really home.[1]

Although all survivors experienced displacement, its meanings differ for hidden children, as revealed in their forms of remembering and expression. Key to understanding this difference lies in the multivalent meanings of hidden in the context of the Holocaust. For many hidden child survivors, as psychologist Sarah Moskowitz observes, "memories may prove too frightening to recall or may have been repressed and never discussed by any subsequent caretakers out of well-meaning efforts to help the child forget."[2] For those who were too young to form and retain cognitive recall, past experiences can remain entirely or partially hidden from their adult consciousness. For adolescents or young adults, creative and critical development took place in isolation from those formative relationships and events that constitute ordinary emotional, social, and intellectual growth. Moskowitz concludes, "For unlike the older survivor who has memory of ordinary peaceful prewar life, the child survivor, especially from countries invaded early, has no such stabilizing recollections" ("Making Sense" 14). The art and writing of hidden children survivors express the ongoing emotional and cultural challenges of these discontinuities as their subjects and as shaping their language and narrative forms. Among the themes Alan Berger identifies as emerging from these discontinuities, stories by hidden child survivors emphasize "the psychic disorientation imposed by a new identity necessitated by the invention of a life history in order to survive [and] silence and a lack of understanding of why this happened to them."[3]

These themes are explored, complicated, and extended in two volumes of autobiographical stories by hidden child survivors who immigrated to the United States and for whom it took sixty years or more to find the language and forms through which to narrate the experiences and responses they did not fully understand and could not share at the time. Ava Kadishson Schieber's collection of stories, drawings, and poems, *Soundless Roar*, and the anthology *Out of Chaos* demonstrate how these themes relate to questions about the shifting boundaries and definitions of modern American Jewish literature as it continues to be shaped by Holocaust writing. For example, Alan Berger and Gloria Cronin situate Jewish American and Holocaust literature as both separate and related genres, showing how "the Holocaust legacy plays a vital role in the psychosocial lives and the imagistic realm of the second generation," but also in the younger generations of Jewish American writers unrelated to the Holocaust.[4] Integrating the art and writing of hidden child survivors into the evolving themes and relationships between Jewish American and Holocaust literature raises the following questions: how do we situate, analyze, and teach the thematic and narrative contributions of hidden child writing and art to American Jewish culture? Jennifer Lemberg maintains that "[t]he very real destruction of Jewish life in Europe and the frightening prospect of its disappearance worldwide made the Holocaust an American Jewish issue, as did the survivors who carried their stories to America's shores."[5]

Written in English, these collections embed and illustrate the hidden child survivor's struggle to remember and represent experiences that at the time and later were often unexplained and remain only partially coherent. Compounding this struggle is a multilingual transcription: from recalling experiences as they occurred in their first language and through the unsteady acquisition of other languages as they often migrated to different locales before settling in the United States and acquiring American English. Of crucial importance to their writing and contribution to Jewish American culture, this struggle for coherence, connection, and credibility constitutes their poetic and narrative forms and is embedded within them. As Lawrence Langer observes of Holocaust survivor testimony, "the urge to tell meets resistance from the certainty that one's audience will not understand."[6] Their accounts include direct or metaphorical references to shards of memory, to a lost sense of a stable childhood and belonging, to the progression of time, and to ruptures from traditional models of ethical guidance and behavior. Denied access to education, especially reading materials, they were also cut off from the cultural traditions and innovations that inspire and shape each generation of writers in all historical contexts. As a result, like other Holocaust writers, for example, Charlotte Delbo, these writers infuse their representations with self-doubt about their tenuous retrievals of the long-distant past and the need to engage readers with accessible narratives. Like Delbo, they implore their readers, "Try to look. Just try and see."[7] Intertwining their Holocaust histories with the challenges of writing, hidden children writers draw attention to their processes of remembering, discovering, conceptualizing, shaping, and conveying their stories.

Hidden children artists and writers insert their voices into Jewish American cultural history, creating another strand of Jewish immigrant experience and evolving identity. Their Holocaust stories complicate the Jewish American history of integration and assimilation with a combination of retaining and abandoning their European identities. As their representations reveal, their identities as persecuted European Jews are indelible and no longer hidden, but memorialized in the transmission of their stories to become integral to the Jewish-American narrative. Having been silenced, they now testify. Having been marginalized, they now build, guide, and occupy key memorial spaces. This is true not only for the genre of Holocaust representation or Jewish American culture, but, as I argue, for modern American culture writ large.

Although over passing decades scholars have continued to examine the thematic, formalist, and psychological distinctions of survivors' Holocaust representations, the writing and art of hidden child survivors extend their findings to argue that if it were not for Holocaust memory as content and as historical and ethical contexts, such experiments and self-reflexivity would accord with many of the aesthetic characteristics of modernism. As Carol Zemel's work demonstrates, there are many examples of twentieth-century Jewish art that share elements of modernism, for example, "sudden and strange perspectives," pictorial fragmentation, and "visual restlessness" (*Looking Jewish* 44, 64). But as any survey will reveal, except for focuses on Jewish-American modernism, there is an almost total lack of interchange between the study of Holocaust representation and non-Holocaust modernist art. This disassociation suggests the possibility for constructing a productive critical relationship between studying Holocaust art and writing and a more comprehensive modernist cultural expression. Exploring this relationship offers an approach to scholarly investigation and teaching that would show how to interpret and analyze the aesthetics and mandates of each in the light of the other. *Soundless Roar* and *Out of Chaos* demonstrate how analyzing and applying the cultural concerns and formal elements of modernism offer a method of teaching Holocaust representation that illuminates its aesthetic challenges, innovations, and achievements. In turn, the historical and experiential contexts informing Holocaust art raise theoretical and cultural historical questions about modernism's celebration of fragmented subjectivity, exile, moral ambiguity, and its rejection of tradition and the past.[8]

Although Holocaust representation and modernist art constitute separate subjects or fields, they share many concerns and expressive forms.[9] In their departure from realist conventions, including recognizable settings, externally detailed characterizations, and self-explanatory plots, both Holocaust and modernist representations challenge readers' expectations for linear progression, coherent characterization, and morally or psychologically satisfying conclusions. Both literary traditions represent the search for a holistic, identifiable, and explicable self, challenges to enlightenment epistemologies, the inclusion of "diaspora's double consciousness," self-questioning narratives, inexplicable temporal and structural shifts, and the dissolution of narrative reliability (Zemel xi). Differences abound, however, between the self-appointed goals and functions of modernist and Holocaust artists. Although Anglo-American modernists and Holocaust artists both responded to the horrors of war, they overturn realist narrative conventions for significantly different reasons. High Modernists like Hemingway and Virginia Woolf rejected the political and ethical values that in their view motivated and produced the chaos of trench warfare and the catastrophic human losses of World War I. To express the ethical failures, emotional disorientations, and misleading patriotic rhetoric of that war demanded that battleground experiences and their traumatic aftermath be rendered in subjective terms. To represent the disparity between the promises of prewar stability and traumatic responses demanded unsettling narrative innovation that challenged the claims for stability embedded in mimetic narrative forms. To proffer messages or lessons would be tantamount to propaganda or dogma, the enemy of art and critique.

In modernist literature and art, imagination reigns, and its support includes deconstructing the very idea of objective realities, including historical documentation and testimony. And so even as modernism has expanded and changed over the last century, it continues to contest realist representation with nonrepresentational, impressionist, expressionist, imagist, and surrealist styles that defy the possibility of rendering impartial investigation. The forms that emerge from these principles might include metanarratives that respond to the aesthetic invitation to reflect on the infinite recesses of subjective experience and interpretation.

Unlike Ezra Pound's modernist manifesto, "Make it new," a rejection of canonical artistic traditions and their insular social and representational codes, Holocaust art and writing are motivated by efforts to recapture the past, including memories of pre-Holocaust cultural and family life and traditions. Even if absent or lapsed memory produces fragments, transfiguring them into graphic details asserts the authenticity of Holocaust experiences and responses. With resemblance to modernist innovations in genre and form, Holocaust artists have searched for the linguistic and pictorial compositions through which to represent and memorialize the past while conveying the psychological and cultural effects of displacement, relocation, and adaptation on their identities and sense of self. Unlike modernist rejection of national political culture as oppressive, the writing and art of hidden child survivors express the embrace of their American identity and wish to become part of the American story. Their rebellion against hegemonic political culture was fulfilled by surviving the Nazi revolution and its reign of terror.

From his own and related clinical experience, Robert Krell testifies: "Many of us were raised in silence, enveloped in silence. A child not noticed might survive. We could not draw attention to ourselves, not in that world."[10] A major challenge for hidden child writers is the residue of silence left by having lost the languages that identified themselves, their parents, and communities. While the youngest had no chance to acquire the linguistic fluency that defined their worlds, older children experienced a linguistic rupture that for many meant a difficult adaptation when they reached the United States. English was rarely learned or used in European Jewish communities before, during, and in the immediate aftermath of the war. Jennifer Lemberg explains how "[t]he nature of the Holocaust further complicated the use of language by defying familiar structures used to narrate human experience by perverting even ordinary language so as to confound our understanding of the everyday" (140). As Ava Schieber and the contributors to *Out of Chaos* demonstrate, however, such complications are not necessarily impediments to artistic expression. Instead, they become integral, even necessary to their testimonial and artistic achievements.

In a recent forum on Holocaust testimony, Sara Horowitz broadens the definition of testimony to include "fiction, poetry, and the discourse of the imaginary," genres that are distinct from the demands of "juridical testimony."[11] Among its many virtues, Horowitz notes, the reliance of imaginative expression on metaphor leads to richly nuanced representations of the "processes and constructions of memory, ethics, inner life" and other such subjective responses that allow the subject to speak in her own self-constructed voice (195). In the writing of many survivors, such as Delbo, Ida Fink, and Tadeusz Borowski, such imaginative voices reconstruct the Holocaust past in expressive forms that suggest critical questions about the possibilities of rendering fragmented and traumatic memories in language or pictorial art.

A Fugue in Five Languages

In 1941, when the Nazis invaded Yugoslavia, Ava Kadishson Schieber's father told his wife and two daughters that their only hope for survival was not to register, as demanded, but to separate and go into hiding. Fifteen-year-old Ava was sheltered for four years in a chicken coop, tending the animals on a small farm south of Belgrade. To conceal her identity as an educated, confident Jewish woman, fluent in German, Serbian, and Hungarian, she adopted the persona of a mute; she avoided eye contact and stood small. As with so many survivors, even liberation was fraught with struggle. As Schieber has said, for four years following the Allies' victory over the Axis powers, until she and her mother, her family's only other survivor, were allowed passage to Israel, they were forced to trade Hitler for Stalinist oppression under Tito.[12] To make the most of this fraught political situation, Schieber studied set design, a craft that would provide work along with an outlet for what she refers to as her "visual memory" and self-expression (2/14/16).

Soundless Roar is written in English, Schieber's fifth language. She acquired the language at the same time that she learned Hebrew, to adapt to her life in Israel. Hebrew, of course, is Israel's official and everyday language, but English was required in her first job at the Cameri Theater designing the set and poster for *The Heiress*, a stage adaptation of Henry James's novella *Washington Square*. An English-language copy of the novella became Ava's textbook and served her creative talents well. Inscribed fifty years later, the lexicon, syntax, and voices of *Soundless Roar* convey a process of learning and translating her multilingual memories of her prewar Yugoslav childhood, of hiding, and of adapting into English. Echoing James's tautly structured, elliptical storytelling and cryptic dialogue, Schieber's writing suggests the translation of an iconic American modernism into a Jewish American Holocaust modernism. Interrelating stories, poems, and drawings, the book's content and structure depict her translation of the losses she endured into graphic and literary images gleaned from shards of memory. In this translation, *Soundless Roar* also addresses a question raised by Glenn Sujo in his study of Holocaust art: "How did the artist cling so tenaciously to her memories which have, as a result of this transcription, become so tangibly, so resolutely her own?" (*Legacies* 76). Instead of chronological development, Schieber's memorial images cohere in their reflexive commentary on each other, while expressing a linguistic strangeness in their intermittently unidiomatic English. An outsider from the moment Ava left her family and home in Novi Sad, she deploys her poetic language to convey that her preferred identity resides beyond the confines of conventionally accessible models and their forms of expression.

soundless roar the title says
construct your own meaning from the image
of mute din
where a vague maze of lines
limited by size and form
just indicates the space it evolved from
no place to fit a key
mind must break open closed entry
and cross the threshold
stare into obscurity of revealed insight
face glare of unfeigned depths
and then the way back to innocence
has lost all road signs
hence time is nameless too
and word's abundant treasure inadequate
even with novel terms

Like many modernists, Schieber conceives her art in formal experiments that defy the claims of realism and challenge meanings of both everyday and poetic language.[13] Her untitled poem and drawing announce the triangular paradoxical relationship between Schieber's urgent desire to represent the Holocaust, its challenges, and its impact on creative expression. Whereas paradox was the mantra of the New Critics' acclaim for Modernism, allowing readers to revel in ambiguous structures for their aesthetic and epistemological pleasures, Schieber's poem and drawing are structured as paradoxical promises that must be betrayed.

The tonal ambiguity in the poem's second line entices and challenges readers to engage with her book's images, but her "maze" entraps them with paradoxes that remain resistant to "meaning," as she suggests the inadequacy of modernist representation and interpretation—"even with novel terms." Instead of affirming "the act of writing—narrating, composing, choosing, interpreting," Schieber's poem refuses "to bestow order on a reality that had none."[14] The poem's self-referential aesthetics are bound by an inexplicable history. How does a reader hear the "mute din" that bombarded Ava's hidden self? How does one read the syntax of a fifth language that omits "key" lexical designations of "this and that," of "a and the," the articles of faith on which we rely to lead us to the subject, the verb, the object of a sentence or line? This is a usage that originates in displacement and replicates it in a form that defies the grammatical rules of American English. It is written primarily for an American audience but keeps its distance, reminding readers "about the mediated nature of our relationship to the Holocaust as well as its continuing impact" (Lemberg 139). Resonating with the sounds of foreign languages, Schieber's poem insists that the reader's "mind must break open closed entry / and cross the threshold" to recognize the Holocaust poet's tenuous identification with modernist Jewish culture. But the Holocaust context and subject of Schieber's book are also defiant. How do non-survivor readers extend their own imaginative capacities to envision the Holocaust experience that lies unresolved across that threshold? By implication, Victoria Aarons addresses this question by arguing that Holocaust narratives must, "by necessity, deviate from traditional forms and expectations of language and design [because] language itself [is] no longer an identifiable measure of reality, words so corrupted, distorted from their original meanings" ("Memory" 187). We can only read on to immerse ourselves in the writing and art that follow.

The accompanying drawing is equally challenging in its labyrinthine structure. It is composed of a single tense but sinuous line that, in a modernist stroke, mirrors the metaphoric opaqueness of the poem in its concrete but abstract elusiveness. Hands and faces are clearly recognizable as such and constitute the sole subject, but, like a child's stick figures, they lack signs of individuality, gender, or sexuality. Rather than building up a sense of self, Schieber maintains that her art takes the self apart to demonstrate the fragmented relationship between inside and outside and between interior dualities. In all, this atomization reflects her "search for understanding" (2/14/16). A distinct feature, Schieber notes, are the eyes of the figures, the starting point and metaphorical center, for each drawing (2/14/16). Eyes and faces look every which way, animated but without direction or engagement with viewers. Schieber attributes her emphasis on eyes to their dominance in the Greek Orthodox icons she viewed in the homes and churches of her childhood friends. Another influence derives from the books of art in her own childhood home, including photographs of classical Greek sculpture and catalogues of Bauhaus architecture and furniture. In combination both aesthetic traditions emphasize simplified, clean lines, a minimalist approach from which natural and constructed objects reveal their essence. These elements are apparent in Schieber's drawings, where one unshaded line connects and disconnects all the etiolated figures, each of whom looks at, looks for, and looks away from the other. As Schieber notes, they reflect her emotional isolation in hiding as well as her yearning for connection (2/14/16). Although bodies in Schieber's drawings have no solidity, neither flesh nor muscle, the lines of which they are composed combine lyrical fluidity, mordant immobility, and a single dimension that intensifies their formal tension.

Despite the influences and engagement with classical, religious, and modernist aesthetics, the Holocaust context and content of Schieber's book occupy a distinctive cultural space. With only a blank white space as backdrop, no accompanying objects, and a flattened, floating perspective, Schieber's figures can easily be interpreted in allegorical terms with universal significance, such as "the inertness of suffering" (2/14/16). They can be viewed as though they have been transported in and to an indefinite time and place, a nowhere in which they remain in a state suggesting either a self-determining modernist exile or a religious sense of eternal oneness. In a book about the uncertainty of hiding from political oppression, however, Schieber's line figures are emblematic of a different iconography. Just as she was both sheltered and trapped, performing hard farm labor while starved of adequate food and comfort, so her figures are frozen, both in repose and in anxiety, isolated from surrounding danger but also suggesting its ghostly effects. As she maintains, "The subject is always there" even when her art verges on the nonrepresentational, but "it is a subject without security" (2/14/16). Just as there is no way into or out of this drawing, no stable position for the viewer, there is no escape for the figures. They entangle meaning in irreconcilable loss.

Although the drawing's position alongside the poem indicates their heuristic relationship to each other, neither elucidates the other. Barbie Zelizer confirms the challenges of visual Holocaust representation to readers and interpretation: "If we view representation as translation work rather than mere reportage, as metaphor rather than index, as incomplete rather than comprehensive, then we admit the frailty of representational codes into our own expectations of what each representational code can and should do" (*Visual Culture* 2). In their defiance of what Zelizer refers to as "schematic, iconic, and simplistic features of a representation," Ava Schieber's drawings offer a paradox. She created *Soundless Roar* with all the benefits of "working at a safe distance," but her art also inscribes "a certain hesitancy, a tentativeness and lack of artifice" that Glen Sujo interprets as characterizing those "stylistic and iconographic choices available to artists in internment, so rigorously proscribed by the severity of their existence" (Sujo 79–80).

Hiding in Silence and the Language of Terror

Ava Schieber's stories encapsulate the tensions and paradoxes of her poetry and drawings in narrative structures that are both triangular and circular in time, the purpose of which is to represent her "search for understanding" the fragmented but insistent presence of the past (2/14/16). The stories often begin with a querulous narrative tone that informs their critical relationship between Schieber's "fragments in my mind . . . from that prewar time" and her method of foreshadowing.[15] In effect, Schieber's method challenges conventional depictions of an idyllic prewar childhood. Carrying this challenge forward, the stories then move to a wartime scenario and conclude with a succinct reflection in the present continuous tense that reveals the irrepressible impact of two world wars on Schieber's consciousness and art.

Her story "Rabbit" begins by relating her Holocaust generation to her grandmother's experiences of displacement and extreme hunger as the Austro-Hungarian Empire fell into chaos. With its reflexive structure, the story tethers Schieber's childhood identity to the lexicon of the Holocaust, as a "second generation survivor of World War I" (2/14/16). Situating her childhood in the liminal position between two world wars produces a critical perspective. Instead of comforting bedtime stories that would "have been the blueprint for a carefree childhood," her grandmother offered history lessons that were "great lessons for a child to learn about the unpredictability of life and politics" ("Rabbit" 29). The structure of "Rabbit" is governed by these lessons, with the retrospective plotting of Holocaust "unpredictability" achieving narrative coherence even as it undermines the possibility for an open ending. The story warns its readers of the necessity of its closed, circular structure at the very beginning by announcing that "in the thirties, before the Second World War . . . signs were already everywhere" and "Hatred of the Jews in Germany was rampant and spreading" ("Rabbit" 30, 31). This ominous contextual commentary shapes the story of the child Ava.

On a visit to a farm with her beloved grandmother, she is given a "fluffy" pet rabbit, a "lovable toy" to which she responds by loving it to death; she hugs it so fiercely, it is asphyxiated ("Rabbit" 32). Although accidental, the form of the animal's death is resonant, recalling the Nazis' gas chambers. With this association, the farm where Schieber is given the rabbit becomes an overdetermined metaphor, fusing hatred of the Jews, Ava's displacement during the war, and the Janus face of love. Although she was saved by the farmers who hid her, the abject conditions that concealed her presence also meant sharing their farm's scant resources with the animals in her care, her only companions and source of emotional comfort. The presence of the childhood past in the Holocaust present illustrates the story's interdependent structure that metonymically suggests a symbiotic ecology representing a political critique. More concretely, this ecological balance stands in opposition to the disorder created by the well-ordered Nazi ideological hierarchies that identified the Jews and other human groups not only as unlovable, but also as threatening animals that must be destroyed.

Political and ethical disenchantment mark Schieber's journey into emotional and intellectual dispossession, isolation, and loss. Hers is no *bildungsroman*, but, as with her other stories, including "Children's Story," the history of two world wars revises the transformative promises of the genre by questioning what it means to develop a sense of self and skills that defied models of ordinary and mythic human development and progress—skills such as suspicion, vigilance, and suppressed emotion. Narrated in "Rabbit," these were the skills she employed when fetching drinking water several miles from her farm and when she observed two small children whose manner of being she recognized as that of her own, of hiding. Hidden between "trees and overgrown shrubs," she sees the "small girl's resemblance to the woman who was leading her out of the house. It must have been her mother. She was also carrying the boy, who was hugging her. The girl walked slowly behind them, holding a doll in one hand and a small suitcase in the other, looking back at the farmhouse" ("Rabbit" 36–37). As Schieber learned, the mother must have succumbed to the Nazis' promise to save the family if she led them to her hidden children.

The reverberating references, relationships, and sites are telling of the sense of fatedness embedded in fables as well as the ominous unpredictability of Holocaust experience. Once again, a farm is the site of both fecundity and death, not as nurturing an organic life cycle but as its subversion. Once again, in this catastrophic time, "hugging" portends the untimely death of childhood innocence. The girl's doll or toy presupposes the Nazi ideology of destroying the nurturing love of unwanted mothers and children. The image signifies neither comfort nor "great lessons about the unpredictability of life and politics," only predetermined and unwilling betrayal and death (29). Narratively, in the story's circular time scheme, a child's life cannot develop over time but is the victim of time running out, of the recalibration of time by the Third Reich's promise of a thousand years for itself and no time for its victims. The nonlinear, nonprogressing narrative structure, the interpellation of each segment of the story into the others, suggest the end of a narrative time in which endings are open to imagined worlds of possibility. The conclusion of "Rabbit" interweaves memories of Schieber's childhood and Holocaust past with questions raised by the mother's hopeful but doomed "decision to lead the murderers to her children's hiding place" ("Rabbit" 37). "With my growing awareness of how hatred became the big killer in the world, I was haunted by a solemn memory from my childhood—that love could kill as well. . . . I have not erased that scene of the two children walking out of the house, from the marginal safety of hiding, into the certainty of doom. I have never forgotten those children, nor have I lost the sadness of their being gone" ("Rabbit" 38).

Reading Schieber's nonlinear plotting, dissonant linguistic patterns, and fragmented memories as aligned with modernist formal experiments offers a guide to analyzing and teaching the aesthetic achievements of Holocaust art and writing. Conversely, the historical imperatives of Holocaust art and writing offer a critical perspective on modernist prerogatives, including the privileging of indeterminacy and instability of signification. Although Holocaust writers and artists attest to the disjointed and unpredictable brutality to which they were subjected, they also proclaim the historical authenticity and significance of their experiences. In "Rabbit," Ava Schieber reflects on the tension between the indeterminacy of Holocaust experience and its tragic stability:

> I often thought about how in wartime, haphazard chance could change the whole pattern of events. At first glance, it certainly seemed that way. Years later I started to believe that there were no random occurrences. Events didn't just happen. There were entire arrays of circumstances which had to exist and fit into what then had the appearance of a predesigned pattern. Those seemingly incidental fragments had to link into each other in their perfect fit. ("Rabbit" 36)

The sense of a determined circumstantial pattern accords with the ideology, policies, and practices that comprise the Nazis' intention to keep their targeted victims in a well-ordered state of disorientation and powerlessness. Even though the decision to hide can be viewed as self-determining, whatever the circumstances, the paradoxical presence of uncertain but predictable danger was the governing force. Like other twentieth-century art, Schieber's Holocaust modernism expresses a search to unravel the nonlinear, associative processes that govern fragmented memories of events so extreme, they defy extant ethical and representational models. Inserting the subject of the Holocaust, however, creates a significant distinction from the mandates of canonical modernism. Whereas canonical modernism constructs its discontinuities to reflect its distance from the problematic ideologies of the past, Schieber's art and writing represent "a lengthening of history into the present" (Aarons, "Memory" 186). All of her art and writing embed critiques of Fascist discourse and dramatize its consequences into and beyond the present. Her multilingual American English embeds the confluence of prewar, wartime, and postwar experience. Offering no consolation, the circular, continuous lines of her drawings and patterns of her poems and stories are expressive pathways to her Holocaust past. Schieber's Holocaust modernism allows us to hear the silenced voices and see the Holocaust experiences that had to be hidden.

Salvaged Memories

One of the great achievements of the collection *Out of Chaos* is its representation of each writer's struggle with language and memory. The anthology is exceptional for several important reasons. The guidance of Elaine Fox, the editor, ensured that its stories and poems expressed the writers' individualized voices and narrative structures, including such genres as brief vignettes, tableaux, poems, stories, and an imagined dialogue between two lost mothers. The anthology represents different memories and reactions to a wide range of experiences in hiding across Europe. The sites of their experiences range from Holland, Belgium, Italy, Germany, Greece, Yugoslavia, Poland, and France. The forms of their hiding and escapes include being on the run, escaping over mountains, and hiding and even sometimes forgetting their Jewish identities in convents and rescuers' homes and hovels, basements and attics. Some were left on their own; others found themselves embroiled in rescuer family conflicts.

Each of these stories is complete in itself even as it represents brief or elongated moments, fragments of memory and experience—what Ida Fink calls "a scrap of time."[16] Some contributors chose to write story clusters, each one capturing a moment or incident and often disconnected by memory or temporal and spatial divides. Some stories offer introductory contexts and footnotes to establish as precisely as the authors can the historical frameworks of their personal experiences and reactions. These include the exact locations of their childhood homes, in *shtetlach* and city neighborhoods that mark the writers' social class, religious observance, and affiliation. The stories' evocations of home become symbols of personal and cultural identity, reminding us that hidden child survivors once belonged to vibrant Jewish communities with rich cultural and social lives. If those places are gone, they have been restored to view in the affectionately conceived details of vivid writing.

Where memory permits, some stories recount defining moments of prewar life with family and community, while some authors admit to the emptiness they feel at having no memory of that time before terror defined their lives. The occasional photographs of childhood places attest to the end of meaningful Jewish life when Poland was invaded on September 1, 1939. The stories and poems capture moments of anxiety, joy, relief, fear, disillusionment, and loss. Some authors have chosen to write about their lives after the Holocaust, while others end their stories in moments of traumatic rupture, encounters with the unknown, and inexplicable occurrences and feelings. Connections between past and present register as life stories that defy all platitudes about "happily ever after." Instead, their different responses reveal how the burdens of memory and loss affect the rich lives they all built in the aftermath in the United States. Their journeys are another example of Victoria Aarons' insight that "the ineradicable effects of the Holocaust . . . have no geographical or temporal boundaries" ("Making" 43). All of the contributors struggle to remember, to memorialize, and to depict the fractured Holocaust past and a present fraught with the attempt to retrieve and retain emotional images of the lost.

Like other Holocaust writers such as Tadeusz Borowski and Charlotte Delbo, some writers in the collection narrate their stories in the present tense, suggesting continuous, never-ending anxiety, a stalled sense of an unfolding future, and the ongoing, often failed struggle to remember. Leoni Taffel Bergman, for example, was born in Berlin but left for Belgium with her parents in 1938, seeking safety. With escalating danger, she and her younger sister were hidden, but their parents perished in Auschwitz. At the end of 1946, the sisters immigrated to New York to endure a bleak experience living with strangers once again.

Leoni was then adopted by a family in Chicago, where she was educated, married, and taught school. She contributed four pieces to *Out of Chaos* that chart her odyssey from its earliest hints of danger in Berlin to the dashed hope for safe harbor and hiding in Belgium, to the moment of arrival in the United States, and, with Marguerite Mishkin, an imagined dialogue between their mothers in the transport train to Auschwitz.

Bergman's first piece, "Earliest Memories: A Walk in the Park," uses the present tense to recount a brief incident that occurred in 1938 Berlin when she was three years old and an ordinary activity turned ominous. Stopping to tie her shoelaces while on a walk, she mistakes a strange couple for her parents and speaks to them in Yiddish, inadvertently defying the warning that to do so in public is dangerous. The psychological and narrative implications of the present tense are multivalent: "These walks are familiar to me" suggests continuity between the subject and the context of the incident, including the linguistic duality that must be adjusted constantly to survive the intensifying dangers of living in Berlin.[17] The incident also retains its position in her memory and resonates in the present of writing. Yet, despite her indelible memory of the incident, she cannot recall its aftermath, a definitive journey to Brussels toward more danger and survival. Notwithstanding its fragmented state and temporal isolation, with no background to explain the use of Yiddish as "the home language," the story does not stand alone ("Earliest Memories" 9). Like Ava Schieber's commentary, Bergman's reflection on the incident immediately follows, offering to complete the story. It does so, however, by undermining the possibility of stability with persistent interruptions exclaiming unresolved tension between a sense of urgency and doubt. Bergman's assertion that "It must be a Sunday" signals the verbal modality of both certainty and necessity, but her repetitions of "Maybe" reinforce the uncertainty inherent in the retrieval of such an early memory, its cultural background, and its translation into a coherent narrative ("Earliest Memories" 9).

The story's discontinuities also undercut the possibility for linear development or containment in the past. Simultaneously, however, the fleeting incident achieves certainty through its lingering affect that shapes Bergman's self-imagining and her story. The "dread" of the moment becomes a lasting "fear" that, as it permeates her future seventy years later, needs no retrieval. Its presence persists in her readiness "to blame [her] inability to foresee negative consequences that could occur when a serious event happens in my life" ("Earliest Memories" 10). In the absence of a linear narrative, the story constructs mnemonic bridges across the Holocaust past and her present. Bergman's use of the indefinite, conditional "could" aligns with the uncertainty of memory to create continuity between the terrors of her Berlin moment and its haunting presence in the present in which the story is written. The story's self-reflexive structure provides continuity, framing the incident so that it is not isolated from its past and from the journey into testimony. Whereas the narrative experiments of canonical modernists eschew the viability of offering testimony, Bergman's story illustrates Lawrence Langer's analysis of the conjunction between Holocaust survivors' urge to bear witness and its expressive forms that necessitate a "lexicon of disruption, absence, and irreversible loss" (*Holocaust Testimonies*, xi). Although this lexicon is shared by modernists, the survivor's urge to transform memory into an intelligible and credible narrative is not. Modernists maintain that because the fragmented, associative nature of memory reflects disjunctions between past and present, it can only be represented as an unstable, tenuous narrative, not as truth. For hidden children survivors, testimony restores the past to the present along with the subjectivity that was fractured and hidden from oneself and others. Langer concludes "that *all* of [the survivors] were telling a version of the truth as they grasped it, that several currents flow at differing depths in Holocaust testimonies, and that our understanding of the event depends very much on the source and destination of the current we pursue" (*Holocaust Testimonies* xi).

Trapped in Transit

Judith Levy Straus was born in Dortmund, Germany, in 1933 and moved with her parents to Amsterdam, where they found only temporary safety. In 1943 the family was deported to Westerbork Transit Camp and then to Theresienstadt, where her father was then transported to Auschwitz and killed on arrival. Mother and daughter survived and in 1949 immigrated to the United States. Straus contributed six pieces to *Out of Chaos*, a vignette charting a moment of hushed family discussion in Amsterdam, three poems expressing a child's confusion about ensuing events, and a retrospective account of a day in Westerbork in 1943. A short poem, "The Transit Camp," offers a retrospective view of a single scene repeated in a circular pattern as victims are carried to their deaths:

> Every Monday it arrives
> Gaping and empty
> The long snake of cattle cars.
> Every Tuesday it leaves
> Locked and full
> With human cargo going east.
> Every Monday in overcrowded barracks
> Terrified faces
> Full of worry, fear.
> Every Tuesday, the faces of those left
> Expressionless, empty . . .

Only six more days till Monday.[18] Like a modernist poem, the formal patterns of "Transit Camp" express its meaning. In a circular movement, the poem's twelve lines echo its depiction of the train's endless cycle of round-trip journeys. For the passengers, the itinerary promises only a one-way trip from terror to murder. The train's destination is no secret; the narrator is a seasoned observer of the cyclical pattern of mechanized transport—so well organized that there is no variation in the two days of its execution or in the responses of those who await their doomed fate. The lines are arrhythmical and succinct but incomplete. Their fragmented and atonal form resembles a modernist convention, ascribing divided identities and consciousness to the failure of modernity's progress, but the poem's context provides a critical gloss. While Holocaust writers would agree that the Final Solution signaled modernity's devolution, the prisoners' fragmented, abject state; totalizing loss of freedom; and impending murder are signs of a strategic plan: to create disorienting environments so that genocide would proceed in an orderly fashion. The prisoners suffer not from divided selves, but from having been reduced to a single identity and consciousness—waiting for their predetermined fate.

The poem's voice is monotonal and monologic; there are no shifts in its register and no signs of address to a listener or expectation that its testimony will be heard. Although the speaker is situated among the many "in overcrowded barracks," she is isolated from meaningful contact. Any sense of companionship and, by extension, community has been decimated. The ellipses ending the penultimate line, "Expressionless, empty . . . ," indicate the loss of hope that accompanies the penultimate step before annihilation. With no expectation that a response is possible, the poem conveys the sense that it is already too late for one. And yet the poem's appearance in this volume identifies it as constructing an American audience as a memorializing community.

Jewish American Holocaust Culture

The testimonial stories, poems, and art of hidden children travel over time, escape, immigration, and translation into a story written in English once again to refigure American Jewish identity, its cultural landscape, voices, and meanings. Their writing and art do not assimilate into the major themes and traditions of American Jewish literature. Focused primarily on their European experiences, their stories do not dramatize, narrate, or reflect on the immigrant experience of cultural conflicts and ambivalence about assimilation to the dominant culture and society. Those conflicts are part of the European Holocaust experience and history that commingle with their Jewish-American identities. Nor do they infuse their writing with "the rich, imaginative expression of *Yiddishkeit*, a character of life and culture infused into the language and literary imagination of postwar writers" (Aarons, "Making" 47).[19] As Schieber, Bergman, and Straus attest, to represent the history they survived and the languages they abandoned and acquired, English becomes the language to express the integration of their hybrid American identities, writing, and art into Jewish American culture.[20]

Notes

1. Robert Krell, "Some Unique Aspects of Child Survivors," *Messages and Memories*, 6.
2. Sarah Moskowitz, "Making Sense of Survival," *Messages and Memories*, 21.
3. Alan Berger, "Hidden Children," *Jewish American and Holocaust Literature*, 13–14.
4. Alan Berger and Gloria Cronin, "Introduction," *Jewish American and Holocaust Literature*, 4.
5. Jennifer Lemberg, "The Holocaust in American Jewish Fiction," *The Edinburgh Companion to Modern Jewish Fiction*, 139.
6. Lawrence Langer, *Holocaust Testimonies*, xiii.
7. Delbo, Charlotte. *Auschwitz and After*, 84.

8. Ranen Omer-Sherman examines modernist Jewish-American poetry as offering various alternatives to national and cultural identity, complicating a postcolonial tendency to view exile as a productively destabilizing condition.

9. This separation is apparent at academic conferences. For example, the Lessons and Legacies Holocaust focuses solely on Holocaust history and culture, while the Modernist Studies Association's conference rarely includes presentations on Holocaust cultural production. The American Comparative Literature conference occasionally features seminars on Holocaust culture, but rarely do scholars in more generalized approaches to modernist culture participate.

10. Robert Krell, "Hiding During and After the War," *Messages and Memories*, 41.

11. Sara Horowitz, "Engaging Survivors," 195.

12. Personal conversation, February 14, 2016.

13. Ava Kadishson Schieber, untitled poem and drawing, *Soundless Roar*, Frontispiece.

14. Gila *Safran* Naveh, "A Speck of Dust Blown," 105.

15. Ava Kadishson Schieber, "Rabbit," *Soundless Roar*, 30.

16. Ida Fink, *A Scrap of Time and Other Stories* (Evanston: Northwestern University Press), 1995.

17. Leonie Taffel Berman, "Earliest Memories: A Walk in the Park," 9, 10.

18. Judith Levy Straus, "The Transit Camp," *Out of Chaos*, 171.

19. Hana Wirth-Nesher offers a modernist textual reading to establish the significance of Yiddish language and culture to the identities and art of first-generation Jewish American immigrant writers.

20. Whereas the idea and practice of hybridity were denounced as promoting and producing mongrelism in Nazi ideology, in postcolonial theory, hybridity is employed as a critique of racial or cultural essentialism. For the foundational postcolonial theory of hybridity, see Homi Bhabha, *The Location of Culture*. For its more recent critique, see Han Nederveen.

References

Aarons, Victoria. "Memory, Conscience, and the Moral Weight of Holocaust Representation." In *Ethics, Art, and Representations of the Holocaust*, edited by Simone Gigliotti, Jacob Golomb, and Caroline Steinberg Gould, 183–98. New York: Lexington Books, 2014.

———. "The Making of American Jewish Identities in Postwar American Fiction." In *The Edinburgh Companion to Modern Jewish Fiction*, edited by David Brauner and Axel Stähler, 43–52. Edinburgh: Edinburgh University Press, 2015.

Berger, Alan, and Gloria Cronin, "Introduction." In *Jewish American and Holocaust Literature: Representation in the Postmodern World*, edited by Alan L. Berger and Gloria L. Cronin, 1–10. Albany, State University of New York Press, 2004.

Berger, Alan L. "Hidden Children: The Literature of Hiding." In *Jewish American and Holocaust Literature*, 13–30.

Bergman, Leonie Taffel. "Earliest Memories: A Walk in the Park." In *Out of Chaos: Hidden Children Remember the Holocaust*, edited by Elaine S. Fox, 9–11. Evanston: Northwestern University Press, 2013.

Bhabha, Homi. *The Location of Culture*. New York: Routledge, 1994.

Delbo, Charlotte. *Auschwitz and After*. Translated by Rosette C. Lamont. New Haven: Yale University Press, 1995.

Fink, Ida. *A Scrap of Time and Other Stories*. Evanston: Northwestern University Press, 1995.

Horowitz, Sara. "Engaging Survivors: Assessing 'Testimony' and 'Trauma' as Foundational Concepts." *Dapim: Studies on the Holocaust* 28, no. 3 (2014): 195–96. http://dx.doi.org/10.1080/232356249.2014.951909.

Krell, Robert. "Some Unique Aspects of Child Survivors." In *Messages and Memories: Reflections on Child Survivors of the Holocaust*, 2nd ed., by Robert Krell, 1–10. Vancouver, BC: Memory Press, 2001. 1–10.

Langer, Lawrence. *Holocaust Testimonies: The Ruins of Memory*. New Haven: Yale University Press, 1991.

Lemberg, Jennifer. "The Holocaust in American Jewish Fiction." In *The Edinburgh Companion to Modern Jewish Fiction*. 138–148.

Moskowitz, Sarah. "Making Sense of Survival: A Journey with Child Survivors." In *Messages and Memories*, 11–26.

Naveh, Gila Safran. "A Speck of Dust Blown by the Wind Across Land and Desert." In *Jewish American Holocaust Literature*, 103–14.

Nederveen Pieterse, Jan. *Globalization and Culture: Global Mélange*. New York: Rowman & Littlefield, 2004.

Omer-Sherman, Ranen. *Diaspora and Zionism in Jewish American Literature*. Hanover, NH: Brandeis University Press, 2002.

Schieber, Ava Kadishson. *Soundless Roar: Stories, Poems, and Drawings*. Evanston: Northwestern University Press, 2002.

Segev, Tom. *The Seventh Million: The Israelis and the Holocaust*. New York: Hill & Wang, 1994.

Straus, Judith Levy. "The Transit Camp." In *Out of Chaos*, 171.

Sujo, Glenn. *Legacies of Silence: The Visual Arts and Holocaust Memory*. London: Imperial War Museum and Philip Wilson Publishers, 2001.

Wirth-Nesher, Hana. *Call It English: The Languages of Jewish American Literature*. Princeton: Princeton University Press, 2006.

Zelizer, Barbie. *Visual Culture and the Holocaust*. New Brunswick: Rutgers University Press, 2001.
Zemel, Carol. *Looking Jewish: Visual Culture and Modern Diaspora*. Bloomington: Indiana University Press, 2015.

3

Reimagining History

Joe Kubert's Graphic Novel of the Warsaw Ghetto Uprising

Victoria Aarons

Ever since the publication of Art Spiegelman's *Maus* (volume I published in 1986; volume II in 1991), there have been a wide range of graphic narratives that attempt to re-create the traumatic impact of the Shoah. An appreciable number of these graphic renditions are written and illustrated by the children and grandchildren of Holocaust survivors, the second and third generation, whose narratives give voice to survivor accounts mediated through a more contemporary lens.[1] In their attempt to extend memory and testimony, these graphic narratives blur conventional genres: memoir, biography, the intersection and juxtaposition of text and image. Narrating the events of the Holocaust from a variety of voices and perspectives, these graphic narratives move between present and past, returning to the sites of catastrophic rupture. In the graphic novel *Yossel: April 19, 1943* (2003), the late comics artist Joe Kubert stages his narrative against the backdrop of the Warsaw Ghetto, creating an extended moment in history memorialized across genres, across time and space.

In *Yossel*, Kubert creates a self-referential counternarrative in which his alter ego, sixteen-year-old Yossel, is a resistance fighter in the Warsaw

Ghetto Uprising and narrates the fictionalized memoir in which the narrator/protagonist is the constructed double of the artist/writer. While Yossel, the fictionalized protagonist of the graphic novel, tells the story of "what happened," the counternarrative that exists alongside the fictionalized events, as Kubert maintains, "could have happened."[2] In introducing the design for the narrative, Kubert writes, "[t]his book is the result of my 'what if-?' thoughts. It is a work of fiction, based on a nightmare that was fact. There's no question in my mind that what you are about to read could have happened" (Introduction iii). The conditional "could have," contingent less on temporality and more on circumstance, creates an amalgam, not only of genres—fantasy, memoir, historical fiction, counterbiographical sketch, illustrated novel—but also of perspectives through which we witness the events as they unfold. The narrative, while fictionalized, is less counterfactual, however, than it is an overlay of fictional characters and imagined dialogue and action onto a distant historical event, a midrashic reinvention of responding to the gaps, animating, vivifying, and extending the narrative of the Warsaw Ghetto Uprising. In doing so, Kubert peoples the increasingly remote event with sound, with an interpretive, fantasized rereading of events and the people who participated in the resistance efforts. History, here, becomes narrative, an extension of the traumatic moment. But such flights of the imagination are reined in by the necessity to remain faithful to that history, thus bridging the gap between distance and proximity, between unfamiliarity and recognition, and between the uncanny condition of awareness and a vicarious participation in events beyond one's reach.

Thus, with the Warsaw Ghetto Uprising as the historical frame of his graphic novel, Kubert imagines a congruent narrative, as Brad Prager puts it, an "allohistorical space between what was and what might have been."[3] Against the backdrop of the uprising, Kubert creates something of an alternate history, an account of the uprising in which he creates a doppelgänger, his alter ego who narrates the events as he participates in them.[4] Kubert fantasizes himself as an "other" existing in an alternative history in order to vicariously—safely, belatedly, and from a distance—experience the trauma of the Shoah. He imagines himself in—draws himself into—the traumatic episode of the uprising. Kubert constructs his projected self as a courageous resistance fighter, taking action on the side of good, a measure of that which the young Kubert living in safety and security in the United States could not have been. In *Yossel*, Kubert constructs a "might have been" narrative, a fantasized "what if" tale in which he imagines himself as someone he might have become save for the accidents of history. Such a literary conceit reveals at once a desire to have been that young resistance fighter, his fear that it could have happened, and his projected apprehension that, had he been the subject of this historical narrative, he would not have had the resilience and fortitude of his doppelgänger, his imagined other—an "if only" conceit turned to "what if," with all the attendant anxieties and self-punishments implied by meditations on loss. In his introductory remarks to the graphic novel, Kubert outlines his own family history as the inspiration for the design of the book. In 1926, the infant Kubert, along with his parents and older sister, fled Europe for the United States. Of his life growing up in Brooklyn, Kubert says, "I was lucky" (Introduction ii). Kubert's position in relation to the events he describes speaks not only to his individual family history but also to his position as a Jew at a fraught time in Jewish and world history. As he explains:

> I've given thought to the idea of what might have happened if my parents had decided not to come to America in 1926. In 1939, I was thirteen years old, attending the High School of Music and Art, in New York City. In 1939, Hitler invaded and conquered Poland . . . the elimination of all Jews in Europe and Russia had begun with a vengeance . . . Between 1940 and 1942, I was still in high school. Wonderful things were happening to me. . . . At the same time in Europe, people were being led into the gas chambers and fed into the ovens. (Introduction ii)

Here Kubert envisions his own life through the lens of a proximate, parallel history; while he and his family were enjoying the relative freedom of their reinvented lives in the United States, Jews were being systematically murdered throughout Europe.

The events taking place in Europe thus create a metaphorical shadow, a counterexistence with a clear, unitary antagonist. Kubert sees his and his family's lives as contingent on the fortuitous and auspicious turn of fortunes. Initially prevented from securing safe passage, Kubert's family, "a persistent lot," eventually were granted visas and set sail for the United States (Introduction i). What perhaps might be considered, to a certain extent, "survivor guilt" is complicated for Kubert by the knowledge that his family's initial deterrence at the port crossing in

England was the result of his mother's pregnancy with him. The family was prevented from departing because of his mother's condition. Their second attempt, after Kubert's birth, was successful, and "[p]ermission was given for the Kuberts to come to the New World. America" (Introduction i). As Samantha Baskind suggests, "As a child who just barely escaped Nazi tyranny, Kubert occupies a unique position—not a Holocaust survivor nor a second-generation witness but still closely attuned to the War's disastrous consequences. . . . As such . . . Kubert . . . has taken the burden of the Holocaust on as his own."[5] Kubert's sense of "what might have been," then, seems to have motivated the creation of the graphic novel. At any number of points, their departure *might have been* aborted. Thus, as he acknowledges, "If my parents had not come to America, we would have been caught in that maelstrom, sucked in and pulled down with the millions of others who were lost" (Introduction ii).[6] Thus, "what might have been" (in terms of the Kuberts' actual lives), "what actually occurred" (the events of the Warsaw Ghetto Uprising set against the wider scope of systematic murder), and "what if" (the invention of Yossel) become conflated. The relation between actuality and imagined reality stage the unfolding of the narrative, blurring genres and complicating the shape of memory.

In an attempt to bridge the gap between fantasy and reality, Kubert, in a gesture toward authenticating his story, outlines the origins of *Yossel*:

> Based on the stories I heard from my parents, the things I read and available historical data, I wrote and drew this book. I've incorporated information in letters my parents received from survivors and relatives during and after the war. I backtracked and reread authenticated references concerning dates, times and places. The experience was very personal. . . . It was something I felt I had to do. (Introduction iii)

Thus, Kubert's narrative is based on a compilation of research, historical data, personal correspondence, "borrowed" memories, and the imagination. As Prager proposes, "the author may be responding to the sense that he ought to have certain memories, yet does not—that he should have partaken of a particular fate, yet did not" (115). Thus, as Prager suggests, through the creation of a fictional counterpart who lives a parallel existence, Kubert "is addressing his own absence of memories, a lack for which he compensates . . . by way of his alter ego" (126).

Kubert creates an imagined rhetorical scenario in which he recreates himself as Yossel, an adolescent boy who, like his creator, loves to draw comics. Early on in the story, Yossel, who narrates the unfolding chronicle of events, explains, "I have been drawing from the time I could hold a pencil. Since I was two or three years old. That's what my mother and father told me. And I always loved to draw. Especially cartoon strips. To see the things I imagined in my mind come to life on paper" (7). In Yossel, Kubert creates a parallel self, a boy born in Yzeran, the shtetl in Poland from which Kubert's parents fled. And here is where their fictional and actual paths diverge. While Kubert and his family set sail for a new life in the United States, the fictionalized Yossel and his family are ordered from their home, now designated "the property of the Reich," and are forcibly incarcerated in the Warsaw Ghetto. During one of the selections, Yossel's parents and sister are deported to Auschwitz, while Yossel's life is provisionally spared because he can draw, "amusing the [guards] with . . . cartoons" (29). For Yossel, art is a provisional escape from deportation and death, a form of protest in which Yossel might temporarily—like the author—"create my own world" and "drive my fears into little corners and crevices" (7, 13). Drawing provides young Yossel with the invented means to take control of his life and thus create a fantasized rescue narrative. As he says, "Even in the ghetto, being able to draw gave me a feeling of salvation. A sense of security" (23). Drawing momentarily offers Yossel a sense of relief, taking him out of himself and his situation: "Often when I drew late into the night, I would fall asleep on my drawings. And then, I would dream that my characters came to life and I was with them. In the jungles, or on the spaceship, or in the big cities, or deep in the earth's core. And it was wonderful" (13). Ironically, while Yossel in fantasy escapes the ghetto, his creator inserts himself into the terror and barbarity within the ghetto walls. So, too, for Kubert, art is a form of protest, of resistance. *Yossel*, then, is a counterfactual narrative, yet one in which the artist/writer places his imagined younger self in a narrative already set by history.

In *Yossel*, Kubert establishes both a direct and an indirect representation of the Shoah through this doubling of voices. The fictionalized Yossel narrates the events of the Warsaw Ghetto Uprising as they occur in the "real time" of the narrative. While the events are narrated through an adolescent's traumatized eyes, such direct "witnessing" is doubled by the implied author's/illustrator's drawings, which provide another perspective overlaid on that of the first-person narrator's account. Although the controlling point of view is governed by Kubert's invented protagonist, the young voice in the midst of the experience is joined by another voice, the perspective of the distanced writer/illustrator, who draws the story that his protagonist narrates. While Kubert gives himself no actual lines in the text, the images he draws establish a lens through which we see the events unfold, a synchronization of narrating voices and perspectives characteristic of the graphic form. Such a multidirectional perspective is complicated by the pairing of the young protagonist's own drawings with those of the graphic artist. Kubert relies exclusively on pencil drawings for the images, explaining, "I felt an immediacy in my pencil drawings that I wanted to retain" (Introduction iii). The images are rendered in shades of black, white, and gray, suggesting a journalistic approach to the events as they are reported. The pages of the graphic novel are dense, images without panel frames, interspersed with rectangular framed text balloons, drawings that border on one another. Such an assault of images creates a felt sense of immediacy and urgency. The compounding of images, a cacophony of sound and sense, produces a claustrophobic effect, reproducing life within the shrinking, suffocating walls of the ghetto and also the experience of hiding underground, in the sewers, where the resistant fighters plan the revolt.

Kubert's drawings are deeply disturbing: varying gradations of black and gray amid the colorless, leaden, deathly backdrop of the ghetto; faces made brittle by jagged lines of despair; hunched, smudged, broken figures; smokestacks bellowing dense, harsh, frenzied, black streaks. There is an ashen, somber quality to the images, all suggestive of the devastating tenor of time running out. Kubert achieves an implied frenetic movement in these jagged cumulative images that contribute to the building of narrative tension and the heightening of an inevitable end. In a discussion of Kubert's distinctive style, Prager argues that:

> The author has avoided using clearly defined lines or crisp blacks and whites. His stray pencil markings, distributed liberally across the image, some light and others dark, suggest that everything in Yossel's world transpires in . . . a gray zone. The gray that characterizes the pages is meant literally, in that it mirrors the washed-out world of the ghetto and the ash produced in the camps. . . . The regularity and precision of his text stands in stark contrast with the rough, imperfect images, and the juxtaposition of the two recalls an

issue specific to the representation of such atrocities: Kubert's decision to represent the horrors of the Holocaust imperfectly constantly reminds readers that the images should not be taken to stand for authentic Holocaust experience. This is not a story as depicted by a witness. (118)

At the same time, however, the rough, blurred edges of the drawings, the pained faces of the victims, and the narrowing confines established through the heavy repetitiveness of unrelenting and escalating terror re-create the conditions of and foreshadow the inevitable outcome of the narrative. Kubert's drawings are unrelenting images of horror: mounds of shoes, eyeglasses, hairbrushes and combs, luggage piled one on top of the other such that the individual items are rendered indistinct, suggestive metonymically of the magnitude of those murdered; bodies being incinerated; enormous tanks that fill up the page; bodies hanging from lampposts, faces obliterated by death.

Significantly, we see these images as if through the eyes of Yossel and the other victims of the ghetto and the camps. Although the narrative takes place in the camps only indirectly—as told by a witness to those incarcerated in the Warsaw Ghetto—the perspective by which the reader views these drawings is that of an insider/outsider. In other words, we are made privy to the horrors through the representative images but from a distance; we remain "outside" the text. At the same time, we are being asked to see the images from the complicated perspective of those who exist "inside" the experience of the text. Most often it is through Yossel's increasingly fractured and traumatized perspective that we either "witness" or "hear" of the atrocities. There is one excruciating moment in which we find ourselves looking onto a scene in which three Sonderkommandos, concentration camp prisoners forced to dispose of bodies, have just placed a corpse into the crematorium (62). In this scene, we are in two places at once. We view the faces of the Sonderkommandos looking directly at us, yet they are looking into the incinerator. The viewer is outside looking in, yet we see the image—the feet as they extend outward—as if from inside the furnace. This is a truly gruesome image, not least because of the complicated angle from which we experience this doubling of vision. In this simultaneity of direct and indirect narrative exposure, we are outside, looking in, but we are also on the other side of the experience, looking at the horrified, hopeless, and pained faces of those looking into the incinerator, that is, looking at us. Kubert thus calls into question the assumed limits of self-protective interiority by multiplying the places of the narrative gaze. The resulting depersonalization of the represented "subjects"—the dead owner of the feet; the scowling, depleted Sonderkommandos; and the others outside the incinerators—provides an image of arresting horror that is less narrated than simply exposed.

Kubert develops these tensions in direct and indirect ways both distant and immediate, narrated and imagined throughout the graphic medium. When, for example, we are introduced to the workings of the concentration camp, we come to such information with preestablished knowledge, but also from the shocked and horrified position of Yossel and others in the ghetto, who have not witnessed such events directly. In this intersection, Kubert creates a juxtaposed "disturbance" in vision and thus in the projected interiority of the subject. We are introduced to the arrival of the messenger, "a stranger," who escaped the camps to tell the tale of horrors (37).[7] Starving and brutalized, "a man, or what was once a man . . . gaunt, filthy, bones pushing against translucent skin and shredded clothes, unable to stand upright . . . such fear, such pain," the stranger reveals himself to be a landsman from Yzeran, the rebbe—not a stranger to Yossel—who was deported to the camps (37). The tale he tells (the story within the story) is one of abject horror: people tattooed, "like animals," shaved heads, men and women separated, "clothes . . . piled up, watches, money, eyeglasses, luggage, anything of value . . . taken," assigned to barracks, to hard labor, "no place to move . . . no place to breathe," beaten, starved, murdered, "fed into ovens" (41, 42, 66). It is here that the rebbe, before miraculously escaping, saw Yossel's mother, father, and sister, who, during one of the selections in the camp, "joined a long line heading toward a building. From a smokestack pouring a stinking black plume. . . . The last time anyone saw them" (80). Kubert's indirect narrating voice is thus created by the images and icons of the experience that Yossel articulates in the text boxes. In setting the drawings outside the text boxes, Kubert creates two developing plot lines that intersect, if not visually, then thematically. When, for example, Yossel hears the rebbe's story of the destruction of the inhabitants of Yzeran, the young protagonist responds by saying, "His words formed vivid pictures in my mind. I could see the things he described, as if they were happening in front of my eyes" (39). In this moment, Kubert creates three interlocking directions of witnessing, of giving testimony: the rebbe's firsthand witnessing—"I have seen this with my own eyes" (50); Yossel's narrative recitation of the rebbe's words, a secondhand witnessing; and the graphic artist's drawing of representative images of the atrocities. Here author/illustrator and protagonist merge in Yossel's insistence that "I **had** to draw so the pictures would sink into my brain. So I could see the things he described" (43).

Bearing witness, thus, is a collective enterprise, a chorused expression of lamentation and moral reckoning and the ongoing articulation and extension of memory. For it is Kubert who visualizes the rebbe's story that Yossel "hears." The image that accompanies the story is frighteningly intense, a collection of faces huddled together, distorted by pain and suffering, against a backdrop of jagged, peaked lines representing the barbed enclosures of the cattle car in which they are imprisoned and the concentration camp that is their destination (39). The shapes of the heads are disproportionate to bodies we cannot see, for the figures are cut off below their faces, a collective expression of the magnitude of suffering Kubert wants to convey, faces imploring, mouths stretched open in soundless lamentation. Words here are unnecessary, to be sure, because the starkness of the image suggests the enormity of the situation, but the lack of intermediating text also suggests that their cries go unheard. These are images unconstrained by panels or frames, suggesting the uncontained disposition of the Nazi genocide, a willful departure from the norms of decency and humanity. Indeed, the two faces at the upper left-hand corner of the image look more animalistic than human.[8] The degradation of all that is human is reflected in a later image of camp inmates, similarly dressed in prison garb, faceless. Walking in the same direction, they represent the descent of humankind. Through the synchronistic chorus of visual images and text, Kubert thus creates a mosaic of narrating perspectives, drawing on a variety of stylistic and recurring Holocaust tropes and conceits that enact the fractured, catastrophic rupture of lives and history.

Such dissonant and arresting images represent the dislocation, upheaval, and eradication of lives, the very tenor of existence for those victims of the Shoah. At one particular juncture in the narrative, there is a disturbing mirror image of discordant icons, the visual doubling of a swastika on the upper left-hand side of one page and the Star of David on the bottom of the facing page (83–84). The one—a symbol of destruction—is on the rise and the other—a symbol of survival—descending. We see these as a piece: what is and what once was. Such iconic tensions and the characteristic jagged lines of the images reflect the escalating Nazi assault, and this escalation of tension continues into the pages drawn of the Warsaw Rebellion. Kubert depicts life in the ghetto in heavy, ominous black tones, dark lines scribbled over shapes to represent the tense, chaotic uncertainty and confusion of the moment of the rebellion. The resistance fighters, gathered in the sewers of the ghetto, are further hidden in the shadows of Kubert's drawings. The frantic motion represented by the characteristic jagged, dark lines suggests the urgency of the moment, the experience of hiding in the sewers and its claustrophobic fear created by the layering of scrawled, overlapping, indistinct marks.

Kubert creates a kind of heaviness in these images, the foreboding weight of the moment. The thick gradations of shades, shadows, and textures represent the gradations of traumatic memory, but also the increasing movement and progression of the Germans as they advance in order "to purge the ghetto, to deport or kill the entire population, to eliminate all signs of an uprising, to destroy the ghetto, to raze it to the ground, to leave no one alive" (113). Kubert draws Yossel and the other resistance fighters waiting in the sewers for the onslaught, submerged under the weight of heavy crosshatching with severe black lines, their faces obscured. Kubert thus creates the desperate, tense moment of the impending arrival of the armed Germans: "They were coming. . . . In a moment they would be here. . . . They were here" (116). Each instant of the Nazis' menacing approach is isolated in a separate rectangular text box, the boxes functioning as footsteps as they march toward the impending confrontation and conflagration. Such a technique—gradations of black and white, crosshatching, and shadowing—throughout the narrative contributes to the tense, heavy, claustrophobic weight of terror and suffering.

Tragically, of course, neither Kubert's nor Yossel's drawings can save the protagonist from the barbarities of history; nor can drawing ultimately protect those brought to life for the performative moment of the graphic novel. Drawing has been in Kubert's text a metonymy for the expression of life and voice, a trope of defense against the immediate reality of their situation. As Yossel admits, "I hold my scraps of paper and pencil close to my chest. Protecting them. As if they were my mother. My father. My sister" (5). Yet the staccato punctuation of the lines anticipates and enacts the fragmentation of his world, shattered as it is spoken. Yossel, after learning of his family's final moments, finds himself no longer able to imagine them onto the page. The rebbe's silence after disclosing the moment in which he saw Yossel's mother, father, and sister walking into the crematorium is a harbinger of the protagonist's inability to represent them through images as well as his own impending silence. Yossel can no longer draw them for they can no longer be imagined back into life, and visualizing their deaths is too painful to imagine. Yossel thus mourns their absence through graphic silence: "I wanted to draw a picture of Papa, Mama, Chaiya. I could see them clearly in my mind. . . . I could not draw them. I could not" (81). Paradoxically, the young artist for whom drawing enabled him to imagine, if momentarily, "a different world" cannot bear to draw their deaths into life (115). Drawing, thus, ultimately fails him, an absence mirrored in the textual silence of the moment: "No one said a word. Only silence. . . . Struck dumb with fear, pain, and sorrow" (82). The absence of creation is made emphatic by the single drawing that fills the entire page on which Yossel is shown holding a pencil up against a blank sheet of paper (81).

Yossel thus anticipates his own death: "If I could not draw, I would not survive" (104). His superheroes—creations who could "tear the German soldiers apart," "vanquish all evil doers . . . make mincemeat of the swastika murderers" (114)—even in fantasy can no longer save him. For the "real monsters" are the Nazis, against whom Yossel's imaginary heroes are impotent, living only on paper and in his wishful fantasies— "if only our heroes were real" (100, 115). The "real heroes," of course, were those like Yossel and Mordecai, the leader of the resistance, who fought and died. Kubert will draw Yossel into life only to erase him. We have anticipated the protagonist's death from the first line of the narrative: "I am going to die here" (2). Ironically, the affirmation of self—"I am"—in the very moment of articulation is reversed, inverted by its dissociative, deafening antagonist. Indeed, as Yossel warns us at the novel's opening, "there is no escape" (2). Thus, at the novel's end, Yossel will narrate his own death.

Hiding in the sewers that stretch beneath the ghetto, the insurgency is insufficiently armed against the Nazis who hunt them down with flame throwers. The repeated images of Yossel's face moments before his death show him to be aging instantaneously (119). Coming into focus from the initial faceless sketch, Yossel is no longer the young, innocent boy in the second iteration of his quadrupled image in this figure. In the final image on the right-hand side of the page, Kubert's double appears aged: exhausted, defeated, eyes heavy-lidded, sunken and darkened. Yossel has, indeed, come to the end of the line. His final word—"M-mama"—is a universal cry, an expression of the most basic of human utterances in the face of inhuman misery.

The narrator's death—which he narrates at the extended moment of his dying—is followed by total silence, an *aposiopesis*, a trope signifying the deliberate cessation of speech. So, too, his death presages the suspension of sound and image, troping the cessation of voice, of bearing witness, a *praecisco*—complete and calculated silence.[9] Yossel's death is followed by a wordless image of armed Nazi guards looming over the dead bodies of the resistance fighters, one of whom retrieves from the burnt cindered ground of the sewers a sheet of paper on which, we are meant to assume, Yossel might have continued to sketch his superheroes in their battle against his shattered world. In a series of four simple etchings, Kubert creates a simulacrum of effortless movement as the Nazi looks down at the crumpled paper on the ground, bends down to retrieve it, casts a glance at it, and, turning away in a gesture of contemptuous indifference, flings the sheet of paper from his grasp, where it drifts to join the rest of the flotsam on the floor of the sewer. The final image on the last page of the book is that of a blank sheet of smudged, torn paper set against jagged black, scrawled marks, a midrashic extension of the charred remains of the dead (121).

The blackened sheet of paper, on which there are no words, is torn, crumpled, and partially scorched by the soot of the flames. Represented silence thus becomes the means by which Kubert reenacts annihilation, creating an after-image of absence that remains long after the speaker is rendered speechless. As Baskind suggests, the final page "is empty, devoid of imagery, just as Yossel is now devoid of breath" (179). Kubert here takes on the complexity of articulating through image and text not only death but also a response to that particular dying. Paradoxically, the absence of text—of the speaker's/character's voice—is a surrogate for speech. The close alignment of graphic novelist and his literary creation allows for the protagonist's voice to extend beyond the conditions of his death. He is rendered silent, and so is Kubert. But the "silent" paper that stands as sentry, as witness to the events that unfolded, extends the life that once was by way of its absence. Indeed, absence implies presence. The blank sheet of paper at the close of the novel thus suggests a visual representation of silence, providing the distanced viewer, as second-generation graphic artist Bernice Eisenstein puts it, with the means "to step into the presence of absence."[10] The understatement inherent in the final image of the blank page creates an extremity of impossible restitution in its utter silence and signals the threat to both historical and personal memory. Kubert thus draws his double and, by extension, himself in and out of history, fracturing the narrative. Voice, after all, signifies remembrance. Thus, at the narrative's close, the cessation of utterance represents the damaged end of testimony. The final moment, then, is a response to silence. Yossel's silence as well as that of Kubert at the graphic novel's end signal the eradication of voice, generations cut off, an interruption in generational continuity and the extension of memory.

Notes

1. See, for example, the second-generation accounts, Martin Lemelman, *Mendel's Daughter: A Memoir* (New York: Free Press, 2007), and Bernice Eisenstein, *I Was a Child of Holocaust Survivors* (New York: Riverhead Books, 2007), and third-generation graphic narratives, such as Jérémie Dres, *We Won't See Auschwitz* (New York: Abrams Image, 2013), and Amy Kurzweil, *Flying Couch: A Graphic Memoir* (New York: Catapult, 2016).

2. Joe Kubert, Yossel: *April 19, 1943: A Story of the Warsaw Ghetto Uprising* (New York: ibooks Graphic Novel, 2003), Introduction iii, page numbers added.

3. Brad Prager, "The Holocaust without Ink: Absent Memory and Atrocity in Joe Kubert's Graphic Novel Yossel: April 19, 1943," in *The Jewish Graphic Novel: Critical Approaches*, ed. Samantha Baskind and Ranen Omer-Sherman (New Brunswick, NJ: Rutgers University Press, 2008), 117.

4. I am indebted to Sandor Goodhart for bringing to my attention the curious—if implied—connection between Kubert's graphic novel *Yossel* and an earlier fictionalized account of the Warsaw Ghetto written by Zvi Kolitz in 1946, the short story "Yossel Rakover's Vendung Tsu G-ot," translated into English as "Yossel Rakover's Appeal to God." Kolitz's story, narrated by a survivor of the ghetto, is written as an eyewitness account of the final days of the ghetto. I have not found a direct link between the stories other than their fascinating parallel conceits, and I am not aware of any evidence that Kubert was familiar with the earlier story, although I suspect that he must have been. There are both similarities and dissimilarities between the two narratives, but both take the perspective of eyewitness testimonies to the horrors of life in the ghetto and to those who died in the resistance. An obvious difference is that, although both Yossels narrate the events, one survives the devastation and the other, at the novel's end, dies in battle. Another key distinction is the implied addressee:

while Kolitz's Yossel appeals to God, Kubert's narrator, knowing that he will, as he says "die here," writes as a last measure of existence, of voice, even as his life plummets to an end. There is no one to hear his appeals save the distanced reader. For a consideration of the peculiar history of Kolitz's story and the confusions about fact and fiction surrounding the publication and reception of the story, see Sandor Goodhart's discussion of the interesting saga of Kolitz's Yossel in *Möbian Nights: Reading Literature and Darkness* (New York: Bloomsbury, 2017), especially 114–20.

5. Samantha Baskind, "Picturing 'The Holiest Thing': Joe Kubert's Children of the Warsaw Ghetto," in *Visualizing Jewish Narrative: Jewish Comics and Graphic Novels*, ed. Derek Parker Royal (London: Bloomsbury, 2016), 181.

6. This sense of being among the "lucky" harkens back to Saul Bellow's fraught American Jewish protagonist, Asa Leventhal in Bellow's second novel, *The Victim*, published in 1947. Feeling the weight of anti-Semitism and his own "survivor guilt," Leventhal, too, considers himself one of the lucky ones, lucky to have, as he anxiously puts it, "gotten away with it" (Saul Bellow, *The Victim* [1947; rpt., New York: Penguin, 1988], 33). Leventhal, throughout Bellow's ominously charged novel, believes himself to have narrowly escaped what might have been his fate. Leventhal remains haunted by "that part of humanity of which he was frequently mindful . . . the part that did not get away with it—the lost, the outcast, the overcome, the effaced, the ruined" (16). A similar apprehension and unease are articulated in Kubert's sense that he might have been, were it not for the fortunes of circumstance and luck, "caught in that maelstrom, sucked in and pulled down with the millions of others who were lost" (*Yossel*, Introduction ii).

7. The figure of the messenger is a recurring trope in Holocaust literature, the appearance of a seeming stranger who returns to tell the tale of what he has witnessed. More often than not, the herald initially is not believed, his account the stuff of horrific and grotesque fantasy, as we see here when the rebbe who appears unbidden and whose account of "death camps" is initially seen by those not there as "another fairy tale," beyond the capacity of a human mind to envision (38). We find such a conceit, too, in Elie Wiesel's *Night* when, early in the narration, a messenger, Moishe the Beadle, will miraculously return to tell the tale of mass murder of Jews in the forest in Poland. But he is not to be believed: "Day after day, night after night, he went from one Jewish house to the next, telling his story . . . He spoke only of what he had seen. But people not only refused to believe his tales, they refused to listen. . . . 'They think I'm mad,' he whispered" (Elie Wiesel, *Night*, trans. Marion Wiesel [1958; repr., New York: Hill and Wang/Farrar, Straus and Giroux, 2006], 7).

8. We are reminded once again of the chilling word of Primo Levi's poem "Shema," which stands as an epigraph to his memoir, *Survival in Auschwitz*: "Consider if this is a man . . . Who dies because of a yes or a no. . . . Consider if this is a woman / Without hair and without name / With no more strength to

remember / Her eyes empty. . . ." (Primo Levi, *Survival in Auschwitz: The Nazi Assault on Humanity*, trans. Stuart Woolf [1958; repr., New York: Touchstone/Simon & Schuster, 1996], 11).

9. Tropes that enact silence, loss, and absence, such as *aposiopesis*, *praecisco*, and ellipsis, are characteristic of Holocaust literature. I have found the following book to lay out the distinctive features of these tropes in useful ways: Arthur Quinn, *Figures of Speech: 60 Ways to Turn a Phrase* (Salt Lake City: Gibbs M. Smith, 1982, 34, 36). A paradigmatic expression of the enactment of silence and annihilation is Dan Pagis's poem "Written in Pencil in the Sealed Railway-Car."

10. Bernice Eisenstein, *I Was a Child of Holocaust Survivors* (New York: Riverhead Books, 2006), 167.

4

Alternate Jewish History
Philip Roth's *The Plot Against America* and Michael Chabon's *The Yiddish Policemen's Union*

Andrew M. Gordon

Judaism is a religion with a very long history, and the Jews, as "the chosen people" perpetually awaiting the messiah, feel they have a special relationship with history. The twentieth century in particular was monumental for the Jews, with the massive immigration from Eastern Europe and the rise of American Jewry, the European Holocaust, and the creation of the state of Israel. In the course of that century, as the Jews struggled to survive and to prosper, they repeatedly had to reinvent themselves. As Philip Roth writes, the Jews were "created and undone a hundred times over" in the twentieth century ("Imagining Jews" 246). Roth has always been fascinated by what history does to the Jews. But if history shapes the Jews, fiction is also capable of reshaping history. According to E. L. Doctorow, "history is a kind of fiction in which we live and hope to survive, and fiction is a kind of speculative history, perhaps a superhistory" ("False Documents" 25).

The subgenre of fantasy and science fiction, the counterfactual novel or alternate history, is an especially powerful form of superhistory, a means of speculating on and reconceiving events. Award-winning novels by Philip Roth and Michael Chabon reimagine twentieth-century Jewish history, showing both the imaginative power of fiction and the contingent nature of history. In *The Plot Against America* (2004), Roth, imitating a memoir, tweaks the American involvement in World War II to imagine a United States sliding toward fascism and a potential American holocaust for the Jews. In *The Yiddish Policemen's Union* (2007), Chabon, imitating the hard-boiled detective novel, invents a post-Holocaust Jewish state, not in Israel but in Alaska. Both novels won the Sidewise Award, which is presented annually for the best novel of alternate history. They are thought experiments, profound commentaries on the fluid nature of events and the special relationship of the Jews to history as well as to the present and future. "Strange times to be a Jew" is the repeated refrain of the characters in *The Yiddish Policemen's Union*; the implication of both novels is that throughout history, it has always been and continues to be a strange time to be a Jew.

Alternate history (AH) derives from the universal human tendency to speculate about the random and arbitrary nature of existence and about how our lives might be dramatically altered if one small event in the past were to change. We do it to congratulate ourselves on our good fortune, to express our fear about the huge role chance plays in human existence, or to wish that our lives had gone otherwise. Says Michael Chabon, "I think all of us are wired to lie awake in bed at night going back over the course of our life, looking at the things that led us to the place where we are now, being able to see sometimes only after only after a period of many years certain key junctures. . . . You can begin to imagine an alternate life for yourself. It's a fundamental part of the way we look at our own history" (Chabon interview by Greenwood). AH simply extends that tendency from rethinking one's own history to reimagining the entire pattern of world events. AH, the practice of positing "what if" history had transpired differently, is both a flourishing subgenre of science fiction and a subfield of history. It has also been called uchronia, allohistory, and counterfactuals. Grammatically, "alternative history" is more accurate, but because this term is used in a specialized sense by historians, such as history viewed from a feminist perspective, the preferred term for the subgenre of science fiction is alternate history.

Science fiction (SF) posits a change in the present or near future and imagines its consequences further in the future. AH, on the other hand, imagines a change in the past and its consequences for the past and the present. AH interests us not only in how the characters develop, but also in how their world changes and develops. Part of the pleasure in reading AH is figuring out at what point the change occurred, then measuring the created world against known history and noting the deviations. "The alternate history is a text placed at the crux of temporality, narrativity, and history; these three points engage in a dialogue that . . . questions these topics by estranging them, by changing events or interpretations to make them unfamiliar" (Hellekson 65). SF seems to be histories of possible futures and AH to be histories of possible pasts, but both are really about the present. Writes Gavriel Rosenfeld, "When the producers of alternate histories speculate on how the past might have been different, they invariably express their own highly subjective present-day hopes and fears" (Rosenfeld 10).

AH permeates contemporary popular culture in both science fiction and fantasy and mainstream novels. There are dozens of websites catering to fans of the genre, with such features as AH role-playing games, instructions on how to create your own alternate timeline, and Rough Planet Guides to Alternate Earths. There are also many AH video and computer games and comic books. On television, there have been series such as *Quantum Leap* (1989–93), about a time traveler who improves people's lives; *Sliders* (1995–2000), about a team who use machinery to travel to many parallel Earths subtly or dramatically different from our own; *Time Cop* (1997), based on a 1994 movie about a policeman who travels through time to correct its course when criminal time travelers alter history for personal benefit; and the recent series based on Philip K. Dick's novel *The Man in the High Castle* (2015–17). And movies such as *Run Lola Run* (1998) and *Sliding Doors* (1998) present a given situation played through repeatedly, yielding different and sometimes completely contradictory outcomes—similar to Philip Roth's novel *The Counterlife* (1986). Although it may saturate our popular culture, AH gets little respect from literary critics, who disdain genre fiction except when it is practiced by serious mainstream writers such as Roth and Chabon.

AH has a long and distinguished lineage beginning with the Greek historian Herodotus, who wondered what would have happened if the Persians had defeated the Greeks at Marathon, and the Roman historian Livy, who pondered what would have happened to the Roman Empire if Alexander had gone west instead of east. The first known AH in English is a chapter in Isaac D'Israeli's *Curiosities of Literature* in 1824. The first novel-length AH, Louis-Napoleon Geoffrey-Chateau's *Napoléon et la conquête du monde*, was published in 1836. Nathaniel Hawthorne's 1845 story "P.'s Correspondence" concerns a man who is considered mad because he sees an alternate 1845. Charles Renouvier's 1857 French novel *Uchronie* introduced the French term for AH. But the best-known AH of the nineteenth century is Mark Twain's *A Connecticut Yankee in King Arthur's Court* (1889), where the alteration is caused through time travel, which in the twentieth century became a favorite literary device to create a changed past or present.

AH really burgeoned in the twentieth century both in the speculations of historians and in the creations of the new genre of SF. Its rules began to be codified as well. Alternate histories basically come in three varieties: the anomaly, the time travel deviation, or the parallel worlds scenario.

First, the alternative reality may be due to an anomaly that is simply given. At some critical juncture in the past, which the critic Karen Hellekson calls "the nexus event" (27) and other critics call "the point of divergence," history deviated from its known course to follow another path, as in Philip K. Dick's classic *The Man in the High Castle* (1962), which takes place in a California governed by the Japanese decades after the Axis won WW II. Both Roth's and Chabon's novels follow this pattern: the AH is an anomaly that is simply a given.

Second, a time traveler may inadvertently or deliberately interfere with the course of events, as in *A Connecticut Yankee* or L. Sprague de Camp's *Lest Darkness Fall* (1941), where a twentieth-century time traveler in sixth-century Rome prevents the Dark Ages by introducing the printing press and other modern innovations. The film series *Back to the Future* (1984, 1989, 1990) deals with branching time lines caused by a time traveler who must keep traveling up and down the alternate time lines to correct his mistakes. The hero of the film *The Butterfly Effect* (2004) also travels back in time repeatedly to alter the present until he attains the desired effect.

Third, there is the possibility of parallel worlds, multiple realities, or a "multiverse," and people may accidentally slip cross-time or else deliberately travel from one timeline to another by machine. These parallel worlds are seen as coexisting but in separate dimensions, and they may be "virtually identical, right down to the people who inhabit them," so that the hero can even encounter different versions of himself (Hellekson 51). H. G. Wells's *Men Like Gods* (1923) may be the first novel about cross-time travel to an alternate universe. Vladimir Nabokov dabbled in the notion of parallel worlds in his novel *Ada, or Ardor: A Family Chronicle* (1969), in which he conjures up an "Anti-Terra" where the Russian and American land masses are connected. A variation on the parallel worlds theme is the time-loop story, in which a character involuntarily reexperiences a portion of his life over and over with different outcomes, as in Ken Grimwood's novel *Replay* (1986) or the film *Groundhog Day* (1993).

British historian John Squire's *If It Had Happened Otherwise* (1931) collected speculations by distinguished historians, including Winston Churchill's sophisticated essay "If Lee Had Not Won the Battle of Gettysburg," in which a historian from an alternate world in which the South won the Civil War imagines what would have happened if the South had lost. This form of alternate history is known variously as "recursive AH," the "double-blind what-if," or the "alternate-alternate history." The most famous example is Ward Moore's classic science fiction novel *Bring the Jubilee* (1955), in which a historian from a twentieth century in which the Confederacy triumphed time travels to witness the Battle of Gettysburg, but in the process of observing unintentionally changes the outcome of the battle. He becomes trapped in a world in which the North wins—that is, in our world, which he has unwittingly helped create.

Starting in the 1960s, the publication of alternate histories increased exponentially, no doubt because, with the coming of postmodernism, history was up for grabs. Doctorow said that "history as written by historians is insufficient and the historians are the first to express skepticism over the 'objectivity' of the discipline. . . . [T]here were not only individuals but whole peoples whom we had simply written out of our history." Theorists such as Roland Barthes and Hayden White began to note the similarity between the strategies of history and fiction. In *Metahistory* (1973), White argued that historians structured their narratives just like novelists. Writers recognized that there was no single "truth" about a period, that who was telling the story and how mattered, and that fiction had much to contribute to our understanding of history.

American writers in the 1960s and 1970s responded by creating not so much alternate histories as a new kind of historical novel that mixed fact and fiction, or history and pure fantasy: John Barth's *The Sot Weed Factor* (1960), Thomas Berger's *Little Big Man* (1964), Bernard Malamud's *The Fixer* (1966), William Styron's *The Confessions of Nat Turner* (1967), Kurt Vonnegut's *Slaughterhouse-Five* (1969), Thomas Pynchon's *Gravity's Rainbow* (1973), and Robert Coover's *The Public Burning* (1977) and Doctorow's *The Book of Daniel* (1971), both of which reimagined the Rosenberg case.

Like these new historical novels, AH rewrites known events, but it goes even further: it rewrites reality. Says Karen Hellekson, "Alternate histories question the nature of history and of causality; they question accepted notions of time and space; they rupture linear movement; and they make readers rethink their world and how it has become what it is. They are a critique of the metaphors we use to discuss history. And they foreground the 'constructedness' of history and the role narrative plays in this construction" (Hellekson 4–5).

Gavriel Rosenfeld suspects that the mainstreaming of AH in recent decades reflects the postmodern discrediting of deterministic ideologies and skepticism about all metanarratives. In AH, everything is contingent and history is open-ended (6). Moreover, according to chaos theory, even a tiny change in a complex system can lead to a cascading series of huge effects. Now that the threat of totalizing systems such as fascism or communism seems behind us, we have the freedom to look back and see how easily it could have turned out differently. Meanwhile, new threats, such as resurgent nationalism, religious fundamentalism, terrorism, and climate change, make the future less certain than ever. "In our current transitional era . . . we recognize that nothing is inevitable at all" (7).

The flood of AH novels since the 1990s includes William Gibson and Bruce Sterling's *The Difference Engine* (1991), in which the Victorian era features gigantic computers run on steam; Harry Turtledove's *The Guns of the South* (1992), in which time travelers try to change the outcome of the Civil War by importing modern weaponry; and Robert Harris' *Fatherland* (1992), set in Nazi Berlin in 1964.

How to explain the turn toward AH among Jewish-American novelists such as Roth and Chabon? One possibility is that contemporary American Jewish experience is too bland. William Deresiewicz, commenting on Roth and Chabon as well as on the work of Jonathan Safran Foer and Nathan Englander, speculates that "[t]he most visible of the current generation of Jewish novelists appear to be avoiding their own experience because their own experience just seems too boring. . . . Better to write about a time or place where there was more at stake." But that, of course, does not entirely explain a turn toward AH. Another possibility is that AH is a way to rethink or to Americanize the Holocaust. What would an American Holocaust look like? Through AH, both novelists find a way of transposing the Holocaust to the United States, or at least to imagine Jews imperiled in the United States like their European counterparts. Valerie Sayers notes that "Roth and Chabon both suggest that we have exhausted our capacity to imagine the Holocaust's realities, and that a more fruitful moral exercise might be to imagine what else might have happened, and what might happen still."

It is not surprising that Philip Roth, with his tendency toward satire and fantasy, might turn toward AH. After all, this is the author who imagined a man turning into a breast, a baseball league that never existed, Franz Kafka becoming a Hebrew teacher in New Jersey, and two Philip Roths meeting in Israel. It makes sense that the man who created Zuckerman's fantasy about an alternate Anne Frank who survived the Holocaust and went to the United States and authored *The Counterlife* might write a counterfactual history of an isolationist United States in 1940–42 under the administration of President Charles Lindbergh. Curiously, Roth seemed to have no awareness of the long tradition of AH when he wrote *The Plot Against America*. He writes, "I had no literary models for reimagining the historical past," as if he were writing in a vacuum. The only novel to which he compares his is Orwell's *1984*, which is SF but not AH. "Orwell imagined a huge change in the future with horrendous consequences for everyone. I tried to imagine a small change in the past with horrendous consequences for a relative few. He imagined a dystopia, I imagined a uchronia" (Roth, "The Story"). Yet if Roth was aware of the term "uchronia," why was he seemingly ignorant of the many examples of the subgenre?

Beginning with the American trilogy, Roth conducted a deep investigation into the nature and patterns of American history and the relationship of the individual to those events. *The Plot* continued the investigation. Roth described *The Plot* as "an exercise in historical imagination . . ." (Roth, "The Story"). For Roth's heroes, American history is not a smooth and inevitable chain of events as in the history books; instead, it is a disaster, sudden, accidental, and terrible, hitting Roth's protagonists when they are totally unprepared. Writes Roth, "History claims everybody, whether they know it or not and whether they like it or not. . . . We are ambushed, even as free Americans in a powerful republic armed to the teeth, by the unpredictability that is history . . ." (Roth, "The Story"). In *American Pastoral*, for example, Roth's narrator, Zuckerman, imagines Seymour "Swede" Levov, a representative twentieth-century Jewish American who is "fettered to history, an instrument of history" (*American Pastoral* 5). Once his daughter bombs the local post office to protest the Vietnam War, the Swede's marriage is destroyed and he becomes a haunted man: "the very thing that must have baffled the

Swede till the moment he died: how had he become history's plaything? History, American history, the stuff you read about in books and study in school, had made its way out to tranquil, untrafficked Old Rimrock, New Jersey. . . . People think of history in the long term, but history, in fact, is a very sudden thing" (AP 87). The Swede, whose life was all carefully planned well in advance as a series of successful steps, cannot deal with the unforeseen disaster that is history: "He could never root out the unexpected thing. The unexpected thing would be waiting there unseen, for the rest of his life ripening, ready to explode, just a millimeter behind everything else. The unexpected thing was the other *side* of everything else" (AP 176). In *The Human Stain*, Coleman Silk too thinks he has escaped history, but is nonetheless finally caught in "the stranglehold of history that is one's own time. Blindsided by the terrifyingly provisional nature of everything" (HS 336).

In *The Plot*, little Philip, the protagonist, sees his father fall apart and cry "because he was powerless to stop the unforeseen. And as Lindbergh's election couldn't have made clearer to me, the unfolding of the unforeseen was everything. Turned wrong way around, the unfolding of the unforeseen was what we schoolchildren studied as 'History,' harmless history, where everything unexpected in its own time is chronicled on the page as inevitable. The terror of the unforeseen is what the science of history hides, turning a disaster into an epic" (*Plot* 113–14). Commenting on *The Plot* and his other novels about American history, Roth said, "In writing these books, I've tried to turn the epic back into the disaster as it was suffered without foreknowledge, without preparation, by people whose American expectations, though neither innocent nor delusional, were for something very different from what they got" (Roth, "The Story"). Like AP, *The Plot* is a story about a Jewish family, all of whose members are profoundly affected, even traumatized, by the unexpected currents of twentieth-century American events. In *The Plot*, he compares two families from 1940 to 1942, as World War II is raging in Europe and Asia: the Lindberghs, upper-class WASPs who occupy the White House in Washington, DC; and the Roths, lower-middle-class Jews living in a modest home in Newark, New Jersey—that is, Philip Roth's own family. Although the two families never meet, they are linked through Evelyn Finkel, Bess Roth's sister, who marries Rabbi Lionel Bengelsdorf, a Lindbergh supporter, and goes to work for the Lindbergh administration. Thus the fortunes of the two families are connected. The Lindberghs are history's darlings, whereas the Roths are in danger of becoming more of history's Jewish victims. As the Lindberghs rise, so the sufferings of the Roths increase.

Even worse for Herman and Bess Roth is that the man they perceive as their enemy, Charles Lindbergh, is idealized by their older son, Sandy. For Sandy, Lindbergh is a substitute father. Lindbergh's landing in Paris after his daring solo flight across the Atlantic "even happened to coincide with the day in the spring of 1927 that my mother discovered herself to be pregnant with my older brother" (Plot 5). Sandy does a drawing to commemorate the event, which resembles a religious "annunciation": his mother clutches her stomach with one hand while the other "is pointing skyward to *The Spirit of St. Louis,* passing visibly above downtown Newark at precisely the moment she comes to realize that, in a feat no less triumphant for a mortal than Lindbergh's, she has conceived Sanford Roth" (5). Lindbergh in *The Spirit of St. Louis* becomes the holy spirit impregnating Bess and thus Sandy's symbolic father. Therefore, Sandy rejects his real father when Herman shows no faith in Lindbergh.

If Sandy's surrogate father is Lindbergh, then Philip's is Franklin Roosevelt, for Philip is born in 1933, the year Roosevelt began his first term in office. By 1940, when the novel begins, Roosevelt is the only president the seven-year-old Philip has ever known, and "the first famous living American whom I was taught to love" (7). Moreover, Philip becomes an avid stamp collector, inspired by Roosevelt's hobby. Roosevelt as Philip's substitute father was actually introduced earlier, in Roth's memoir *Patrimony* (1991). In that book, soon after the death of Herman Roth, the fifty-five-year-old Philip dreams about a disabled American warship, "a ghostly hulk of a ship," drifting into a pier at Port Newark as "we on the pier who may or may not have been children gathered together to be evacuated. The mood was heartbreaking in exactly the way it had been when I was twelve and . . . President Roosevelt died of a cerebral hemorrhage." Then he wakes up and realizes that "my father *was* the ship" (*Patrimony* 235–36). To Roth, the dream had "crystallized my own pain so aptly in the figure of small, fatherless evacuee on the Newark docks, as stunned and bereft as the entire nation had once been at the passing of a heroic president" (237).

Fitting for a novel about American history, *The Plot* has three characters who are chroniclers of history. First is Shepsie Tirschwell, the projectionist at the downtown Newark newsreel theater, which Herman attends to keep up with current events, especially as the war rages. Once Philip sneaks into the theater without permission. He views spliced-together scenes of the carnage of war, a hell on earth. This is history in the raw, the nightmarish procession of disasters, which for Roth epitomizes history:

> The same inferno again and again. . . . Picture after picture of misery without end: the mortars bursting, the infantrymen doubled over and running, marines with raised rifles wading ashore, airplanes dropping bombs, airplanes blown apart and spiraling to earth, the mass graves, the kneeling chaplains, the improvised crosses, the sinking ships, the drowning sailors, the sea in flames, the shattered bridges, the tank bombardment, the targeted hospitals sheared in two, pillars of fire coiling upward from bombed-out oil tanks, prisoners corralled in a sea of mud, stretchers bearing living torsos, bayoneted civilians, dead babies, beheaded bodies bubbling blood. . . . (*Plot* 200)

The second chronicler of history they encounter is Verlin Taylor, the Roth family's guide on their disastrous visit to Washington, DC, which turns into a series of humiliations. Ominously, as soon as the Roths enter Washington in their car, "we made a wrong turn." They run into the Capitol building, "the biggest white thing I had ever seen" (57). "Inadvertently, we had driven right to the very heart of American history, and whether we knew it in so many words, it was American history, delineated in its most inspirational form, that we were counting on to protect us against Lindbergh" (58). But American history will not protect them. The Roths are Jews, not white enough for the "big white thing" that is Lindbergh's United States. A motorcycle cop escorts them away from the Capitol. Later they will be evicted from their hotel by an anti-Semitic clerk, and twice Herman Roth will be denounced in public as a "loudmouth Jew." When Herman is insulted by an anti-Semite at the Lincoln Memorial, "[i]t was the most beautiful panorama I'd ever seen, a patriotic paradise, the American Garden of Eden spread before us, and we stood huddled together there, the family expelled" (66). The Roths do not belong in this American pastoral. Wherever they go in Washington, they cannot escape the shadow of the omnipresent, oppressive Lindbergh, who occupies the skies in his airplane. Lindbergh always hovers overhead, like a god surveying his kingdom—or like Hitler amid the clouds as his airplane flies to the Nuremberg rally at the beginning of Leni Riefenstahl's Nazi propaganda film, *Triumph of the Will* (1935).

Verlin Taylor, their guide in Washington, DC, is a good man who helps the Roths find a hotel after they have been expelled and even stands up to an anti-Semite who provokes Herman in a restaurant. But his version of history is limited, "American history, delineated in its most inspirational form," a false notion of the United States that will not protect the Roths. Taylor, a college history professor who lost his job in the Depression, is now reduced to guiding tourists; American history has not been kind to him. He spouts dates and facts like a walking history book, but his idealized United States is contradicted by reality. At the Lincoln Memorial, he tells the Roths to "prepare ourselves to be overwhelmed" (63), and they are, but not in the way he intended. Christian Americans mock Herman Roth, and a woman says, "'I'd give anything to slap his face'" (65). Scenes of blatant anti-Semitism are among the most painful in Roth's fiction, like the episode in *The Counterlife* in which Nathan Zuckerman is insulted in a London restaurant. As Roth writes about *Plot*, "In this book it's the humiliation that helps to tear apart and very nearly disable the family. . . . How do you try to remain strong when you are not welcome?" ("The Story").

The third chronicler in the novel is the gossip columnist Walter Winchell, the quintessential "loudmouth Jew" who broadcasts the latest hot news in his radio program and fearlessly speaks out against the Lindbergh administration's secret plot against the Jews. When Winchell is forced off the air by political pressure, he runs for president, boldly addressing crowds across the country until he is assassinated by an anti-Semite. At the memorial service, New York Mayor Fiorello LaGuardia eulogizes Winchell as the anti-Lindbergh. Where Lindbergh is "pure as Ivory soap," Winchell is hopelessly impure. But because Lindbergh is a fascist sympathizer and Winchell is "the enemy of the fascist," then "by comparison Walter's vulgarity is something great, and Lindbergh's decorum is hideous" (Plot 304–5). Roth develops the same theme in the American trilogy, especially in *The Human Stain* and *I Married a Communist*, that impurity is preferable to purity. American Puritanism would deny "the human stain" and so deny life. "Because everything that lives is in movement. Because purity is petrifaction. Because purity is a lie" (IMAC 318).

The Plot Against America is a frequently dark, frightening, and scathingly corrosive novel portraying a dystopian United States sliding into fascism. Yet, ultimately, it is not a depressing novel. First, it is frequently funny because of the naiveté of the protagonist, little Philip, who perceives everything with the intense but distorted perceptions of a boy from the ages of seven to nine. Second, it has a colorful cast of characters, including a wonderfully pompous rabbi—Roth has always loved to mock the rabbinate—and Newark Jewish gangsters. Third, Herman and Bess Roth are believable and sympathetic heroes who keep the family together through all their trials and provide the book with its moral compass. Their basic decency and faith in American democracy prevail. Roth says one of the reasons he wrote the book was that "it provided me an opportunity to bring my parents back from the grave and restore them to what they were at the height of their powers" ("The Story"). Fourth, the novel has a happy ending: Lindbergh vanishes, Roosevelt is restored to power, the United States enters the war, and history returns to its actual course after this awful two-year detour. Roth writes, "The American triumph is that . . . it didn't happen here. Though a lot of things that didn't happen here did happen elsewhere" ("The Story").

Why then did Roth choose to write this alternate history, to flirt with the notion of an American Holocaust only to return things to normal at the end? I think it was to demonstrate that the history books are only fictions and that the imaginative truths of fiction may constitute a superior history, or what Doctorow would term "a superhistory." The American events of *The Plot Against America*, because they never happened, are as unforeseen by the reader as they are by the characters, so that we experience in reading some of the same shock they do—or that real people do as they are confronted with the unexpected, with history as it is happening. He could not have had the same effect if he had written about events that were already fixed and well known. In the age of Trump, *The Plot Against America* can almost be read as prophecy.

The Yiddish Policemen's Union is a novel of great charm, a hybrid of the tough-guy detective novel and Jewish humor. It is—pardon the language—a jeu d'esprit. It features the bleak, nocturnal cityscapes of Chandler and Hammett—fleabag hotel rooms, garbage-strewn alleyways, cheap diners—peopled with their typical cast of characters—tough, sentimental, or corrupt cops; gangsters and thugs; lowlifes, petty crooks, and informers—all delivered with a wry Jewish twist. Chabon's crew is replete with crooked rabbis, *alter kockers*, *goniffs*, *luftmenschen*, *vontzes*, *momzers*, *shtarkers*, *shtinkers*, and total *meshugenahs*. His detective hero is a depressed, alcoholic schlemiel adept at wisecracks even as he is being beaten up. It is the shtetl revisioned as film noir. Chabon says his inspiration was Isaac Babel: "I . . . immediately felt the kinship between his prose style and his narrative stance and those of the American hard-boiled tradition. The use of outrageous but perfect simile, the handling of violence with aplomb, the wiseass chill—I heard Chandler in it, but it was a Jewish voice, too" (Chabon/Hasak-Lowy). Not since Daniel Fuchs's *The Williamsburg Trilogy* (1934, 1936, 1937) have we seen such mordant, witty ghetto comedy set in the United States.

The premise of Chabon's alternate history is that, beginning in 1940, European Jewish refugees were allowed to settle in Sitka, Alaska, where they established a Yiddish-speaking state and became known as "the frozen chosen." The few Jews in Palestine were driven out in 1948, so the state of Israel never existed. The catch is that, starting in 1948, the Jews were only given a sixty-year lease in Sitka, after which the territory reverts to the United States. The time is 2007, and the lease is set to expire for several million Alaskan Jews. "They are like goldfish in a bag, about to be dumped back into the diaspora" (YPU 202).

The plot involves a mystery. The night manager of Hotel Zamenhof finds a guest murdered in a room. He rouses another occupant of the hotel, the hard-drinking, hard-boiled detective Meyer Landsman of the Sitka Homicide Squad. Landsman soon discovers that the dead man was Mendele Shpilman, a heroin addict (he tied off with tefillin) and the alienated gay son of Rabbi Heskel Shpilman, leader of the Verbovers, a Hassidic sect and organized crime syndicate. Rabbi Shpilman, a physical monstrosity, is a crime lord on the scale of Don Vito Corleone. Not only that, the dead Mendele was reputed to be a miracle worker and the Tzaddik Ha-Dor, potentially the Jewish messiah. Unraveling the murder leads Landsman and his partner (who is also his cousin), the half-Jewish, half-Tlingit Indian detective Berko Shemets, to discover a far-reaching conspiracy involving the Verbovers and the US government to blow up the Dome of the Rock in Jerusalem prior to establishing a Jewish state there. Thus, like Roth's novel, Chabon's also concerns a secret US government plot, this one not so much against the Jews as exploiting the Jews.

Both Roth and Chabon write about Jews in a precarious situation, facing the perennial crisis of Jews for thousands of years: they are about to be expelled. Herman Roth actually quits a good job in an insurance company rather than be relocated from Newark to Kentucky. Says Chabon, "This story, I think, is about the status quo of the Jews, who are always on the verge of being thrown out, of being shown the door. . . . That's the Jewish story and I guess what I came to realize in writing the novel is that it's still the Jewish story" (Chabon/Goldstein).

Both also choose as the point of divergence from actual history the year 1940. "By creating nightmare scenarios that very well could have happened, they seem to be asking why Jews have been able to avoid broad-based repression that the U.S. government . . . has nonetheless managed to hoist onto other minorities. Moreover, both seem to think that the period around World War II was crucial, a make-or-break time that American Jews managed to navigate safely" ("Friday Column"). In *Plot*, the Jews are actively oppressed by the American government; in *Yiddish Policemen's Union*, they are merely shunted aside in Alaska and neglected.

But whereas Roth's novel covers only the period from 1940 to 1942, Chabon's story takes place in an alternate 2007. Chabon explains, "I don't understand the impulse of setting an alternate history in the past the way Roth did. The whole point of alternate history, to me, is to concoct, thereby, an alternate *present*. To set off the present by means of comparing it to its hitherto unknown freakish twin. I thought Roth pulled his punch at the end of the novel, spent too much time in the past. I wondered if he was aware of Philip K. Dick's *The Man in the High Castle* and was afraid that if he came too far forward into the scary 'reality' of a *judenrein* America, he would bump up against Mr. Dick" (Chabon/Hasak-Lowy). Despite Chabon's complaint, there is no rule that alternate histories must be set in an alternate present; in fact, many are set in alternate past, such as *The Difference Engine*, which takes place in an alternate Victorian England, or *Lest Darkness Fall*, set in sixth-century Rome. And it is unlikely that Philip Roth was trying to compete with Philip K. Dick, given Roth's apparently blissful ignorance of the entire subgenre.

Both wrote their novels in homage to family and to the Jewish past: Roth to his parents and Chabon to his grandparents. Chabon says that after his grandparents died, "I started to turn back a little. . . . And also not only look at what I had left behind, but what my parents and grandparents had left behind. The world, the language, they had left behind, the culture and civilization" (Chabon/Greenwood). Although Chabon grew up hearing Yiddish, he couldn't speak it. Then in a bookshop he stumbled across a Yiddish phrase book, *Say It in Yiddish: A Phrase Book for Travelers*. He tried to picture the imaginary country where one would need "a phrase book that instructed you how to say, in Yiddish, 'I need a tourniquet'" (Chabon/Greenwood). Thus, he invented the Yiddish-speaking Sitka. Chabon studied Yiddish before writing the novel.

Both novels are also based on a grain of real history. Lindbergh was indeed an anti-Semite, an admirer of Hitler, and a leader of the American isolationists during the early years of WW II. One the speeches he gave in 1941 is duplicated in the novel, but moved back to 1940. And some Republicans flirted with the notion of drafting him to run for president in 1940. And as for settling Jews in Alaska, "Harold Ickes who was secretary for the interior under FDR proposed it. He prepared this report and issued this finding that it could be a useful way of killing two birds with one stone, of exploiting Alaskan resources and also of solving this refugee problem" (Chabon/Greenwood). In fact, this same Harold Ickes, a friend of the Jews, is mentioned five times in *The Plot Against America*. In real life, the representative from Alaska voted down Ickes's proposal. In his novel, Chabon disposes of this obstacle by having the legislator conveniently run over by a taxicab before he can cast his vote.

Whereas *The Plot* concerns a dystopia, *The Yiddish Policemen's Union* concerns a failed utopia. Sitka is a sad city, filled with abandoned projects and unfulfilled hopes. For example, Landsman lives in the Hotel Zamenhof, named for the Polish Jew who created another failed utopian scheme, the proposed international language Esperanto. All that remains of Zamenhof's language in the hotel is an elevator sign that reads "Elevatoro." When Landsman's ex-wife, Bina, now his boss in the Homicide Squad, visits his shabby room in the Zamenhof, she asks, "'How do you say 'shit heap' in Esperanto?'" (YPU 164). Another difference between the novels is that Roth uses his to attack Jewish neoconservatives, whereas Chabon attacks right-wing zealots. Roth's satiric target is Rabbi Lionel Bengelsdorf, the quisling who "koshers Lindbergh for the goyim" (Plot 40). The pompous, sententious Bengelsdorf is a "court Jew" who rises to a high position in the Lindbergh administration. Chabon uses Rabbi Shpilman, who is both a physical and moral monstrosity, to criticize radical Zionists.

Finally, the fundamental difference between these two alternate Jewish histories lies in their views of history. In Roth's novels, one always comes face to face with the unknowable. For example, in *American Pastoral*, we never know the real relationship, if any, between the Swede's daughter, Merry, and the radical who calls herself "Rita Cohen." And in *The Human Stain*, we never know if Coleman Silk and his lover, Faunia Farley, were killed by her crazed ex-husband, Les Farley, or died by accident. Similarly, the mystery surrounding Lindbergh in *The Plot* is never resolved: did he die in a plane crash, or was he killed or kidnapped by Nazis? Moreover, was his infant son kidnapped and killed by Bruno Hauptmann, or was he abducted and taken to Germany to be used as leverage against the future American president? What exactly was Lindbergh's "understanding" with Hitler, and what were his plans for American Jews? But in choosing to write an homage to the murder mystery, Chabon is obliged to follow the conventions and to resolve the mystery. By the end, Meyer Landsman does find out who killed Mendel Shpilman as well as the probable killers of Meyer's sister, Naomi, a pilot who helped Mendel. And he uncovers the plot to blow up the Dome of the Rock—not, unfortunately, in time to prevent it. At the end of the novel, the fate of the Jews after "the Reversion" of Sitka to the United States is uncertain—as the fate of the Jews is always uncertain. But history for Chabon is ultimately knowable, whereas for Roth, history remains a mystery.

Let me give the last word to Michael Chabon, who provides a lucid explanation for the recent interest of Jewish novelists in AH:

> Judaism is all about history and what happened to us and how we got where we are. The patterns of our history and the crucial moments—the destruction of the temple, the expulsion from Spain, Kristallnacht, these dates that both seem to change everything and yet merely were repeating, in some way, the last time. And yet at the same time Judaism, in its truest form, is very focused on the future, on the coming of the Messiah, on the redemption of the world. . . . [I]n a way the Messiah story is kind of the ultimate science fiction; it's kind of a prediction of this brave new world that is always yet to come. . . . To have that sort of simultaneous sense of looking backward and looking forward—I think it does definitely lend itself to the kind of speculative, hypothetical thinking of the counterfactual novel. You're looking at history and asking, "Where are the moments where things changed, where history forked and it could have gone this way?" (Chabon/Goldstein)

References

Chabon, Michael. "Jews on Ice." Michael Chabon interviewed by Sarah Goldstein. Salon.com, May 4, 2007. http://www.salon.com/books/int/2007/05/04/chabon/print.html.

———. "Michael Chabon Interview." Helen Greenwood. Sydney, Australia *Morning Herald*, May 3, 2007. http://www.smh.com.au/news/books/michael-chabon-interview/2007/05/03/1177788267982.html.

———. "The Language Deep, Deep in Chabon's Ear." Michael Chabon interviewed by Todd Hasak-Lowy. Jbooks.com. http://www.jbooks.com/interviews/index/IP_HasakLowy_Chabon.htm.

———. *The Yiddish Policeman's Union*. New York: HarperCollins, 2007.

Deresiewicz, William. "The Imaginary Jew." *The Nation*, May 10, 2007. http://www.thenation.com/doc/200070528/deresiewicz/print.

Doctorow, E. L. "False Documents." E. L. Doctorow: Essays and Conversations, edited by Richard Trenner. Princeton: Ontario Review Press, 1983.

"Friday Column: Michael Chabon's *The Yiddish Policeman's Union* and Alternate History." March 30, 2007. http://www.conversationalreading.com/2007/03/friday_column_m.html.

Hellekson, Karen. *The Alternate History: Refiguring Historical Time*. Kent, OH: Kent State University Press, 2001.

Rosenfeld, Gavriel David. *The World Hitler Never Made: Alternate History and the Memory of Nazism*. Cambridge: Cambridge University Press, 2005.

Roth, Philip. *American Pastoral*. Boston: Houghton Mifflin, 1998.

———. *The Human Stain*. Boston: Houghton Mifflin, 2000.

———. "Imagining Jews." In *Reading Myself and Others*, by Philip Roth, 215–46. New York: Farrar, Strauss and Giroux, 1975.

———. *I Married a Communist*. Boston: Houghton Mifflin, 1998.

———. *Patrimony: A True Story*. New York: Farrar, Strauss and Giroux, 1991.

———. *The Plot Against America*. Boston: Houghton Mifflin, 2004.

———. "The Story Behind *The Plot Against America*." *New York Times*, September 19, 2004. http://www.nytimes.com/2004/09/19/books/review/19ROTHL.html.

Sayers, Valerie. "The Chosen Frozen." *Commonweal* 134, no. 16 (September 28, 2007): 26–27.

5

Reading the Shema

Jewish Literature as World Literature

Naomi B. Sokoloff

By examining modern poems that draw on and respond to the Shema, Judaism's basic declaration of monotheistic belief, students can learn how recent literary works revisit and reconsider traditional sources and how, in the process, writers across languages and geographical boundaries enter into a kind of conversation with one another. The Shema continues to inspire and energize contemporary writing. Poems by, for example, Marcia Falk, Marge Piercy, Eliaz Cohen, Hava Pinhas-Cohen, and Primo Levi demonstrate how this foundational Jewish text has been understood anew in today's world. Starting by pointing out that reinterpretation has always been an integral part of Jewish thinking, teachers can engage students with poetry to encourage close reading, to strengthen understanding of Jewish literature, and to explore ways in which Jewish literature fits into the study of world literature. The poems under discussion form a translingual and transnational body of work that addresses wide audiences. Jewish literature is a global phenomenon, and this poetry focuses on the kind of universal themes that have an important role to fill in undergraduate education.

Translating the Shema

Whether or not students have knowledge of Hebrew, looking at multiple translations of the Shema can help them grasp its fundamental meanings and also appreciate that the Hebrew does not map seamlessly onto English. The differences between translations, then, can lead to discussion regarding the name of God, gender in the language of prayer, conceptions of hierarchy in relations between humans and the divine, uses of metaphor in Jewish liturgy, and, most importantly, the unity and singularity of God.[1]

The first line of the Shema comes from Deuteronomy 6:4:[2]

Shema Yisra'el Adonai Eloheinu Adonai Echad.

Here are several translations:

1. Hear, O Israel! The LORD is our God, the LORD alone.[3]
2. Hear, O Israel, the Lord is our God, the Lord is One![4]
3. Hear O Israel: Adonai is our God; Adonai is One.[5]
4. Hear, O Israel: HASHEM is our God, HASHEM, the One and Only.[6]

Translation 1 focuses on exclusive fidelity to God, as it states that "the LORD alone" is Israel's God. In contrast, translation 2 expresses the idea of a unity that encompasses all the diverse and even conflicting aspects of the world and of human experience. Both ideas about God's oneness—fidelity and unity—have been integral parts of long-standing Jewish interpretations of the Shema, but the translations here differ in emphasis. An element that the two translations do share, notably, is their reference to the "Lord." Both versions conceive of God in terms of kingship, a metaphor prevalent in the Ancient Near Eastern context from which the Biblical text emerged. The capitalization of LORD then conveys respect for majesty, and it also nods to the ineffability of the name of God, a name too holy to be pronounced aloud or even spelled out in the Hebrew. The original text offers, instead, the substitute word that is pronounced "Adonai." Translation 3, then, retaining that word in transliteration, insists on the specificity of the Jewish name for God. (For congregants not familiar with Hebrew, this formulation may actually muffle or obscure the reference to a masculine image of kingship.) For the Orthodox congregation, addressed in translation number 4, even "Adonai" is too sacred a word to be spoken outside of the act of prayer itself and thus is replaced here simply with "HASHEM"—that is, "THE NAME." The Orthodox formulation also distinguishes itself by referring to God as the "One and Only," a phrase that may emphasize both unity and singularity. Another meaningful facet of these translations is the different use of punctuation in each. In Deuteronomy, the Shema conveys a conversation. God (through Moses) speaks, "Hear O Israel," and the people respond with their affirmation of faith and devotion. Translation 1 here with its exclamation point, most closely captures the division of the biblical verse into two voices. Translation 2, however, obscures the dialogic dimension of the words and loses that sense of dramatic exchange. Versions 3 and 4 present variations that are not self-evident as dialogue, but compatible with it.

A version of the Shema that reinterprets it not through translation into English but through the layout of the Hebrew words on the page presents the traditional text as a haiku. David Carasso has separated the words into three lines, noticing that they thereby form a syllable pattern of 5-7-5: She-ma Yis-ra-'el / A-do-nai El-o-hei-nu / A-do-nai E-chad. Moreover, the Shema fulfills not only the formalistic conventions of the haiku, but also many of the other characteristics of this particular kind of poetry. Carasso comments:

> It is about nature, or rather the nature of the universe. It is very concrete, and consists of strong nouns and a strong verb, with no modifiers. It deals with the here and now. Its three lines each express a complete thought. There is an imaginative distance between two distinct sections: The first section (Israel) is finite, and yet connects with the second section, God the Infinite.[7]

In short, Carasso gleans spiritual insight and a renewed sense of understanding by reading the Shema as poetry—specifically as a genre that features brevity and understatement in order to convey capacious perception and astute observation.

American Sign Language and the Shema

ASL presents an especially captivating case of translation. The Shema is perhaps the best-known part of the Jewish liturgy, recited by Jews around the world even in the most far-flung locations,[8] yet ASL, in a jolting way, raises questions about inclusion and exclusion; how do the words "Hear, O Israel" resonate for the deaf and the hearing impaired?

Rabbi Darby Jared Leigh's version of the Shema, available online, addresses this issue directly.[9] Leigh points out, first, that he interprets the word "hear" as "pay attention." This understanding encompasses all avenues of perception, not just listening. And, as he explains, "The Lord Your God, the Lord is One" is a concept that can be dramatized beautifully through hand motions. As fingers open and close, they dynamically express diversity within unity while also emphasizing the singularity of God. Recognizing the multiple manifestations of God's works and declaring fidelity to the One God are central aspects of the Shema; ASL energetically reaffirms these Jewish monotheistic beliefs in a visual and highly accessible way.

The distinctive power of ASL also emerges from the next section of the Shema, known as Ve'ahavta—the first word of the passage, meaning "And you shall love."

> You shall love the Lord your God with all your heart, with all your soul and with all your might.
> And these words which I command you today shall be upon your heart.
> You shall teach them diligently to your children, and you shall speak of them
> When you sit in your house, and when you walk on the road, and when you lie down and when you rise.
> You shall bind them as a sign upon your hand, and they shall be for a reminder between your eyes.
> And you shall write them upon the doorposts of your house and upon your gates.
>
> *Ve'ahavta et Adonai Eloheikha bekhol levavkha uvekhol nafshekha uvekhol me'odekha.*
> *Vehayu hadevarim ha'eileh asher anokhi metzavkha hayom al levavekha.*
> *Veshinantam levanekha vedibarta bam*
> *beshivtekha bevetekha uvelekhtekha vaderekh uveshakhbekha uvekumekha*
> *Ukeshartam le'ot 'al yadekha vehayu letotafot bein einekha.*
> *Ukhetavtam' al mezuzot beitekha uvish'arekha.*

Most striking, in a signed version provided by Jewish Deaf Multimedia,[10] is the verse "You shall bind them as a sign upon your hand" (*ukeshartam le'ot 'al yadekha*). "Them" refers here to "*hadevarim ha'eileh*"—that is, the Commandments—and this part of the Shema explains how to enact belief by remembering what God has commanded. Traditionally, in accordance with this verse, Jews lay tefillin, binding the leather straps of the phylacteries about an arm. In ASL, binding on the hand is vividly enacted, mimicking the action of laying tefillin and so bringing to life the connection between the words of the text and Jewish custom. Furthermore, in ASL the words "*had'varim ha'eileh*" literally become signs upon (and of) the hand.

Yet more resonances stem from the fact that *devarim* in Hebrew can mean "words" or "things" and also "acts." In ASL, verbal constructs not only become embodied; in addition, because they are concretized as palpable shapes and movements, the actions of signing bridge the gap that English supposes to exist between words and things. In this way, it turns out, the ASL version captures more of the authentic Hebrew meanings than does the English version.

Finally, this ASL Shema exerts special power, as it refers to loving God "with all your heart, with all your soul, and with all your might." The physical strength evident in the signer's rendition of this verse conveys meaning with a kind of literal force that neither spoken nor written words can capture in quite the same way. And, to refine this observation a bit further: keep in mind that the word translated as "might"—*me'od*—is an intensifier. It has devolved in Modern Hebrew into the adverb meaning "very." Though the connotations of the biblical word "*me'od*" are tricky to translate into English, the ASL Shema handily captures intensity, as it demonstrates, quite physically, the effort of putting one's physical being into declaring love for God.

ASL has its own distinctive poetic qualities—qualities achieved through movement, three-dimensionality, and semantic layers that have no exact equivalent in spoken or written English. These infuse the signed Shema with a unique kind of immediacy and vitality. These same qualities demonstrate that the deaf have much to teach the hearing world about language and perception. People who are not hearing impaired can learn from ASL to reread "Hear O Israel." As the Shema calls on Jews to recognize and acknowledge the diverse manifestations of one God, ASL renditions of the Shema serve as a pointed reminder to honor diversity.

American Jewish Poets Rewrite the Shema

Moving beyond translation, several American Jewish poets have reworked the Shema in compositions designed as new liturgy. Marcia Falk, for instance, in her *Book of Blessings*, offers both English and Hebrew versions of the Shema for use in worship. She also provides extensive and informative notes explaining the choices she has made as a translator/poet. Notably, she eschews masculine God-language and avoids the hierarchical metaphor that equates divinity with kingship. In addition, she explicitly celebrates the diversity within unity that the traditional Shema implicitly declares.

> Hear O Israel—
> The divine abounds everywhere
> and dwells in everything:
> the many are One.

Then, in her rendition of "*Ve'ahavta*," she deliberately includes mention of daughters as well as sons among those who should receive instruction; similarly, she avoids the sexist language inherent in the gendered Hebrew verb "*veshinantam*" ("you shall teach them"), which addresses a masculine singular "you" (referring to the people, Israel). Instead, she substitutes "*neshanenam*" (a gender-neutral verb form meaning "we will teach them"). She also replaces the word "*devarim*" with "promises," emphasizing not ritual, but parents' obligation to be reliable and responsible to their children. Among those things that children should be taught, she spells out justice, peace, kindness, and compassion; all are values of traditional Judaism, but not itemized in the original Shema. Falk includes as well a distinctly contemporary environmental awareness and call for stewardship of the earth.[11]

Another poet who reenvisions prayer is Marge Piercy. Some of her work has indeed found its way into prayerbooks, such as the Reform movement's High Holiday mahzor, *Mishkan Hanefesh* (2015). Her version of the Shema features a decidedly humanist emphasis. Unlike Falk, she does not avoid the word "God," but she does focus emphatically on human experience, declaring:

> Hear, Israel, you are of God and God is one.
> Praise the name that speaks us through all time.[12]

Piercy likewise shies away from highlighting God's commandments. Instead, she uses second-person plural as she urges the community to do what is right. The result is not "And you shall teach them diligently to your sons" but "we must teach our children." At the same time, she does embrace the word "*Ve'ahavta*" in transliteration—as opposed to Falk, who rejects the masculine verb form that means "and you shall love"—and so Piercy reaffirms her connections with traditional language.

This poet both acknowledges and modifies tradition by choosing the words "you shall love what is holy with all your courage, with all your passion, with all your strength," which recall but are not identical with the conventional formulation: "you shall love the Lord your God with all your heart, all your soul and all your might." And, as Piercy valorizes the transmission of Jewish teaching, she also adds her own emphases, notably a contemporary focus on environmental concerns. She praises "clear precious water" and remarks, "Heaven and earth observe how we cherish or spoil our world." In the last portion of her Shema, she sprinkles the text liberally with references to various parts of the Torah, with injunctions to "love our neighbors as ourselves," "love the stranger," "choose life," and listen to "a still small voice." This compendium of inspirational sayings forms an alternative to the emphasis on ritual and ritual objects (tefillin and mezuzah) that Orthodox interpretations consider an integral part of the traditional Shema.

Israeli Poetry and the Shema

Turning to Israeli poets, consider now how writing in the Hebrew language offers special possibilities for allusion to the Shema. Take, for example, this poem by Eliaz Cohen:

Hear, O Lord.
(prayer for the days of awe)

Hear, O Lord, Israel your people, Israel is one
And you shall love Israel your people
With all your heart
And with all your soul
And with all your might
And these sons who are being killed for you daily shall be

upon your heart
And you shall teach them diligently in your heavens
And you shall talk of them:
When you sit in your house
And when you walk by the way
And when you lie down and when you rise
And you shall bind them as a sign upon
your hand (phosphorescent blue numbers) and they shall
  be as frontlets
between your eyes (like the sniper's shot)
And you shall write them (in blood) on the doorposts of
  your house
And on your gates[13]

This poem has special impact because it so closely mimics the original biblical text, using archaic verb forms and turns of phrase and combining those with Modern Hebrew—for example, "*vehayu letotafot beyn eyneikha (kemo pegi'at tselafim)*"; "and they shall be as frontlets / between your eyes (like the sniper's shot)." To be sure, the poem retains much of its force in English, too, as it dramatically reverses the roles of God and the Jewish people. Here the people do not acknowledge the oneness of God; instead, the poet implores God to recognize the oneness of the Jewish people, not to allow them to split apart or to have one faction turn against the other. Nonetheless, some components of the text cannot be translated easily. The epigraph is especially tricky because of its multivalence in Hebrew. "*Yihud le yamim nor'aim*" means not just a special prayer for the Days of Awe (the period between the New Year and the Day of Atonement), but also, in everyday Hebrew, a prayer for "terrible days." Composed during the second Intifada, a time of terror and intense political violence, this poem issues an anguished outcry; the poet seems uncertain about where God is in the midst of such terrible events.[14] In addition, while "*yihud*" is the term used for affirming the unity of God, here it suggests an attempt to connect with God. Rather than declaring the oneness of God, this poem expresses a yearning for God to be at one with the Jews, attentive to their suffering. Indeed, the poet seeks a kind of reciprocity, asking for God to empathize with and learn from humans, not only—as the traditional Shema articulates—for people to honor God's teachings. The mention of blue numbers underscores the need for empathy, as it recalls the Holocaust and ties past suffering to continuing violence against Jews. In this way, not with tefillin on the arm but with tattooed numbers of the Shoah, the poet asks to bind God closer to the people of Israel. The word "*yad*" in Hebrew works well in this case, because it connotes "arm" or "forearm" as well as "hand." One further nuance of the Hebrew likewise binds God and man: while the English notes that sons are being killed "for you," the Hebrew states "*nehargim 'aleikha.*" This wording has more punch, because the same preposition, "'*al,*" also appears in the phrase "'upon your heart" ("'*al levavekha*"). That is to say, "for you" and "on you" are the same in Hebrew; the parallel verbal construction reinforces the idea that the death of the young, who were devoted to God, should leave a mark on God's heart, in other words, be taken to heart by God.

Unlike the Hebrew in "Hear O Lord," some of the lines in Hava Pinhas-Cohen's "You are Loneliness" ("*Atah habedidut,*" 2003) stand out because they move away from biblical cadences while still alluding to the Shema. Her Hebrew shifts toward contemporary colloquial diction, and that is part of the charm of this text. Because Israeli Hebrew is so close to the ancient language yet also distant from it, modern poetry gains creative options not so readily available in English.

> Hear
> O Israel, I say,
> and you are silent
> Japanese headphones cover your ears
> that consume sweet music
> like Turkish nougat
> covered in raisins and cinnamon.
>
> Hear, oh Israel, I do not
> whisper the holy Name
> to you I preach rain
> while you smile to the everlasting face
>
> I learned to say to love, sleep here tonight
> *Mashiach* now, a blue ox *Mashiach*
> tomorrow, I will open the window for you
> you'll depart like a bird.[15]

Sharon Hart-Green's accomplished translation here echoes the opening words of the traditional liturgy: "*shema Yisr'ael*" (Hear O Israel). Another option for translation, though, underscoring the everyday sound of the words in Modern Hebrew, could be "Listen, Israel" or even "Hey, Izzy, listen up." In Hebrew, the poem opens in the linguistic register of conversation between familiars. This tone contrasts with the exchange between God and the Israelites in the context of prayer. Embedded for so long in formal ritual, the words "*shema Yisra'el*" in synagogue have taken on inescapable gravitas and a ceremonious tone. However, because "Israel" is a common first name among Hebrew speakers, these same words in the modern poem can be understood as a mother speaking to a teenaged son raptly intent on the music in his headphones (or any woman speaking to a loved one). Indeed, Pinhas-Cohen's allusion to the Shema suggests the importance of paying attention and of mindfulness, much as did the ASL translation of the Shema. Pinhas-Cohen's Hebrew even intensifies those connotations through the word "*mahrish*." It means both "to be silent" and "to drown out" or "to silence" something else. Here, Israel sits in his own world, not just staying quiet, but also tuning out the woman speaking to him. Strikingly, the text acknowledges a kind of encounter with the divine; the words "Smiling to the everlasting face" (or the "infinite face") suggest that he experiences profound delight and spiritual transport. However, this is a solitary experience, not the communal act of declaring Shema in public. Also, strikingly, the woman's stance is more one of understanding than of taking offense at being ignored. She describes herself as "preaching rain," which recalls the second (less often recited) section of the Shema—Deuteronomy 11:13–21—which promises reward to those who obey God's commandments, especially in the form of rain and plentiful crops. In Pinhas-Cohen's poem, if we imagine a mother with a son, it is noteworthy that the speaker does not demand discipline or respect from the child, nor does she insist on transmitting tradition ("I do not whisper the holy Name," she says). Rather, she emphasizes her hopes for the boy's welfare. Wordplay in the phrase "*metifa geshem*" enhances this idea. "*Metifa*" can mean "preach," but it can also mean "drip" or "trickle"—that is, the speaker wishes to rain goodness down upon the son. Significantly, his is a globalized world. Although this is a short text, the poet deliberately finds room to mention Japanese headphones and Turkish sweets—both of which Israel finds more compelling than any preaching the mother might offer about "el Shaddai" (translated here as "the holy Name"). Her focus, then, is less on strict religious observance or transmitting Jewish culture to her son than on her desire for him to experience blessings and well-being—even in a world that distracts him from Torah.

Clarifying this point, the final verse is overtly expository. The woman explains that what she has learned, and what accounts for her attitude here, is that love may not last, that loved ones will fly away in their own time (most likely too soon). The last line in the Hebrew reads "*tets'i*"—that is, love "will leave." This future-tense verb (second person) could also be understood as a kind of gentle imperative: "go ahead, leave." She gives love permission to take its own path. As a parent, she is willing to let go of the son. At the same time, she does yearn for him to be present and to acknowledge her, and, to formulate those feelings, she borrows a phrase from a prominent slogan of the Chabad movement, "*Moshiach akhshav*" (Messiah now).[16] She exhorts Israel to be alert to her now, which would feel redemptive, but she nonetheless casts this request as somewhat unrealistic. To demand that he pay attention to her right away is to ask for a blue ox—that is, like the tall tales about Paul Bunyan, this is the stuff of legend. Her deep wanting to overcome loneliness is heartfelt, but she senses that holding on and letting go at the same time is the very definition of parental love.

All in all, while retaining the exact words "*shema Yisra'el*" and recalling the reference to rain in the second part of the Shema, the poet here has adapted the ancient text in a variety of ways. She has changed the register, made the words multivalent in an intensely personal way, and shifted the focus from inherited tradition to private, individual experience. Finally, while the Shema in Jewish liturgy deals with the diversity of the world and the oneness of God, Pinhas-Cohen's poem presents a mother's love as a variation on the notion of unity and difference. Fidelity here, of a mother to her son, means a desire for closeness and a simultaneous recognition of having to let go; consideration of the parental role means not only teaching diligently, but also letting children lead their own lives.

Primo Levi's Shema and the Holocaust

Perhaps the best-known modern poem based on the Shema is the one that appears at the opening of Primo Levi's 1946 memoir *Survival in Auschwitz* (*Se questo e un uomo*). The forthright use of allusive elements of the text and the title in English translation ("*Shema*") explicitly recall the liturgy.[17] The speaker here, a survivor, calls on all those who have not themselves experienced the Shoah to attend to those who are suffering and to remember the suffering caused by the Holocaust. The people who live in comfort are enjoined to teach these values to their children, at home and outside the home, when lying down and when getting up, just as the Torah charges Jews to teach the Commandments. The ending of the poem then offers a curse, recalling the verses of the Shema from the book of Numbers that promise negative fortune to those who disregard the Commandments. One commentator has remarked on this ending:

> listening is not enough. The verb *shema* carries additional meanings—it also denotes doing, obeying, performing, acting. Perhaps Levi . . . wanted to jolt his reader, through graphic and painful images, into action.[18]

The Italian original of Levi's poem evokes this interpretation by explicitly using the word for command, "commando." The widely read English version, though, by Ruth Feldman and Brian Swann,[19] translates that word as commend ("I commend these words to you"). This way of putting things has a softer connotation: of recommending and also encumbering, of charging someone with a responsibility. The translation is, in its own way, felicitous; it allows the poem to express less a demand for obedience than an insistence that it is wise to pay attention to these matters. This recommendation, furthermore, is inseparable from a keen awareness of the importance of transmission, of passing along the duty to bear witness.

In stating its case, this poem patently addresses a wide audience ("You who live secure / In your warm houses") and lays claims to universal significance, as it poses fundamental questions about personhood, humanity, and inhumanity. Remembering a prisoner at hard labor "Who fights for a crust of bread / Who dies at a yes or a no," Levi asks us—as the title in Italian indicates—if this degraded creature is still human. However, the language here is distinctly gendered: "Consider whether this is a man." The poem thereby presents divisive pronouncements, offering broad generalizations about manhood and womanhood. It attributes agency (and its loss) first and foremost to the purview of men, while it defines women primarily in terms of appearance and bodily experience—especially motherhood. The woman prisoner is associated with loss of hair, "empty eyes," and a womb no longer fertile. In evidence here is the kind of binary thinking about what constitutes masculinity and femininity that current gender theory rejects. Recent cohorts of students prefer instead to think in terms of fluid gender categories and a plethora of nuanced terms for identities that go beyond "male," "female," and "transgender." The original Shema, because it is a Hebrew text, inevitably poses issues of gender; gender is built into the grammar of the language. The result is to emphasize masculinity. In addition, the Shema excludes specific reference to women, and it does not directly address them. Levi, by contrast, includes women along with men in his considerations of what is most valuable and must be taught diligently to the next generation. He does so, though, in a way that no longer seems au courant. Today's students have found new prisms through which to read his poem and new perceptions that strain against the constraints of his "Shema." Each generation no doubt will seek out its own path to expression and new responses to traditional sources.

Conclusion

From translations of the Shema to reworkings of it in new liturgy, to poems more loosely reflecting on the Shema or alluding to it, this discussion has suggested ways in which Jewish literature, composed in a variety of languages and in connection with a variety of literary traditions, remains in dialogue with shared foundational texts. The Shema has moved from the context of traditional Jewish worship to modern experiment with prayer, to new and specifically Jewish cultural settings and then beyond, addressing and reaching broader audiences.[20] In the process, each of the texts examined here in some way illuminates or puts into relief, by way of contrast, how the others relate to the original Hebrew. Together these texts indicate aspects of the original Shema that have spoken emphatically to contemporary writers. Forming a kind of transhistorical textual community, these pieces enhance one another and therefore lend themselves well to study in the field of world literature.[21] This is a rubric that has been growing in popularity at universities across North America in recent years. Literature increasingly is being read in worldwide contexts, and more and more educational programs have been examining how works of literature travel across time, space, languages, and media. Jewish literature, transnational and translingual as it is, provides rich opportunities to discuss the global circulation of culture.

Material related to the Shema is, by the same token, well suited for use in courses that feature not only comparative literature but also cross-disciplinary approaches. Students are less likely to sign up for a course on Jewish poetry than for a course that asks big questions, such as, what is prayer? Why do people pray? What do people do when they pray? What does prayer look like in different religious traditions (for example, in Judaism, Christianity, and Islam)? How does modern writing respond to and reinterpret those traditions? In an era of plummeting enrollments in the humanities, wide conceptual frameworks such as these, together with broad thematic inquiry, can provide intellectual as well as pragmatic solutions to curricular challenges. My argument, fundamentally, is that solid grounding in broadly humanistic study can bring students to close readings—an important and indispensable skill too often at risk in a world of shortened attention spans—and then help them move from specific texts back to overarching concepts and the kind of big-picture thinking that an undergraduate education, at its best, can provide. The Shema invites special scrutiny in this regard. Its reference to the ineffable name (what cannot be said) defies translation, and so this text puts into relief both the importance and the limitations of translation. Moreover, it focuses pointedly on the importance of transmission and the teaching of tradition; as the Shema continues to elicit new responses from contemporary writers, it seems only fitting to reflect on how this text itself has been transmitted and transformed. Finally, as it presents both particular and universal claims, and as it travels the globe in new interpretations, this text can resonate with Jewish and non-Jewish audiences alike.

Notes

1. For a valuable pedagogical tool that introduces the Shema, its history, its implications for Jewish worship and belief, the gender issues it raises, and the translation challenges it poses, see *My People's Prayerbook*, vol. 1: *The Shema and Its Blessings*, ed. Lawrence A. Hoffman (Woodstock, VT: Jewish Lights Publishing, 1997). A very useful, brief introduction to the Shema can be found in the comments by Alan Mintz at http://www.myjewishlearning.com/author/alan-mintz/. See also Mintz's essay on prayer in *Back to the Sources*, ed. Barry W. Holtz (New York: Simon and Schuster, 1984), 403–29.

2. The term "*Shema*" can refer to this one biblical verse (Deuteronomy 6:4) or to three passages from the Torah (Deuteronomy 6:4–9, Deuteronomy 11:13–21, and Numbers 15:37–41), or to a unit of prayer in which the biblical selections are combined with a series of blessings.

3. *The Torah: A Modern Commentary*, ed. W. Gunther Plaut (New York: Union of American Hebrew Congregations, 1981).

4. Chaim Stern, *Gates of Prayer: The New Union Prayerbook* (New York: Central Conference of American Rabbis, 1975).

5. Hoffman, *The Shema*, 82.

6. Nosson Scherman, *The Complete Art Scroll Siddur* (New York: Mesorah, 1984).

7. David Carasso, "The Jewish Haiku," http://www.aish.com/ci/a/48932982.html.

8. Students can benefit from seeing videos of diverse congregations reciting the Shema. A particularly striking one of tribesmen in New Guinea who say the Shema while holding Christian beliefs has been posted online, https://www.youtube.com/watch?v=yZkK-iOzh9k.

9. https://www.youtube.com/watch?v=MDUU4vy2tmM.

10. http://jewishdeafmm.org/shema/. The English translation of *Ve'ahavta* cited here is the one presented in subtitles in this same video.

11. *The Book of Blessings: New Jewish Prayers for Daily Life, the Sabbath, and the New Moon Festival* (Harper, 1996; Beacon, 1999), 170–73. Copyright © 1996 by Marcia Lee Falk.

12. *The Art of Blessing the Day: Poems with a Jewish Theme* (New York: Knopf, 1999).

13. Eliaz Cohen, *Hear O Lord: Poems from the Disturbances of 2000–2009*. Trans. Larry Barak (New Milford, CT: Toby Press, 2010). This is a bilingual edition of the poems; the English and the Hebrew can be found on facing pages, 14–15. The poem is reprinted here with permission.

14. Some readers have also taken the poem as a plea for Jewish political unity and, in particular, for retaining control over territories captured in 1967.

15. Hava Pinhas-Cohen, *Bridging the Divide*, ed. and trans. Sharon Hart-Green (Syracuse: Syracuse University Press, 2014), 162–63. The excerpt is reprinted with permission.

16. Online videos may help students may understand the "Moshiach now" phenomenon: https://www.bing.com/videos/search?q=you+tube+we+want+moshiach+now&view=detail&mid=802D9EDD76010FD6F271802D9EDD76010FD6F271&FORM=VIRE, accessed February 6, 2017.

17. Primo Levi, *Collected Poems*. Translated by Ruth Feldman and Brian Swann (London: Faber and Faber, 1992).

18. Dorothy Richman, http://ajws.org/what_we_do/education/publications/dvar_tzedek/5768/vaetchanan.html accessed January 13, 2013.

19. Levi, *Collected Poems*, 19.

20. Additional examples of modern poems that engage with the Shema include Pinhas-Cohen's "He who sees it says: that is it" and "From Songs of Home" "A" and "B." A very useful resource for discussion of Hebrew poetry is David A. Jacobson's book *Creator, Are You Listening: Israeli Poets on God and Prayer* (Bloomington: Indiana University Press, 2007).

21. Robert Alter uses the term "transhistorical textual community" to characterize ways in which disparate modern Jewish literatures share foundational source texts. See *Canon and Creativity: Modern Writing and the Authority of Scripture* (New Haven: Yale University Press, 2000), 5.

6

The "Story Without an Ending"

Art, Midrash, and History in Dara Horn's
The World to Come

Sandor Goodhart

[W]hat if . . . [the dead and those about to be born] know each other, . . . [if] the already-weres and the not-yets of our world, the mortals and the natals, are bound together somewhere just past where we can see, in a knot of eternal life?[1]

I. The End of *The World to Come*

The plot of Dara Horn's book is simple. A piece of art—a small painting by Marc Chagall known as "Study for *Over Vitebsk*"—is stolen from an art gallery in New York City (where it is on exhibition from its home in the Soviet Union). The item is taken during a singles reception by one of the attendees, and some time later a forged copy of the painting is returned to the museum "from a busy New Jersey post office with a fake return address" (272). Horn's plot is based on newspaper reports of an actual heist that took place in June 2001 in which the same painting by Chagall is stolen in New York City, then recovered some six months later in a post office in Topeka, Kansas, although in newspaper accounts the missing painting was discovered by accident. In both cases, the returned artwork was said to be authenticated—"the real thing" (272), the narrator notes—but in the fictional account we know the returned item to be a forgery. Horn's report of the newspaper account is given in a few pages following chapter 19, which thereby allows it to serve in effect as the book's final chapter.[2]

The energy driving the plot in this book is the back story. Woven within Horn's fictional account of the theft by Benjamin Ziskind and its reacquisition by the gallery's young curator, Erica Frank, are a wide variety of other stories. In alternating chapters, we read about Ben's childhood with his now-deceased mother, Rosalie (Raisya by birth), and father, Daniel, amid the difficulties of living within a metal brace from the ages of eleven to seventeen. We hear the story of Ben's relation to his twin sister, Sara, and her new husband, a burly Russian immigrant, Leonid Sheharansky (with whom Ben formerly conducted a pen-pal correspondence). We learn the story of Rosalie's courtship with her future husband, Daniel, who predeceased her as the result of a war injury, as well as the story of Daniel's relationship with his own parents, and especially his experience in Vietnam, where he fought alongside an American soldier who initially challenged his masculinity and then died trying to save him.

Perhaps most significantly, we learn the story of Rosalie's father, Boris, who, as an orphan in postwar Russia, saw his mother killed before his eyes (his unborn sibling "torn from his mother's knifed-open belly and thrown through the smashed bedroom window" [19]). He then spent time in a Jewish colony for orphaned children, where he met the painter Marc Chagall, who taught an art class at the school and gave him the small painting that eventually landed in the New York City museum, and the Yiddish writer Pinkhas Kohanovitch (more widely known under the pen name "Der Nister" or "the Hidden One"), who recited midrashim to the children and whose own family later was tragically decimated by poverty, the premature death of his wife, and the violent rape of his daughter at the hands of a group of local young hoodlums shortly before his own arrest and death in a postwar anti-Semitic political sweep. Finally, we learn the story of Boris's own betrayal and arrest in front of his daughter Raisya (followed by his imprisonment and death), an episode engineered by a Russian neighbor, Sergei Popov, who, posing as a friendly neighbor, turned out in fact to be a government agent and art curator eager to implement Russia's new anti-Semitic policy, and who later tracked down and secured the elusive Chagall painting, which had passed with Raisya (later Rosalie) and her mother, Tatiana, to the United States.

Within and around this rich and complex narrative tapestry, and moving the governing plot forward—at ninety degrees perpendicular to it, so to speak—are a series of some five additional stories, traditional midrashim, which are told diegetically. We find, for example, stories told by Rosalie to her children, Ben and Sara; stories told by the book's omniscient narrator, the authorial voice that offers from time to time midrashic accounts, proverbial wisdom, and the like; stories contained within the books that Rosalie writes (based on those she has read in books by authors such as Der Nister or learned about from her parents); stories contained in the various letters circulated throughout this volume; and miscellaneous other stories and narrative genres on generous display in this work. Recovering from his war injuries, Daniel remembers a story he and Rosalie used to read: "It was a story with many stories inside it, he remembered now, stories within stories within stories" (172). That characterization applies amply to Dara Horn's book.

By anyone's account, the book is extraordinary. Five generations of characters (if we include Boris's mother and Sara's unborn child, Daniel), countless narrative forms in which their histories are offered to us, and two or three serious thematic issues presented to us (and developed for us) by a competent, trustworthy narrator make this book one of the most complex and exciting on the contemporary scene. One of those issues is ownership. Ben steals a painting he feels was stolen from his family. In its place he returns a forgery—a facsimile painted by his twin sister, Sara. But there is some indication that the Chagall painting itself may have been a forgery. Ben suspects as much in his conversations with his sister (188). And the basis on which Sergei Popov gains possession of it from Rosalie may have involved such an assumption (if we are to trust the letter Ben finds from his mother—after her death—to the individual who arranged the deal with the Russian buyer [186–87]). Because we are not given the history of the ownership of the painting beyond its acquisition by Boris at the orphanage, its transfer to Rosalie upon Boris's demise, and its transfer to the United States with Rosalie, it is difficult to say more. The Chagall painting in question was of course already only a "study," a sketch, a draft of the larger work. Boris comes to possess it as a trade for giving Chagall a drawing of his own, a sketch he developed as a child thinking perhaps about the story his mother told him (itself taken from the Talmudic tractate *Niddah*) and about the fate of the unborn child in her womb whom he would never know and who took unexpected "flight" one day when his mother's murderers arrived (19). The drop of blue paint that drips onto the canvas from either Boris's or Chagall's palate (the narrative is unclear about its origin), which becomes later a trademark of Chagall's work, confuses the origin of this work further (27–28).

Such questions about authorship of the painting (and the trademark) parallel concerns about the authorship of midrashic stories. Does Talmud "own" the story from the tractate *Niddah* of the happiness of babies before birth? Does Der Nister, who recites it to the children of the orphanage? Does Rosalie, who signs her name to it in a book of such borrowed writings? Does Sara, who retells it from memory in a modernized version? Does Boris, who hears it from his mother in response to the violence swirling around her and is inspired by it as a basis for his drawing? Does his mother? Does the author of this book, who tells all of these tales?

But there is a second issue aside from proprietary rights in this book, which may shed light on the first: the relation of the specific Talmudic midrash of the prenatal schooling of children to the idea of the "world to come," which provides the title for the book at large. The most astounding instance of the problematic nature of this relation occurs within the sequence—the story within a story—that concludes it. The narrator (the "implied author," as Wayne Booth was wont to say), who identifies herself as a repository of received wisdom, tells the midrash recited by the rabbis of what happens to souls between conception and birth into the universe identified as "the world to come," linking it with "the world to come" in the future of the life we are living. She collapses, in other words, the final chapter of the world (the world to come) within its pre-history (the midrash of prenatal schooling).

It is, then, to this final chapter of Horn's book, and the premises on which it is based, that we turn in the section that follows. Given an inside that is continuous with the outside, and a future that is continuous with the past, this final chapter of her book (to the extent that it remains separable from the author's note succeeding it) would seem uniquely bound up with all that occurs to that point in the novel, one in which the "world to come" serves in effect as both the container and the contained, or perhaps more precisely as the container within the contained.

II. The Problem of the Ending

But as soon as we turn to that chapter, we encounter a problem. How are we to read it? The book to that point is rich, textured, and extraordinarily complex. Its diegetic use of a wide variety of narrative styles is unmatched on the contemporary American literary scene. Then we get chapter 19, where we learn that in the world of the "not-yets" and the "already-weres," the not-yets attend school, where they do science experiments by observing in the lab the growth of "small cells of betrayal" in Petri dishes (286). Or they take field trips "to the sky" to visit "the storehouses of snow" (287). Or they go to the public baths where they soak in "liquid emotions" and especially "the warm pool of love and the steam of friendship" (288). Or they sleep in beds and hammocks "made of music" (291). Or they visit restaurants where "the cuisine is artwork" (291). Or they attend a bar where the drinks to be consumed are "bottled books"—often biblical scripture—and drunks are identified as "biblioholics" (295–99). Or in the final sequence they build bridges "upon their mistakes" (304).

How do we read such prose? Horn is not speaking metaphorically here. The final episode is not about saying creatively that people are hungry for art, that newborns have just learned (and in the manner of rabbinic midrashim) how fast betrayal spreads, or that the way to traverse difficult patches in life is to learn from our mistakes. That would take far fewer sentences. But these quirky mixtures of metaphors and literalisms continue for pages. After the intensity of the writing preceding it—describing the imprisonment, torture, and death of Boris; the betrayal, imprisonment, and death of Der Nister; the sense about the subsequent career of Chagall that he was a "sellout" to the Yiddish writers with whom he worked as an illustrator (because he decided to tour Europe while they returned to Russia and in most cases to their imminent deaths); the traumatic experiences of Daniel in Vietnam (where he lost a leg) and later when he attempted to face that trauma; the early childhood experience of Ben living within a portable medicinal metal cage; and other disasters in the lives of these characters—these final lighthearted pages could easily seem fatuous.

Some moral theorizing on the author's part near the book's conclusion would seem fitting (although she has been doing that implicitly throughout). But after the complexity and subtlety of the book's handling of questions about authorship and originality (and their relation to the rabbinic understanding permeating this narrative), these final pages feel spurious, especially arriving as they do after chapter 18, in which the curiously hopeful narrative of Ben's relationship with Erica seems incomplete, and we are encouraged to wonder what is to follow.

Chapter 19, in short, could easily seem an instance of bad writing, a piece of "inelegant" prose, to use Horn's own word in another connection (43), and it is not difficult to imagine why some readers who have approved of the rest of the book have suggested that at this moment in the novel, after handling so much so well, the author simply "ran out of steam." Indeed, at first glance, it is hard to argue otherwise. It is difficult to imagine, for example, that this young author could not do better because she did infinitely better somewhat earlier in her career and earlier in this book itself.[3] And other readers, less ready perhaps to criticize the gesture, have elevated it to a level of mystical or spiritual ephemera or largely ignored it, as if the book in fact ends with chapter 18, where we are left in the dark regarding the future, but in a place where authors sometimes leave their audience, to the frustration of otherwise devoted readers or viewers.[4]

Finally, the difficulties of the book's ending—the narrative unsettledness in which the budding romance between Ben and Erica in chapter 18 is left and the insertion of a piece of oddly laborious prose in chapter 19 in place of a continuation of the unfinished narrative or a more august set of reflections—are complicated by the fact that to readers who have complained publicly about the ending, the author has responded in her own defense, which simultaneously alleviates and compounds frustration. Chapter 18 is "deliberately ambiguous," she asserts. "Both possibilities—the possibility that Ben dies, and the possibility that he survives and continues his life with Erica—exist in the book, and the reader gets to choose." This ending is what she dubs "the Der Nister ending—the open-ended possibility, where the reader is forced to ask the question about what the story might mean and which ending feels the most real." But in chapter 19, she says, we discover another ending, "a 'Chagall' ending (a redemptive ending)" or happy ending. The "last two paragraphs," she notes, have "the child falling to the earth laughing"—although in that final chapter we also learn "that the supernatural 'world to come' is only a fake, a copy of the real world to come—which is this world." And she summarizes her assessment as a matter of "two kinds of readers—the Chagall readers, as I call them, who prefer the happy or redemptive ending; and the Der Nister readers, who appreciate the open-ended possibility and the challenges it presents."[5]

But is her assessment a review of readers or of her book? It is hardly our place as critical readers of Dara Horn's book to judge whether or not the ending succeeds in accord with some external moral, narratological, or readerly standard. But it is within our province to interrogate Horn's "implied authorial intention" with the final chapters and wonder whether what she has given us meets expectations the book itself has constructed. Because she has offered us an explicit commentary, what we are asking is whether we can discern an internal structural necessity for the two contrastive concluding chapters so that they do not count as a breach of her achievement to that point, a logic that allows at once for the characters to be both dead and alive (perhaps in the manner of "Schrodinger's cat" [42–43 and 281]), at once Der Nister–like and Chagall-like, open-ended and redemptive.

In fact, I suggest, we can. The ending is not unanticipated. We have been prepared for it repeatedly, and it might be instructive, in considering this ending and its relation to the whole, to identify that preparation.

III. Waiting for the End

The premise of chapter 19 is that souls of these incipient people to be (or "not-yets") are educated in the nine months between conception and birth with all the knowledge of the world they are about to enter (and thus the book's surprising title); then, just before they are born, an angel touches them on the face and they forget all they have learned. The plan is that all they are about to experience will be in fact only a rediscovery of what has always already been known, a remembering of what the angel effectively blocked from their consciousness, which is to say, in short, the "world of our fathers." But in at least one instance in the book in which the story is told, the angel is drunk (237), and the gesture intended to block knowledge from the head of this soul to be fails to attain its goal. As a result, the individual is born into the world-to-come (i.e., our world) with full knowledge retained from the other one.

The final chapter plays on this idea. The chapter occurs, in the first place, at an entirely unexpected moment in the narrative. The artwork has been stolen from the museum. A promise for its return has been made. The plan is for Ben to return the work to the gallery's young curator, Erica Frank, with whom he has developed something of a romantic attachment. But Ben has in fact delivered not the original—which he feels belongs rightfully to his family, from whom it was stolen earlier (by his grandfather's neighbor, Sergei Popov, who, in later years, came to the United States and through a mediator proffered a large sum of money to his mother, Rosalie, to obtain it)—but a forgery painted for the occasion by his twin sister, Sara, herself an accomplished artist.

His sister's artwork is sent to the curator. At Sara's request, Ben attends a reception (accompanied by Sara and her husband) where it is on display, a reception not unlike the one with which the book opens. In the course of their admiration of her work, there is a terrible explosion, and the narrative account of Ben's relation to the curator—along with the details of the aftermath of the return of the painting—is suddenly (and decisively) interrupted. He safely escorts his sister and her husband outside the building and then descends to check on the curator, who has not yet appeared. But as he opens the door to her room, the narration suddenly stops. And we learn nothing further about their relationship (or the painting) by the book's conclusion than we know already: "'Erica,' he called, and listened for her answer. And then he opened the door and entered the world to come" (282). What happens next? Is there a second explosion? Is that why the text "goes dark"? And if there is an explosion, does he die in it? Is "the world to come" a reference to the world after death (after his death) or, at the very least, to death itself? Or, to look at the text differently, is the phrase an allusion to what is to follow in this world? Perhaps he does not die. Perhaps there is not even another explosion, and the words refer to his musing about the future potential of their affection for each other—the world their love could conceivably create for them.

What we know for sure is that the chapter ends. And our assumption as readers must be that we will get our answer momentarily—if not in what immediately follows, then sometime later. Horn's technique, like that of many contemporary fiction writers, is to switch the scene on us, and we are prepared to accept that narratological gesture here as we have previously in the book, so long as the information is delivered to us eventually. But, in fact, nothing of the sort occurs. We learn nothing further about the matter—about their relationship to each other, about either of them individually, about Sara and Leonid, who are presumably waiting outside, or indeed about any of the major characters still presumably alive at this moment of the drama—than we know already. What we get instead is something entirely different. In place of the expected knowledge of the world to come for them (whatever world that is for them), we get the final chapter, a story that turns out to be a version of "the world to come" of a very different sort, a midrashic variant of it, suddenly presented to us as if it is a realistic novelistic narrative continuation.

Is Dara Horn reproducing the scene of the art theft she read about in the newspapers? In place of the ending we expect, we seem to find a "fake" (her word), a forgery, a piece of "bad" writing. Think of Andy Kaufman's comedy, which is based on the presentation of ineptitude.

Let us turn, then, to that chapter itself and reflect on the way it brings together the two dimensions of midrashic tapestries operative throughout this book: the diegetic stories told by the characters themselves to each other and the substories of the novel's plot that are also its history.

IV. The End before the End

The story informing all of chapter 19 is first presented to us earlier in several variant versions. In the first place, there is the rabbinic midrash, the story echoed repeatedly throughout the book. The Talmudic rabbis tell the story that before a child is born, while it is still within the womb, it learns everything about the world that is to follow. And then, just before birth, the angel touches the child and all is forgotten. Here is a passage from Tractate, *Niddah* 30b:

> R. Simlai delivered the following discourse: . . . there is no time in which a man enjoys greater happiness than in those days, for it is said, O that I were as the months of old, as in the days when God watched over me; now which are the days "that make up months" and do not make up years? The months of pregnancy of course. It is also taught all the Torah from

beginning to end . . . As soon as it sees the light, an angel approaches, slaps it on its mouth and causes it to forget all the Torah completely, as it is said, Sin coucheth at the door.[6]

Why would the Rabbis invent such a story? A midrash responds to a gap or tear in the primary text in such a way that constitutes a material extension of that text. To what text is this midrash responding? Torah. How? By pointing to the world as we know it, the world that for these "pre-babies" is still to come. One answer, in other words, is that the midrash is a creative way of saying there was a time when I was happy, when God watched over me, moments when I felt secure in my mother's womb, and when I learned Torah all day long. Would that I were able to return to those times that are so different from my own—in which God may not be watching, in which I am not secure, in which Torah is not read (or practiced), and in which happiness is fleeting if even available.

How does that midrash from *Niddah* inform Horn's book? Here is an early instance of the story from chapter 2:

> Before being born, his mother explained, babies go to school. Not a school like Boris's, but a different kind of school, where all the teachers are angels. The angels teach each baby the entire Torah, along with all the secrets of the universe. Then just before each baby is born, an angel puts its finger right below the baby's nose—here she paused to put her finger across his lips (could he see the blood under her skin, or did he only imagine it?)—and whispers to the child: *Shh—don't tell.* And then the baby forgets.
>
> "Why does he have to forget?" . . . She pulled her hand away from his face, resting it on her own stomach. "So that for the rest of his life," she said, "he will always have to pay attention to the world, and to everything that happens in it, to try to remember all the things he's forgotten." (26)

Not God but angels, who are God's agents. Angels are divine messengers, pure deeds in the Jewish tradition. Moreover, it is not some abstract learning context but "school," and the curriculum is expansive. Babies learn "the entire Torah, along with "all the secrets of the universe," as if the second half is secondary serving to illuminate the first, that the Torah is indeed the "blueprint of the world."

And we gain something from the context in which the story functions. He forgets, she tells him, "So that for the rest of his life," she said, "he will always have to pay attention to the world, and to everything that happens in it, to try to remember all the things he's forgotten." Perhaps because she feels she did not pay sufficient attention, did not read the handwriting on the wall in time, and as a result, they are in the situation they are in. The fact that Boris remembers this repeated episode with his mother, that his parents were subsequently killed, and that he was found astride a grave, within it and outside it, lends a special irony to this potential (20).

In subsequent passages, in the colony, Boris will paint a picture of what he remembers—a baby seated within a womb at a table before a large book (presumably Torah) with an angel floating next to him—a picture that will strike the fancy of the young Chagall, who is teaching art at the colony where orphaned children like Boris are staying and who asks to keep it in exchange for another he will give to the child. Is this sequence another version of the story? An artistic version? Something of a transition between the mother's midrash and the painting that Chagall offers the child in exchange?

In any event, the same story is presented to us in chapter 5, which explores the history of Der Nister:

> Der Nister had been taught . . . There are no days in a person's life that are better or happier than those days in the womb. When those days must end, an angel approaches the child in the womb and says, *The time has come*. But the child refuses—wouldn't you? (Didn't you?) *Please*, the child begs, *please don't make me go*. And then the angel smacks it under the nose so that it falls from the womb and forgets—which is why babies are always born screaming. But before that they are happy and they wait. (81)

Der Nister's version retains elements from the Talmudic and shares features with the version related by Boris's mother. No days are happier (Talmudic). The agents of the action are angels, not God (maternal). The enemy in Der Nister's account, however, is time. The time has come, he says, whereas in Boris's mother's version it was more a matter of natural process. And in this version, the child rebels, refuses, and then begs, and violence results. He is "smacked" and enters the world screaming. The lesson he retains is not attentiveness but impotence before fate and an overpowering authority.

The same story is told somewhat differently again in chapter 8, where we hear what Der Nister himself learned:

> The hand that dents each child's face below the nose just before he is born, Der Nister had once learned, is a familiar one. The day before the child's birth, the very same hand scoops up the child and takes him on a tour all over the world, from morning until evening, showing him everything he will ever see—the place where he will be born, the places where he will live, the places where he will travel, and, at the end of the long day as the dusk slips between the fingers of the hand, the places where he will die and be buried. The child sees all this in a single day. The owner of the hand reminds the child that against his will he was created, and against his will he will be born, and against his will he will live, and against his will he will die, and against his will he will someday have to give a full and complete accounting of everything he has done with all that was given to him against his will. And the child is frightened—not of dying, but of living. He is so frightened that he refuses to be born, spitting on the hand until it smacks him across the face, removes his memory and casts him out (131).

The violence of the final interaction bears a trace on the body: the dent below the nose. Moreover, it is no longer an angel, a messenger of God, who smacks him, but a disembodied "hand." And it is the same hand that a moment before educated him so that an element of betrayal has entered the picture. Moreover, Torah seems to have dropped out of the picture entirely, and what the child sees becomes all-important. "The very same hand . . . takes him on a tour . . . showing him everything he will ever see."

Finally, the denial of freedom in the expulsion is emphasized. "The owner of the hand reminds the child that *against his will* he was created, and *against his will* he will be born, and *against his will* he will live, and *against his will he will die*, and *against his will* he will someday have to give a full and complete accounting of everything he has done with all that was given to him *against his will*" (italics added). Six times the same phrase is spoken. What is the consequence of this denial of choice? "[T]he child is frightened—not of dying, but of living. He is so frightened that he refuses to be born, spitting on the hand until it smacks him across the face, removes his memory and casts him out." Der Nister's account is in this telling is strikingly different finally from both the Talmudic version and the version Boris's mother offers her son.

The story comes up again a fourth time, a fifth if you count Boris's youthful drawing. In "My Last Day in Paradise" at the beginning of chapter 16, Sara recalls the story Rosalie published when Sara was in college as her "favorite" (237), and one that presumably her twin brother Ben heard as well (234–36). The story combines elements from earlier versions with a twist. Here is its opening:

> The days I spent in paradise were the most beautiful days of my life. Even today, my heart flutters a bit and tears come to my eyes when I remember that joyful time. I often close my eyes and relive those years which will never return. In those dreaming moments I even forget how my wings were shorn off before I left that other world, and I spread out my arms and try to fly. It's only when I fall on the floor in pain that I remember that I only had wings in paradise. Why did I leave, you might ask, if I was so happy there? Well, I'll tell you one thing: it wasn't up to me. (234)

In some ways, it draws upon all three earlier versions and seems a kind of compendium of all of them. Angels are an essential part of the scene. Although the word "school" is not used, the story appears to identify the setting as educational. The time before birth is identified as "the most beautiful." This version reports that the leaving "wasn't up to me," an idea that aligns itself with the second version attributed to Der Nister.

But there are also important differences. We notice immediately that this story is cast autobiographically. A first-person narrator living after the events recalls them. We even get a sense of the current life of that narrator—and thus of the context in which it is told. It now seems to me as a "dreaming moment," with "wings" of my own whose memory encourages me to think I can still "fly," and it is "only when I fall on the floor in pain" that I remember the limitations of the world in which I currently reside. We also note a heightened degree of self-consciousness (jumping back and forth between what was going to happen and what had not yet happened: "on the day I was going to be removed") and of a modernistic framing. One of the angels is named "Sammy," a modern diminutive for Samuel. Another, "Pissant." A third, "Simon." None of the characters in any of the three earlier versions was named, and none appeared in the Talmudic midrash from *Niddah*. And the sense that these characters have names creates an entirely different feel: the potential for an evaluation of the angel who will expel them (he is characterized at one point as "a murderer" [235]) and the introduction of a strategy of deception that uses the inevitable fate to gain some advantage (in this case, the clay nose that will allow the child to remember all that has occurred). There is no hint of characterization of the angels in any of the prior versions or of strategy on the part of the human to be. Horn has cast the midrash in this presentation as the story of a battle. The humans will outwit the divine agents—the angels, God—and survive what they perceive to be strategies of betrayal on the part of the divine agents.

V. The World to Come of *The World to Come*

Then we encounter chapter 19. Ben is the only major character whose name does not appear. A reference seems to be made to him as the "uncle" of the not-yet (300) and then, conceivably, again, in a photograph as the man standing "between" a bride and groom, "holding them together" (302). Nor does he show up as an "already-were." Is he alive? Is it Erica whom he is "watching" (302) behind the photographers? The chapter maintains affinities with all of the previous accounts but differs in important ways.

The chapter is divided into eleven small sections. In the first, the moralizing narrator considers the possible construction of the world to come. What if those who have died and those who have just been born know each other, if in fact those who died educated those who have just been born from the moment of their conception to the moment of their birth, a knowledge barred from them just before they entered our world? Then our existence is a circle. When we die, we partake as "already-weres" in educating the "not-yets." That connection is the first way in which the chapter differs from its midrashic predecessors.

In the second section, that potential is worked out through one extended example. Daniel Ziskind Sheharansky, son of Leonid Sheharansky and Sara Ziskind, is hurried to "school," where he learns something about the history of his maternal great-grandfather, Boris Kulbak; his father, Leonid; his mother, Sara; his maternal uncle, Ben; and his maternal grandfather, Daniel, whose name he has inherited. In the third (and subsequent) sections, we learn more about his schooling: field trips to the sky, the baths, the restaurants, the bar, and most spectacularly to the tree of eternal life, guarded by the ever-turning sword. In the final moments of the sequence, he obtains the fruit of the biblical tree of life, which he is encouraged by his maternal grandmother to discard, and falls to earth.

Whatever else it is, the chapter is a compendium of ideas from the earlier versions of the story. The setting is paradise, as in Rosalie's account. The natals go to school, as in Boris's mother's version. The child tours the universe—the natals are educated in the ways of the world, in people, things, and language—which conforms to all the stories. For a while, the not-yet considers not leaving, a gesture that aligns itself with Der Nister's stories, in which the child refuses to leave and comes into the world screaming. And finally the child falls at the conclusion into the world below, a gesture that conforms as well to all the other stories.

But there are significant differences. Although in the rabbinic midrash and most of the stories the child is touched by another and forgets what he has experienced, in this one he falls on his own as the consequence of conscious choice. Although in others angels are the instructors in school or the agents of his removal for birth, here there are "already-weres," mortals, individuals who have already lived and made choices. But most significant are the references to the Book of Life with blank pages in which his deeds will be written.

Why the difference? To the midrash from *Niddah* (which Horn linked to the Chagall painting and all other versions) Horn has added the redemptive story of the world to come. And linking the two stories—the mortals and the natals—changes everything.

The phrase "the world to come" retains something of an ambiguous status in the rabbinic literature. It is often invoked to mean the messianic age, the age following the arrival of *Maschiach*. In that sense, it is about the future of our world, our world in the future, after the coming of the Messiah. The Talmudic tractate *Sanhedrin* uses the phrase that way. Even when the phrase is used in this sense, however, there is some ambiguity about it. Some rabbis speak of it as the age following the arrival of the Messiah—the age that begins with the Messiah's arrival and includes that arrival. Others speak of it as the world that follows that one, the world strictly after the Messiah has arrived and excludes that arrival, not the messianic age, in other words, but subsequently, understanding that the messianic age itself could last a thousand years.

It is also used in a third more immediate sense to mean the world to come for each of us after death, the future in which, according to the rabbis, we will each be judged for our earthly deeds. "If the person [is] good," the stranger says to the narrator of *The Dead Town*, if he makes good choices and does good deeds, "the soul is rewarded in the world to come" (108). A fourth sense sometimes attached to this third renders the phrase a reference to the moment in the afterlife at the end of time when all will be resurrected. Maimonides famously comments on this sense.[7]

Dara Horn's book employs all four of these rabbinic understandings but to this panoply introduces another. Setting the scene of the world to come within the midrash of the education of prenatals, she loops the two together. If the world to come is the future, then, from the point of view of the past, the "world to come" is the present. And if the world in which this binder works is her fictional world, then her novel is that world to come. Her title thus reorients readerly attention to whatever present world in which the characters function, and her book works as a midrash does: responding to a fundamental gap in a prior text in such a way that it constitutes a material extension of it.

In other words, if the world to come and the world from which we are born are the same, time is closed within an unexpected circularity. Consequently, the world to come (from the point of view of the past) is our world, and historical time is an illusion. What we experience as history is only *our* time after which we pass into the next world as "already-weres," ready to instruct enthusiastic "not yets" along their journey. The register of the lives and events of people who have traversed the path between birth and death is necessarily partial, an abstraction based on selective way stations while they complete their apprenticeships and enter the real world of the already-weres. And there are, then, finally, only two registers: the world from which we have come and to which we are going (which are the same), and our own world, with the latter observed by the former. Horn's novel, in which this journey is described, constitutes as a result its midrashic extension.

But there is a second consequence of her invention of the union of natals and mortals. The linking of the two stories at the end of her book makes the book a performance of the art theft it is describing, a fictional staging of the missing painting in the world. The ending we expect has been snatched away just as we were contemplating the romance of Ben and Erica, and in its place remains a forgery, a fake, a copy, an imitation of Yiddish writing, not unlike Rosalie's book of ghost stories that retains the same title (180), a book that Sara and Ben agree was a forgery (187–90), and that contained within it a story about "the world to come" (192). The world to come is this book. This book is the place where the staging of the art theft occurs. We read and expect a "happy ending," a redemptive moment that Chagall would like (38), as Horn suggests. Instead we get a "fake," a piece of sallow and pallid prose that does more to confuse and confound than to clarify and resolve matters at hand.

The novelistic staging is not simply a parallel to the art theft described within, but its continuation: "stories within stories within stories" (172) in an infinite loop. Including presentations of Der Nister's work as a representative sample of the generation of Yiddish writers lost after the war when Stalin decided to murder the Yiddish writers of his generation, Horn's book constitutes the place where the generations are at once dead and alive. The world of Horn's novel, the fictional world constructed here as an extension of the fictional worlds lost through the efforts of the National Socialists and Stalinists, comprises at once the past, present, and future of the world to come.

In sum, the three strands we have followed—Chagall's art, the Der Nister–like rabbinic midrash of the prenatals, and the redemptive Chagall-like midrash about the afterlife once history has run its course—are united in the final chapters. And the book itself, as a bringing together of five historical generations in which these stories and this artwork—about those alive, dead, and unborn—comes to count as a new commentary. More than novelistic fiction, the book as a whole becomes itself a midrash. But not just midrashic, or midrash-like, in the way we commonly speak. Rather the book becomes a commentary on the heist that is also an extension or performance of it, the "back story" of the art theft, so to speak. The whole becomes an extension of the part, the container lodged within the contained.

But that result leads us to a third. The way the book enacts the art heist, the theft of the object we have come to observe, is by becoming that object. Dara Horn's *The World to Come* reproduces in writing Chagall's painting, aligning itself with the *ut pictura poesis* tradition. Chapter 19 is the happening of the impossible and directly follows an explosion in chapter 18. But is it any more impossible than the villagers flying over the city in Chagall's painting "Over Vitebsk"? Chagall's painting, we are told, was painted in response to brutalizations that took place at the hands of governmental forces in his native city of Vitebske (82), just as the midrash told to the child Boris by his mother was recited while disaster swirled around her in the explosion of her realities and onslaught of impossibilities that constituted events eventually characterized as the Holocaust.

The performance of the explosion in chapter 18, in other words, and the impossible narrative structure succeeding it in chapter 19 constitutes a duplication of the process reflected in the painting of Chagall and of which the painting is the consequence. The whole reproduces a part, the container within the contained. What is explored in *The World to Come* is the dynamics between art, midrash, and history. In the ending, historical authenticity, midrash, and the painting come together. The novel reproduces the painting. The painting reproduces the midrash. The midrash reproduces the disaster. And all four—novel, art, midrash, and historical catastrophe—are linked in a chain in which each is at once original and derived, fictional and historical, written and painted, utterly conceptual and utterly real in our ongoing engagement with the world in which we live and our understanding of how and why it works (or fails to work) for its willing and unwilling participants.

Constructed as the midrash of a theft, performing an explosion of the realities sustaining it, Dara Horn's novelistic history resides alongside the newspaper report added by the author.

We began by noting the problem of the book's ending. As documentary realism, the story is confusing. In a strange narrative gesture, chapter 19 explodes everything that precedes it. But the dissolution of that confusion results from understanding an explosion followed by a midrash in a manner not unlike the way trauma may be followed by fanciful stories that both conceal and protect it but also disclose it in ways that allow it to be read, the way, for example, we may learn to read Jerzy Kosinski's novel *The Painted Bird*, in which a young protagonist is buried in a field up his neck by a peasant woman, after which he is attacked by a flock of ravens and reports later that he "gave up" and, freeing his "chilled wings," "joined the flock of ravens" to fly with them.

VI. Conclusion

We leave the last word to Boris, whose experience with abject historical disaster, images of horrid human flight, and midrashic stories of a "God of wombs" replacing a God of mercy started it all. When his erstwhile friendly neighbor arrives at his home with an armed government militia to haul him away to imprisonment and death, he faces his young daughter, who is screaming, "Daddy, don't go!" (270), and thinks of an abyss, broken wings, a ladder, a narrow bridge, and learning how to fly:

> What do you say to a child you will never see again? That there really is an abyss? That it is easy to fall into it? That the only way to stay out of the filth is to learn how to fly, or to collect the broken wings of the ladder and build them back again? That the whole world is nothing more than a narrow bridge, and that the most important thing is not to be afraid? Boris could think of nothing; his imagination failed him. He looked at Raisya and said only what he saw.
> "Baby," he whispered. And walked out the door. (271)

Notes

1. Dara Horn, *The World to Come* (New York: W. W. Norton and Co., 2006), 283. "A Story without an Ending" is the subtitle in Yiddish of "The Haunted Tailor" by Sholem Aleichem, http://www.facebook.com/note.php?note_id=276468180611.

2. Horn's account of the details of the actual theft is given in the "Author's Note," 311–14. For an example of the newspaper accounts, see Thomas J. Lueck, "Museum's Stolen Chagall, Or a Good Fake, Turn up in Topeka Mail," *New York Times*, January 23, 2002.

3. Her first novel, *In the Image* (New York: Norton, 2002), was hailed as a major achievement in the literary world and won her numerous prizes.

4. Think of the ending of John Sayles's brilliant film *Limbo* (Screen Gems, 1999) and its fate among reviewers.

5. For Horn's posted internet note, see http://www.facebook.com/note.php?note_id=276468180611.

6. http://www.come-and-hear.com/niddah/niddah_30.html.

7. See, for example, Maimonides, in the Talmudic tractate *Sanhedrin*, chapter 10, in *A Maimonides Reader*, ed. Isadore Twersky (Springfield, NJ: Behrman House, 1972), 402–23.

7

Midrash and Social Justice

Sol Neely

It began with an interpretation of history from a single aspect, then made that aspect absolute, and finally reduced all of history to that one aspect. The exciting variety of history was discarded in favor of an orderly, easily understood interplay of "historical laws," "social groups," and "relations of production," so pleasing to the eye of the scientist. But this gradually expelled from history the very thing that gives human life, time, and thus history itself a structure: the story. And the story took with it into the kingdom of unmeaning its two essential ingredients: uniqueness and ambiguity. Since the mystery is the articulated mystery of man, history began to lose its human content.

—Václav Havel, "Stories and Totalitarianism"[1]

History is amoral: events occurred. But memory is moral; what we consciously remember is what our conscience remembers. History is the Totenbuch, The Book of the Dead, kept by the administrators of the camps. Memory is the Memorbucher, the names of those to be mourned, read aloud in the synagogue. History and memory share events; that is, they share time and space. Every moment is two moments.

—Anne Michaels, *Fugitive Pieces*[2]

Václav Havel observes that the emergence of a pervasive, one-dimensional, evasive thinking is given alibi by the destruction of story. With contemporary Jewish American and Holocaust literature, we realize—*again*—that midrashic reading restores story in existentially and politically complex ways and thus guards against such one-dimensional totality. I write that we realize this significance of story *again* because the pedagogical and moral aspects of story that midrash recovers is not new, but it has found renewed articulation and urgency in the seventy years since the Shoah. That which gives impetus to this recovery is what Monica Osborne calls "the midrashic impulse"[3]—which carries within it a pedagogical impulse that helps orient our pedagogies toward restorative justice (*tikkun olam*). Here I coin the phrase "ontology of story" as a means of articulating this restoration of story, which I contrast with an "ontology of truth" that already, to much despair, shapes much of our phenomenological and pedagogical projects.

In what follows, I offer a set of complementary critical meditations informed by Emmanuel Levinas, Sandor Goodhart, Martin Matuštík, and Monica Osborne, wherein I argue that recovering a midrashic "ontology of story"—indexed to what Levinas calls a "consciousness termed hearing"[4]—opens the condition by which bearing witness as substitution must be enacted. In short, I aim to theorize midrash through its radical potential for enacting justice by translating the requirements of midrash through Levinas's "phenomenology of sociality." In so doing, I rely on a number of contemporary accounts of the midrashic today, but I also aim to render the relation of midrash and social justice in more explicit ways—explicitly drawing "the midrashic impulse" into concrete concerns for economy and politics. After the prologue, in which I account for my first studies in midrashic reading, I then move through two meditations—the first of which gives focus to the phenomenological, and the second of which gives focus to the midrashic. Finally, by way of *excursus*, I describe ways by which my work has continued to develop at the intersection of midrashic studies and social justice through my experience teaching midrash and phenomenology in the prison. In the end, we discover through the requirements of the midrashic uncanny sources of inspiration for exodus away from social orders of sacrifice and toward the political restoration of responsibility in our public and pedagogical spheres.

Prologue: Encountering Midrash Through Levinas

The best teacher lodges an intent not in the mind but in the heart.

—Anne Michaels, *Fugitive Pieces*[5]

As a graduate student in Purdue University's Philosophy and Literature PhD program, I gained my first sustained critical attention to midrashic thinking in a fall 2005 seminar led by my teacher, Sandor Goodhart. The seminar was titled "Midrashic Reading in Literary, Philosophic, and Religious Study."[6] While the seminar drew inspiration from a number of influential contemporary thinkers—such as Geoffrey Hartman, Gerald Bruns, Michael Fishbane, and Claire Katz—the seminar was largely concerned with close readings of Levinas's *Nine Talmudic Readings*. At that time, there was heightened philosophical and critical concern among Levinas's North American exegetes for the question of what a "Levinasian politics" might look like—and, given my interest in social-political philosophy, I adopted this question in my own studies and activism. Even a decade later, this question about what a Levinasian politics might look like is typically taken up by Levinas's more secular readers, who attended primarily to Levinas's overtly philosophical texts without giving much attention to his Talmudic readings. Of particular influence, during the time of our seminar, were two recently published opposing points of view that framed the problem of a Levinasian politics in alternating supportive and critical terms. First, in 2003, William Simmons published his book *An-Archy and Justice: An Introduction to Levinas' Political Thought*, a supportive account of how Levinas's ethics as first philosophy can intervene against a politics for its own sake.[7] This work inspired my own projects—but, as Simmons himself observed, it was an admittedly limited and introductory account of Levinas's political thought that drew only from philosophical texts such as *Totality and Infinity* and *Otherwise Than Being*. The following year, in 2004, Simon Critchley published a more critical article in *Political Theory*—titled "Five Problems in Levinas' View of Politics and the Sketch of a Solution to Them"—in which he claims that politics is Levinas's "Achilles heel."[8] Intuitively, I could not agree with Critchley's description of Levinas's work, so at the end of the fall 2005 semester, as our course on Levinas and midrashic reading came to a close, and we announced the founding of the North American Levinas Society (NALS), I suggested that our inaugural conference take up as its theme "Levinas and the Political."[9] The conference, which brought together more than 120 presenters from six continents, occasioned a rich discussion of what a Levinasian politics ought to look like, drawing primarily from liberalism, Marxism, postcolonialism, phenomenology, and anarchistic influences. What seemed to be missing, however, was a thinking of a Levinasian politics through the other half of Levinas's oeuvre—namely, his Talmudic readings.

The fall 2005 seminar marked my first foray into Levinas's Talmudic readings and my first encounter with midrashic reading. I came to the class already with a substantial erudition in Levinas's philosophical texts, but I had not yet sketched out a comprehensive articulation of what a Levinasian politics might look like. What became clear to me over the semester was that a qualitatively different kind of political content was present in Levinas's Talmudic readings as opposed to the more philosophical (and secular) half of his authorship, which influential thinkers such as Robert Bernasconi, William Simmons, Enrique Dussel, and others had already addressed. What I found in Levinas's Talmudic readings was not so much a prescription for political praxis but a rich source of political *inspiration* articulated concretely through a modality of story shaped by a vocation for justice. This was my first real encounter with Judaic learning, and our seminar enacted the very modality of reading that we studied. We were encouraged to think of midrashic reading in extensional ways, beyond its strict application to scripture, so that we could adopt midrashic values with other literary and political texts. And, as we struggled to arrive at a sense of what was required by "midrashic reading" across literary, philosophical, and religious horizons, I became very interested in how the midrashic enables more than a hermeneutical approach. Midrashic responsiveness demands a kind of "attitude" or "vigilance," which calls for an existential responsiveness, in the wake of disaster, to the address of the other. I discovered that I was already compelled by "the midrashic impulse"—which, Osborne writes, "is not just a form of exegesis; it's a form of life with a text that summons all of us, as a community, into its dialogue."[10] In short, I discovered that midrash is always already pedagogical and concerned for social justice and healing.

Meditation One: Translating Midrash and Postsecular Phenomenology

Translation is a kind of transubstantiation: one poem becomes another. You can choose your philosophy of translation just as you choose how to live: the free adaptation that sacrifices detail to meaning, the strict crib that sacrifices meaning to exactitude. The poet moves from life to language, the translator moves from language to life; both, like the immigrant, try to identify the invisible, what's between the lines, the mysterious implications.

—Anne Michaels, *Fugitive Pieces*[11]

I did not witness the most important events of my life. My deepest story must be told by a blind man, a prisoner of sound.

—Anne Michaels, *Fugitive Pieces*[12]

Given that Levinas identifies his own task as one of translation—of translating "Judaism into Greek"—I adopted as my project a concern for translating that rich political content of Levinas's Talmudic readings into an "ethical-existential" discourse developed in the interest of a postsecular critical theory. The notion of "postsecular" is one I borrow from Martin Matuštik, who calls for us to harness the advantage of living in our "postsecular condition" characterized by the coexistence of "various religious and secular phenomena."[13] According to Matuštik, by adopting such "postsecular sensibilities," we can better leverage an *internal* critique of the "myriad phenomena of willed human destruction" that marks our age.[14] The notion of an "internal" critique is important, as it safeguards against the kind of sacrificial, scapegoating violence that "external" critiques tend to foster and thus compels us away from the sacrificial toward responsibility. Translating the political content of Levinas's Talmudic readings into a critical theory is necessarily a postsecular endeavor. However, as Sandor Goodhart has extensively commented, the internal and external topographies are not exclusive but continuous with one another in a möbian relation.[15] In other words, if we index Levinas's philosophical works to phenomenology and his Talmudic readings to midrash, the point is not to translate *midrash* into *phenomenology* but to take up phenomenology *midrashically*. Translating the political content of Levinas's Talmudic readings into a postsecular critical theory, then, becomes a midrashic endeavor.

Although Levinas tended to distinguish his philosophical and Talmudic writings, there are occasions where the values of each intersect in rich ways. In one of his last essays, "Diachrony and Representation," Levinas brings his midrashic and phenomenological dimensions together, claiming that his work has developed toward a "phenomenology of sociality."[16] Sociality, for Levinas, is a third term otherwise than the ethical or the political—neither anarchic enough for the ethical, as an obediential relation of two in the face-to-face, nor reducible to representation and intentionality as instantiated by the political in a relation of three. Sociality, Levinas writes, bears a quality of the diachronic, "irreducible to the immanence of representation" and "other than the sociality that would be reduced to . . . knowledge."[17] This "prior" or "forgotten" sociality is the "sociality of *saying* [*dire*]" as opposed to the sociality of *the said*.[18] It is that in which "responsibility is made concrete," and it is the space of writing—or *L'Espace littéraire*, to borrow from Blanchot—in which both the midrashic and Levinas's phenomenology (of sociality) are articulated. The phenomenology that attends to this sociality requires postsecular sensibilities in accord with the interrogative qualities of midrashic reading. By relocating the starting points of phenomenology in midrashic values, Levinas's phenomenological impulse adopts three new starting points that differentiate it from those phenomenological and eco-phenomenological enterprises still beholden to Husserlian intentionality.[19] The new starting points move us from intentionality to inspiration; a consciousness of seeing to a "consciousness termed hearing"; and an *ontology of truth* to an *ontology of story*. Briefly, I explore each in turn:

1. *From intentionality to inspiration*: For Levinas, the first movement of phenomenology is neither intentionality nor apprehension—but inspiration. Inspiration is linked to the literalness of respiration, whereby, as Levinas writes in *Otherwise Than Being*, the body is "the distinctive in-oneself of the contraction of ipseity and its breakup." He writes: "This contraction [of respiration] is not an impossibility to forget oneself, to detach oneself from oneself, in the concern for oneself. It is a recurrence to oneself out of an irrecusable exigency of the other, a duty overflowing my being, a duty becoming a debt and an extreme passivity prior to the tranquility, still quite relative, in the inertia and materiality of things at rest."[20] In his "translator's preface" to *Otherwise Than Being*, Alphonso Lingis distinguishes this "openness upon the air" of Levinas's inspiration against Heidegger's thinking of existence as being in an openness. To find oneself in the openness of a clearing in the forest is to find oneself already in the space of light, seeking illumination as the primary model of thinking—and thus of sociality.[21] For Levinas, there is always something prior to the contours of openness marked out by illumination. Prior to space filled with light, there is space filled with air. "I am inspired," Levinas writes succinctly.[22] And this inspiration is indexed to the cadence of an openness—not of light but of deep respiration—as that which is described already by Edmond Jabès:

> What you call "distance" is but the time of breathing
> in, of breathing out.
> All the oxygen man needs is in his lungs.
> Empty, the space of life.[23]

This "openness in which being's essence is surpassed in inspiration" is "an openness of which respiration is a modality or a foretaste, or, more exactly, of which it retains the aftertaste."[24] Perhaps this is how we can invoke a sense of social justice as an inspired justice: "Outside of any mysticism, in this respiration, the possibility of every sacrifice for the other, activity and passivity coincide."[25] Through inspiration, "I exist through the other and for the other, but without this being alienation"—"I am summoned as someone irreplaceable."[26]

2. *From a consciousness of seeing to a "consciousness termed hearing"*: In "Diachrony and Representation," Levinas notes that human consciousness, as historically conceived by Continental philosophy, amounts to an "aiming of thought"—one that aims, embraces, and perceives "all alterity under its thematizing gaze." This aiming of thought is what we call "intentionality," which first indicates a "thematization of seeing" but also indicates "aspiration, finality, and desire, a moment of egotism."[27] Opposed to a consciousness of seeing, Levinas articulates a "consciousness termed hearing"—one that breaks from the egology of intentionality, aspiration, and the "self-complete world of vision and art."[28] In "The Transcendence of Words," Levinas writes,

> In sound, and in the consciousness termed hearing, there is in fact a break with the self-complete world of vision and art. In its entirety, sound is a ringing, clanging scandal. Whereas, in vision, form is wedded to content in such a way as to appease it, in sound the perceptible quality overflows so that form can no longer contain its content. A real rent is produced in the world, through which the world that is *here* prolongs a dimension that cannot be converted into vision."[29]

According to Levinas, the violence of the philosophical is in the bringing of alterity under the panorama of the *noesis-noema* structure of intentional consciousness of which Husserl writes. Levinas notes that "vision is essentially an adequation of exteriority and interiority": "[I]n [vision] exteriority is reabsorbed in the contemplative soul and, as an *adequate idea*, revealed to be a priori, the result of a *Sinngebung*."[30] The totality of philosophy is predicated on assumptions of shared presence across a common horizon of visibility. Comprehension is linked to presence: A shared presence (*com-presence*) demarcates the space of comprehension. Within a consciousness of seeing, this shared presence always risks usurping the place of the other.

Of course, in the wake of the Shoah, Levinas is not alone in his critique of the sacralization of a consciousness of seeing. Maurice Blanchot also stayed critical of what he describes as the "optical imperative that in the Western tradition, for thousands of years, has subjugated our approach to things, and induces us to think under the guaranty of light or under the threat of its absence."[31] If philosophy takes shape under the imperatives of vision, midrash—along with Levinas's phenomenology of sociality—takes shape through the inspired cadences of a "consciousness termed hearing." This is a radically different starting point, both midrashically and phenomenologically. As Gerald Bruns notes, "Philosophy has no place for sound. Sound is foreign. It is always outside the world, threatening to invade it, like anarchy."[32] Anticipating a point I develop in the next meditation, Levinas rehabilitates the vocabulary of vision through his acts of translation, and there are two prominent moments within his authorship worth highlighting—moments that reveal ways by which "the midrashic impulse" opens an intrigue for social justice. The first comes in Levinas's properly philosophical work *Totality and Infinity*, in which he famously claims "ethics is an optics" before qualifying it: "But it is a 'vision' without image, bereft of the synoptic and totalizing objectifying virtues of vision, a relation or an intentionality of *a wholly different type*."[33] The second comes from one of his Talmudic readings, "The Temptation of Temptation," where he also invokes ethics as an optics, but here he describes it as a "direct optics—without any mediation of any idea—[and which] can only be accomplished as ethics." Only through a consciousness termed hearing does the revelation become legible because Torah is given not through the mediation of idea but concretely *"in the Light of a face"*—"the epiphany of the other person."[34]

3. *From an "ontology of truth" to an ontology of story*: A phenomenology of sociality that takes as its starting point inspiration, linked concretely to the literalness of respiration, and escapes the thematization of a consciousness of seeing occasions what I call an "ontology of story."[35] In this sense, I oppose "ontology of story" to ontology of truth that saturates literary and pedagogical traditions from Aristotle to Mat-

thew Arnold. Sandor Goodhart has written extensively on this in his efforts to recover a rich sense of the literary in its anti-sacrificial and midrashic dimensions from its philosophical conditioning.[36] Indeed, in one of his more recent essays, "From Sacrificial Violence to Responsibility: The Education of Moses in Exodus 2-4," Goodhart addresses this sacralization of an *ontology of truth* against an *ontology of story* by drawing from comparative genealogies of education founded in Plato and Judaism. Here, he notes that as Plato challenged the educational system in place at that time—very much still headed by Homer and the ancient tragedians and still exhibiting all the qualities of an ontology of story—he substituted "for an older oral culture founded on an elaborate system of mnemonics," which privileged "an aural or hearing-centered culture," one that was "founded more decisively upon writing and the alphabet"—thus inaugurating "a visual or video-centric cultural organization."[37] Within an ontology of truth inaugurated by and predicated on a consciousness of seeing, the educator appeals to "the language of reason, and to the realm of the ontological as the context in which the true [can] be defined."[38] Thus, the hallmarks of story, those borne by the midrashic endeavor itself, evaporate. In its place, we encounter only impoverished literacies of representational thinking and sacrificial politics.

Within an ontology of truth, "truth" is understood only in epistemological terms. Within an ontology of story, truth is unhinged from the *merely* epistemological and is straightway *ethical*. But we ought not simply oppose the two within a synchronic framework—for it is indeed the case that the two relate diachronically in what Goodhart calls a möbian relation.[39] It is not the case that an ontology of truth is opposed to an ontology of story because to make such a claim is to adopt the very Platonic gesture that Plato makes when he opposes the two and, in the wake of that opposition, enacts the sacrificial by banishing the poets. Rather, an ontology of truth is a moment *within* an ontology of story, but Western literary and pedagogical traditions have scandalously forgotten this genealogy, this diachrony, and assumed the opposite. An ontology of truth thus affects everything from our literary pedagogies to our phenomenologies still too beholden to intentionality. Instead of opening to the possibility of revelation and substitution, they enable only struggles for recognition and fetishize egological comprehension, which demands false pretense of mastery and thus evaporates the possibility of vulnerability and radical passivity, the sine qua non of midrash. Within an ontology of story, however, story remains—in the final instance—

irreducible to history, memory, and representation. It is always read, like Torah, in the *light of the face of the other*.

As a first step in staging social justice through the imperatives of midrash, I follow Levinas's example of translating Judaism into Greek by meditating on what it means to undertake a postsecular translation of the midrashic and the phenomenological. By adopting Levinas's starting points for his phenomenology of sociality—by which we move (1) from intentionality to inspiration and (2) from a consciousness of seeing to a consciousness termed hearing—we are delivered *uno tenore* (in one breath, in an instant) to an ontology of story, the very *epoché* of the midrashic. Inspiration, linked to the literalness of respiration, not only compels our phenomenological descriptions of sociality beyond a consciousness of seeing, but it also remains resolutely embodied (material, economic, somatic) in a way post-Cartesian subjectivities and the phenomenological projects derived from them cannot accommodate. A phenomenology of sociality is thus "embodied" but not "reducible to flesh." It entails a radical passivity that is more passive than the opposite of action.[40] Receptive to revelation and unconcerned for the struggles of recognition, such postsecular phenomenology (of sociality) discovers itself in "the midrashic impulse" and restores, as Goodhart describes by appeal to Martin Buber, a "Hebrew humanism": "To be open to the Hebrew Bible, for Buber, does not mean necessarily to be open to a specified content. . . . But it does mean rather to be open to its word, to its language, to that which encloses content, to its capacity as address, to what Buber calls the 'mystery of its spokenness (*Gesprochenheit*)."[41]

Thus, we return again to Havel's claim bracketed in the epigraph at the top of this chapter: totalitarianism is given alibi by the loss of story, which takes with it "into the kingdom of unmeaning its two essential ingredients: uniqueness and ambiguity." Insofar as I am summoned to respond in responsibility to the face of the other, I am *phenomenologically* summoned as *irreplaceable*. Nobody can bear the burden of my indeclinable responsibility. And insofar as midrash always entails reading not in the light of Plato's sun but in the light of the face of the other person, calling for a consciousness termed hearing, I am *midrashically* compelled to remain open to the "mystery of its spokenness"—which, as Havel writes, "is the articulated mystery of man." In this way, we restore to history its human content.

Meditation Two: Midrash and Sociality

Questions without answers must be asked very slowly.

—Anne Michaels, *Fugitive Pieces*[42]

While the German language annihilated metaphor, turning humans into objects, physicists turned matter into energy. The step from language/formula to fact: detonation to detonation. Not long before the first brick smashed a window on Kristallnacht, physicist Hans Thirring wrote, of relativity: 'It takes one's breath away to think what might happen to a town if the dormant energy of a single brick were to be set free . . . it would suffice to raze a city with a million inhabitants to the ground.

—Anne Michaels, *Fugitive Pieces*[43]

If the first meditation gives greater emphasis to the phenomenological, the second turns more concretely to the midrashic. Here I want to emphasize the claim that midrash and Levinas's phenomenology of sociality arise from the same intrigue for social justice and healing the world (*tikkun olam*). Sociality is thus something other than ethics or politics. Like midrash, we read it—when legible—in its symptoms and in the wounds of historical, humanly engendered violence. A phenomenology of sociality is, like a phenomenology of hunger, concretely concerned with the material welfare of the other. In this way, Levinas's richest source of political expression derives, to my mind, from his Talmudic readings because in his midrashic texts we best encounter this ontology of story. To attend to a phenomenology of sociality through midrashic apertures, I invoke two distinct but related passages from Sandor Goodhart in which he describes, in alternating contemporary and historical terms, the requirements of midrashic responsiveness: In the first instance, I look to his essay "'A Land That Devours Its Inhabitants': Midrashic Reading, Emmanuel Levinas, and Prophetic Exegesis" for a succinct description of the five qualities of midrashic reading. In the second instance, I turn to his essay "Back to the Garden: Jewish Hermeneutics, Biblical Reading, PaRDeS, and the Four-Fold Way" to draw on what I perceive to be a profound contribution Goodhart makes toward thinking about midrash explicitly in terms of social justice. Between these two key passages from Goodhart, I want to invoke what has been perceived as a Levinasian conundrum concerning the relation of the ethical and the political.

To give pedagogical contour to this meditation, I begin with the first essay, in which Goodhart gives a more contemporary account of five qualities that constitute midrashic reading—"the lack of any one of which," he writes, "would diminish its capacity to be characterized accurately as 'midrashic.'"[44] Goodhart broadly describes midrash "as a story told in response to a gap or tear or a break in a prior or previous text in such a way that constitutes a material extension of that earlier text."[45] He then adumbrates these five qualities, which I abbreviate here: (1) "In the first place, a midrash is a story. It is not something other than a story. It is not a piece of expository prose, for example"; (2) "A midrashic story itself is necessarily secondary in status; there is always a prior text to which it is a response"; (3) Midrash is always connected to that prior text as a response (response-ability) or supplement. It "issues from the primary text and responds to it"; (4) That in the prior text to which midrash responds "is a gap or tear or hole or discontinuity of some kind; a wound, or silence, or absence, or lack"; (5) As a material extension of the prior text—and as a response to that wound, or silence, or question—midrashic responsiveness "is of a particular kind (and not just any response)." Goodhart notes that midrash "is not, for example, a filling in or patching over of the missing piece"—which I read as a way of saying that midrash, as material extension of the text, also materially extends the very question that occasioned the midrashic response in the first place.[46] In other words, we can say that the midrashic, following Blanchot, occasions an *infinite hermeneutics* and that such infinite hermeneutics expresses, following Levinas, an *infinity within the finite*, as Goodhart's appeal to the möbian demonstrates.

To Goodhart's five qualities of midrashic reading, however, I want to add a sixth, which is articulated by Claire Katz: midrashic reading brings us in proximity to God.[47] It is not that Goodhart misses this sixth quality by any means. It remains implicit in all of his work, but I want to render it explicit here with one important qualification. As Levinas everywhere reminds us, proximity to God entails nothing more than the effectuation of the ethical—which, in turn, must be effectuated economically and materially. The work of Enrique Dussel is particularly compelling on this point.[48] Quoting Rabbi Israel Salanter, Levinas insists, "The Other's material needs are my spiritual needs"[49]—which is another way of articulating the revelation of Torah in the light of the face of the other person. In *Otherwise Than Being*, Levinas writes that within the ethical, "in corporeality," is to be found "the duty to give to the other even the bread out of one's own mouth and the coat from one's shoulders."[50] Taken together, the requirements of midrash adumbrated here occasion the very exigencies that make justice concrete.

But what does it mean to talk about a "midrashic impulse," as Osborne does? Without losing the specificity of textual references, in what ways can we adopt the values and articulations of "the midrashic impulse" and turn them toward effectuating social justice? I want to argue that these requirements of midrash make legible our descriptive endeavors, characterized by postsecular sensibilities, within the kind of phenomenology of sociality that Levinas describes in "Diachrony and Representation." In other words, what if we read this "prior text" to which the midrashic responds as *sociality* itself? Such possibility, I believe, is richly articulated by Edmond Jabès, who writes,

> (*I speak . . . but to whom? And why speak? For whom? How? With what aim, in which light, which perspective? To speak—under what pretext, to which end? Ah, to go up to where and where from? To stop at which frontier, in which dark or flame, on which beach or mountain?*
>
> *To speak—under what circumstances, after what silence, wave, or incomparable path in mid-ocean, after what question, desert, exile, before which dawn?*
>
> *I speak—in what summer, after what long winter, what call, what failure, before what scream?*
>
> *—After what death, before what death?*)[51]

I want to propose that such questions here are neither rhetorical nor abstract. They demonstrate all of the ceaseless interrogations of midrash, as inquiry and investigation. Moreover, they are the questions that enact what Levinas describes in "A Religion for Adults" as the ritual self-discipline requisite for the midrashic endeavor and response-ability.[52] They signal a distress of sorts, but it's a distress that is immediately transformed by the exigencies of "the midrashic impulse." On the one hand, the questions Jabès articulates with some urgency respond to the distress of sociality, of the distress of political economy and historical violence (*After what death, before what death?*). Such distress—as the questions concretely realize—does not always come into representation, which is why a phenomenology of sociality is necessary in the first place (*I speak—in what summer, after what long winter, what call, what failure, before what scream?*). But Levinas also highlights what he calls "the aspiration to a just society" commanded in Judaism, adding that "personal responsibility of man with regard to man is such that God cannot annul it."[53] For Levinas, the distress of political economy—in its alienation, despair, and empty freedoms—transforms into a distress of another kind. It is a distress of the psalmist who cries out to the commandment, not unlike the speaker in Jabès' poem: "I am a sojourner on earth; hide not thy commandments from me."[54]

In "The Temptation of Temptation," Levinas starkly writes, in a manner not unlike Jabès: "In the beginning was violence."[55] This is not a theological claim but a phenomenological description with religious accents. We always already begin in the wake of humanly engendered violence. From the start, then, midrash is irrevocably occasioned by the vocation of social justice born from an immemorial past (*under what circumstance, after what silence?*). And although Levinas's philosophical writings are rigorous in their own way, we discover in his Talmudic readings a qualitatively different kind of political content that restores story in its rich postsecular dimensions. From a "consciousness termed hearing" we find ourselves devoted to the other so that, as Osborne notes, midrash is "not just a form of exegesis." It is calling to interrogate the sources of human misery in order that we might repair them and transform the world.

The midrashic and the phenomenological, as I've attempted to describe them here, coincide in the moment of witnessing—in the embodied, hermeneutical, and economic articulations of "Here I am" (*hineni*)—by the subject who confesses it. To read midrashically in the light of the face of the other—to confess these questions, as Jabès does—means that the revelation of the face of the other individual is expressed in the transcendence of words that is embodied but not reducible to flesh. How is this possible? Because, as Levinas writes, the transcendence of words, revelation, more exterior than any exteriority of being, "does not come to pass save through the subject that confesses or contests it."[56] Here, Levinas writes, "there is an inversion of order: the revelation is made by him that receives it, by the inspired subject whose inspiration, alterity in the same, is the subjectivity or psyche of the subject."[57] Phenomenologically, in other words, my subjectivity is constituted by (subjected to) my becoming inspired, by revelation, which bears with it a fundamentally different experience of time than the tranquility in the inertia and materiality of things at rest. Sociality is thus "fundamental historicity"—the irruption of the diachronic (as *saying*) not reducible to representation (*the said*) but still falling back into it. What is revealed through a phenomenology of sociality made legible through the ritual self-discipline of the midrashic are my obligations—uniquely mine as indeclinable and irreplaceable—of a lived corporeality situated by this "fundamental historicity."

To make better sense of this, and before turning to Goodhart's second text on midrash and PaRDeS, I want to address a common conundrum of sorts within Levinasian scholarship. Too frequently, a great deal of Levinasian scholarship and activism builds on some difficult confusions between the relation of *the ethical*—the relation of the two, the face-to-face, which is a relation of obedience to the call of the other—and *the political*—the relation of the three, which is a relation of hermeneutics as opposed to obedience, and requires us to compare the incomparable. What is frequently missing from this tension is any sustained focus on sociality and why, as a third term, it is so important to Levinas's work. Levinas takes up the problem in many areas, but let's look at an early and relatively simply articulation of the concern. In *Ethics and Infinity*, Philippe Nemo asks Levinas about his "phenomenology of face," but Levinas immediately corrects Nemo and notes that phenomenology is about what appears and that the face never appears as such. Levinas says,

> I do not know if one can speak of a "phenomenology" of the face, since phenomenology describes what appears. So, too, I wonder if one can speak of a look turned toward the face, for the look is knowledge, perception. I think rather that access to the face is straightaway ethical. You turn yourself toward the Other as toward an object when you see a nose, eyes, a forehead, a chin, and you can describe them. The best way of encountering the Other is not even to notice the color of his eyes![58]

Later, he adds, "The face is signification, and signification without context."[59] Commenting on this notion of the face of the other encountered as signification without context, Oona Eisenstadt and Claire Katz write that "ethical responsibility arises not between a person of this kind and a person of that kind, but whenever the self is faced with any other human being, prior to a definition of who or what that being is, such that the face shows itself non-empirically as a 'nudity stripped of form.' "[60]

But what, then, do we make of claims such as those that insist we attend to others in their embodied situations—whether we are concerned with Black Lives Matter, the welfare of Palestinians, indigenous sovereignty claims, or the alarming rise of anti-Semitism of late? Eisenstadt and Katz write, "One can, of course, dispute this idea [of the face as signification without context], and many scholars have taken up Levinas on the point, uneasy, for instance, with an ethics that has no place for ethnicity, and therefore takes no account of what might be a history of injustice based on that ethnicity."[61] They go on to note that when we attend to the other as "named or categorized"—whether we are talking about "the Palestinians" or a prisoner—we are dealing with political situations rather than ethical ones. As Levinas notes in his interview with Nemo, "the face can surely be dominated by perception, but what is specifically the face is what cannot be reduced to that."[62] In other words, even in the context of the prison, the ethical calling of the face of the other means the incarcerated person is not reducible to that context—that the other remains incommensurable with that situation and not reducible to their history. Time and again, Levinas insists that we not confuse the ethical and the political—and that the whole history of Western literary, pedagogical, and political philosophies is nothing but a history of such confusion. To be sure, as Eisenstadt and Katz remind us, a political situation "remains one in which one is called on to strive for justice! But it is not a face-to-face encounter."[63]

Beyond reiterating this insistence on not confusing the ethical and the political, I want to return to the question of sociality and Levinas's stated concern for articulating a "phenomenology of sociality" in order to discover how midrashic responsiveness enriches our political (material, economic) attentiveness to historical healing and social justice. Here I find particular inspiration in Goodhart's essay "Back to the Garden: Jewish Hermeneutics, Biblical Reading, PaRDeS, and the Four-Fold Way." In this essay, Goodhart details the history of the Jewish four-fold hermeneutics (PaRDeS) as it emerges in historical parallel with the medieval Christian four-fold exegesis. These four levels as pertaining to midrashic reading from a Jewish rabbinic point of view include the following: (1) *peshat*—or the literal or scriptural; (2) *remez*—or the symbolic or allegorical; (3) *derash*—or the ethical or moral; and (4) *sod*—or the prophetic or providential. In each tradition, Goodhart invites us to think about the relation of the component parts to the whole in terms of a möbian relation: while "allegory" is a moment within the Christian four-fold exegesis, the four-fold is also contained with the operations of allegory as a container carried by the contained. Similarly, although *derash* is a moment within PaRDeS, PaRDeS is simultaneously contained within the requirements of the midrashic.

To my mind, however, the richest potential for thinking midrash, phenomenology, and sociality—in efforts to effectuate social justice—comes in Goodhart's articulation of how *peshat* and *remez* relate. First, Goodhart writes, "Peshat is the words of the text, what it says, what it is saying. But as Emmanuel Levinas would commonly remark in his Shabbos morning talks on Rashi, the *peshat* never exhausts all that a text says or, more precisely, 'The text never exhausts itself in what it has said.' Why? Because *peshat* is in a sense *le dire*, the 'to say,' the saying."[64] By contrast, Goodhart observes, "*remez* refers to the meaningful or symbolic contexts or codes in which *peshat* functions, the allusions it contains that may not be apparent on the surface that allow it to become meaningful at all."[65] Peshat, as *the saying*, is in a sense illegible until it is contextualized by the symbolic codes and contexts of *remez*. "Beginning as a saying, *peshat* is domesticated by what comes after it, which determines in retrospect what has transpired."[66] Reading this articulated relation of *peshat* and *remez* is critical to how we understand the face of the other as an *ethical* relating before and beyond the political. This is the meaning of Levinas's idea that the face is "signification without context." The face is the origin of all signification—the light by which Torah must be read.

As with the relation of *peshat* and *remez* in PaRDeS—by which *remez* "describes the way a saying assumes meaning in a context"[67]—so too is the face of the other domesticated by the *remez* of their sociality, by the context and situation into which they are born that carries the "fundamental historicity" of the diachronic. As Goodhart notes, "a different *remez* means a different *peshat*."[68] Although Goodhart's descriptions of PaRDeS in this sense aren't explicitly linked to the intrigue for social justice, we can nevertheless elicit it. Goodhart writes, "The medieval commentators who said they were supplying *peshat* (and they were) were supplying *remez* in order that *peshat* be known."[69] Similarly, a phenomenology of sociality supplies the *remez* by which the face of the other, as *peshat*, becomes legible. This is why we cannot speak of a "phenomenology of the face," only a phenomenology of sociality. Researchers and activists who advance descriptions of Levinas's ethics as having no place for ethnicity miss this critical point supplied by Goodhart. The concern for ethnicity, history, and context arrives with the *remez*, a social *remez* or what Goodhart calls a "*remezed peshat*."[70] And although the face of the other can be dominated by perception or its social and historical context, in no way is the face of the other reducible to such political categorization.

Upon establishing this relation between *peshat* and *remez*, Goodhart attends to the other two aspects of PaRDeS that follow—*derash* (the ethical or moral dimension) and *sod* (the prophetic or providential dimension):

> As *derash* delimits the ethical status and *remez* the symbolic code (what the text is saying), *sod* draws the unforeseen consequences of a given text, what is coming down the road as a result of it: its historical implications as opposed to its present obligations, what it prophesies as opposed to what it imposes, the sense of things known only to God. Like *remez* it is hidden, but like *derash* it leaves the context in which a meaningful saying appears and speaks of its effect on the future. To speak of *sod* is to speak of time.[71]

In terms of relating midrash to a phenomenology of sociality, we can summarize these relations explicitly in terms of social justice: (1) The face of the other is signification without context, a *peshat*. The face of the other is never a character or a political category but absolutely transcendent to such context; (2) Nevertheless, the face of the other becomes legible through sociality, the social *remez*, or the *remezed peshat*. We encounter the other through social contexts and codes such as ethnicity; (3) With *derash*, I know what I ought to do, how to enact my responsiveness and muster the resources for my response-ability to the other, who calls to me out of the social *remez* but is irreducible and incommensurable with it. In this way, I too am given context. The face of the other *addresses* me—and I read this notion of address as both verb (the other calls to me, addresses me) and noun (for which "address" is like a mailing address—which is to say, I am situated by the call of the other). In response, I am given a "here"—as in "Here I am" (*hineni*); (4) Finally, *sod* concerns the effects of *derash* and *remez* on the future. As Goodhart writes, "To speak of *sod* is to speak of the future."[72] He adds,

"*Sod* describes what will have been. If *remez* is hidden from view because it is a code, *sod* is hidden from view because it has not fully occurred as yet. The messianic is a *soddic* modality."[73] Goodhart's description of sod is not unlike Levinas's description of the "eschatological vision" as that which "breaks with the totality of wars and empires in which one does not speak."[74] This is a "vision"—"bereft of the synoptic and totalizing objectifying virtues of vision"—that does not proceed from the experience of morality but *consummates* it.[75]

Excursus: Teaching Midrash and Phenomenology in Prison

> Never trust biographies. Too many events in a man's life are invisible. Unknown to others as our dreams. And nothing releases the dreamer; not death in the dream, not waking.
>
> —Anne Michaels, *Fugitive Pieces*[76]

In 2012, I started a prison-education program that brings university students into the prison for mutual collaboration and study with the inmates. The first texts we read were by Václav Havel, Martin Matuštík, and Emmanuel Levinas. During the second semester of study (Spring 2013), Matuštík attended class with us inside the prison—at which point the incarcerated students decided to call our project "The Flying University" after the post-1968 student dissident movement in Prague of which Matuštík was a part. Matuštík has since given his full blessing to our second iteration of the "Flying University," recognizing it as sharing an existential and pedagogical genealogy with the first. A year later (Spring 2014), Sandor Goodhart also attended class inside the prison, concretizing the midrashic service on which our pedagogy is based. When we published our first volume of prisoner poetry for the Flying University, I composed this sentiment as part of the volume's introduction:

> Václav Havel writes that every prisoner has a story. Emmanuel Levinas tells us that none of us are reducible to our histories. They mean the same thing, that each of us bears a genealogical depth with rich colorations of self that cannot be accommodated by the reductive logic of identity and "choice" that governs our contemporary carceral system. Each of us bears within us a secrecy of sorts, an incommensurability with the

institutions we inhabit, with our histories, and with the psychological compositions that come to represent our institutional identifications. The work of the Flying University, then, begins with this assumption: When we go inside the prison, we are called to bear witness to lives irreducible to their histories. This irreducibility, this incommensurability between a person's life and their history, is the space of transformation, however small such space might be.

Prison, much like the university, too frequently becomes the space in which *place* is put under erasure—where the *remez* is never fully attended to with the vigilance requisite of a robust phenomenology of sociality. By putting place under erasure, we foreclose the possibility of address, of articulating the "*Here* I am" of bearing witness. Like the university, prison is also a place where story is expelled in favor of reductive histories that bear little of that "articulated mystery of man" invoked by Havel in the epigraph at the top of this chapter. Because story is asserted only through the impoverished modalities of a consciousness of seeing, we risk sustaining a certain tone deafness to a quality of human suffering carried—even if "hidden from view" at first, as Goodhart writes of *remez*—by story.

As I meditate on how the midrashic helps us recover complex ways of attending to story—through its existential and economic exigencies—I am reminded of a feature of Martha Nussbaum's "capabilities approach," which she articulates in an interview for the documentary *Examined Life*.[77] There, Nussbaum observes that when we are tasked with mustering the material and economic resources that enable a person to develop their capabilities, we cannot simply turn to the individual and make an inquiry of his or her desires because our desires are already deformed by political economy. I think about this in the prison too, as the prison—sustained on false political pretense of rehabilitation—only deforms the individual's desires. The question, then, is by what means do we determine, politically and economically, what kinds of resources we need to effect social justice and the terms by which those resources are mustered? The answer, according to Nussbaum, is that we go to story, the story of the other, a story born of sociality irreducible to the political but always already situated by the social *remez* that shapes it. A phenomenology of sociality that attends to a person's story requires midrashic values to discern that quality of sociality not yet reified by the demands of the political. Even in the context of the prison, we encounter the face of the other irreducible to the institutionalization. That space of incommensurability is the secrecy we afford the other. It is the space of transformation, however small and however hidden from view it might first appear. In this way, we find uncanny sources of inspiration. Rather than opposing ethics and ethnicity, then, we learn finally their proper sequence. It is no wonder that I find a particularly receptive audience for teaching midrashic values inside the prison.

Epilogue: Midrash and the Pedagogical Foundations of Social Justice

> It's Hebrew tradition that forefathers are referred to as "we," not "they." "When we were delivered from Egypt. . . ." This encourages empathy and a responsibility to the past but, more important, it collapses time. The Jew is forever leaving Egypt. A good way to teach ethics. If moral choices are eternal, individual actions take on immense significance no matter how small: not for this life only.
>
> —Anne Michaels, *Fugitive Pieces*[78]

In meditating on the possibilities of social justice at the intersection of the midrashic and the phenomenological, I attempt to further Levinas's stated effort to translate Judaism into Greek. In his essay on "The Education of Moses," Goodhart distinguishes the education of Plato from the education of Moses, which I addressed briefly in my first meditation. Goodhart notes that the word "education" comes from the Latin, *educare*, meaning "to lead out" or "to bring up."[79] The question is whether this education is put in service of the state, and thus made to serve "the totality of wars and empire," or if this education is put in service of justice. In the first case, as in Plato, justice is made to serve the state. In the second case, as demonstrated in most of Levinas's *Nine Talmudic Readings*, the state exists only to enable the vocation of justice. In the case of Jewish education, Goodhart writes, the latter entails an accounting of exodus: "Both in founding patriarchal stories, and in its historical exodus accounts, Judaism . . . defines itself as the giving up of social orders that have become inefficacious, and the reorientation towards . . . an antisacrificial perspective that wanders progressively away from the gods and lays human responsibility at the hands of human agents."[80]

Each part of this chapter is prefaced with an epigraph from Anne Michael's masterful novel *Fugitive Pieces*. I have situated the novel in proximity to this chapter purposively for the simple reason that its insights are rich and haunt my meditations on the midrashic and sociality. But I do not, here, offer a midrash of the novel; instead, I see the novel as already giving the midrash on sociality—in terms of drawing into midrashic scrutiny our relation to language, pedagogy, memory, ancestry, and time as they enable genocidal violence or move decisively away from it. I conclude with the passage cited above for its specific invocation of ancestry—by which we discover the diachronic and lived understanding of what it means to say that sociality is "embodied" but not "reducible to flesh."

The words "exodus" and "education" share something of a common etymology in this notion of "leading." But if we trade an inspired accounting of consciousness predicated on hearing (one indexed to an "ontology of story") for an intentional model of consciousness predicated on vision and visibility (indexed to an ontology of truth), the resources for attending to story are lost, and we call down an invidious totality. In "giving up of social orders that have become inefficacious" and giving up "the totality of wars and empire," we discover a more difficult reading, in the restoration of story, that demands to be fulfilled through our material and economic commitments to the welfare of others. This, in the final instance, is what it means to read in the light of the face of the other.

Notes

1. Václav Havel, "Stories and Totalitarianism" in *Open Letters: Selected Writings, 1965–1990*, ed. John Keane (New York: Vintage, 1992), 335.

2. Anne Michaels, *Fugitive Pieces* (New York: Vintage, 1996), 138.

3. Monica Osborne, "The Midrashic Impulse: Reading Cynthia Ozick's *Heir to the Glimmering World* Against Representation," *Studies in American Jewish Literature* 26 (2007): 28.

4. Emmanuel Levinas, "The Transcendence of Words," in *The Levinas Reader*, trans. Seán Hand (Oxford: Blackwell, 1989), 147.

5. Michaels, *Fugitive Pieces*, 111.

6. The group of students enrolled in the seminar—which included Monica Osborne, Dara Hill, Katherine Ludwig, Rebecca Nicholson-Weir, Octavian Gabor, Michael Paradiso-Michau, and me—went on to found, with Professor Goodhart, the North American Levinas Society (NALS), which held its inau-

gural conference at Purdue in 2006. NALS is the direct legacy of this Fall 2005 seminar, which enriches the historical significance of the seminar.

7. William Paul Simmons, *An-Archy and Justice: An Introduction to Emmanuel Levinas' Political Thought* (Lanham: Lexington Books, 2003).

8. Simon Critchley, "Five Problems in Levinas' View of Politics and the Sketch of a Solution to Them," *Political Theory* 32, no. 2 (2004): 172–85.

9. For that inaugural conference, we invited William Simmons to be part of what has become a tradition of NALS: our annual "pedagogy session." Historically speaking, NALS took root at the intersection of midrash, pedagogy, and social justice.

10. Monica Osborne, "The Midrashic Impulse: Reading Cynthia Ozick's *Heir to the Glimmering World* Against Representation," *Studies in American Jewish Literature* 26 (2007): 28.

11. Michaels, *Fugitive Pieces*, 109.

12. Ibid., 17.

13. Martin Beck Matuštík, *Radical Evil and the Scarcity of Hope: Postsecular Meditations* (Bloomington: Indiana University Press, 2008), 10.

14. It is worth noting that many of the students in Professor Goodhart's Fall 2005 seminar were also taking courses with Martin Matuštík. As the acknowledgements to *Radical Evil and the Scarcity of Hope* attest, Goodhart's influence on Matuštík's appeal to the midrashic in his own work are indelible.

15. See Sandor Goodhart, *Möbian Nights: Reading Literature and Darkness* (New York: Bloomsbury Academic, 2017).

16. Emmanuel Levinas, "Diachrony and Representation," in *Entre Nous: Thinking-of-the-Other*, trans. Michael B. Smith and Barbara Harshav (New York: Columbia University Press, 1998), 169.

17. Ibid., 164.

18. Ibid.

19. For an extended discussion on this, see Sol Neely, "On Becoming Human in *Lingít Aaní*: Encountering Levinas through Indigenous Inspirations," *Environmental Philosophy* 13 (2016).

20. Emmanuel Levinas, *Otherwise Than Being, or Beyond Essence*, trans. Alphonso Lingis (Pittsburgh: Duquesne University Press, 1981), 109.

21. Ibid., xxviii.

22. Ibid., 114.

23. Edmond Jabès, *A Foreigner Carrying in the Crook of His Arm a Tiny Book*, trans. Rosemarie Waldrop (Hanover: Wesleyan University Press, 1993), 3.

24. Levinas, *Otherwise Than Being*, 110.

25. Ibid., 115.

26. Ibid., 114.

27. Levinas, "Diachrony and Representation," 159.

28. Levinas, "The Transcendence of Words," 147.

29. Ibid., 148.

30. Emmanuel Levinas, *Totality and Infinity: An Essay on Exteriority*, trans. Alphonso Lingis (Pittsburgh: Duquesne University Press, 1969), 295.

31. Maurice Blanchot, *The Infinite Conversation*, trans. Susan Hanson (Minneapolis: University of Minnesota Press, 1993), 27.

32. Gerald Bruns, *Maurice Blanchot: The Refusal of Philosophy* (Baltimore: Johns Hopkins University Press, 1997), 107.

33. Levinas, *Totality and Infinity*, 23.

34. Emmanuel Levinas, "The Temptation of Temptation," in *Nine Talmudic Readings*, trans. Annette Aronowicz (Bloomington: Indiana University Press, 1990), 47.

35. I first coined this phrase in my dissertation, written under the supervision of Sandor Goodhart. See Sol Neely, "Revolutionizing Maieutics: Literary, Philosophical, and Political Pedagogies in a Time of Disaster," PhD diss., Purdue University, 2009.

36. Sandor Goodhart, *Sacrificing Commentary: Reading the End of Literature* (Baltimore: Johns Hopkins University Press, 1996), 246.

37. Sandor Goodhart, "From Sacrificial Violence to Responsibility: The Education of Moses in Exodus 2-4" in *The Prophetic Law: Essays in Judaism, Girardianism, Literary Studies, and the Ethical* (East Lansing: Michigan State University Press, 2014), 118.

38. Ibid.

39. In some sense, Goodhart's use of the term "möbian" is his way of articulating (or translating) midrash into secular terms.

40. Emmanuel Levinas, "Useless Suffering," in *Entre-Nous: Thinking-of-the-Other*, trans. Michael B. Smith and Barbara Harshav (New York: Columbia University Press, 1998), 92.

41. Sandor Goodhart, "From Sacrificial Violence to Responsibility: The Education of Moses in Exodus 2-4," in *The Prophetic Law: Essays in Judaism, Girardianism, Literary Studies, and the Ethical* (East Lansing: Michigan State University Press, 2014), 121.

42. Michaels, *Fugitive Pieces*, 159.

43. Ibid., 143.

44. Sandor Goodhart, "'A Land That Devours Its Inhabitants': Midrashic Reading, Emmanuel Levinas, and Prophetic Exegesis," *Shofar: An Interdisciplinary Journal of Jewish Studies* 26, no. 4 (2008): 18.

45. Ibid.

46. Goodhart, "A Land That Devours Its Inhabitants," 13–35.

47. Claire Katz, *Levinas, Judaism, and the Feminine: The Silent Footsteps of Rebecca* (Bloomington: Indiana University Press, 2003), 11.

48. See, especially, Enrique Dussel, *Ethics of Liberation in the Age of Globalization and Exclusion*, trans. Eduardo Mendieta, Camilo Pérez Bustillo, Yolanda Angula, and Nelson Maldonado-Torres (Durham: Duke University Press, 2013).

49. Richard Cohen, "Introduction: Humanism and Anti-humanism—Levinas, Cassirer, and Heidegger," in *Humanism of the Other*, trans. Nidra Poller (Urbana: University of Illinois Press, 2003), xxxiv.

50. Levinas, *Otherwise Than Being*, 55.

51. Edmond Jabès, *The Book of Questions*, vol. 2, trans. Rosemarie Waldrop (Hanover: Wesleyan University Press, 1991), 136.

52. Emmanuel Levinas, "A Religion for Adults," in *Difficult Freedom: Essays on Judaism*, trans. Seán Hand (Baltimore: Johns Hopkins University Press, 1990), 18.

53. Ibid., 20.

54. Ibid., 19.

55. Levinas, "The Temptation of Temptations," 94–119.

56. Levinas, "The Transcendence of Words," 156.

57. Ibid.

58. Emmanuel Levinas, *Ethics and Infinity*, trans. Richard Cohen (Pittsburgh: Duquesne University Press, 1985), 85.

59. Ibid., 86.

60. Oona Eisenstadt and Claire Elise Katz, "The Faceless Palestinian: A History of an Error," *Telos* 174 (2016), 16.

61. Ibid.

62. Levinas, *Ethics and Infinity*, 86.

63. Eisenstadt and Katz, "The Faceless Palestinian," 16.

64. Sandor Goodhart, "Back to the Garden: Jewish Hermeneutics, Biblical Reading, PaRDeS, and the Four-Fold Way," in *The King James Bible across Borders and Centuries*, ed. Angelica Duran (Pittsburgh: Duquesne University Press, 2014), 47.

65. Ibid., 48.

66. Ibid., 47–48.

67. Ibid., 48.

68. Ibid.

69. Ibid.

70. Ibid.

71. Ibid., 49.

72. Ibid., 50.

73. Ibid.

74. Levinas, *Totality and Infinity*, 23.

75. Ibid.

76. Michaels, *Fugitive Pieces*, 141.

77. *Examined Life*, dir. Astra Taylor (2008; New York: Zeitgeist Films, 2010), DVD.

78. Michaels, *Fugitive Pieces*, 159.

79. Goodhart, "From Sacrificial Violence to Responsibility," 117.

80. Ibid., 119.

Part II

TEACHING

8

The Midrashic Legacy

Monica Osborne

> ... Midrash is not satisfied with the text as it stands, and while it refuses to produce a new or transformed writing it looks for more of the original in the original, for more story, more words within the words.
>
> —Geoffrey Hartman, "Midrash as Law and Literature"

If one is incredibly lucky in the world of academic graduate study, there will be a class that surprises—an experience that reshapes and reconfigures one's mind and heart. When I was working on my master's degree, courses with Holli Levitsky at LMU set my scholarly path in motion and confirmed for me that I wanted to work in Jewish and Holocaust literature. And later, when I was a PhD student at Purdue University, Sandor Goodhart's "Midrashic Reading" course became, in many ways, the midrashic response to my earlier graduate work because it gave me a new—though admittedly ancient—lens through which to read the literature of trauma, particularly trauma connected to the Holocaust. To delineate here all the ways in which the concept of midrashic reading (and thinking and writing) influenced my teaching and scholarship would be impossible because it left none of my scholarly impulses untouched.

My recent book, *The Midrashic Impulse and the Contemporary Literary Response to Trauma*, would not exist without Goodhart's class on midrashic reading. The question of what in fact constitutes an ethical response to the Holocaust and other traumatic historical moments is the basis for my book, and in this chapter I share some of my thoughts on this topic as well as articulate how an understanding of midrashic thinking has transformed the way I teach not only the Holocaust but also all literary and cultural studies courses, whether they deal with historical moments of trauma or not. Whether through incorporating a section on midrashic reading into my critical theory course at Pepperdine University or simply teaching literature students to learn to raise questions rather than to pursue answers, the midrashic mode, as Goodhart calls it, is a powerful pedagogical tool because it has the capacity to deepen students' understanding of any text and, perhaps most importantly, allows them to begin to consider their own sense of ethical responsibility in our world.

Midrashic thinking, reading, and writing always pull us back to the beginning, to origins. Perhaps, as Goodhart often suggested in the course, it also always begins in violence—it is rooted in a darkness that has always been with us. I think back to a time when, as an undergraduate, I found myself sitting on the floor of a local bookstore, completely immersed in and overwhelmed by works written by poets Marge Piercy and Alicia Suskin Ostriker. I was not entirely familiar with this strange word: midrash. At the very least, I understood only that it had something to do with ancient Jewish texts. Yet here were collections of what was being called contemporary midrash, written not from the perspectives of the ancient sages and rabbis, but from a contemporary position—a perspective that takes into account the struggle and turmoil of the twentieth and twenty-first centuries. In particular, both Ostriker and Piercy write from the perspective of contemporary women in general and contemporary Jewish women more specifically. "The text is bare bones," Piercy suggests, "and midrash puts the flesh on those bones" (Piercy n.p.). Given my personal and scholarly connections to biblical texts, the idea that there was more there than what readily presented itself—that there was meaning between the lines and letters, within the white spaces—made a profound impact on me. In some ways, this was indeed a moment of violence to which I always return—the ripping and tearing away of former habits of reading, a tear in my text. And Ostriker's assertion that women in particular must "enter the tents/texts, invade the sanctuary, uncover the father's nakedness" through interrogating the text, turning it and mining it for evolving meaning, changed everything within me (7). I sensed the power of midrash and midrashic inquiry, though I didn't yet fully know what to make of it, as I encountered it in the context of poetry, prose, memoir, fiction, and, of course, biblical exegesis. Sufficiently intrigued, I decided that I wanted to study midrash as part of a doctorate in English—not the likeliest of pairings, but when I discovered that a scholar named Sandor Goodhart was doing midrash in an English department, my scholarly future materialized.

The work of Emmanuel Levinas figured largely into Goodhart's course and is now a consistent part of all my teaching and scholarship—so much so that it is difficult to imagine that I never heard of Levinas before embarking on a study of midrash in a literary context. In my post-World War II German film class, for example, which I have taught at both the University of California, Los Angeles and Pepperdine University, an analysis of the movie *The Tin Drum* is incomplete without a Levinasian reading of it, particularly given that it is a film that responds indirectly to Germany's dark role in the Holocaust and World War II. But it is a reading that is imbedded in the midrashic, for we must determine how to read Oskar's resounding scream, piercing and distressing though it may be, for what is not readily apparent. Employing a midrashic mode of reading, students learn in this way to interrogate the text. But, at least in the case of Oskar, we find that such textual interrogations bring us back to the question of ethical responsibility and to Levinas. For the character of Oskar may be read, among other things, as a representation of German citizens who failed to accept responsibility in the wake of WWII, choosing instead to act as children, lacking in the awareness of the responsibility to which they are (we all are) no doubt called. Students also discover that there is something primal about the scream, something that returns us to our origins and to the ethical struggle into which we are all born; for, as Levinas suggests, we know that responsibility precedes ontology and preexists our origins.[1] So we are inevitably brought back to questions of our own responsibility.

I suspect that any course dealing with Holocaust or post-Holocaust literature or film does not progress without students wondering what they would have done had they been average citizens in Hitler's Germany, watching as Jewish, homosexual, or other friends and neighbors were dragged away to almost certain deaths. To suggest that one knows what he or she would have done in such circumstances is certainly presumptuous and naive. Such speculation in fact often leads to one deriving comfort from the potentially false assumption that he or she would have been one to resist and confront the barbaric actions of the Nazis. We revel in the deceptive comfort of knowing that we would not have behaved like all of the others. And yet it is an exercise that is not completely futile if we raise the question "What would I have done?" without providing an answer, and if such a question becomes consequently grounded in the contemporary moment. The question of what one would have done in Hitler's Germany becomes rather a question of what our responsibility is regarding current suffering around the world, which is ongoing and which we see happening now in this particular historical moment. How can and should we respond to the Syrian refugee crisis, for example, or to American racism and anti-Semitism? An analysis of the past is meaningless if it cannot be applied to the present and the future. Reading midrashically, we learn, is reading with an awareness of our own responsibility: for the text, for our neighbor, and for ourselves.

Levinas's idea of the "thou must which takes no account of the thou can" figures into questions of responsibility and is particularly useful in class discussions with undergraduate students. We are summoned to responsibility, to demonstrate responsible behavior. This idea generally makes sense to students, but quite often as discussions evolve it becomes an almost impossible request. For example, when I ask students how many of them would wish to see a world at peace, with no wars, violence, terrorism, starvation, and poverty, every hand is raised, as expected. When I subsequently ask whether they think such a thing is in fact possible, the response is a collective and unanimous "no." Levinas's insistence that our call to responsibility is not predicated on whether the desired outcome will be achieved, and that instead it is critical that we work toward and strive for that outcome, is important in enabling students to fully comprehend the notion of responsibility. The question of the possibility of world peace and whether its impossibility suggests that we should cease striving for this outcome is a useful way into Levinas's ideas. It transforms students' understanding of their responsibility as simply whatever they can reasonably accomplish into a conceptualization of responsibility as something that transcends the question of whether the desired outcome is possible. As Judaism inherently teaches, it is not the ends or the outcome that is most significant, but the means by which we work to achieve the outcome. We work constantly and consistently toward peace, even if it is not at all possible. We work in all ways toward a world in which there is no suffering, no war, no violence, even while we know such a thing is likely impossible. It is the striving that is important—the process as opposed to the product. Even this understanding is midrashic in nature. Midrashic thinking resists products, answers, and final outcomes, privileging instead the ongoing nature of continual questioning and response.

At the heart of midrashic thinking is the urge to uncover the more within the less. Or, as Geoffrey Hartman puts it, midrash is never satisfied with the text "as it stands, and while it refuses to produce a new or transformed writing it looks for more of the original in the original" (210). Students in my Holocaust film and literature courses at both UCLA and Pepperdine have been disturbed by the iconic silent scream of the character Sol Nazerman, a Holocaust survivor who owns a pawn shop in east Harlem, in Sidney Lumet's film *The Pawnbroker* (based on the novel of the same name by Edward Louis Wallant). Nazerman, having witnessed the deaths of his family during the Holocaust, is a character engaged in a number of inner struggles. He inhabits, as is the case with survivors of collective tragedies and traumas, two places at once. For while one may have been liberated from the concentration camp and may have escaped death, one cannot ever fully leave. A survivor of any major collective trauma arguably always inhabits two worlds simultaneously. This, we know, is how trauma works, rendering a person simultaneously broken and whole.

In this sense, readers of Jewish-American literature will likely recall Cynthia Ozick's Rosa in the second part of *The Shawl*. A survivor of the Holocaust, Rosa's post-Holocaust narrative begins with her smashing her own store—an action that is perhaps impossible to understand. Should she not be thankful she survived the camps and that she has somehow found the opportunity to start her life over? This is a question that is often asked by students. They wonder why she would do such a terrible thing, and they are irritated with her. But she is the quintessential survivor in this case: she appears whole but is simultaneously a body and mind made up of invisible cracks and wounds. One explanation for her actions is that she struggles to find a language with which to address the trauma of her past. One must remember that Rosa, in addition to being held in a concentration camp, witnessed the death of her young daughter, Magda, as she was hurled against an electrified fence by a Nazi guard. This moment in the text has always been, for me, the premise for my own personal "What would I have done?" inquiry. I imagine only a scream coming from my own throat, primal and not under my control, as I run toward what is gruesome and what robs me of everything.

Still, we are told that Rosa did not run. She did not run because "if she tried to pick up the sticks of Magda's body they would shoot, and if she let the wolf's screech ascending now through the ladder of her skeleton break out, they would shoot." Instead of speaking or even screaming, Rosa takes Magda's shawl and pushes it into her own mouth, "stuffed it in and stuffed it in, until she was swallowing up the wolf's screech and tasting the cinnamon and almond depth of Magda's saliva." Rosa, then, "drank Magda's shawl until it dried" (10). And this is the final line of the first part of *The Shawl*. The final moment in this part of the text, which also happens to be our last image of Rosa before the second part of the novella, which opens with her smashing her shop, is one of silence and suppression. The survivor here does not speak.

But reading midrashically means reading the smashing of Rosa's shop for what it does not say—that is, for what Rosa does not say. The smashing of the shop is violent and catastrophic. It says without saying. Rosa often writes to her niece, Stella, who was also in the concentration camp and whom Rosa blames in part for Magda's death, given that Stella stole Magda's shawl, causing Magda to come running out of the barracks only to be discovered and subsequently murdered. Rosa writes in Polish, which she calls a "living language: all at once this cleanliness, this capacity, this power to make a history, to tell, to explain. To retrieve, to reprieve." But it is also this language—the language of her past, the language of before—that allows one "to lie" (44). Rosa's letters are articulate, her Polish exceptional. And yet to write in the language of her past—the language of before, before the concentration camps, before the brutal execution of Magda—culminates only in misrepresentation of the past, which is not truly, as Rosa says, the past but the "during that stays"; what others might call Rosa's past is for her a permanent during (59). We see here a perfect example of the breakdown of language and of representational thinking. Despite Rosa's vast Polish vocabulary, and despite her ability to write clearly and articulately in the language of her childhood, what emerges is merely the potential for a lie. Words fall short. She is betrayed by language and representational thinking, which is the antithesis of midrashic thinking. For representation claims to know the unknowable, to articulate what cannot be articulated. It amounts to one thing standing for another, acting as if the distance between the two does not exist. Unlike midrashic thinking, it does not attempt to highlight and read that absence. In this way, every attempt becomes a lie, a betrayal. What Rosa calls "a living language" in fact lacks the capacity to articulate the experience of trauma. It reveals nothing, instead obscuring what is at the heart of the traumatic experience. It is no wonder, then, that she chooses to smash her shop.

In the afterword of Cathy Caruth's *Literature in the Ashes of History*, she writes about the theory of catastrophic history, suggesting that it may "ultimately be written in a language that already lingers [in texts responding to trauma] after the end, in a time that comes to us from the other shore, from the other side of the disaster" (92). I have often wondered if what she is getting at is the language of midrash, if this is the language that comes to us from "the other side of disaster." It is a language and an impulse that precedes all we wish to articulate. It is an extension of the primary text rather than a representation of it. And one might argue that the language of midrash lingers in so many texts that deal with and respond to (or try to articulate) the experience of trauma, particularly collective trauma. In a biblical context, midrash is what deepens and fills out the biblical text. It is what makes it matter, makes it meaningful. It "infers from ellipses or condensations a very human story and introduces dialogues that draw God deeper into the affairs of mankind" (Hartman 209). It is meant to bring us closer to the event we call God. And in the context of writing and thinking about trauma, midrashic thinking has the capacity to bring us closer to the experience of trauma about which we cannot speak.

Returning to *The Pawnbroker*'s Sol Nazerman, we find something exceptionally compelling about his silent but intense expression of grief. Neither language nor sound is appropriate in this context. And so we bear witness to the silent scream that is heavy with meaning, heavy with stories that cannot be told but that nevertheless remain with the character. Here is a scream that cracks us wide open without making a sound. What, one might ask, is there to read in this display of nothingness? But we read midrashically in this moment a shocking utterance of absence. Perhaps Sol Nazerman's entire life is unreadable except through this moment of the silent scream. Perhaps Rosa's is similarly unreadable but through the lens of her smashed shop. Let us learn to read silence, I often tell my students. Let us learn to read what isn't there, but what is nonetheless buried within the cracks and wounds of the text. Let us, as Levinas suggests in "The Temptation of Temptation," rub the text "in such a way that blood spurts out," so that we might "arrive at the life it conceals" (46). And, finally, let us learn to read the more within the less and to resist the impulse of satisfactory readings that would allow us to falsely assume we now know the extent of the trauma.

Perhaps no Talmudic story resonates more deeply with the work I do with my students than the one explicated by Levinas in "The Temptation of Temptation." Near the end of Tractate Shabbath (88a and 88b), which responds to Exodus 19:17,[2] we read about a spying Sadducee who sees Raba immersed in study. Raba is so engrossed in his reading that he absentmindedly rubs at the skin beneath his foot. He does this so intently and urgently that, unbeknownst to him, blood begins to spurt from it. "How do we read this moment?," I remember Goodhart asking his graduate class. The answer, of course, is that this is a midrashic moment that teaches us how to read, a moment that reveals to us the potential for violence that resides in any text and our reading of it. The midrashic impulse, after all, is one that is always a response to a violence that comes before it. The biblical narrative itself, for example, begins with a world that is "wild and waste," with darkness obscuring "the face of Ocean" until God's words intrude on the chaos, splitting the light from darkness, waters from heavens.[3] There is an inherent sense of violence in the rhetoric of these very first biblical moments. The language does not allow for any imagined scenario in which a divine figure lovingly and peacefully creates the world and brings us into being. Our origins are, instead, violent and tumultuous—not unlike the violence of childbirth. A child is born into the world by way of blood, darkness, screams, and the pain of sometimes cut and torn flesh as the body of the child is separated permanently from the body of its mother. Are we not all born out of and into violence? Is it not violence that precedes and fashions us as we come into this world? It is a subtle reminder to all of us: this is how the world came into being. Imaginably this is also how words that matter come into being—always already through violence. And so these first words of the biblical tradition are a subtle reminder to all of this. Perhaps everything that follows these first verses of Genesis is a response to this initial chaos. For reading in such a way is to respond to the wounds within the text—to bear witness to its tears and ambiguities and to acknowledge them. Levinas talks about the "violence done to words to tear from them the secret that time and conventions have covered over with their sedimentations, a process begun as soon as these words appear in the open air of history" (47). This is the layer that must be removed so that the reading can begin.

My first exposure to midrash, as I've said, was in its biblical context. The Jewish rabbinic tradition has long been comfortable with acknowledging the gaps, silences, and inconsistencies of the Hebrew Bible. There has never been an impulse to obscure these textual issues, make excuses for them, or act as if they simply don't exist. Instead, the rabbis and sages of antiquity sought to bring these issues to light through the creation of *Midrashim*, the collections of stories that reveal and respond to these gaps and silences. Forming along with the Talmud an expansive body of rabbinic biblical commentary, midrash and all of its proposed scenarios, unresolved quarrels, and unanswered questions is incapable of amnesia, and it disallows the possibility of amnesia within the reader as well. It prohibits the possibility of forgetting, as its existence is possible only because of a wound in the text that calls for response. One midrashic account does not stand in for another midrashic account. Instead, they stand together, in this way highlighting and presenting the original gap or absence and putting it at the forefront. It addresses and responds to this absence, this wound in the text, without claiming to resolve it. And because of this, we are drawn into the wound. The absence is made visible, finally, so that we can read it. Here we are as close to it as we can possibly be.

In an age in which technology has put more information at our fingertips than ever before, the idea of midrashic reading becomes increasingly paradoxical. Midrash is about preserving silences and absences, and such an impulse seems incompatible with contemporary urges to know everything, to become somehow omniscient in the context of everything from global current events to dinnertime decisions and fashion choices of social networking friends. When it comes to information and data in this age, we want for nothing thanks to the pervasiveness of the Internet and its numerous search engines. We can (almost) truly know everything now, it seems. We have the luxury of presuming to fill in any and all gaps in our knowledge. We can brazenly peer into the past simply by typing in a few keywords or phrases, perhaps "Holocaust," "concentration camp," "Nazis," and "9/11" or even "slavery" or "Native American genocide." In so doing, we imagine that the gaps in our own limited understanding of some of the most unimaginable historical events of our time become smaller and less pronounced as we fill them with images and textual summaries gleaned from electronic searches. But a midrashic awareness reminds us that such information, while critical to historical and cultural memory, is but a vast supply of representations of traumatic events. Even a photograph of a moment within a concentration camp is but a representation of that moment. And as I have said in other places, representational modes do very little to bring us closer to an actual event. Instead, they give us permission to claim knowledge we cannot possibly have, inevitably distancing us from what it is we wish to know. For this reason, the metonymic and diachronic nature of midrashic reading is perhaps a more ethical and authentic tool for looking into the past and envisioning the future.

But what shape does this take in the classroom? The novel I teach most often, in a number of my courses, is Anne Michaels's *Fugitive Pieces*, which tells first the story of Jakob Beer, a child survivor of the Holocaust, and, in the second part of the novel, of Ben, a child of survivors. My students are always struck by the distinctly different writing style of each section. In the first part, Jakob, who is writing his memoir, states, "I did not witness the most important events of my life. My deepest story must be told by a blind man" (17). Michaels, a poet who has now written two spectacular novels, writes a character who writes midrashically.[4] Jakob demonstrates an awareness of his own blindnesses and shortcomings, and in his careful acknowledgement of them he becomes a responsible reader of his own trauma because he begins in an acknowledgment of his failure (which is also Michaels's acknowledgment of her own failure, as a writer, to ever fully evoke the horrors of the Holocaust). Jakob never claims to know what even the survivor cannot know, and it is in this admission that the midrashic moment materializes.

The very existence of midrash, in its sacred and classical manifestation, implies a failure in the primary text (the biblical text) to recount a complete and fully authentic story. The Hebrew bible, it seems, even as it functions as the blueprint of the world according to the rabbis and our Jewish tradition, has a blind spot. It has failed in some sense. But midrash brings this failure to the forefront and functions as what Goodhart calls a "material extension" of the biblical text (18). Classical midrash is not an addendum to the biblical text; rather, it is a mode that reaches back into the contradictions and ambiguities of the biblical text and brings to light what already resides there in those spaces and ellipses. Perhaps without midrash the biblical text would be little more than a cultural artifact—a representation of something that once was. Midrash is permission to question and interrogate even the most sacred texts or ideas. For example, when in Genesis 22 God says to Abraham, "Pray take your son, your only-one, whom you love, Yitzhak, and go-you-forth to the land of Moriyya/Seeing, and offer him up there as an offering-up," should we not bristle at this suddenly silent Abraham who in every other instance was willing to push back against God's requests and to argue with him, but when told essentially to execute his son had nothing to say?[5] While the Christian tradition typically reads this moment and what follows as an example of Abraham's faith being tested, with him ultimately passing the test, the Jewish tradition is not satisfied with the text or with this interpretation. Indeed, Christians most often refer to the story as "the sacrifice of Isaac," whereas Jewish readers tend to refer to it as "the binding of Isaac." The difference in wording here is critical. The act of sacrifice implies finality. But the idea of a binding as opposed to a sacrifice suggests that there is a struggle to be had, that it is an ongoing struggle. I like to read this as a metaphor for what Hartman calls a "struggle for the text."[6] The silences in this crucial text about Abraham and his son Isaac become more pronounced when read midrashically. Various midrashic texts suggest the possibility that Abraham did in fact answer God. Others suggest the ram caught in the thicket, which would replace Isaac as a sacrifice, was placed there by Sarah. There are countless midrashim on this moment, both classical and contemporary. But what is most important here is that such responses to the text resist representational models of biblical response and exegesis that attempt to silence or cover up the ellipses, instead bringing those to the forefront and moving us toward dialogue.

The idea of representation as the antithesis to midrashic reading and writing is important. When my students encounter the second half of *Fugitive Pieces*, narrated by Ben, a child of survivors, they describe an experience of being pushed away from the text. Students often feel confused by their own emotional response to the text. They marvel at how, despite the fragmented and broken nature of Jakob's narrative—and the subsequent return to traditional narrative format in Ben's—they find difficulty connecting with Ben. They feel suddenly disconnected from a novel that had in the first part taken hold of them in the most meaningful of ways. Whereas Jakob knows "the power of language to destroy, to omit, to obliterate," Ben seeks to represent the experience of his parents, unknown to him as it really was (79). "I see now," Ben says, "that my fascination wasn't archaeology or even forensics: it was biography" (221). He attempts to reconstruct the stories of trauma that are not his, and it is in this implicit claim to know what he cannot know and to simultaneously act on it that his efforts become anti-midrashic.

Or they become simply representation, which, functioning as one thing standing for another, always distances us from the very thing about which we want to know more. Ben, like Jakob, fails. But Ben, unlike Jakob, is unaware of his failure, and without this awareness and acknowledgement of the blindness that must always accompany such undertakings, readers of his narrative are kept at an arm's length, staring at what amounts to little more than a simulation or facsimile of the traumatic moment.

The midrashic mode of reading, I tell my students, is not about finding answers or filling in gaps. Some people misunderstand midrash as an attempt to fill in rather than respond to gaps in the biblical text. The distinction is critical. If we read to fill in gaps, then we read to complete a process and to present ourselves with a final product, the logic of which is antithetical to midrashic reading, which is always concerned with questions as opposed to answers. Process is privileged over product, always. Of Jakob Beer, another character (in fact Ben's girlfriend, Naomi) says that he "looks like a man who has finally found the right question" (234). Certainly the opposite is true in the context of the university, where students are often conditioned to cram for exams, making use of short-term memory in an effort to supply all of the necessary answers to prove that they have learned something. But midrash cares little for answers because answers are almost always a foreclosure of dialogue and discussion, where the deepest meaning is to be found. "The question creates," writes Edmond Jabès, "The answer kills" (37). When a midrashic story responds to a gap in the biblical text, it does not provide an answer, but rather a possibility, and even as it provides that possibility, it simultaneously extends the gap it seeks to fill. The dialogue never ends, and the text it surrounds remains alive for this reason.

Hartman, one of the first literary scholars to recognize the importance of midrash not just to the Jewish and biblical traditions but also to literary studies in general, writes, as I have said, that midrash "infers from ellipses or condensations a very human story and introduces dialogues that draw God deeper into the affairs of mankind" (209). I would suggest that what we want most from our students is an ability to engage in thoughtful, intelligent, and meaningful dialogue with others. An understanding of midrash and midrashic reading in general creates for students an environment where this is not only welcome but also necessary if we are to truly learn together.

When we read midrashically, we are engaging in the work of memory—but not memory in the way that undergraduates usually understand it (that is, the struggle to remember material on which one might be tested). Reading midrashically means taking account of the secondariness of every text. Midrashic texts are "citational to an extreme degree," suggests Hartman, "They reject amnesia and cryptomnesia" (217). We are necessarily haunted by what comes before, by what is primary. Perhaps this is what students find so distressing about Ben's narrative in *Fugitive Pieces*—it acts as if it were primary, as if the representation were more than simulacra. I often wonder if the students suspect the farce. His narrative—his representation!—rings false for those who have learned to read midrashically.

Ben is born to survivors of the Holocaust, so he has in many ways inherited the trauma of this disaster. The very notion of what we call disaster evokes a falling apart, a tearing away of words from the wounds they struggle to describe. And yet the means by which Ben seeks to understand and respond to the disaster that both is and is not his achieves the opposite of the task he sets out to accomplish. In the context of our many books, films, and other artistic attempts to approach the Holocaust, we are not unlike Ben in many cases. We create simulations of the disaster—in this case the Holocaust—but these replicas ultimately become disguises for the wounds about which we cannot, perhaps should not, speak. In struggling to remember and understand the original event, we begin a dangerous process of forgetting, of muting the silence that should instead be at the forefront. We do this while telling ourselves that we are remembering, that we are recalling events to which there are no witnesses, piecing things back together for a greater good. Some of us even imagine that we are engaged in a process of finding meaning in the suffering of others despite the knowledge that such a claim is transgressive and that, as Levinas suggests in "Useless Suffering," we may not find meaning in the suffering of another, but only in our own suffering. In struggling to identify or assign meaning and erect it in such a way that it will achieve permanence, we chip away at the structure of memory. Reading midrashically, however, prevents this chipping away, instead preserving memory, even when memory is but a series of voids and absences.

I suspect there are some for whom this idea of midrashic reading—no longer tethered solely to biblical exegesis and commentary—is wildly inappropriate or even dangerous. And certainly there was a sense in Goodhart's "Midrashic Reading" course that we were doing something that was both new and ancient. Midrash is neither literature nor commentary. And yet it is *both* literature and commentary, or simultaneously inside and outside the text, as Goodhart so often told us, using a Möbius strip as a visual example and tracing his finger along the outside that merged seamlessly with the inside, transgressing neither border nor boundary. Perhaps the Möbius nature of such an endeavor makes it difficult to situate in a specific discipline. But we were certainly not alone. In the concluding lines of Hartman's "Midrash as Law and Literature," he remarks briefly on the "field that may eventually be created by the awareness that Midrash and literary study take of each other" and concludes that a "knowledge of Midrash will prove more interesting for the literary critic than a knowledge of literary criticism for the scholar of Jewish texts" (217–18). It has indeed proven interesting to me. And as I pass on to my own students this mode of thinking, reading, and writing—simultaneously ancient and modern—I remember Marge Piercy's comments that spoke to me so early on, and I think, yes, we're putting the flesh on these old bones.

Notes

1. For more on this, see *Ethics and Infinity: Conversations with Philippe Nemo*.
2. "And they stopped at the foot of the mountain . . ." (qtd. in Levinas 30).
3. Genesis 1:2 (from Everett Fox's excellent translation of the first five books, *The Five Books of Moses*).
4. *The Winter Vault* is Michaels's second novel.
5. Translation from Everett Fox's *The Five Books of Moses*.
6. Hartman published an essay by this name in *Midrash and Literature*. It was subsequently republished in other collections, including most recently Hartman's *The Third Pillar: Essays in Judaic Studies*. It is also a phrase he uses throughout much of his work.

References

Caruth, Cathy. *Literature in the Ashes of History*. Baltimore: Johns Hopkins University Press, 2013.

Fox, Everett. *The Five Books of Moses: Genesis, Exodus, Leviticus, Numbers, and Deuteronomy*. New York: Schocken, 1983.

Goodhart, Sandor. "'A Land that Devours Its Inhabitants': Midrashic Reading, Emmanuel Levinas, and Prophetic Exegesis." *SHOFAR* 26, no. 4 (Summer 2008): 13–35.

Hartman, Geoffrey. "Midrash as Law and Literature." In *The Geoffrey Hartman Reader*, edited by Geoffrey Hartman and Daniel T. O'Hara, 203–22. New York: Fordham University Press, 2004.

Jabès, Edmond. *The Little Book of Unsuspected Subversion*. Translated by Rosmarie Waldrop. Stanford: Stanford University Press, 1996.

———. *The Third Pillar: Essays in Judaic Studies*. Philadelphia: University of Pennsylvania Press, 2011.

Levinas, Emmanuel. *Ethics and Infinity: Conversations with Philippe Nemo*. Translated by. Richard A. Cohen. Duquesne: Duquesne University Press, 1995.

———. "The Temptation of Temptation." In *Nine Talmudic Readings*, trans. Annette Aronowicz, 30–50. Bloomington: Indiana University Press, 1990.

———. "Useless Suffering." In *Entre Nous: Thinking-of-the-Other*, translated by Michael B. Smith and Barbara Harshav, 78–87. London: Continuum, 1998.

Michaels, Anne. *Fugitive Pieces*. New York: Vintage, 1996.

———. *The Winter Vault*. New York: Vintage, 2009.

Ostriker, Alicia Suskin. *The Nakedness of the Fathers: Biblical Visions and Revisions*. New Brunswick: Rutgers University Press, 1994.

Ozick, Cynthia. *The Shawl*. New York: Vintage Books, 1980.

Piercy, Marge. "Email Conversation." February 2, 2017.

9

Anne Frank, Figuration, and the Ethical Imperative

Aimee Pozorski

> Her diary is beloved and still read by young people in schools around the world. We all know that. But what is less remarked upon is that she has become a trope for the Holocaust in American fiction.
>
> —Rita D. Jacobs, 2016

A May 2016 visit to the Anne Frank House in Amsterdam emphasizes the power of the memory of Anne Frank in the contemporary global imagination. Open from 9:00 a.m. to 10:00 p.m., the house boasts a perpetual line for admission that wraps around the corner from sunup to sundown. Nearby, Mari Andriessen's Anne Frank statue at Westermarkt features throngs of tourists wanting to get a view of the girl's image up close, many visitors being so bold as to take a selfie beside the statue. When I have asked students if this is a blatant sign of appropriation, they answer with an emphatic, "No," explaining that their generation feels an affinity for Anne Frank, one born out of a sustained reading of her diary in high school and a shared sense of worry about what the world has in store for their own generation.

Coinciding with the contemporary affinity for Anne Frank, this chapter focuses on specific ways in which the image of Anne Frank has been used in fiction to connote not only an insecurity about the future, but also a more writerly concern about what fiction might offer contemporary generations in the wake of a century marred by genocide. Just as Adorno worried about the status of poetry after Auschwitz, the figure of Anne Frank betrays fiction writers' anxieties about Holocaust representation. Via close readings of such authors as Philip Roth and—in a more sustained way—Nathan Englander, a relatively new (or newly valued) voice in contemporary literature, I argue that the figure of Anne Frank allows us to engage students in this debate about how literature can help convey the history of the Holocaust.

I am not the first professor and scholar to notice that our interest in Anne Frank has evolved from historical person to literary trope. In fact, I seem to be one of many in the summer of 2016. For example, in a blog post titled "72 Years On: The Fictional Afterlife of Anne Frank," Rita D. Jacobs returns us to Roth's 1979 treatment of Anne Frank as a survivor in *The Ghost Writer* before calling attention to "the Anne Frank tropes used by the third generation authors, who had to have read the diary well after its first publication. Witness Nathan Englander's 2011 short story, 'What We Talk About When We Talk about Anne Frank' and Shalom Auslander's 2012 novel, *Hope: A Tragedy*."[1] Sanford Pinsker, in his review of Englander's story and Auslander's novel together, has noted that "[a]s a rite of passage for hundreds of thousands of teenagers who learn about her tragically short life from the printed page, the silver screen, or the Broadway stage, Anne Frank has become, for better or worse, the poster child of the Holocaust."[2]

I am interested in a further consideration of what it means to think about Anne Frank as a "poster child"—an exemplary case in order to fit a stereotype—or as a "trope," to use Jacobs's term, or as a figure, to use my own. In these cases, "trope" and "figure" (and even, to some extent, "poster child") are examples of literary writing that require readers to see beyond the literal denotation of the word. In twenty-first-century literary studies, particularly studies of representations of the Holocaust, there seem to be enormous stakes in looking past Anne Frank's lived history and seeing in that history potential for literary figuration. I am interested in asking students not only what Anne Frank as a metaphor might mean in the larger sense, but also what is to be gained and lost in terms of understanding the Holocaust—and even representation—when we turn a living, breathing girl into a metaphor for something else. Ultimately, I wonder: Is it ethical to use Anne Frank as a literary figure in fiction about the Holocaust? The short answer, I would contend, is both yes and no. But the longer answer involves a consideration of ethics, not only after the Holocaust, but now, more than seventy years later, in our post-9/11 landscape. In linking the figuration of Anne Frank with what I am calling "the ethical imperative"—a phrase borrowed from disciplines as far ranging as the law, medicine, philosophy, and business—I argue that authors such as Roth and Englander have used Frank as a figure to emphasize the ways in which we are responsible for the well-being of one another, a relationship between self and other that is not entirely different from the relationship between writer and reader, calling attention to the critical role of storytelling itself.

A 2012 collection edited by Barbara Kirshenblatt-Gimblett and Jeffery Sandler titled *Anne Frank Unbound: Media, Imagination, Memory* has accomplished much in terms of this larger consideration of Anne Frank's role in popular memory, especially during a cultural moment when Anne Frank studies seems to be experiencing a resurgence. According to the editors:

> The Anne Frank phenomenon shows no sign of abating. Tributes to Anne Frank now reach to the heavens (an asteroid was named for her in 1995), she has become a fixture of new social media (a Facebook page was created for her in 2008), and her diary garners ever more prestigious accolades (it was added to the UNESCO Memory of the World Register, along with the Magna Carta and the Nibelungenlied, in 2009). As this book went to press, two writers, Shalom Auslander and Nathan Englander, published works of fiction in which Anne Frank figures prominently, as an immortal presence haunting a contemporary American Jewish family's home and an epitomizing test case of personal loyalty, respectively.[3]

Here too is the key word, "figures," taken to mean not only that Anne Frank's presence is felt throughout the works, but also that she has evolved, in the span of nearly seventy years, from victim of history to household name to a metaphor in third-generation literary works. It seems significant that authors and critics are noticing it now, in this twenty-first century moment—a moment, as Englander's fiction makes clear—that is hyperaware of the loss, still, of the World Trade Center Towers on September 11, 2001.

In addition to Pinsker's, Kirshenblatt-Gimblett's, and Sandler's work from 2012, and emerging alongside Jacobs's essay in the summer of 2016, two additional discussions of the place of Anne Frank in contemporary American fiction have advanced the conversation—and they have done so by reminding us of a significant early voice of dissent regarding the use of Anne Frank in fiction: Cynthia Ozick. In the July 2016 newsletter of the *International Journal of Humanities and Cultural Studies*, for example, Alexandra Strukova and colleagues argued that

> [i]n the second half of the twentieth century two prominent American authors turned to the image of Anne Frank. These are Philip Roth in his novel *The Ghost Writer* (1979) and Cynthia Ozick in her essay "Who Owns Anne Frank?" (1997). The idea they reveal is the same: public opinion and Mass Media have turned Anne into an idol devoid of human features and credibility. The majority of people have forgotten or never realized the fact, that *The Secret Annex* is a work of literature, unfinished but possessing undoubted aesthetic value.[4]

The key words here are "image," "idol," and "work of literature," reminding us of the dangers of appropriating a living being for the use of sending a larger message. The risk, for Strukova, is that Anne Frank becomes, in contemporary memory, "devoid of human features and credibility"—which may be another effective way to acknowledge the "poster child" effect Pinsker recognizes above. A June 26, 2016, interview with Ozick herself reminds us of this fact. Published in advance of the appearance of Ozick's latest book, *Critics, Monsters, Fanatics, and Other Literary Essays* (2016), the interview, "The Fanatic," revisits the topic of cultural memory explored in her much earlier essay "Who Owns Anne Frank?," which downright condemns contemporary American culture's emergent fanaticism (in the sense of fan culture as well as overwhelming enthusiasm or devotion) surrounding the life and writing of Anne Frank. In this interview, Giles Harvey writes, "In a marvelously indignant essay on Anne Frank, she protests the diarist's assimilation by mainstream culture, the way in which she has been 'infantilized, Americanized, homogenized, sentimentalized, falsified, kitschified, and, in fact, blatantly and arrogantly denied.' Sapped of quiddity, she has become 'an all-American girl.'"[5]

Because Ozick can be credited for the important insight that Anne Frank has been thoroughly assimilated into mainstream culture, it is important to return to that original *New Yorker* essay. Looking back at it, it becomes clear that Ozick is also interested in Anne Frank's legacy, not only for what her story tells us about the history of the Holocaust, but also for what it tells us about the role of the writer in documenting traumatic events. Early in the essay, Ozick writes, "even if she had not kept the extraordinary diary through which we know her it is likely that we would number her among the famous of this century—though perhaps not so dramatically as we do now. She was born to be a writer."[6] Here we have an important contemporary Jewish writer worrying about the legacy of another important contemporary Jewish writer; in this essay, Ozick resolutely rejects an interpretation of Frank's diary as optimistic, reparative, or uplifting. Ozick argues that the diary's "reputation for uplift is, to say it plainly, nonsensical" (78).

In indicting the mainstream appropriation of Frank's diary as a way to assuage American guilt, Ozick continues by arguing that

> the diary itself, richly crammed though it is with incident and passion, cannot count as Anne Frank's story. A story may not be said to be a story if the end is missing. And because the end is missing, the story of Anne Frank in the fifty years since "The Diary of a Young Girl" was first published has been bowdlerized, distorted, transmuted, traduced, reduced. (78)

She cites in particular Alvin Rosenfeld, a scholar of the reception of the adaptation of Anne Frank's diary for Broadway, who acknowledges that "[t]he Anne Frank whom thousands saw in seven openings in seven cities 'spoke affirmatively about life and not accusingly about her tortures.' No German in uniform appeared on stage. 'In a word,' Rosenfeld concludes, 'Anne Frank has become a ready-at-hand formula for easy forgiveness'" (87).

Here too—as early as 1997—we see a profound ambivalence about the rise of Anne Frank in cultural memory. The idea that she is "a ready-at-hand formula" emphasizes the ways in which her suffering in history has been reduced to an idea easier for many to accept—that, at least when she was writing to Kitty—she was a forgiving, all-American teenager, not yet jaded by the genocidal world around her.

The words associated with Anne Frank's legacy, then—among them "image," "idol," "work of literature," and "ready-at-hand formula"—all point to a deep discomfort with the ways in which her name is used as a figure in Holocaust literature, which provides an important opportunity to reflect with students on the role of the figure more generally in literary fiction and rhetoric. The most literary-centered definition of figuration from the *Oxford English Dictionary* is associated with ancient Greek rhetoric: "In various uses, representing the technical applications of Greek σχῆμα; any of the various 'forms' of expression, deviating from the normal arrangement or use of words, which are adopted in order to give beauty, variety, or force to a composition."[7] In deviating from the literal or historical use of Anne Frank's name—and what she experienced—it seems that contemporary American writers, as exemplified by Roth, Auslander, and Englander, use the figure of Anne Frank to emphasize instead the vexed role of the author and the author's relationship with ethics overall.

More basic definitions of figuration still are the Poetry Foundation's definition: "An expressive, nonliteral use of language";[8] and Walter Kalaidjian's from the anthology *Understanding Poetry*: "Tropes are figures of language that depend or 'turn' on describing one thing in terms of something else. Figurative language works through . . . comparisons and verbal substitutions where a particular word or phrase stands in for some other intended meaning."[9] What does it mean to "turn" the identity of Anne Frank into something else in fiction? What can be gained in terms of the "other intended meaning"?

In considering the specific cases of the use of Anne Frank as a figure in Roth's *The Ghost Writer* (1979) and Englander's "What We Talk About When We Talk About Anne Frank," I argue, in other words, that the connotative dimension, or the intended meaning, has shifted. Whereas we might say that Roth's use of Anne Frank points to the writer's plight primarily, certainly the powers of the writers' imagination and their effect on the self, Englander's twenty-first-century use of Anne Frank points to the relationship between self and other, and—within that relationship—the role of storytelling in calling attention to historical or ethical failings.

From Englander's self-referential title alone, we are asked to consider "What We Talk About When We Talk About Anne Frank." What we—or Anne Frank stories—talk about has to do with a commitment to others; the figure of Anne Frank, as late as 2012, is a relational figure, asking ultimately: Who among us would save someone if his or her life were in danger? Roth has been considered the self-referential, inward-gazing writer of his generation; and while Englander looks inward, he also looks outward. The "Anne Frank game" at the heart of his story is not merely the game of the writer (although it is that); it is also about shifting loyalties and the claim one person makes on another. It is, in short, about the ethical imperative.

The relationship between stories and ethics has been well documented in the theoretical work of Adam Zachary Newton, whose 1995 monograph *Narrative Ethics* uses the word "narrative" not as an adjective to describe ethics but as a noun equivalent with ethics itself. He writes: "A narrative is ethics in the sense of the mediating and authorial role each takes up towards another's story . . . Storytelling lays claim upon all its participants, those circumscribed within the narrative as well as those . . . witnesses and ethical co-creators from without—its readers."[10] In this sense, stories implicate the reader in bearing witness to whatever history a writer tells; stories make the reader responsible for the text. Stories about Anne Frank, if I may be permitted to go even further, are effective in appealing to the readers' sense of affinity for her and her story. In facing the figure of Anne Frank, the reader becomes more invested in the narrative experience—understanding the ways in which the one story, Anne Frank's story, might give us access to the stories of 6 million more who perished during the Holocaust while simultaneously warning against appropriating them.

The language of witness and ethics emerges also in trauma theory during the same time in Cathy Caruth's 1995 edited collection *Trauma: Explorations in Memory* and her 1996 monograph *Unclaimed Experience*. In the latter text, Caruth writes, "we can begin to recognize the possibility of a history that is no longer straightforwardly referential (that is, no longer based on simple models of experience and reference). Through the notion of trauma . . . we can understand that a rethinking of reference is aimed not at eliminating history but at resituating it in our understanding, that is, at precisely permitting *history* to arise where *immediate understanding* may not."[11] Ultimately, that seems to be the case with the figure of Anne Frank as well: in turning her from a literal, historical fact to a literary device that is no longer straightforwardly referential, we are able to reposition ourselves in relation to traumatic history. We are able to see history, in other words, in a new way—this time, not with relation to the story of one girl, but also, as in the case of Englander, with relation to how the story of the girl reflects on our relationships and willingness to help others to this day. When reading Roth's and Englander's literary works that draw on the figure of Anne Frank alongside Caruth's defense of writing that is not straightforwardly referential, we may in part exonerate them from Ozick's critique.

Roth's *The Ghost Writer* and Englander's "What We Talk About" are exemplary cases also in the sense that they allow teachers to address questions of representational ethics in Holocaust fiction. Much has been written about Philip Roth's treatment of Anne Frank in *The Ghost Writer*.[12] In what remains of this chapter, I briefly discuss Roth's 1979 treatment of Anne Frank—extending my earlier publication from 2005 on the topic—and then go on to focus on Nathan Englander, a rising Jewish voice in twenty-first-century American literature who also represents the lingering centrality of Anne Frank in the American literary imagination.

In my 2005 reading of Roth's representation of Anne Frank in *The Ghost Writer*, I reveal the ways in which Roth's alter ego, Nathan Zuckerman, fantasizes that Anne Frank had indeed survived the death camps and was living with his mentor, E. I. Lonoff—an arrangement that would make possible Zuckerman's relationship with the greatest Jewish author in history in order to assuage his parents. But there was a second reading I wanted to espouse, too, namely that Roth was an underappreciated Holocaust writer, revealing how we remain haunted well into the twenty-first century by the memory of six million dead. I suggest that, "[d]espite Zuckerman's lengthy Anne Frank fantasy and its suspension of any simple reading of *The Ghost Writer* as a bildungsroman, very few critics are willing to classify Philip Roth as a Holocaust novelist" (90).[13]

On my original reading, I argued that

> the Anne Frank fantasy recalls not just Anne Frank and her family in hiding but also the concentration camps, death by typhus, and the genocide of six million Jews. The first ghost that *The Ghost Writer* "conjures," in other words, is the ghost of Anne Frank and the inassimilable experience she represents. . . . This darker side of Zuckerman's imaginings reveals that even for a comic writer like Roth, the Holocaust still consumes Jewish Americans—and, indeed, all of us—living relatively safe lives in the United States.[14]

For me, more than a decade ago, the novel revealed, through traumatic repetition of the Anne Frank trope, the fact that the death of this girl seems to weigh on our collective conscience even still. A closer reading of Roth's project, however—one that allows for a reading of *The Ghost Writer* through the prism provided by the Englander story—reveals that it is also about the responsibilities or burdens of being a writer; all three contemporary texts, *The Diary of a Young Girl*, *The Ghost Writer*, and "What We Talk About When We Talk About Anne Frank," are works about writing and the effects of the imagination. They are, in other words, self-referential to the core.

The centrality of the Anne Frank figure in Roth's novel comes into full view in chapter 3, "Femme Fatale." At first, it becomes clear that Roth is, like Ozick, concerned about the easy association between Anne Frank and forgiveness. In the Anne Frank fantasy sequence, she says to Lonoff, after seeing her diary transformed for the stage, "It wasn't the play—I could have watched that easily enough if I had been alone. It was the people watching with me. Carloads of women kept pulling up to the theater, women wearing fur coats, with expensive shoes and handbags. I thought, this isn't for me. . . . it was the women who frightened me—and their families and their children and their homes.'"[15] What appears to be frightening is the fact that high-society New York women, in their expensive coats and accessories, found, in Anne Frank on the stage—already on her way to becoming a figure—an easy way to forgive themselves for not taking a larger part in accepting Europe's refugees. Such an observation also casts contemporary students' affinity for Frank in a slightly uncomfortable light. Do they, too, find an easy way to forgive past and current American foreign policy as it relates to immigrants?

In the Roth novel, the adaptation of *The Diary of a Young Girl* is staged at the Cort Theater (125); while there, "[t]he women cried. Everyone around me was in tears. Then at the end, in the row behind me, a woman screamed, 'Oh no'" (123). The "Oh no," as vocalized by Anne, seems to be coming from her own unconscious; the theater women are reacting to melodrama, but Anne herself is reacting to the way her own words have been mishandled and taken out of context. For her, it is as much a writer's problem as it is a problem of history. As Nathan continues to fantasize, Amy says to Lonoff: "'It's like one of your stories. An E. I. Lonoff story . . . called . . . oh, you'd know what to call it. You'd know how to tell it in three pages. A homeless girl comes from Europe, sits in the professor's class being clever, listens to his records, plays his daughter's piano, virtually grows up in his house, and then one day, when the waif is a woman and out on her own, one fine day in the Biltmore Hotel, she casually announces . . .'" (124).

Roth's experimentation with perspective is important here: Roth imagines the story of Zuckerman imagining the story of Anne Frank, who in turn imagines the similarity of her story with E. I. Lonoff, the mentor of both her and Zuckerman. "It's like one of your stories," points up the fact that everything, at some level, is crafted—just as are the layers of Roth's invented work. The promise and perplexity of the writer's life, for Amy Bellette, the actual girl who inspires Zuckerman's Anne Frank fantasy, is further reinforced on discovering that her diary did not have her intended effect—and now was out of her hands. Zuckerman imagines that she imagines, "All her reasoning, all her fantastical thinking about the ordained mission of her book followed from this: neither she nor her parents came through in the diary as anything like representative or religious or observant Jews" (142); the lament goes on for several pages, culminating four pages later with:

> She was not, after all, the fifteen-year-old who could, while hiding from a holocaust, tell Kitty, I still believe that people are really good at heart. Her youthful ideals had suffered no less than she had in the windowless freight car from Westerbork and she in the barracks at Auschwitz and on the Belsen heath. She had not come to hate the human race for what it was—what could it be but what it was?—but she did not feel seemly any more singing its praises. (146)

Roth points up here, using very different devices than Cynthia Ozick's lacerating essay, that Anne Frank's story is not complete unless we understand fully the effect of the experiences of Auschwitz and Belsen. Her true story, if it ever could be written, includes horror, starvation, and death by typhus—which would presumably lead any young girl to refrain from singing the praises of humanity.

What follows, however, is Zuckerman's description of the effect his own fiction about Anne Frank has had on him. His reality has been altered. He sees people differently. He confesses, "But I could not really think of her as Amy any longer. Instead I was continually drawn back into the fiction I had evolved about her and the Lonoffs while I lay in the dark study, transported by his praise and throbbing with resentment of my disapproving father—and, of course, overcome by what had passed between my idol and the marvelous young woman before he had manfully gone back to bed with his wife" (157). I like the phrase "drawn back into"; it is as if his own fiction had pull over him. The word "evolved" too evokes a sense of building, of maturation, of refinement.

This fiction is also motivated as much by the girl's presence as it is by Zuckerman's own experiences: his meeting with his disapproving father, his discovery that his mentor is having an affair. But when everything is taken into consideration, it is the story that lasts—the story of Anne Frank that is decidedly not the story of Anne Frank; it is the story about the effect of stories.

Nathan Englander's 2012 story works in a similar vein, but ends up ultimately wondering about the effect of stories on other people, rather than on the writer himself. Englander's work has earned comparison with Roth in the past, most notably by Sanford Pinsker, who was among the first to connect Englander's "What We Talk About" to Roth and Shalom Auslander via Anne Frank in an early review of the latter two (2013). In this review, Pinsker defines the "What if?" school of fiction as fiction that imagines alternative histories. Pinsker writes, "With regard to Anne Frank, the What if? School imagines a scenario in which Anne Frank survives the concentration camp at Bergen-Belsen and appears in America years later."[16] In fact, echoing Pinsker's language for recent alternative histories, Central Connecticut State University student Michael Leone, during a recent discussion, has said that he finds this figurative representation of Anne Frank deeply unsettling. For Leone, "Anne Frank should not be looked at from a 'what if' perspective, but how she was able to survive for that long of time. . . . This is not right to say ask 'what if Anne was able to survive or to live on?' We should honor what she did and how she was able to keep track of a number of events, while waiting for a downfall."[17] Even in this reading, it seems, students like Leone—who also align themselves with Ozick—see the value in Anne Frank not only as a voice of the Holocaust but also as a writer as well.

Like Pinsker, Michiko Kakutani compares Englander with Roth in an early review, in part because of their interest in Anne Frank. Kakutani suggests that Englander "can be as funny and outrageous as Philip Roth in describing the incongruities of modern life. The two couples in the title story, one secular and one Hasidic, sit around a kitchen table in Florida, smoking pot (filched from one woman's son) rolled up in a paper tampon wrapper."[18]

While there has been so much said about Roth's descriptions of the incongruities of modern life, little to date has been said about the impact of this new Jewish American author who appears to have very large shoes to fill following Roth's retirement. Englander has been compared with

Roth as well as with Raymond Carver—not only as a result of the obvious influence of "What We Talk About When We Talk About Love" but also "Cathedral." Writing on "What We Talk About," for example, Emily Hoffman suggests that "Englander's story is better understood as a hybrid homage that relies on elements of Carver's 'Cathedral' to execute its devastating ending. In creating this hybrid homage, Englander reverses the life-affirming conclusion of 'Cathedral.'"[19]

While I would go further about the significance of Englander's work than pointing up his representation of "the incongruities of life," I agree with Kakutani and Hoffman that Englander is both dark and comedic—a master of dialogue in the tradition of Carver and of drawing out important philosophical questions, particularly about the role of the story, in the tradition of Roth.

Englander's title alone—"What We Talk About When We Talk About Anne Frank"—pays tribute to Carver, but also delivers a philosophical question that gets to the heart of our national obsession with Anne Frank. Like the character of Deb in the story, we too seem deeply entrenched in the legacy of the Holocaust, not simply to master its memory, but also to consider how we got there and what to do to prevent a twenty-first-century genocide, considering the sudden creep of nationalism in the last several years. Now, more than ever, the threat of the extinction of a particular race is always on our minds. What would we be willing to do when fascist, racist, intolerant rules became the law of the land? I think, in many ways, that is what we wonder when we wonder about the legacy of Anne Frank. Via Englander, Anne Frank becomes the figure of philosophical and ethical discourse made possible by literary writing.

We might even go as far as to say that Englander's story asks what we talk about when we talk about Anne Frank after the 9/11 terrorist attacks, as the story reminds us repeatedly about the role of Mohammed Atta in the attacks on the Pentagon and the World Trade towers. After the 2016 election, when Donald Trump became president of the United States, Englander's story reminds us that Trump's early plan to identify all Muslim Americans feels dangerously close indeed to the origin of the Anne Frank story.

The story takes place in South Florida and is an extended conversation between two couples: one, the narrator and Deb, who live currently in Florida; and another couple, Mark and Shoshana, as the narrator calls them, Orthodox Jews who are visiting from Jerusalem. They are connected by the fact that the two women were close friends since childhood. The Florida husband narrates the story, calling into question his reliability as the story progresses from the couples' small talk over glasses of vodka and, later, hits of marijuana.

By the second page, the competitive banter of the two men escalates. The narrator is not sure whether he likes the new couple. In discussing his hosts' south Florida residence, Mark says, "'Yes, you've got it all now,'. . . . 'Even terrorists'" and later reminds them that one of the organizers of the 9/11 terrorist attacks lived in their midst: "'Wasn't Mohamed Atta living right here before 9/11?' Mark says, and now he pantomimes pointing out houses. 'Goldberg, Goldberg, Goldberg—Atta. How'd you miss him in this place?'"[20] It is with the second jab that it becomes clear that "What We Talk About" is not only a post-Holocaust story, but also a post-9/11 story—a trait shared by other recent fiction such as Jonathan Safran Foer's *Extremely Loud and Incredibly Close* and Anna Winger's *This Must Be the Place*, also written by emergent Jewish American writers.

At the heart of the story, however, is the narrator's wife's "obsession" with the Holocaust, an obsession that moves from worries over the death of the surviving generation to worries about what would happen in the case of another genocide. The narrator tells us, the readers, that "Deb is very interested in Mark's parents. They're Holocaust survivors. And Deb has what can only be called an unhealthy obsession with the idea of that generation being gone. Don't get me wrong. It's important to me, too. I care, too. All I'm saying is, there's healthy and unhealthy, and my wife, she gives this subject a lot, *a lot*, of time'" (8). The narrator does not come right out and say that Deb's obsession is unhealthy—how can worry about the loss of a generation be unhealthy?—but it does set us up for a central moment in the story: a story within the story about what constitutes proper treatment of the Holocaust.

Mark, at this point, takes over the narration; only he has access to this memory. It is about what happens when he visits the locker room of the golf club house his father belongs to. Mark notices that a man in the locker room has a camp number tattooed into his arm that is one digit away from Mark's father's camp number. He says: "That's the only difference. I mean, they're separated by two people" (10). Later in the passage, he continues:

"Around the world, surviving the unsurvivable, these two old guys end up with enough money to retire to Carmel Lake and

> play golf every day. So I say to my dad, 'He's right ahead of you,' I say. 'Look, a five,' I say. 'And yours is an eight.' And the other guy looks and my father looks, and my father says, 'All that means is, he cut ahead of me in line. There, same as here. This guy's a cutter. I just didn't want to say.' 'Blow it out your ear,' the other guy says. And that's it. Then they get back to putting on socks." (11)

The word "unsurvivable" here carries heavy weight; technically not a recognizable word, it nevertheless points up the experiential truth of the Holocaust camps. Here are two men who shouldn't have been able to survive the horror they witnessed, but they did survive nevertheless. And what remains is a kind of playful, jaded banter to undercut the trauma that echoes the banter of the two couples in a suburban Florida home.

What's more important, however, is that Mark's story gives the narrator a way to comment on his own story about the meeting between couples happening in the present time. Reclaiming the story, the narrator says:

> Deb looks crestfallen. She was expecting something empowering, some story with which to educate Trevor, to reconfirm her belief in the humanity that, from inhumanity, forms. So now she's just staring, her mouth hanging on to this thin, watery smile.
>
> But me, I love that kind of story. I'm starting to take a real shine to both these two, and not just because I'm suddenly feeling sloshed. (11)

Englander seems to be winking here at the reader who might also expect an empowering story about the Holocaust, especially if it contains the name Anne Frank in its title. Mark's story, like the narrator's and Englander's stories, does not carry the ability to empower or educate or reconfirm belief in humanity. Already, though, we know from the voice of the narrator that he is not as sentimental as his wife. That he loves this kind of uneasy story also tells us something about Englander's fiction. At first glance, we are not going to get a lesson via the figure of Anne Frank. The narrator underscores this point in case it is not already clear: "'She won't tell you, but she's a little obsessed with the Holocaust. And that story, no offense, Mark, it's not what she had in mind'" (12).

Later, Mark warns against the kinds of stories that teach Judaism only via the Holocaust. In a way, here, he too is talking to the reader about identity, history, and figuration in Holocaust literature: "'What I'm trying to say,'" he remarks, "'whether you want to take it seriously or not, is that you can't build Judaism only on the foundation of one terrible crime. It is about this obsession with the Holocaust as a necessary sign of identity. As your only educational tool. Because for the children, there is no connection otherwise. Nothing Jewish that binds'" (22). This moment, like Roth's critique of New York high society's finding comfort at the theater, offers another place to disrupt students' unquestioned affinity with Anne Frank. If you are looking for education and affirmation here, Englander's story seems to tell us, you will not find it. And yet the story does conclude with a final message that hinges crucially on the motif of Anne Frank, and it is introduced as coming-of-age stories traditionally are: "the sky darkens in an instant. It is a change so abrupt that the ladies undo their hug to watch, so sharp is the sudden change of light. . . . And then the skies open up and torrential tropical rain drops straight down, battering" (25). The change of light and the torrential rain both seem to signal a moment of cleansing and illumination—as if to foreshadow that some great insight is about to come. "Somehow," the narrator says, "we've formed a broken circle. We've started dancing our own kind of hora in the rain" (26).

The rain leads the couple to the pantry, which is stocked to the brim with food in case the family has to go into hiding, as Anne Frank and her family went into hiding. The narrator and Shoshana compare notes again about the Holocaust obsession of Deb: "'I know what you're going to say,' I tell her, and I'm honestly excited. 'The game, yes? She played that crazy game with you?'" (28). To hear Shoshana say, "It's the Anne Frank game'. . . . 'Right?" seems at once refreshing and sacrilegious (29). Games are associated with fun and leisure, yet we have a sense that what is about to unfold is not that kind of game—it is more a test of humanity that reflects a worry about where we are in the present day. Deb underscores this point when she says, "'It's not a game," and the narrator is happy to "hear her say that, as that's just what I've been trying to get her to admit for years. That it's not a game. That it's dead serious, and a kind of preparation, and an active pathology that I prefer not to indulge'" (29). What became a casual conversation among four middle-aged people has suddenly taken a very dark turn. Perhaps we were prepared for this to be a Holocaust story after all, but the narrator's casual tone has led us to take our guard down. When the narrator tries to defend his wife's interest, he says the wrong thing: "'No, it's not a game. It's just what we talk about when we talk about Anne Frank'" (29). The "just" here is the most telling word in that sentence because, in fact, there is no "just" about it.

There is nothing simple about the kind of questions the game provokes or necessitates to proceed: "'That, in the event of an American Holocaust, we sometimes talk about which of our Christian friends would hide us'" (29). Here we are very far afield from Carver, who nevertheless has his characters talk about love and death, too. The anticipation of having to go into hiding seems somehow darker and more desperate than Carver. Shoshana, perhaps unwittingly, takes the game to an entirely new level when she says: "You could play against yourselves, then. . . . What if one of you wasn't Jewish? Would you hide the other?" (31).

Once again, this story turns into a story about reading—text and other. Deb now reads her husband as we read him, and the language in front of us. Will this narrator we have come to mistrust pass the test? How does he fare in the Anne Frank game? He is ready to be studied and judged:

> I stand up straight, put my shoulders back, like maybe I'm in a lineup. I stand there with my chin raised so my wife can study me. So she can really get a look in, and get a think in, and decide if her husband really has what it takes. Would I really have the strength, would I care enough—and it is not a light question, not a throwaway question—to risk my life to save her and our son? (31)

It is not with a little relief that we come to learn the truth via his wife, Deb: "Of course," she says, without a question (31). He has what it takes. He would risk his life.

Then comes the story's climax, when Shoshana evaluates Mark according to the rules of the game:

> And you can tell Shoshana is thinking of her kids, though that's not part of the scenario. You can tell that she's changed part of the imagining. And she says, after a pause, yes, but she's not laughing. She says, yes, but to him it sounds as it does to us, so that he is now asking and asking. But wouldn't

> I? Would I hide you? Even if it was life and death—if it would spare you, and they'd kill me alone for doing it. Wouldn't I?
>
> She does not say it. And he does not say it. And from the four of us, no one will say what cannot be said—that this wife believes her husband would not hide her. What to do? What would come of it? And so we stand like that, the four of us trapped in that pantry. Afraid to open the door and let out what we've locked inside. (32)

The story ends with the two couples in the pantry, having discovered that there is one among them who has not fared well in the Anne Frank game. The knowledge that someone, maybe someone we love, would not hide us as someone hid Anne Frank is knowledge that seems too frightening to let into the world. The string of questions here for me is the most compelling part: The five repeated versions of "Wouldn't I"—but wouldn't I hide you?—are turned on the reader, too, as if to say: How would you do playing the Anne Frank game? Would the people you love hide you, too? In using the second-person "you" throughout the story and walking you through the game, the story itself becomes the Anne Frank game, and it is also a story about stories, about what we talk about when we are perpetually afraid of what the future holds. Ultimately, however, it is a story about the reparative or anti-reparative effects of stories that draw on the figure of Anne Frank.

While Roth's Zuckerman talks about fiction in terms of "the fiction I had evolved"—with a focus on the first-person "I"—Englander's story seems to serve a larger purpose, one that has to do with the self in relation to another, and the reader in relation to the text. As Pinsker has so insightfully noted, "Nathan Englander knows enough to know that Anne Frank is a ghost who haunts those who have little trouble imagining a second Holocaust and who wonder if there are any righteous Gentiles left."[21] Englander's story is haunting in the sense that it raises such questions as: What would it mean to imagine oneself as someone who would risk her life to help others in the case of a "second Holocaust"? Ida Fink's 1983 story "The Shelter" goes a step further to suggest that, rather than plan for a second Holocaust, "righteous Gentiles" would do better to work to prevent that from happening in the first place.[22] The figure of Anne Frank demands, in this twenty-first-century text, that we all engage such questions in an attempt to look from inside out, from the past to the future.

This post-9/11 story's repeated gestures to the future lead me to a final point about the evolution we may find in the figuration of Anne Frank—one that signals a new way of reading rising contemporary Jewish American writers. This evolution links the ethical imperative to a new value for the future. According to Amir Eshel, "As cultural and literary critics, we have a choice between holding on excessively to a distanced, analytical position that takes delight in judging works of art for their retrospective merits (or lack thereof) and, alternatively, recognizing in books, films, memorials, or paintings their potential for shaping our lives."[23] In reading Nathan Englander as a new voice in Jewish American literature, I also read him as asking us, to use Eshel's language, to "discover in art's engagement with modernity's recent, deeply troubling past a way to embrace contingency and take up our uncertain future" (23). Even though, for this new generation of writers exemplified by Englander, the future is indeed uncertain, it also carries with it great potential. To face the figure of Anne Frank is to face the others in our midst, to know that you—like Englander's narrator—would do the right thing even if others perhaps would not, in order to tie one's future to something larger than yourself.

Notes

1. Rita D. Jacobs, "72 Years On: The Fictional Afterlife of Anne Frank," *Signature*, August 1, 2016, http://www.signature-reads.com/2016/08/72-years-on-the-fictional-afterlife-of-anne-frank/.

2. Sanford Pinsker, "Anne Frank and the 'What If?' School of Fiction," *Sewanee Review* 122, no. 2 (2014): 340–41.

3. Barbara Kirshenblatt-Gimblett and Jeffrey Sandler, "Introduction: Anne Frank, the Phenomenon," in *Anne Frank Unbound: Media, Imagination, Memory*, ed. Barbara Kirshenblatt-Gimblett and Jeffery Sandler (Bloomington: Indiana University Press, 2012), 2.

4. Alexandra Vladimirovna Strukova, Olga Olegovna Nesmelova, and Olga Borisovna Karasik, in "Anne Frank as an Icon: Fictionalization of the Image in the Works of Literature and Visual Arts," special issue, *International Journal of Humanities and Cultural Studies* (July 2016): 651.

5. Giles Harvey, "The Fanatic," *New York Times Magazine*, June 26, 2016, 57.

6. Cynthia Ozick, "Who Owns Anne Frank?," *New Yorker*, October 6, 1997, 76. Subsequent page references to this work appear in parentheses in the text.

7. "Figure, n.," *Oxford English Dictionary*, August 2, 2016, http://www.oed.com.

8. "Figure of speech," *The Poetry Foundation*, August 2, 2016, https://www.poetryfoundation.org/resources/learning/glossary-terms/detail/figure-of-speech.

9. Walter Kalaidjian, "Figurative Language," in *Understanding Poetry* (Boston: Houghton Mifflin, 2005), 39.

10. Adam Zachary Newton, *Narrative Ethics* (Cambridge: Harvard University Press, 1999), 48, 24.

11. Cathy Caruth, *Unclaimed Experience: Trauma, Narrative and History* (Baltimore: Johns Hopkins University Press, 1996), 11, italics in original.

12. See Lily Corwin, "Exit Shoah: Amy Bellette and Fading Cultural Memory in *Exit Ghost*"; James Duban, "Guardians of Order and Declarations of Independence"; Rachael McLennan, "Enabling Fictions: Philip Roth's Prosthetic Anne Franks"; Duco van Oostrum, "A Postholocaust Jewish House of Fiction"; Sanford Pinsker, "Marrying Anne Frank: Modernist Art, the Holocaust, and Mr. Philip Roth"; and Taylor Loomis, "Nathan Zuckerman: The Tantalized and Tantalizing Hero of History." These essays share an interest in the scholarly debate over Roth's treatment of Anne Frank as survivor.

13. To date, such writers as Sophia Lehmann, Sanford Pinsker, Steven Milowitz, and Michael Rothberg remain the few scholars who have pursued this argument. See in particular Lehmann, "'And Here [Their] Troubles Began'"; Pinsker, "Jewish-American Literature's Lost and Found Department"; Milowitz, *Philip Roth Considered*; and Rothberg, "Reading Jewish."

14. Aimee Pozorski, "How to Tell a True Ghost Story: *The Ghost Writer* and the Case of Anne Frank," in *Philip Roth: New Perspectives on an American Author*, ed. Derek Parker Royal (Westport, CT: Praeger, 2005), 98.

15. Philip Roth, *The Ghost Writer* (New York: Random House, 1979), 123. Subsequent page references to this work appear in parentheses in the text.

16. Pinsker, "Anne Frank and the 'What If?' School of Fiction," 341.

17. Michael Leone, email message to author, August 8, 2016.

18. Michiko Kakutani, "Nude Rabbis and Tales of Revenge," *New York Times*, February 9, 2012, http://www.nytimes.com/2012/02/10/books/what-we-talk-about-when-we-talk-about-anne-frank-stories-by-nathan-englander.html?_r=0 Review.

19. Emily Hoffman, "The Hybrid Homage: Nathan Englander's 'What We Talk About When We Talk About Anne Frank," *Explicator* 72, no. 1 (2014): 45.

20. Nathan Englander, "What We Talk About When We Talk About Anne Frank," in *What We Talk About When We Talk About Anne Frank* (New York: Alfred A. Knopf, 2012), 2, 4. Subsequent page references to this work appear in parentheses in the text.

21. Pinsker, "Anne Frank and the 'What If?' School of Fiction," 341.

22. Ida Fink, "The Shelter," in *Scraps of Time and Other Stories*, trans. Francine Prose (Evanston, IL: Northwestern University Press, 1995).

23. Amir Eshel, *Futurity: Contemporary Literature and the Quest for the Past* (Chicago: University of Chicago Press, 2013), 22. Subsequent page references to this work appear in parentheses in the text.

References

Caruth, Cathy. *Unclaimed Experience: Trauma, Narrative, and History*. Baltimore: Johns Hopkins University Press, 1996.

Corwin, Lily. "Exit Shoah: Amy Bellette and Fading Cultural Memory in *Exit Ghost*." *Philip Roth Studies* 9, no. 2 (2013): 77–83.

Duban, James. "Guardians of Order and Declarations of Independence: Roth's *The Ghost Writer*, Hawthorne's 'My Kinsman, Major Molineux,' and the Diary of Anne Frank." *Papers On Language and Literature: A Journal for Scholars and Critics of Language and Literature* 52, no. 1 (2016): 34–62.

Englander, Nathan. "What We Talk About When We Talk About Anne Frank." In *What We Talk About When We Talk About Anne Frank*, by Nathan Englander. New York: Alfred A. Knopf, 2012.

Eshel, Amir. *Futurity: Contemporary Literature and the Quest for the Past*. Chicago: University of Chicago Press, 2013.

"Figure." OED Online. http://www.oed.com.

"Figure of Speech." *The Poetry Foundation*. https://www.poetryfoundation.org/resources/learning/glossary-terms/detail/figure-of-speech.

Fink, Ida. *Scraps of Time and Other Stories*. Translated by Francine Prose. Evanston, IL: Northwestern University Press, 1995.

Harvey, Giles. "The Fanatic." *New York Times Magazine*. June 26, 2016, 32–35; 57.

Hoffman, Emily. "The Hybrid Homage: Nathan Englander's 'What We Talk About When We Talk About Anne Frank." *Explicator* 72, no. 1 (2014): 45–48.

Jacobs, Rita D. "72 Years On: The Fictional Afterlife of Anne Frank." *Signature*, August 1 2016. http://www.signature-reads.com/2016/08/72-years-on-the-fictional-afterlife-of-anne-frank/.

Kakutani, Michiko. "Nude Rabbis and Tales of Revenge." *New York Times*, February 9, 2012. http://www.nytimes.com/2012/02/10/books/what-we-talk-about-when-we-talk-about-anne-frank-stories-by-nathan-englander.html?_r=0 Review.

Kalaidjian, Walter. *Understanding Poetry*. Boston: Houghton Mifflin, 2005.

Kirshenblatt-Gimblett, Barbara, and Jeffrey Sandler. "Introduction: Anne Frank, the Phenomenon," in *Anne Frank Unbound: Media, Imagination, Memory*, edited by Barbara Kirshenblatt-Gimblett and Jeffery Sandler, 1–24. Bloomington: Indiana University Press, 2012.

Lehmann, Sophia. "'And Here [Their] Troubles Began': The Legacy of the Holocaust in the Writing of Cynthia Ozick, Art Spiegelman, and Philip Roth." *CLIO* 28, no. 1 (1998): 29–52.

Loomis, Taylor. "Nathan Zuckerman: The Tantalized and Tantalizing Hero of History." *Philip Roth Studies* 5, no. 2 (2009): 179–88.

McLennan, Rachael. "Enabling Fictions: Philip Roth's Prosthetic Anne Franks." *Comparative American Studies: An International Journal* 7, no. 3 (2009): 253–67.

Milowitz, Steven. *Philip Roth Considered: The Concentrationary Universe of the American Writer.* New York: Garland, 2000.

Newton, Adam Zachary. *Narrative Ethics.* Cambridge: Harvard University Press, 1999.

Oostrum, Duco van. "A Postholocaust Jewish House of Fiction: Anne Frank's *Het Achterhuis (The Diary of a Young Girl)* in Philip Roth's *The Ghostwriter.*" *Yiddish* 9, nos. 3–4 (1994): 61–75.

Ozick, Cynthia. "Who Owns Anne Frank?" *New Yorker.* October 6, 1997, 76–87.

Pinsker, Sanford. "Anne Frank and the 'What If?' School of Fiction." *Sewanee Review* 122, no. 2 (2014): 340–44.

———. "Jewish American Literature's Lost and Found Department: How Philip Roth and Cynthia Ozick Reimagine Their Significant Dead." *Modern Fiction Studies* 35, no. 2 (1989): 223–35.

———. "Marrying Anne Frank: Modernist Art, the Holocaust, and Mr. Philip Roth." In *Literature, the Arts, and the Holocaust,* by Sanford Pinsker and edited by Jack S. Fischel (Greenwood, FL: Penkevill, 1987.

Pozorski, Aimee "How to Tell a True Ghost Story: *The Ghost Writer* and the Case of Anne Frank," in *Philip Roth: New Perspectives on an American Author,* edited by Derek Parker Royal, 89–102. Westport, CT: Praeger, 2005.

Roth, Philip. *The Ghost Writer.* New York: Random House, 1979.

Rothberg, Michael. "Reading Jewish: Philip Roth, Art Spiegelman, and Holocaust Postmemory." In *Traumatic Realism: The Demands of Holocaust Representation,* by Michael Rothberg, 187–220. Minneapolis: University of Minnesota Press, 2000.

Strukova, Alexandra Vladimirovna, Olga Olegovna Nesmelova, and Olga Borisovna Karasik. In "Anne Frank as an Icon: Fictionalization of the Image in the Works of Literature and Visual Arts." Special issue, *International Journal of Humanities and Cultural Studies* (July 2016): 651–57.

10

Nathan Englander's "Anne Frank" and the Future of Jewish America

Hilene Flanzbaum

The wordy and colloquial title of Nathan Englander's 2011 story "What We Talk About When We Talk About Anne Frank" unabashedly mimics a classic of late twentieth–century American literature: "What We Talk About When We Talk About Love," Raymond Carver's 1981 masterpiece. A story widely anthologized and taught, "Love" appears again and again in classrooms where students read American literature, learn about the short-story genre, or practice the craft of fiction writing. For fledgling creative writers, the story models valuable tools of the trade: clean, clear prose in a "Hemingway-esque" fashion (which Carver repopularized), spare but effective scene setting, and hyperreal dialogue. In literature classes, "Love" easily leads to a conversation about the students' favorite subject: relationships. As a graduate student in fiction at the Iowa Writing Workshops in the nineties, Englander was no doubt weaned on this story. It seems likely that he teaches it to his own students. His own story "Frank" has some of the same virtues; yet for teachers of Jewish-American and Holocaust Literature (JAHLIT), it also offers a lot more. In just thirty-two pages, Englander rounds up a host of hot-button topics in Jewish-American life and culture.[1] His short but profound text might well introduce a class to the contemporary state of Jewish-American identity—and thereby invoke the complicated and controversial topics of Holocaust representation, ethnicity, religious practice, and the state of Israel. Moreover, discussion of "Frank" easily encourages broader applications about hyphenate identity in the United States. For the teacher of JAHLIT, Englander's story triggers an avalanche of provocative questions that could engage a class for weeks, or perhaps months. Further, the writer shows little interest in resolving the problems he presents. In the tradition of Talmud, a serious reading of the text demands that the students ask important questions . . . and then argue about the answers.

With the title itself, Englander launches the opening salvo. By taking Carver as his literary forbearer, rather than Shalom Aleichem or Amos Oz, Englander claims "American" as his primary identity. In fact, his adoption and slight alteration of Carver's title might well be compared to how the adjective "Jewish" modifies the noun "American." Such a declaration does not signal Englander's patriotism (though he may well be patriotic); instead, it clarifies his subject position. Everything you are about to read, Englander warns, every controversial claim that he is about to examine, comes through an American lens. While the reader can never assume that author and narrator speak with the same voice, in this case the two *do* share a national identity: both had an American education; they studied Abraham Lincoln in history class, not Golda Meir. They both live under the laws of the United States Constitution and not the Hebrew Bible. Before we read a word of his story, Englander's invocation of a great American short-story writer demands that we reexamine the very term "Jewish-American."[2]

Because twenty-first-century students have been inundated by issues of identity politics and are asked to struggle with radical injustices, racism, colonialism and trauma, an investigation of where ethnicity or race or religion intersects with American identity can prove invaluable. Rather than a scorching treatise on civil rights or discrimination, Englander's story proves so useful because it scrutinizes the terms on which identity is based. "Frank" ultimately strips Jewish identity claims to their barest bones. In the counterfactual "game" the characters play at the end of the story, they have to decide whether or not people they know, or they themselves, could have hidden Anne Frank. This final narrative crisis lends itself to a discussion of what makes us human, instead of Jewish or American or Hindu or French. Like the Carver story, "Frank" ultimately leaves the reader asking, "What makes us human?"

In the setup of the story as well, Englander follows Carver. In both, two middle-aged couples leisurely sit around a table in a quiet suburban backyard, getting progressively more drunk and stoned, and sharing conversation that grows uncomfortably intense. In terms of subject matter, however, the stories go their separate ways. While in one, the couples argue about what "love" really means, in the other, the conversation circles around what it means to be Jewish. While most of us, going all the way back to Plato, would agree that the definition of love is hard to pin down, Englander takes a more controversial leap when he assumes that "what it means to be Jewish" is equally debatable. And while theologians and scholars may be familiar with such squabbles, most students, including Jewish students, will not be. Rather, they will be surprised to learn that this particular question—"Who is Jewish?"—has animated debate for thousands of years and remains critical in 2016. In the secular world, if not the Hasidic one, Jewish identification can include widely divergent practices and beliefs. If the end of the Carver story reveals that we have no idea what we say when we say we "love" someone, the Englander story reveals that we are similarly confused when we say we are "Jewish." That such a controversial discussion takes place in the shadow of Anne Frank, and by extension the Holocaust and its memory, raises the stakes substantially; with this connection, Englander tells us that such definitions are not merely semantic, but can acquire deadly consequences.

Talking about the Holocaust

In the title of the story itself, Englander shows irreverence toward an event once deemed both too recondite and too holy for irony or fiction.[3] Yet in 2011 in southern Florida, the setting of "Frank," the Holocaust is neither hidden nor holy. In fact, the narrator believes, as many people do, that the Holocaust is everywhere, and Jewish-Americans have been oversaturated with information. "She's a little obsessed with the Holocaust," says the narrator, describing his wife Deb, a Jew from New York:

> It's like she's a survivor's kid, my wife. It's crazy the education they give them. Her grandparents were all born in the Bronx, and here we are twenty minutes from downtown Miami but it's like it's 1937 and we live on the edge of Berlin. (12)

To the narrator, Deb's obsession with the Holocaust is unnatural; and it is quite possible that Englander shares his narrator's indignation here. On the other hand, as the story progresses, it becomes clear that the narrator is *himself* obsessed with his wife's so-called obsession. "'Don't get me wrong. I mean, I care too,'" he says, "'but there's healthy and unhealthy'" (8). While Deb often tries to turn the conversation to more cheerful topics, the narrator won't let the Holocaust drop. He demonstrates a strong wish—perhaps even a need—to talk about the historical past with the Israeli couple visiting their home. Holocaust fever, Englander suggests, is difficult to avoid, for American Jews—including those with moral reservations about such voyeurism.

As *Sophie's Choice, Schindler's List, Life Is Beautiful, The Grey Zone, The Pianist, Defiance,* and dozens of other movies; and thousands of books, both documentary and fictional, including Wiesel's *Night* as an Oprah selection, attest, the narrator is right: the Holocaust is everywhere. Well documented, the American love affair with the Holocaust shows no signs of letting up. Controversial Jewish-American writers, including Peter Novick and Norman Finklestein, have argued that the Holocaust has come to occupy a destructive place in Jewish-American culture. Critics have often been made nervous by such arguments, which, they argue, can lapse all too easily into anti-Semitism—or provide fodder for anti-Semites.[4] Your students, however, might agree with the narrator here. Holocaust education has indeed become ubiquitous. Whether or not it is *too* visible (i.e., whether our obsession is, in the narrator's terms, "unhealthy") remains a matter of debate. In any case, personal experience and fellow teachers' anecdotes confirm that students do know quite a bit.

This familiarity, or overfamiliarity, with the Holocaust is a relatively recent historical development. When I began teaching Holocaust literature in 1992, classroom conversation did not get very far—at least in terms of "literature." Students just had too many questions about what actually happened. Sometimes I felt more like a historian or sociologist than a critic. When we discussed D. M. Thomas's *The White Hotel*, we spent more time on Babi Yar than on poetry, dreams, or Freud. For class sessions on *Survival in Auschwitz*, it was necessary to cover both the Italian Resistance and the actual conditions at the concentration camps—which left little time to analyze Primo Levi's detached, scientific language. Shock, curiosity, and astonishment were as far as my students could get. And, of course, those emotions were entirely justified.

The gap between what my students knew even ten years ago and what they know now is as wide as an ocean. Those who have worked hard to make the Holocaust known must feel a great sense of accomplishment. Students certainly know "what happened"; they have seen *The Pianist* and read *Night* in middle school and *Survival in Auschwitz* in Humanities I. And they know more imaginative renderings as well: as children, they may have encountered *The Boy in the Striped Pajamas* or *Number the Stars*.[5] A good many students, even those from Indiana, have visited the Holocaust Museum (which opened in 1993), and they remember the piles of hair and shoes. Of course, most students will have read the quintessential symbol of Holocaust education, *The Diary of Anne Frank* (which is sometimes assigned as early as the fifth grade); some will have seen a stage play version (or even performed in it).[6] And some students are already fatigued. "Not this again," they say, my husband, a high school teacher, reports.[7] Those who don't turn away may become like the narrator's wife: "unhealthily" obsessed with all things Holocaust (although Deb's particular fascination is with survivors).

Students will be surprised to learn that in the first three decades after the war, survivors who lived in the United States and elsewhere were virtually invisible. How Holocaust survivors evolved from the Sol Nazerman of *Pawnbroker* fame—a man who lived on the margins, repressed his memories, and was virtually forgotten by his children—to become classroom and synagogue celebrities is a wonderful example of the changing phenomenon of the Holocaust.[8] Our students no doubt believe, as Deb does, that survivors are like saints on earth, symbols of endurance, even miracles. Englander does a masterful job of skewering these attitudes.

In Englander's story, the Israeli character Mark, the child of survivors, has a much more realistic view.[9] When Deb inquires about his parents, Mark replies resignedly, "What can I say? My mother's a very sick woman" (8). Perhaps the darkest and most surprising moment in "Frank" comes when Mark relates an anecdote about waiting for his father to change his clothes in a locker room at a golf club, where another elderly man appears:

> And I see, while I'm waiting, and I can't believe it—I nearly pass out. The guy next to him, the number on his arm, it's three before my father's number. You know, in sequence . . .
> I mean the number tattooed. It's the same as my father's camp number, digit for digit, but my father's ends in an eight.

And this guy's, it ends in a five.... And to my father I say, "Do you know this gentleman? Have you two met? I'd really like to introduce you, if you haven't." And they look each other over for what, I promise you, is minutes. Actual minutes. It is—with kavod I say this, with respect for my father—but it is like watching a pair of big beige manatees sitting on a bench, each with one sock on. They're just looking each other up and down, everything slow. And then my father says, "I seen him. Seen him around." The other guy, he says, "Yes, I've seen." "You're both survivors," I tell them. "Look. The numbers." And they look. "They're the same," I say.... "He's right ahead of you. Look, a five," I say. "And yours is an eight." And my father says, "All that means is he cut ahead of me in line.'" (4)

We look to survivors for stories of affirmation and empowerment. But this excerpt reveals that survivors shun such narratives. Mark's parents don't feel powerful; they are old and sick and cranky. The narrator reports that Deb is "crestfallen" by Mark's anecdote (a reading of her facial expression, which she, significantly, disputes). According to the narrator, Deb does not want to hear this kind of Holocaust story, which has the rhythm of a vaudeville joke. If we accept the narrator's take on the situation, that means that Deb, like other Americans, is more interested in Hollywood versions of the genocide, which focus on righteous Gentiles and happy endings. This "sugarcoating" of the Holocaust, as Alvin Rosenfeld calls it, is one of the consequences of Americanization.[10]

As for Anne Frank, however, her saintliness remains intact. As a metaphor for unfair persecution and senseless death, her name is still useful.[11] Whether they are annoyed or obsessed, know too much or too little, students recognize Anne Frank as a heroine and understand that she is conventionally paid homage as a universal symbol of victimhood. In the lower grades, study of Anne Frank is often tied to a more universal discussion of prejudice and oppression. This "universalization" of the Anne Frank mythos was recently dramatized in the film *Freedom Writers*, where a teacher uses the *Diary* to teach her inner-city students that they can rise above persecution.[12] Several students have recounted to me a classroom exercise they did in middle school to experience persecution "first-hand" during which students with brown eyes were given privileges that students with blue eyes did not get.

As long as the *Diary* has been taught, teachers have been drawing these kind of connections to contemporary issues. Until recently, this pedagogical practice was at odds with the outlook of scholars, who insisted upon the specificity and incomparability of the Nazi-administered genocide.[13] For the first quarter-century after World War II, it was sacrilege among scholars to say that the Holocaust was like anything but itself—a restriction known as "the uniqueness" argument. It is notable that such thinking has all but disappeared except among the most conservative of cultural critics. For as time went on—as the historical narrative solidified, while genocides continued to be carried out—how could anyone make an argument for the continuation of Holocaust education if its message could not be applied to more contemporary injustices? Ironically, what was so obvious to teachers in the lower grades from the start eventually reached scholars at the highest rung of education. This is precisely the tactic of contemporary scholars like Michael Rothberg, whose much praised book *Multi-Directional Memory* charts the Holocaust's relevance to other atrocities. More and more, Holocaust studies appears inside a newly born discipline in the humanities, "trauma studies," where it is often recognized as being formative.[14] Like other scholars writing now, Rothberg recognizes that the memory of the Holocaust will inevitably fade if we fail to draw connections between what happened in twentieth-century Europe and what is still going on around the world. Englander is precisely on this message when he ends the story as he does: indeed, the crisis is no longer about Jews or even the Holocaust but about the limits of humanity, a subject addressed shortly.

For too long, the discussion surrounding the Holocaust and higher education has been immune to the commonsense notion that what we need to do in the classroom *this semester* differs from what we needed to do twenty-five years ago. Once the "multidirectionality" of the Holocaust takes the place of the uniqueness doctrine, educators will have license to adapt to the present. In fact, to historicize the Holocaust—as I have suggested one might do with "survivors"—can be extraordinarily productive with respect to Anne Frank. For instance, your students will be shocked to learn that for the original stage play, the producers—who were Jewish—would not permit the characters to be labeled as such. Most Americans of the 1950s, they wagered, would have trouble identifying with Jews.

It is possible that the producers overestimated the xenophobia of their audience. On the other hand, such reluctance to talk about hyphenate identity typified American culture in the forties and fifties—a fact that may astonish students who are coming of age in educational settings where multiculturalism, gender politics, and diversity studies have long been firmly embraced. That Anne Frank was Jewish and that the Holocaust primarily "happened" to Jewish people they are well aware. In fact, in Indiana, where I teach, that may well be all they know about Jews. I have had several students who did not even know that Jews lived in the contemporary era, instead viewing them as another conquered tribe of history. Those who teach in one of the seven cities where 98 percent of the United States' Jewish population live—New York; Los Angeles; Miami; Philadelphia; Chicago; Washington, DC; and Boston—will not find students who have such misconceptions.

Before we leave Anne Frank, we should make one more stop for those interested in the continuity of Jewish-American literature. An earlier invocation of Frank's ghost appears in 1979, when Philip Roth first played fast and loose with Frank's sainthood. In *The Ghost Writer*, the young novelist Nathan Zuckerman boards at the home of his mentor, E. I. Lonoff (perhaps a version of I. B. Singer or Henry Roth—or some other Jewish literary ancestor). A female student is also staying with Lonoff, and Zuckerman imagines that she is Frank herself. Night after night, lying in bed, Zuckerman imagines seducing this young woman, one of the most inspirational figures of the twentieth century.[15] A further benefit of marrying her, Zuckerman imagines, would be to get him out of the doghouse with the Jewish-American community, which was appalled by his earlier novel (an allusion to Roth's own scandalous *Portnoy's Complaint*). Thus Roth becomes the first to make the observation that weakening ties to Judaism and Jewish identity can be fortified by finding a connection to the Holocaust. Because Roth portrays Zuckerman's fantasy as immature and comic, he demonstrates the absurdity of fetishizing real-life tragedy. Roth is among the first to scrutinize how desperately Jewish-Americans have clung to images and memories of the Holocaust as some sort of anchor to Jewishness—a subject that is still urgent for Englander, forty years later.

II. What We Talk About When We Talk About Being Jewish?

When tackling this question, those of us fortunate enough to be teaching in the "seven cities" where students have likely seen many varieties of Jewish experience will have fewer hurdles than those of us in the Diaspora. The uninitiated may wonder why there is any controversy about this at all, assuming that Jewish people are those who practice the religion; or conversely, they might believe that Jewishness is a race, that one is "born" Jewish. It is even more likely that they have not given the matter much thought at all, believing simply that people are Jewish if they say they are. So non-Jewish students may be surprised by the controversy that takes up a good deal of "Frank." As for your Jewish students, they may know enough to be already confused—a confusion that Englander readily exploits. For the fact is that a good many people who say they are Jewish cannot say exactly why. In a 2013 study, Jews cited a range of personal attributes as "essentials of Jewish identity," including remembering the Holocaust, caring about Israel, having a sense of humor, observing Jewish laws, and eating Jewish foods.[16] Englander, who knows that finding a seamless definition of what it means to be Jewish can be frustrating, gleefully opens this can of worms.

In "Frank," Englander presents polarized forms of Jewish experience: Hasidism, the most orthodox, versus the narrator's and his wife's secularism. Additionally complicated is that each couple has disdain for the other's brand of Judaism, though Mark is more vocal about his discomfort with secular Jews than the narrator is about his alienation from the ultra-religious. Nonetheless, the reader has access to the narrator's thoughts and thus reads a barrage of criticism. After confessing that he has turned his once-Orthodox wife secular, he tells the reader that

> Lauren met Mark and they went off to the Holy Land and shifted from Orthodox to ultra-Orthodox, which to me sounds like a repackaged detergent—ORTHODOX ULTRA, now with more deep-healing power. (4)

The narrator has no shortage of skepticism toward Hasidic practice. His censure is clearest when observing how this sect polices the relationships between men and women. Not only is Mark "in charge" of Lauren, but "neither of them will put a hand on the other in public . . . Not to put out a fire" (page). The narrator's perturbation here illustrates what he holds most dear. What *he* believes in, so to speak, is the sanctity of his relationship with his wife—a motif continued throughout the story and no doubt familiar to our students and most Americans. And yet the story would be weaker if it were clear that the narrator is right and Mark is wrong. Fortunately, Englander complicates the discussion. Secular readers may agree with the narrator that the Hasidic laws that restrict sexual behavior are archaic and ridiculous, but the discussion does not end there. Ultimately, the debate focuses on the future of Judaism: Will it even continue to exist if left to Jews like our narrator?

First, Englander asks readers to consider the doctrine of matrilineal descent that held sway for almost five thousand years, but today seems operative only in the most Orthodox of communities. As Mark says to Deb, "Because you're Jewish, your son is, he is as Jewish as me. No more, no less" (24). But such pronouncements little satisfy contemporary readers, who, unless they are themselves Orthodox, will not automatically accept Orthodox beliefs. On a philosophical level, the contemporary reader may have additional objections. Are we prepared to say that Jewish identity is conferred by genetics? To do so aligns us with the kind of racialist thinking central to Nazi ideology and other types of barbaric tribalism. With any luck, students will balk at such a suggestion, as it invokes a biological essentialism that they have been trained to reject because it leads to bigotry and racism on a wider scale. An enlightened student might suggest, as Mark eventually and paradoxically does, that Jewishness is not "genetic" but a religion, and that therefore those who practice Jewish rituals are Jewish.

This is a practical solution to the question "Who's Jewish?" Yet to leave it there ignores the ethnic history of Jews in the United States. For the better part of the twentieth century, a prominent majority of Jews defined their Jewish identity as "ethnic" through behaviors that were not traditionally seen as "American." What they ate, how they talked, what they wore, what they valued—it all signaled "other." Even as synagogue attendance diminished, Jewish ethnicity was a lively and meaningful category of difference.[17] There is a reasonable explanation for this, of course. Approximately 85 percent of Jews in the United States could trace their roots back to Eastern Europe. Thus, what we think of as "Jewish-American" culture is in fact derived not from scripture or genetics, but from a specific geographic region with a specific history. Food that is seen as generically "Jewish," such as borscht and blintzes, was in fact made popular in the United States by Eastern European Jewish immigrants. Likewise, the Jewish taste for self-deprecating and dark humor is derived from the historical experience of discrimination and pogroms—not from any religious doctrine, much less from DNA.

Even if one could firmly grasp what it means to be ethnically Jewish, these behaviors do not endure beyond the third generation. Deb does not say she is ethnically Jewish, but uses a term with which your students will be more familiar: she says she is still "culturally" Jewish—a descriptor that many Jewish-Americans might accept. Mark, of course, points out the flaws in such designations:

> Judaism is a religion. And with religion comes ritual. Culture is nothing. Culture is some construction of the modern world. It is not fixed; it is ever changing, and a weak way to bind generations. It's like taking two pieces of metal, and instead of making a nice weld you hold them together with glue. (22)

This feels like a cogent piece of analysis from Mark, and like the narrator, we can occasionally sympathize with him. Even some of Mark's most offensive comments have a ring of truth. He explains:

> Our concern is not the past Holocaust. It is the current one. The one that takes more than fifty per cent of the Jews of this generation. Our concern is intermarriage. It's the Holocaust that's happening now. You don't need to be worrying about some Mormons doing hocus-pocus on the murdered six million. You need to worry that your son marries a Jew.
> "Oh my God," Deb says. "Are you calling intermarriage a Holocaust?" (24).

While to do so is obviously wrong-headed in half a dozen ways, Mark is not alone when he worries about the "vanishing Jews" of America. In 2009, the Israeli government spent $800,000 on an advertising campaign about the threat posed by foreign Jews who choose to marry non-Jews. Israeli citizens were encouraged to call a hotline, which would help them to connect their endangered foreign friends to government programs that subsidized visits to Israel. "Together, we will strengthen their connection to Israel, so that we don't lose them," promised a television ad, rather ominously.[18] In the 1970s and 1980s, a weaker form of coaxing, sponsored by the United Jewish Appeal, appeared on ads in American subway cars and on billboards along suburban highways: "If you are Jewish, there is only a 25% chance that your grandchildren will be."

Here is another rich opportunity to broaden discussion of the story. This experienced teacher of ethnic studies is no doubt thinking about Werner Sollors's theories of consent versus descent, which, arguably, is at the heart of "Frank." Using Sollors's framework, one can usefully compare the experience of Jewish-Americans with those of other hyphenate groups—both more and less imperiled. In 2016, for instance, the students who identify as Irish-American make a choice they are in control of and incur no costs in doing so, though one could find a time when this was not so—a historical phenomenon worth exploring in class. Of course, many ethnic and religious groups in the United States have no choice whether to self-identify or not: Hijabs identify some Muslim women immediately; and Somalis, Mungs, and Haitians are visibly different and are therefore subject to prejudice.[19] In the twenty-first-century United States, people of Jewish descent can choose to live a Jewish life or to practice Judaism; they can also choose not to. Someone who wears the uniform of the Hasidim makes a choice to identify with the religion and to make that identity clear to others. For Mark, such a getup is not, in Herbert J. Gans's lexicon, "cost-free," but it is his choice.[20] For other immigrant groups, difference is not a choice, because it is immediately apparent, and it comes with a ready-made set of assumptions, most of them negative. Englander's narrator is not visibly different, nor does the theory of descent hold much power for him. What he "consents" to about his Jewish identity is left ambiguous by Englander. With the exception of the narrator's acknowledgement that he knows what Sukkot is, we know nothing of his background or beliefs. One might rightly ask: Why do we think the narrator is Jewish at all? Without any traces of ethnicity, without reliving the Holocaust, without embracing the theory of matrilineal descent, without attendance at synagogue or the observance of Shabbat—why should we agree that he, or anyone else like him, *is* Jewish? In the United States, what sustains Jewish identity at all?

To some degree, this concern has been answered by the Jewish-American embrace of Israel. Indeed, given the climate on today's campuses, this is the biggest can of worms Englander opens. Take a deep breath before opening. In 2016, a classroom discussion about the Jewish state is surely the one most likely to go off the rails. While students may know little about sects of Judaism or twentieth-century Jewish-American life and culture, they may still have an opinion about Israel. The unpopularity of Israeli politics and Israel itself need not be recapitulated here, for most of us are living it. For whatever reasons, just or unjust, many of our students and colleagues view Israel as an oppressive imperialist force. Englander may think so too, but that is not *all* he thinks. Subtly rendered, the argument about Israel in "Frank" leads to a harsh indictment of the United States.

Lest anyone question whether Israel is really on Englander's mind, I remind the reader that it makes an appearance in the very first line of the story, as the narrator observes: "Two minutes in the door and we are already arguing about the Israeli occupation" (3). The dissection of that sentence alone could take some class time. "The Israeli occupation" in this story is double-edged, because it could also refer to the "occupation" of the narrator's house by the Israeli couple. Additionally, Englander has some fun escalating the "talk about" in the title to "arguing about." We expect a Carver-esque suburban vignette, but right away we are thrown into the most intractable geopolitical conflict on the planet.

In the word "occupation" itself (as opposed to something like "nation" or "settlement"), Englander makes the narrator's position clear. Although the argument is not staged within the body of the story, we have a pretty good idea of what was said. If we have been sentient beings at any time since the Yom Kippur War, we get it. In the last ten years, as the Israeli government has continued to authorize settlements on the West Bank (territory won through warfare), the so-called "occupation" has been viewed by some as illegal and immoral at best, and at worst as vicious and imperialist. We can assume that the narrator's position falls somewhere therein. We can also assume that Mark staunchly defends Israel's colonization of the West Bank by virtue of "Israel's right of return," a doctrine originating in biblical times.

Englander only alludes to this familiar conflict—its pieces are too often the source of heated and irrational argument—to raise a peripheral issue: in these issues of imperialism and capitalist expansion, Israel only takes after its model and benefactor, the United States. "You *do* have what we have," the narrator tells Mark, referring to similarities between Israel and Florida: "All of it, sun and palm trees. Old Jews and oranges and the worst drivers around" (3). Mark agrees. "And yet," he says, "look at all this space . . . Space upon space'" (4). What Israel continues to fight for is only what the United States fought for in earlier centuries. Indeed, the sprawling lands of the United States were also obtained as the spoils of war and give Americans a freedom of space that Israelis, at least so far, have not enjoyed. In their high school classrooms, students were probably not taught that their own country was an imperialist monster or that "manifest destiny" was American chauvinism, though more politically minded (or "woke") students probably think so now.

And if they don't, it may be worth talking about the Mexican-American War or the Battle of Wounded Knee. Certainly Americans know that building a great nation does not include ceding land.

One salient distinction between the two nations, however, Englander makes clear. According to Mark, at least, Israel has kept Judaism alive. He issues a diatribe about the deleterious effects of American life: "In Jerusalem we don't need to busy ourselves with symbolic efforts to keep our memories in place. Because we live exactly as our parents lived before the war. And this serves us in all things, in our relationships, too, in our marriages and parenting" (23). The narrator does not seem entirely resistant to Mark's argument, yet he also has serious reservations about both Israel and Hasidism. In one interpretation, the story could be understood to be about the conflict the narrator feels between his liberal values, with regard to gender especially, and his desire to live a more stable, traditional, devout existence. The narrator *agrees* with Mark's claim that secular American society is incoherent ("glued," not "welded") and he sees the attractions of Hasidism. But he cannot accept the entrenched male-female hierarchies of this fundamentalist sect. Ultimately, the story will call into question Mark's claim that "liv[ing] exactly as our parents lived" leads to stronger marriages.

Of course, anyone familiar with Judaism knows that Hasidism and secularism are the furthest distances apart and that the narrator could choose a more moderate way: why not be a Reform, Conservative, or Orthodox Jew? These modifications to ultra-Orthodoxy, one could argue, have managed to keep Judaism alive; or one might conversely argue that such alterations of strict religious law begin the slippery slope toward complete secularism.[21] Maybe, but the point is moot. Englander's concern that the ability to live a Jewish life, to maintain the rituals of the religion, and to feel "ethnically" Jewish are jeopardized by living in the United States. It is not a new claim, though in the early twenty-first century it may have been acquiring increased urgency. If students have a background in Jewish-American literature, they have been well versed in the crushing pressures of assimilation, even if they themselves cannot recognize how their own histories have been affected by such.

IV. Ground Zero

At its conclusion, "Frank" expands and deepens the philosophical crisis its author has been courting all along. If the narrator remains watchful and undecided about many of these issues, the final gesture of the story will compound the reader's confusion.

"So would I hide you?" Mark asks his wife, who has adopted the Hasidic name Shoshana "Would I, Shoshi?" (32). And although these two couples are playing the "Anne Frank" game, suddenly the story is no longer about Anne Frank, the Holocaust, or being Jewish; rather, the question cuts to the very essence of humanity. In the event that you were being mercilessly hunted by mechanistic state-sanctioned forces, who would hide you? And, conversely, at the risk of your own life and family, whom would you hide? To our students, born at least half a century after World War II, such scenarios may seem more the stuff of nightmares or real life.

Most important, for students of any religion, race, or ethnicity, it is exactly the place where any discussion of the Holocaust should lead. Englander has structured the story in such a way that all questions of religious identity pale when juxtaposed with this existential one: *What would you have done, and how can you be sure? What laws would you break to do the right thing? What discomforts would you endure to give food and shelter to a political refugee? And what are you doing now about similar situations?* The discussion can thus broaden to include Huck Finn's "crimes" in literature as well as actual crises: from the unlawful riots of 1968, to the "pro-life" movement, to Black Lives Matter—all are pertinent to a discussion of the responsibilities of individual conscience and its vexed relationship to the will of the majority and the mechanistic forces of national governments.

As for the future of Judaism, here too students can speculate. Englander has toppled familiar touchstones. Might he be suggesting that new, more authentic connections to the ancient religion be found—those that are neither sexist nor chauvinistic? Or does the story imply that religion in any form supplies little sustenance? After all, the characters' joy is found through alcohol and marijuana, not religious experience. I do not yet have the answer to this question, and I have found no better teaching strategy than telling my students that. What I cannot tell my students, I can ask them. For them and for me, these types of discussions are always the most rewarding.

Notes

I would like to thank my research assistant, Melissa Tuckman, PhD, Princeton University, 2017.

1. "What We Talk About When We Talk about Anne Frank" first appeared in *The New Yorker* (December 12, 2011), 1–32; a year later in Tom Perrotta, ed., *The Best American Short Stories* (Boston: Houghton Mifflen Harcourt, 2012), 40–60; and as the title story in Englander's collection (New York: Alfred A. Knopf, 2012). Internal citations refer to the collection.

2. Because Englander was raised in an Orthodox family, it is safe to assume that he also had a rigorous religious education—not something we can assume about the imaginary narrator.

3. Claude Lanzmann, who directed *Shoah*, has reflected on the inherent difficulty, and perhaps the impossibility, of faithfully representing the Holocaust. Regarding Steven Spielberg's *Schindler's List*, he once wrote: "The holocaust is unique in that, with a circle of fire, it builds a border around itself, which one cannot transgress, because a certain absolute kind of horror cannot be conveyed. To pretend that one is nevertheless conveying it makes one guilty of an offence of the utmost rudeness. Fiction is a transgression, I am deeply convinced that there is a ban on depiction." A translation of Lanzmann's essay by Rob van Gerwen can be found at http://www.phil.uu.nl/~rob/2007/hum291/lanzmannschindler.shtml. On the other hand, Lanzmann has also been forthright about the way he used artifice in *Shoah*, which he has referred to as "a fiction of the real." Richard Brody, "Witness: Claude Lanzmann on the Making of Shoah," *New Yorker*, March 19, 2012.

4. Novick's *The Holocaust in American Life* (Boston: Mariner Books, 1999) documents how, in the decades following World War II, the Holocaust was transformed from a historical event into a cultural myth, amenable to certain American political agendas. In *The Holocaust Industry: Reflections on the Exploitation of Jewish Suffering* (London: Verso, 2000), Finkelstein raises similar concerns while pointing out that those who write critically about the Holocaust are in danger of being slandered as Holocaust deniers. Reviewers attacked both authors for their tone and line of argumentation. Writing in the *New York Times*, Michiko Kakutani accused Novick of "deliberate cynicism" and glibness. In the same newspaper, Omer Bartov noted with horror a resemblance between Finkelstein's argument and the rantings of those who believe in a global Jewish conspiracy. See Michiko Kakutani, "The Holocaust in American Life: Taking Aim at the Symbolism of the Holocaust." *New York Times*, August 17, 1999; Omer Bartov, "A Tale of Two Holocausts, *New York Times*, August 6, 2000.

5. John Boyne, *The Boy in the Striped Pajamas* (Oxford: David Fickling Books, 2006); Lois Lowry, *Number the Stars* (Boston: Houghton Mifflin Books for Children, 1989).

6. Anne Frank's diary, often published under the title *Diary of a Young Girl*, has been translated into more than sixty-five languages and published in hundreds of editions. More than thirty million copies have been sold. It is probably one of the most widely read books in the world and has been adapted

into virtually every art form, from movies to stage musicals to operas. It was added to the UNESCO Memory of the World Register in 2009. For more on the diary's publication history and influence, see Barbara Kirshenblatt-Gimblett and Jeffrey Shandler, eds., *Anne Frank Unbound: Media, Imagination, Memory* (Bloomington: Indiana University Press, 2012).

7. And, of course, the uniqueness argument, so imperative to earlier discussions of the Holocaust, is no longer even desirable to make, for reasons we discuss shortly.

8. In terms of the Americanization of the Holocaust, there may be no more fascinating history than that of survivors. A particularly good source is Henry Greenspan, *On Listening to Holocaust Survivors: Beyond Testimony* (Saint Paul: Paragon House, 2010).

9. For a more realistic treatment of survivors by their offspring, I refer the reader to Melvin Bukiet's *Stories of an Imaginary Childhood* (Madison: University of Wisconsin Press, 2002); or to Art Spiegelman's *The Complete Maus* (New York: Pantheon, 1996).

10. Alvin H. Rosenfeld, *The End of the Holocaust* (Bloomington: Indiana University Press, 2011).

11. According to its website, the Anne Frank House still draws more than a million visitors a year. The *Diary* is still in print and selling briskly after seventy years. Nicholas Kristof's recent op-ed in *The New York Times*, "Anne Frank Today Is a Syrian Girl," has been reposted more than 100,000 times on Facebook. The piece was originally published on August 25, 2016.

12. In *Freedom Writers* (Paramount, 2007), a teacher at an inner-city school teaches her students about the Holocaust as an indirect way of addressing local racial tensions and a climate of violence. Anne Frank becomes an important point of reference in the classroom. Frank's famous words "In spite of everything, I still believe people are good at heart" are often remembered, despite the fact that her estimate of human morality may well have changed after her experience in the concentration camps. Carol Ann Rittner reports on a visit by Frank's best friend, Hannah Pick, to Stockton College in 1996, where she was asked by a student, "If Anne Frank had survived, would she still believe people were good at heart?" Pick replied, "No." Carol Ann Rittner, *Anne Frank in the World: Essays and Reflections* (New York: Routledge, 2016).

13. For instance, the construction of the Holocaust Museum stalled for a decade as scholars fought over whether the Holocaust should be represented as a unique event or made pertinent to other worldwide oppressions. Elie Wiesel resigned from the commission when it eventually decided that the Museum would take a more universal approach.

14. For an investigation of the Holocaust as the mother of Trauma Studies, see Robert Eaglestone, *Postmodernism and the Holocaust* (London: Oxford University Press, 2005).

15. Roth, Philip, *The Ghost Writer* (New York: Vintage International, 1995).

16. *A Portrait of Jewish Americans* (Pew Research Center, 2013), 57.

17. There are approximately 6.8 million Jews in the United States, 2.2 percent of the general population, with 22 percent describing themselves as having no religion. Approximately one-quarter of Jews said religion is very important to their lives. Fewer than a third of American Jews reported belonging to a synagogue; 23 percent reported going to synagogue at least once or twice a month; 76 percent reported attending services during the High Holidays.

18. Jonathan Cook, "Israel Gets Tough on Intermarriage," *The National*, September, 7, 2009.

19. Werner Sollors, *Beyond Ethnicity: Consent and Descent in American Culture* (New York: Oxford University Press, 1986).

20. Herbert J. Gans, "Ethnicity, Acculturation, and Assimilation," forward to Neil Sandberg, *Ethnic Identity and Assimilation* (New York: Praeger, 1974), vii–xiii, cited in Thomas J. Ferraro, *Ethnic Passages: Literary Immigrants in Twentieth-Century America* (Chicago: University of Chicago Press, 1993), 8.

21. I point the reader to Bruce Jay Friedman's incisive story on the "slippery slope": "When You're Excused, You're Excused," collected in *Jewish American Literature: A Norton Anthology*, ed. Jules Chametzky, John Felstiner, Hilene Flanzbaum, and Kathryn Hellerstein (New York: W.W. Norton & Company, 2001).

11

Narrating the Past in a Different Language

Teaching the Holocaust through Third-Generation Fiction

Jessica Lang

It seems as if the Holocaust should be easier to teach with each passing decade. Survivors who have long kept silent finally are recording their experiences; historical documents are being released and made electronically available; and references to the Holocaust are being made in every form of record available to us today, from social media to print scholarship to fiction and film. It appears that, after seventy-five years, the Holocaust has been revealed and is accessible, approachable, and, consequently, eminently teachable. Indeed, at the conference that serves as the launching pad for this volume, the Jewish American Holocaust Literature Symposium, one increasingly hears, both informally and formally, resistance regarding a by now well-established position that the Holocaust is unapproachable, unimaginable, and unspeakable. "How so?," advocates of this position argue. What is so hard about understanding racism, genocide, and anti-Semitism? For something that cannot be understood, the Holocaust has generated an enormous amount of analysis, debate, and scholarship, not to mention its growing place in more casual interfaces such as Facebook and Twitter.

Yet, as I argue here, the proliferation of Holocaust texts, films, memorials, social media contributions—in short, the inexorable rise of Holocaust materials—in fact has the countereffect of the one described above. Instead of the plethora of material about the Holocaust increasing its accessibility and making it, as a subject, more approachable and teachable, precisely the opposite happens: it moves us away from the hard truths and inner workings of genocide, those that not only defy imagination but remain cloistered in a place beyond access, beyond the power of descriptive language, and outside a reader's purview. The accessibility of some of these materials make teaching the Holocaust paradoxically even more challenging; yet, of course, not teaching it, speaking it, or writing it simply is not an option. I propose here that, while acknowledging the vast literature available, we must acknowledge the limitations found in teaching and studying materials related to the Holocaust. These limitations have become harder to decipher and often are not recognized at all. By recognizing these and other limits, we teach students about the destruction of European Jewry as wholly and as fully as possible.

In an effort to be as honest as possible in thinking about teaching the Holocaust, I turn here not to the most widely taught Holocaust texts, which are texts that bear direct witness to that terrible history—Primo Levi's *Survival in Auschwitz*; Elie Wiesel's *Night*; Anne Frank's *Diary of a Young Girl*—but rather to the near opposite end of the spectrum, to four semifictional/semiautobiographical stories by authors who identify themselves as third generation and who were largely raised and currently write in countries geographically far from where the events of the Holocaust took place. I do this because as difficult as eyewitness testimony is to read, its very difficulty makes teaching it in many ways an easier experience. Indeed, its inaccessibility and struggle with meaning are themselves among the most central and important features of these works. The fact that students wrestle with Levi's exacting language, with Wiesel's deceptive simplicity, and with Frank's voice is itself a starting point for discussion, analysis, and interrogation of the text. What eyewitness testimony points to again and again is that language is a poor tool—even if it is the only one available—to describe genocide. And if firsthand accounts are limited, then surely, one tells one's students, our own removed readings are even more impoverished.

One powerfully vocal and visual example of the limits around language and comprehension can be found in Lanzmann's epic documentary film *Shoah*. As Gabriela Stoicea notes, *Shoah* employs more than one method of translation. There is the "consecutive interpretation by trained professionals" who are often visible to viewers; there are subtitles; and then Stoicea makes the case for a third kind of translation, "a type of translation performed not by an outside agent, such as the translator/interpreter, but by the speaker him- or herself."[1] Stoicea makes the point that the many different languages that are pointedly included in *Shoah* emphasize the "radical foreignness of all traumatic experience even to its own participants."[2] Stoicea continues:

> In *Shoah*, testimonial accounts carry the full dimension of their foreignness in relation to Jewish survivors themselves, many of whom painfully try to articulate traumatic experiences in broken, heavily accented English, German, or even French. The banishment into a language other than their mother tongue(s) of all Jewish survivors but one in this film already entails an initial process of internalized translation from one language into another, which in some cases is followed by a translator mediated transposition into yet another foreign language. In the case of internalized translation, the positions of speaker and translator are collapsed into one, as if to suggest that working through a trauma always involves some sort of translation.[3]

In teaching *Shoah*, it is crucial not only to think about language as it is used in the film, but also to consider how this act of near constant translation impacts the viewing of the film. Lanzmann's interviewing technique, in which he at times presses forward, urging his subject to continue, and at times circles back, urging his subject to repeat him- or herself, together with the various kinds of translation used in the interviews, creates a sense of circularity that is disorienting. This sense of disorientation is compounded by the film's editing, where what was filmed as a single interview on a single day is broken into parts, and the viewer unexpectedly returns to past figures to hear more of their past stories—and all of this reliving is, of course, taking place in the present.

Both Dominick LaCapra and Shoshana Felman investigate this distorted sense of time where the past and present lean heavily on one another. LaCapra asks

> whether Lanzmann . . . tends to confine performativity to acting-out and tends even to give way to a displaced, secular religiosity in which authenticity becomes tantamount to a movement beyond secondary witnessing to a full identification with the victim. This full identification would allow one not only to act out trauma vicariously in the self as surrogate victim but cause one to insist on having the victim relive traumatizing events, thus concealing one's own intrusiveness in asking questions that prod the victim to the point of breakdown.[4]

In other words, LaCapra understands Lanzmann's intent in pushing survivors to recount and retell even when they express reluctance to do so as a sort of compression of time and history, a means of "concealing" the intrusive presence of the audience through the both past and immediate experience of trauma by the survivor. Felman, in her well-known and lengthy essay on *Shoah*, also addresses this issue, though to a different end: "*Shoah* addresses the spectator with a challenge. When we are made to witness this reenactment of the murder of the witness, this second Holocaust that appears spontaneously before the camera and on the screen, can we in our turn become *contemporaneous* with the meaning and with the significance of that enactment? Can we become contemporaneous with the shock, with the displacement, with the disorientation process that is triggered by such testimonial reenactment? Can we, in other words, assume in earnest, not the finite task of making sense out of the Holocaust, but the infinite task of encountering *Shoah*?"[5] What Felman asks here is for the viewer/spectator to understand him- or herself as a witness, with all the weightiness that word implies, and with the presence of the witness on the screen before us.

    I raise the viewing of Lanzmann's film *Shoah* here because it offers both a useful counternarrative and a useful parallel to how we can, and even should, read contemporary Holocaust literature, especially that of the third generation. *Shoah*'s commitment to translation, along with its recognition of an active role for the reader/viewer, are very much a part not only of third-generation writing, but also of our role as readers of contemporary Holocaust writing. One unique aspect of third-generation literature is the partnership it often assumes between writer and reader, which I examine in greater detail later in this chapter. In addition to these features, I wish to point to one more, little-talked-about result regarding the impact of translation within *Shoah*, and its connection to third-generation literature. That the film, at nine and a half hours, is radically long, has been duly noted. One simple but important consequence of the film's commitment to multivalenced translating and the circularity of its interviews means that the viewer is found in a posture of perpetually waiting: waiting for some sense of linguistic understanding, for a story to be complete, for comprehension to take hold. It is this posture that students often need help identifying but then grasp onto almost anxiously: waiting to see, an aspect of the film never gratified, is a powerful means of talking about and teaching the Holocaust, an ironic point of access to a work and an event that itself defies access. And waiting for some sense of illumination, for a full understanding of their grandparents' history, is also very much a feature of third-generation writing. Lanzmann notes, "I began precisely with the impossibility of recounting this story. I put this impossibility at the beginning. What there is at the beginning of this film is on the one hand the disappearance of traces: there is no longer anything . . ."[6] Eduardo Halfon echoes these sentiments in thinking about the figure of the Polish boxer whose advice to his grandfather while the two were imprisoned in Auschwitz saved his life: "The Polish boxer . . . is a figure that is barely present, or not present at all. Yet he is. He's like a specter, or like a breath that permeates the book. Something you can't point to, that you can't really see, but that you can feel. And that's what my grandfather's story was to me. It was this huge story that was barely present."[7]

The contrast between works written by or narrated by survivors and contemporary Holocaust fiction written by their descendants is noteworthy and is worth exploring in the classroom. Most obviously, third-generation Holocaust fiction is written by authors raised in different countries from those their grandparents (or other members of their grandparents' generation) fled, with different native languages, in a different culture and a different era. Even more telling, third-generation Holocaust fiction is wide-ranging and tends to attract popular audiences who race through their pages with ease and, at times, enthusiasm. These are texts that do not typically cause disorientation; their contents tend not to make us hesitate, slow down, cause discomfort, or otherwise disrupt or shift our reading experience, as so often happens with eyewitness narratives. It is precisely this quality of difference that connects third-generation literature with its origins. There can be no other way. The traumas experienced by the survivor generation are passed onto their descendants by these very divergences in experience, which are attended by a pronounced sense of loss, an absence of wholeness, and a need for translation that never quite encompasses the past in its entirety. I raise this here because while survivor literature holds a unique status in the genre of Holocaust literature, the genre has grown and continues to grow in multiple directions. Alvin Rosenfeld and Robert Eaglestone present two useful and complementary definitions of Holocaust fiction as a genre: First, Rosenfeld's point that Holocaust literature, more than "a loosely arranged collection of novels, poems, essays, and plays about a *subject* . . . is an attempt to express a new order of consciousness, a recognizable shift in being," one that is revealed through "shards and fragments . . . that together add up to something larger than the tragic sense implies."[8] And, second, Eaglestone's understanding that Holocaust fiction is a genre because it is a "way of reading. . . . It is to be read with a specific range of questions, responses, demands, and issues in mind."[9] These definitions make clear that third-generation literature deserves to be included and taught in Holocaust literature courses. Indeed, I would even go so far as to make the case that because contemporary Holocaust literature has acquired such a large and diverse audience, many of whom treat these books more as entertainment than anything else, teaching readers to think more deeply and carefully about them serves to develop and extend crucial ideas around memory and history that are integral to survivor literature and the genre of Holocaust literature more broadly.

Precisely because third-generation Holocaust fiction has at this point in time traveled the furthest from the original form in the field—namely, testimony—I have chosen to focus the remainder of this chapter on four contemporary Holocaust stories. Written by authors who identify themselves as third generation, who hail from three difference countries, and whose native languages are all different (although two write in English), these stories bear the markers of Holocaust literature even as they move away from some of the difficulty and challenges, and so move away—necessarily—from the impenetrable truths that these original texts present to readers. They are "An Animal to Memory" in Canadian (Latvian-born) author David Bezmozgis's collection *Natasha and Other Stories* (2004); the title story, "The Quiet American, or How to Be a Good Guest," and "Lebensraum" in American author Erika Dreifus's short-story collection *Quiet Americans* (2011); and the title story of Guatemalan author Eduardo Halfon's collection of short stories, *The Polish Boxer* (2012), the first of his books to be translated into and published in English.

Narrated primarily from the grandchild's perspective, these stories emphasize both a sense of distance—remoteness, even—to the language of the Holocaust as well as a deep connection to the past. Importantly, the narrator's past is not limited to "family history." Rather, the narrator's past is a collective past to which in one way or another all readers can connect. Bezmozgis's story, surely influenced by Philip Roth's "Conversion of the Jews," describes the violence of Holocaust Day at the thirteen-year-old narrator's Canadian Jewish school. As noted by Derek Parker Royal, the story is deliberately placed in the middle of the collection "and in this way can be read as a pivotal moment" in the narrator's development.[10] Dreifus describes a longing for home through a narrator who travels back to her grandparents' native Stuttgart and through her grandfather's first foray into the American Midwest. Halfon's "The Polish Boxer" interpolates a grandfather's first-ever vocalization of his Holocaust experience with his grandson narrator's thoughts on growing up in Guatemala. For a course that spans Holocaust literature for the past seventy years, the works by Levi, Wiesel, Frank, and Lanzmann would fall in the first half, while the works by Halfon, Dreifus, and Bezmozgis would serve as productive concluding reading assignments. They illuminate the contradictory qualities of contemporary Holocaust literature: how far we have come and how much we have lost. If we teach and read them as they deserve to be taught and read—by acknowledging what they do not and cannot say—as much as we consider and investigate what they do, we will enlarge our students' understanding of the Holocaust through a multitude of voices and silences.

Tough Love: Violence in Bezmozgis's Short Fiction

Mark Berman, the narrator in *Natasha* who as the stories progress ages from a six-year-old immigrant freshly arrived in Toronto from Riga to a young man, outlines the rough contours of Bezmozgis's own history. The fourth story in the collection, "An Animal to the Memory," is narrated by seventh grader Berman, a kid who reluctantly attends a Jewish school where he is occasionally targeted as a "dirty Russian" by schoolmates (68).[11] His response, which he hopes will lead to a transfer to the local public school, is to become the local hoodlum, someone who "glowered in the hallways, and, with the right kind of provocation, punched people in the face" (70).

"An Animal to the Memory" opens on a railway platform in Vienna, with the Berman family in mid-migration from the Soviet Union. The grandparents head to Israel as their children and grandchildren decide to go "someplace that was not Israel" and arrive in Canada (67). The reader learns nothing else of Berman's biological grandfather in the story, but another grandfather moves into his place: the father of Rabbi Gurvich, the school's principal, a "frail and mild" man who survived the Holocaust and who, just that year, had "published his memoirs" about his Holocaust experience (72). The narrator describes "the old man" perching "himself behind the teacher's desk" and smiling "benignly" as he autographs copies of his memoir "with the double imperative: *Yizkor; al tishkach*! Remember; don't forget!" (72–72). As Bettina Hofmann notes, "Personal history intersects with professional aims of education when the school's principal, Gurvich, presents to the class members his father, a Holocaust survivor, who has written a book of his memories. 'We were all encouraged to buy the book' (72), recalls Mark, which the author then signs in class. The laconic quote points to a moral ambiguity here. The survivor's need to testify becomes intertwined with the promotion of his book, while the principal's recommendation constitutes a form of coercion. Indeed, he even profits from marketing his father's Holocaust story."[12] The survivor's mild manners stand in sharp contrast to his "dark, unsmiling" son, whose "primary role was that of disciplinarian" and whose one contribution to the education of his students was Holocaust Day, a day spent in prayer, reflection, and special related activities. During the Holocaust Day service, Berman describes Rabbi Gurvich's recitation of *El Maleh Rachamim*, the funeral prayer traditionally recited graveside, as so "filled with grief . . . his voice seemed no longer his own; his voice belonged to the six million. The sounds he made were dictated by centuries of ancestral mourning. I couldn't understand how it was possible for Gurvich not to cry when his voice sounded the way it did" (74). Rabbi Gurvich's recitation of the prayer of mourning entrances Berman, not only bringing him closer to those murdered in the Holocaust, but also connecting him to larger ancient Jewish traditions around loss and mourning.

These thoughts are interrupted, as are the general cadence and tone of reverence painted by the narrator, by a classmate who calls out to Berman, "'What are you looking at, assface?'" (74). It is a moment of narrative disruption that turns to violence as both the reader and narrator are jolted from the sacred by the profane, from remembering to the present, from the Holocaust, with its iconic imagery (Berman describes looking at a portrait of Mordechai Anilewicz, the leader of the Warsaw Ghetto resistance and a figure Berman clearly identifies with, just before being confronted by his classmates) to the daily tedium of school. A convoluted and complex sense of identification is initiated here, one that, to Bezmozgis's credit, is never fully resolved even at the story's conclusion. Holocaust Day is scheduled just shortly after Berman has returned to school after being suspended for fighting—he gave another boy a concussion—with the caveat "that this was never to happen again" (70). (The dark irony of this earnestly delivered statement, together with the story's profanity, punctuates the narrative with a tone of illicit humor—just the sort of laughter that, if expressed, would get one in trouble with the principal.) Within minutes of being called an "assface," Berman is pushed by a friend of the boy he injured a few days before, loses his balance, and shatters a memorial candle. "The sound of the breaking glass" recalls Kristallnacht, with Berman playing the role of the perpetrator. A fight between Berman and three other kids breaks out in the middle of the Holocaust exhibit, and Berman lands one of the boys in a chokehold. Gurvich pulls Berman off and sends him to his office to wait. Berman is upset and wants to win back Gurvich's favor but also feels unfairly victimized.

A half-hour later, Gurvich appears and demands that Berman return to the Holocaust exhibit. Once there, Rabbi Gurvich tells Berman to "look around" and asks, "'what do you see?'" (76). Berman looks. He responds: "'The Holocaust'" (76). "'And does this make you feel anything?,'" responds Rabbi Gurvich. "'I don't believe you feel anything . . . Berman, a Nazi wouldn't do here what you did today'" (76). Gurvich grabs Berman's shoulder and turns him around, tightening "his grip on [his] shoulder until he saw it hurt" and asks Berman to answer the question "What are you?" (76). Berman responds quietly, but Gurvich physically and verbally goads him to answer loud enough, "'[s]o that my uncles hear you in Treblinka!'" (77). Berman, sobbing, complies and shouts: "'I'm a Jew!'" (77). And then the reflective voice of the narrator draws us back to the complexity of the moment: "I had screamed it in his face wishing to kill him, but he only nodded his head. He kept his hand on my shoulder and waited until I really started to sob . . . Finally, Gurvich removed his hand and backed away a half step. As soon as he did, I wanted him to put his hand back" (77). Adam Rovner argues that from this interaction, "Berman learns that being Jewish means being weak, passive, and fearful." I would suggest a more nuanced reading: Berman's self-identification as a Jew, and with it his sense of belonging to Jewish history, is made both spitefully and longingly.[13]

One compelling feature of "An Animal to the Memory" is its repeated willingness to draw near to history while also articulating a wish to be free of it. Bezmozgis accomplishes this through physical and verbal violence and dramatic and disruptive changes in pacing and tone. Berman's willingness to hurt other students is met with the accusation that his actions are beneath even those of a Nazi. The narrator is regularly forced to shift from an internal exploration of his thoughts regarding memory and history, including his own history as an immigrant, to the present moment through pejorative language and schoolboy pranks. This shift itself is sudden, jerking readers along with the narrator from past to present, from reverie to a defensive posture. Finally, Berman's declaration of Jewishness—the reason he has left Latvia, the reason he is in a Jewish school in Canada, the reason he observes Holocaust Day—is a declaration that is both defiant and wrenching. He screams it out of spite, love, and anger, and the emotions encapsulated in that statement, "I'm a Jew!," relay a filial and cultural duty—"*our* history of oppression," he notes in describing the history of Holocaust Day (my italics)—and resentment.

Self-Imposed Exile: *Heimat* (Homeland) in Dreifus's *Quiet Americans*

Erika Dreifus's short story "The Quiet American, or How to Be a Good Guest" opens with a finger pointed at the reader, a gesture that is powerfully maintained throughout the story: "You will go to Germany. You will go, after years and years of refusing to go . . . ." Written (as few texts are) almost entirely in the second person, the narrator reveals herself only through (or perhaps as) her reader and establishes the following details regarding her own history: with much ambivalence, she decides to return to her grandparents' native country. She finds herself in Stuttgart, the city her father's parents traveled to "in the late 1930s, to apply for their visas at the American Consulate" (114).[14] The story shifts between the more recent past, referencing details about the narrator (again, told through commands that are directed toward the reader); the historical past, revealing her grandparents' history; and the present: sitting on a tour bus with a group of strangers all listening to a German tour guide named Greta narrate what amounts to a deeply sanitized history of the place. "Greta with the green beads seems to be a good guide. She tells you that more than five hundred thousand people reside in Stuttgart; she praises its many parks, its ballet, its zoo. She describes all the buildings the bus passes . . . As the tour continues there's a refrain. Again and again Greta says, 'This building had to be rebuilt after the war. The original was destroyed by the bombings'" (116).

The narrator detects a faint accusation in the guide's voice and, while feeling some sympathy for what Greta's family may have suffered in the war, determines that "[b]uildings don't quite equal civilian lives" (117). As the narrator's discomfort grows, so does her silence; the two responses compound each other. She says nothing, other than thanking Greta at the tour's end. She is, after all, a good guest. But another member of the tour does speak up, and in so doing confirms the anxiety of our narrator. A Briton and World War II veteran of the Royal Air Force is also on the tour and he takes it on himself to confront the tour guide: "I cannot say that I am responsible for these particular bombings to which you continue to refer. But if I were, I would hardly be ashamed" (120–212). The narrator's final action is to catch the British veteran and his wife as all the tourists are dispersing to simply say, "Thank you" (121).

Many of Dreifus's stories concern themselves with the landscape of home—a concern that questions both what (and where) home is and how we conceive of it. In "The Quiet American, or How to Be a Good Guest," the landscape of the war is largely invisible—and this is the central problem of not only this story in particular, but Holocaust narratives more broadly. The original buildings have been largely destroyed by the war and since rebuilt; once robust Jewish communities that have disappeared no longer appear in any form—neither as what they once were nor as what they might have been. The American Consulate that once provided "your" grandparents with visas no longer exists in the city that was once their hometown—although it, too, is unrecognizable. The German tourists on the bus look remarkably like any grandparents. And the tour guide, well, maybe "you [are] just being, as you've been told you can be, paranoid"; she is knowledgeable but also seems "angry at the Allies for having 'destroyed' her country's property" (116; 119).

Instead of seeing the hometown that once existed and the residents as they once were, the granddaughter narrator relies on emotions, none of which comes through more clearly than the tightly controlled righteous anger of a spokesperson telling her reader how the future will (and must) play out. If the German tour guide leads the narrator through a false sense of history, the Jewish narrator leads the reader through its corrected version, pointing out verbal miscues and once important buildings that enabled her grandparents to escape. The use of the second person is effective in illuminating the complexity of Dreifus's own position as third generation. Simultaneously confrontational and didactic, authoritative and vulnerable, the narrator moves against history by willing herself into action—her exhortations to the reader and herself—and with history by embracing inaction and remaining a good, quiet guest. The second-person voice links the narrator with the reader, just as the reader (willingly or not) identifies with the narrator. This comes together most powerfully in the final words uttered by the narrator to the British veteran, which are the final words of the story: " 'Thank you—so much' " (121). The "you" moves from the reader to the figure willing to speak up, a man willing *not* to be a "good guest," a person who vocally marks a landscape that otherwise would have left history behind.

In contrast to the invisibility of the past in "The Quiet American," in the story "Lebensraum" the symbols of war are easy to identify—in the American Midwest. The story is based on the history of Dreifus's grandfather, a German refugee who, as a recently naturalized citizen, finds himself working as a baker for the US Army in Camp Clarinda, Iowa. The narrator describes "how empty this Camp Clarinda seemed. How much quiet. How much land . . . In the distance he could see the barracks, and watchtowers. The barbed wire, of course, he could nearly touch. But there were trees, too, and grass that seemed to reach so very far." Dreifus's Midwest, for all of its expansiveness, is interrupted by the imagery of war and the symbols of the Holocaust: the barbed wire, the watchtowers, the barracks. These features of the landscape are put into place by Americans—Josef, the figure modeled on Dreifus's grandfather, himself is a part of this infrastructure—but they unmistakably shift and transform our sense of perspective, shortening the distance between place and time. Not only the reader and Josef but also Josef's granddaughter must look through that barbed wire fence to see the vast expanse of prairie that reached "so very far." The title of the story, "Lebensraum," confirms the sense that Dreifus is unable to see landscape as pure or untouched—indeed, the very idea of this resonates uncomfortably with the Third Reich agenda of Lebensraum. For Dreifus, the vastness of the prairie is broken, marred, by the infrastructure of Camp Clarinda but also, more symbolically, by the landmarks of the concentration camps. There is no escape, Dreifus suggests. Not even "[i]n America. In Clarinda. The country's basket of bread. How much quiet. How much land" (80). Those final sentences start as questions and end as statements: "How much quiet. How much land." They invoke an accent but refer to middle America. The quiet is both reassuring—the sounds of war are remote—and ominous: imposed silence is not freedom. How much land, indeed! How much Lebensraum. And a small Jewish refugee family must call it home.

Hearing Others as Yourself: Or, How to Listen to the Voice of the Survivor

The first characters recorded in Eduardo Halfon's story "The Polish Boxer" are numbers—the numbers tattooed on his grandfather's arm that were never spoken about except playfully until one afternoon, sixty years after they had been inscribed, with no solicitation, the grandfather says simply to his narrator grandson: "'It was in Auschwitz'" (80).[15] And with his long, self-imposed silence ended, the grandfather, deep in reverie, proceeds to tell his grandson about the two camps he survived, Sachsenhausen and Auschwitz. In Sachsenhausen he had been made the "stubendienst of our block. Three hundred men. Two hundred and eighty men. Three hundred and ten men. Every day a few more, every day a few less" (83). The grandfather fills in some of the details—beatings, punishment, a bribe that went wrong, and the consequent deportation to Auschwitz, where he was locked up in Block 11, a set of cells whose inhabitants were mostly executed. In the cell, the grandfather meets a fellow Jew from Łódź, a boxer, whom "the Germans kept alive because they liked to watch him box" (90). Speaking in Polish, the boxer tells the grandfather exactly what to say when he is put on trial—and what not to say. The grandfather follows the boxer's instructions precisely and lives, never meeting up again with the man who saved him.

In this quiet story about narration, the survivor grandfather speaks out loud, and the survivor's grandson speaks internally. There are gestures that connect them, most of them around the whiskey the grandfather drinks while talking and the cigarettes the grandson smokes while listening. But far more noticeable is the absence of contact between them, even though the affection they have for one another is clearly pronounced by both. After his grandfather initiates the conversation about the Holocaust, the grandson thinks to himself, "I would have liked to ask him what it felt like when, after almost sixty years of silence, he finally said something truthful about the origin of that number. Ask him why he had said it to me. Ask him if releasing words so long stored up produced some liberating effect. Ask him if words stored up for so long had the same taste as they rolled roughly off the tongue. But I kept quiet, impatient, listening . . ." (80).

The grandson's silence takes hold again after he poses the first of three questions to his grandfather. After learning of his grandfather's appointment as stubendienst of his block, the person "in charge of cleaning, of sweeping, of changing the cots . . . of removing the bodies of the men who were dead in the mornings . . . of receiving the new Jews when they arrived in my block" (83), the grandson inquires, "'Why you, Oitze?'" (his affectionate name for his grandfather) (83). His grandfather stares at him "as if we suddenly spoke different languages . . . And on his old face, in his old hand, which had now stopped gesturing and gone back to covering up the number, I saw all the implications of that question. I saw the disguised question inside that question: What did you have to do for them to put you in charge? I saw the question that is never asked: What did you have to do to survive?" (83–84). His grandfather's minimal response—a frown, a slight closing of his eyes, the covering up of his number tattoo—reposition the grandson's perspective from one of confidante to one of interrogator. In this moment, the grandson narrator recognizes the different language his grandfather speaks, the chasm between their two histories, as does his grandfather. Their responses reveal this understanding, the grandfather through a smile and a shrug: "'One day, our lagerleiter, the camp commander, just told me that I'd be in charge, and that was it'" (84); and the grandson through silently recognizing the impossibility of his grandfather answering such a question: "As if you could speak the unspeakable" (84).

As the grandfather continues to narrate his wartime history, the grandson's thoughts shift from thinking about what he would like to ask but chooses not to to his own memories of his grandfather: the whiskey he liked to buy and store "in case there's a war"; his grandfather's weekly manicures given to him by his grandmother; the traffic lights in Guatemala City and the uncomfortable questions the narrator as a child used to pose to his mother while stopped at them; his first sexual encounter, a number of which remind the narrator of the perpetual feelings of "solitude and abandonment" that he felt as a child (88). The grandson's thoughts are prompted by his grandfather's narration. He refills his grandfather's whiskey glass several times during the story; the elegant hands of the lagerleiter, one of the few details the grandfather can recall, prompts the grandson to describe his grandfather's "impeccable" hands (84). The "feeling of solitude and abandonment" that marks important points of maturation are recalled as the narrator thinks about "the claustrophobic image of the dark, damp, crowded cell stuffed with whispers where my grandfather was locked up, sixty years ago, in Block Eleven, in Auschwitz" (88).

While the grandson mostly defers asking his grandfather for answers, he continues to attempt to translate his grandfather's narrative into a series of images that are familiar to him as a means of accessing them. His questions accumulate as his grandfather proceeds, but the grandson settles on one final question at the conclusion of his grandfather's testimony: "I wanted to ask him something about the number or about that young Jewish man who had tattooed him. But I only asked what the Polish boxer had said. He seemed not to understand my question, and so I repeated it, a bit louder, a bit more anxiously. What did the boxer tell you to say and not say, Oitze, during that trial?" (90). One critic notes that "the idea of a boxer saving Oitze is a relic, like a phoenix rising from the ashes, and he holds tightly to the hopes that something or someone will come along to save him too."[16] Perhaps.[17] Although the anxiety expressed by the narrator, his wish for the narrative to continue, his sense of urgency for an answer to his questions, all of these suggest to me a recognition that not all questions can be answered, not all stories can be told, not all people can be saved. His is the position of the third generation at its most authentic: longing to know, to hear, to tell, to write, and yet, like the quiet quest in Dreifus's story and the longing for contact with history in Bezmozgis's story, unable to do just that.

In a 1994 pedagogy article, a German-language instructor investigates the possibility—the merits and challenges—of including materials on Nazism and the Holocaust as part of the curriculum in introductory German-language courses. One of his students is Erika Dreifus, who interviews her grandparents in their native language with questions designed by the class. An edited version of this interview is included in an appendix to the article. Dreifus introduces her grandparents in English by stating that "the stories they tell are their own, and should be understood as such. Theirs are not the definitive voices on the Weimar Republic, or the Kristallnacht, or on emigration from Germany. But they are authentic voices, speaking in a language they have not ceased to consider their own more than a half-century after leaving Germany."[18] Nearly twenty years later, Dreifus's collection of short stories presents her own authentic and definitive voice, one that reflects on her grandparents' history effectively in translation—a quality that emphasizes the limitations of these reflections. The quietness found in the title, the narrative's reserved sensibility, and her search for what she cannot see all speak to Dreifus's understanding around the limits of language and representation and the impossibility of a complete translation.

Similarly, Eduardo Halfon quiets his own voice in the face of his grandfather's. Recognizing that his questions have unintended effects, he contents himself with listening to his grandfather's story and drawing as near to it as he can—recognizing his inability to know it or repeat it in its entirety. In a recent interview, Halfon acknowledges the absence of language that marks his grandfather's story: "[My grandfather] saved himself at Auschwitz by saying what a Polish boxer told him to say, and by not saying what he told him not say . . . My grandfather didn't remember [these words], or he didn't care. He just used them once and they were done."[19] Halfon's story tellingly starts with numbers. His mode of representing his grandfather's history is filtered through time, space, and the narrator's own experiences. Like Dreifus, this form of listening creates a space to acknowledge what is "barely present," what cannot be pointed to, clearly seen, or definitively narrated.

The youngest narrator of all four stories conveys David Bezmozgis's sharply drawn re-creation of Holocaust Day. Replete with shattering glass, accusations of evil, and a sobbing declaration of selfhood, "An Animal to the Memory" creates a startling disruption to the sense of quiet reverie present in all three authors' works. Mark Berman's internal reflections of the images he sees commemorating Holocaust Day echo the silence found in "The Quiet American" and "The Polish Boxer." More than Dreifus and Halfon, Bezmozgis is willing to identify where and how memorializing the Holocaust has gone wrong in recent years—and also its necessary place in the development of a young boy's identity. Central to the success of all of these stories, in how they are both read and taught, is an acknowledgement of the incomplete quality that recent Holocaust literature bears: what is lost in translation is as important as what remains.

Notes

1. Gabriela Stoicea, "The Difficulties of Verbalizing Trauma: Translation and the Economy of Loss in Claude Lanzmann's 'Shoah,'" *The Journal of the Midwest Modern Language Association* 39 (2006): 44.
2. Stoicea, "The Difficulties of Verbalizing Trauma," 45.
3. Stoicea, "The Difficulties of Verbalizing Trauma," 46.
4. Dominick LaCapra, "Lanzmann's 'Shoah': 'Here There Is No Why,'" *Critical Inquiry* 23 (1997): 245.
5. Shoshana Felman, "The Return of the Voice: Claude Lanzmann's Shoah," in *Testimony: Crises of Witnessing in Literature, Psychoanalysis, and History*, by Shoshana Felman and Dori Laub (New York: Routledge, 1992), 268.
6. Claude Lanzmann, "Le Lieu et la parole," in *Au sujet de Shoah* (Paris: Belin, 1990), 295. Found in LaCapra, "Lanzmann's 'Shoah,'" 244.
7. Joshua Barnes, "No Borders: An Interview with Eduardo Halfon," *Sampsonia Way*, December 10, 2012, accessed August 20, 2016, http://www.sampsoniaway.org/literary-voices/2012/12/10/no-borders-an-interview-with-eduardo-halfon/.
8. Alvin H. Rosenfeld, *A Double Dying: Reflections on Holocaust Literature* (Bloomington: Indiana University Press), 12; 33. Italics in the original.
9. Robert Eaglestone, *The Holocaust and the Postmodern* (London: Oxford University Press, 2004), 107.
10. Derek Parker Royal, "Cyrillic Cycles: Uses of Composite Narrative in the Russian Émigré Fiction of Ellen Litman and David Bezmozgis," *Studies in American Jewish Literature* 31 (2012): 244.
11. All quotes are from David Bezmozgis, "An Animal to the Memory," in *Natasha and Other Stories* (New York: Farrar, Straus and Giroux, 2004), 65–77.
12. Bettina Hofmann, "David Bezmozgis—Muscles, Minyan and Menorah: Judaism in Natasha and Other Stories," *Studies in American Jewish Literature* 25 (2006): 106.
13. Adam Rovner, "So Easily Assimilated: The New Immigrant Chic," *AJS Review* 30 (2006): 318.
14. All quotes are from Erika Dreifus, *Quiet Americans* (Boston: Last Light Studio Books, 2011), 113–21.
15. All quotes are from Eduardo Halfon, "The Polish Boxer," in *The Polish Boxer*, trans. Daniel Hahn, Ollie Brock, Lisa Dillman, Thomas Bunstead, and Anne McLean (New York: Bellevue Literary Press, 2012), 78–91.
16. Julie Morse, "'The Polish Boxer,' by Eduardo Halfon," *The Rumpus*, October 11, 2012, accessed August 20, 2016, http://therumpus.net/2012/10/the-polish-boxer-by-eduardo-halfon/.
17. I echo Erika Dreifus's gentle skepticism here. Erika Dreifus, "A Special Kind of Kinship: On Being a '3G' Writer," in *Third-Generation Holocaust*

Narratives: Memory in Memoir and Fiction, ed. Victoria Aarons (Lanham, MD: Lexington Books, 2016), 1–16.

18. William Collins Donahue, " 'We Shall Not Speak of It' ": Nazism and the Holocaust in the Elementary College German Course," *Die Unterrichtspraxis / Teaching German* 27 (1994): 100.

19. Dwyer Murphy and Eduardo Halfon, "Origin Stories: Dwyer Murphy interviews Eduardo Halfon," *Guernica / a magazine of art & politics*, April 15, 2013, accessed August 20, 2016, https://www.guernicamag.com/interviews/origin-stories/.

12

A Complicated Curriculum

Teaching Holocaust Empathy and Distance to Nontraditional Students

Jeffrey Scott Demsky and N. Ann Rider

Introduction: Memorializing the Holocaust in American Culture

Soon after World War II ended, survivor intellectuals and scholars expressed concerns that the Nazis' war on Jews, a program of murder later called the Holocaust,[1] might someday fade from public memory. Such fears were not without merit. During World War I, Armenian Christians endured genocide at the hands of Ottoman Muslims.[2] Although Western powers at the time condemned the killings, the expressions of concern soon fell silent. Such forgetfulness taught a powerful lesson. No less an observer than Adolf Hitler is reported to have remarked, "Who, after all, speaks today of the annihilation of the Armenians?"[3] Theirs was a catastrophe with one and a half million victims but only spotty remembrance. To guard against this amnesia, stewards of Jewish losses have memorialized the Holocaust as a universal tragedy. Particularly in the United States, this push for collective commemoration is apparent. As Peter Novick explains, remembering the victims—and the role

Americans played in liberating the death camps—constitutes a core part of national World War II memory.[4]

So great is this Americanization of the memory[5] that the German journalist Henryk Broder noted, "a naive observer might reasonably conclude that the Nazi Holocaust took place in the United States, and Americans feel obliged to come to grips with this dark chapter of their history."[6] While incisive, Broder overlooks a subtler process. The war on Jews did not directly impact Americans, but its legacy has come to buoy wider aspects of their national identity. In 1979, President Jimmy Carter spoke to this point:

> Although the Holocaust took place in Europe the event is of fundamental significance to Americans. It was American troops who liberated many death camps, and who helped to expose the horrible truth of what had been done there . . . We feel compelled to study the systematic destruction of the Jews so that we may seek to learn how to prevent such enormities from occurring in the future.[7]

Such declarations might be said to capture the nation's traditional duty to memory. It is an empathic, close imagining, more fashioned that factual,[8] that casts the United States government in a constructive light. In contrast to the many traumas of the 1970s—Vietnam War, Watergate, and Iranian hostage affair—stamping an American imprimatur on Jewish survival reminded citizens of past instances of national goodness.[9]

Unlike earlier empty expressions of concern for Jewish welfare,[10] President Carter's words moved policy. He impaneled an official Commission on the Holocaust that recommended building a federal museum; the United States government donated the land for this institution.[11] Again, in these steps, we observe a government once complicit in turning away now openly affecting intimacy. On the state level, during the mid-1980s, lawmakers in California, North Carolina, Georgia, and Nevada mandated that their public schools teach about the Holocaust. Over the next two decades, more than three dozen additional states followed suit. One quarter of the visitors to the Washington, DC, memorial have been school-aged children.[12] Countless more have toured similar repositories spanning Los Angeles, California, to Terre Haute, Indiana. Online delivery platforms—notably the USC Shoah IWitness collection, the Facing History and Ourselves project, and the Simon Wiesenthal

Center website—offer students everywhere streaming access to scholarly and survivor sources.

Far from the feared marginalization, postwar Americans write about the Holocaust so prominently that some critics term the effort a "cottage" industry.[13] While this interpretation is provocative, people still must choose to engage the Holocaust. If they are unwilling to bear witness— taking on what Landsberg terms prosthetic memory—no abundance of artifacts will convey the trauma.[14] The increased visibility of the Holocaust may even achieve the exact opposite end, deconstructing the truth to such a point that it appears trite. This may be why, in 1994, the complimentary *Schindler's List* screening provided to Oakland, California high schoolers elicited laughter rather than reverence.[15] Although the cultural opportunity for memorialization was present, the empathy required for this process to succeed was missing. A few months later, perhaps in an example of life/art imitation, writers for the *Seinfeld* television show also tweaked the film's cultural relevance. During the "Raincoats" episode, Jerry's passionately kissing his girlfriend while screening *Schindler's List* had a humorous intent, blazing a path to his later comeuppance with Jerry's parents and his soon-to-be-ex-girlfriend's.[16] However, the episode's writers may also have been messaging a subtler point, namely desacralizing Holocaust taboos and calling into question the wider practice of stirring audiences' empathic reflexes.

There is evidence of additional memory "evasion"[17] in Jewish American fiction. Phillip Roth's Alexander Portnoy exclaims, "Jew Jew Jew Jew Jew Jew. It is coming out my ears already, the saga of the suffering Jews! Do me a favor, my people, and stick your suffering heritage up your suffering ass!"[18] Such breaking away from a Jewish primary reference group can also index separation from the received narrative of Holocaust trauma. This is not forgetting, but rather indicates that secularized American Jews had different lived experiences than their European forefathers. This is the *Heeb*-reading[19] crowd that grew up in predominately secular social environments where anti-Jewish talk was something they heard discussed among their families, but was not something they encountered as part of everyday goings-on. Such shifts evidenced larger changes in postwar American Jewish life, as the "neighbors in conflict" narrative that Ronald Bayor sketched out during the 1970s gradually gave way to the "strangers no more" trope that scholars like Ira Katznelson have unpacked in more recent times.[20] Consequently, hearing horrific tales of Nazism may have conveyed more a sense of their parent's anxieties than a practical life lesson. Yosefa Loshitzky develops this idea more boldly, arguing that Jewish American witnesses see in the approximately five million thriving American Jews—their demographic—the reincarnation of their murdered European cousins.[21] In this light, the destruction of European Jewry appears less as a tragic end than as the start of an unlikely renaissance, which in turn anticipates how these learners will envision the Holocaust.

In this churning, we perceive a pedagogical opportunity. Namely, this may be the time to think about selecting texts that do not stoke students' empathic impulses. Teaching books that require readers to think about, rather than feel, the writers' words might be more effective. Contra empathy tropes, this approach is something that we are calling a literature of distance. Ruth Klüger's Holocaust memoir *Still Alive* points us to this end. "Dear readers," she implores, "don't wax sentimental."[22] Her story, unlike most, denies solace or closure. Klüger does not permit "the obvious drift of my story away from the gas chambers and the killing fields toward the postwar period, where prosperity beckons."[23] This restriction engages readers intellectually, not sentimentally, teaching them that, ultimately, no amount of well-intentioned empathy can help them to "know" what the Holocaust was like. Tova Reich's novel *My Holocaust* is another example of steering readers toward "unknowable" lessons without employing emotionalism.[24] Her book offers no empathy, insisting instead that readers confront her acrid and disturbing visions head-on.[25] We do not conclude that one narrative representation or another is preferable.[26] Ours is a conversation about how the two differing reconstructions might better reach twenty-first-century learners, especially those who appear nontraditional in the sense that they do not exhibit the expected emotional investment in the history. At times, confronting this sort of reality may prove disagreeable and infuriating, and offer no canned answers. But we cannot celebrate only the success of the dominant tropes. Moving students beyond "safe spaces" and toward judgments brought on by the maintenance of one's emotional control represents both a pressing challenge and a promising opportunity.

Modeling Empathy in American Holocaust Memory

Authors of the initial genocide literature betrayed little interest in, or empathy for, Jewish victimhood. Commenting during the 1950s, Philip Friedman,[27] one of the first survivor intellectuals to write about his experiences, lamented that most publications were "solely concerned with the subject of anti-Jewish hostility and its effects."[28] In these renderings, Jews were simply objects slated for murder, and murdered they were. Little effort was made to establish readers' closeness to the victims. Raul Hilberg's 1961 work *The Destruction of European Jews* encapsulates this approach. Unpacked exclusively through Germans' eyes and words, Hilberg's Jews present as "helpless."[29] Nowhere in his narrative does Jewish intentionality, resistance, or survival garner mention. Expunging Jewish agency overlooks a great deal of facts and lore that existed at the time and has persisted in received memory, the kinds of stories Daniel Torday interweaves in *The Last Flight of Poxl West*.[30] Furthermore, by the early 1960s when Hilberg was writing, current events seemed to indicate that portraying Jews as simple sheep to the slaughter was out of touch with the times.

Hilberg's seminal work in fact appeared during the same period that Israeli courts stood in judgment of Adolf Eichmann, the SS official responsible for managing the deportation trains. Eichmann's trial was not significant for the justice that it imposed on a middling bureaucrat. Rather, as philosopher Hannah Arendt recognized, his capture, judging, and eventual execution repositioned existing perceptions of Nazi invincibility and Jewish vulnerability.[31] As her book's title stated, Eichmann was in Jerusalem. He was imprisoned in the Jewish state's capitol, far removed from any vestiges of past authority. While residue of his sinister deeds still scarred untold millions, his current ramblings held little power. By asserting Jewish dominion over their former captors, Israeli Jews and their "Never Again"[32] American cousins could now celebrate both Jewish suffering and endurance. This might be said to represent the traditional American commitment to witness, one formed by second-generation daughters and sons.[33]

Some American poets, notably Gerald Stern, William Heyen, and Sylvia Plath, brought the Holocaust to the public through their writings.[34] They conflated memory of the victims' loss to their own feelings of suffering. In *Daddy*, which Plath penned during the Eichmann trial, just a few months before her suicide, the verses repeatedly conflated her aching with prisoners'.[35] Hers is a self-directed empathy, but one that also indexes Jewish loss. "An engine, an engine. Chuffing me off like a Jew. A Jew to Dachau, Auschwitz, Belsen. I began to talk like a Jew. I think I may well be a Jew."[36] Such approximations were not simply creative license. The words animate her pain as a daughter and wife. Prior to writing *Daddy*, Plath had already lashed out at her parents in both her private journals and published fiction. There is a moment in

The Bell Jar when Plath's character, Esther Greenwood, is talking about her mother with her doctor and blurts out: "I hate her." Her doctor says, "I suppose you do."[37] That by her life's end Plath found in Holocaust contexts her method for conveying despair speaks both to her personal torment and the memory's growing social significance.[38] Such writings contrasted directly with Theodor Adorno's judgment that all poetry after Auschwitz was "barbaric," pointing instead to American cultural producers valuing the loss as a muse.[39]

Also during the 1960s and 1970s, scriptwriters for American television programs, as Jeffrey Shandler has demonstrated, mined the Holocaust for content.[40] These were episodes that reminded viewers that the fight against German fascism had been in part a fight against anti-Semitism. The 1963 *Twilight Zone* episode "He's Alive" conveyed this message.[41] Aired just six months after Adolf Eichmann's execution, the show cast Dennis Hopper as an American Nazi named Pete Vollmer.[42] In the episode, Vollmer is a rabble-rouser who spends his days spewing anti-Jewish bigotries. In line with the *Twilight Zone* genre, Adolf Hitler soon appears to Vollmer in the flesh and mesmerizes him. "You invoked my name, You took my ideas," the Hitler figure bellowed. "Now, we are immortal!"[43] During the episode's closing monologue, the show's Jewish American creator and lead writer, Rod Serling, a World War II veteran, discussed his script's leitmotif. Abiding ethnoracial prejudices, he explained, put Americans at risk of resuscitating Hitlerism, perhaps in a domestic context. During the Cold War, pointing out overlaps between Nazi and Soviet totalitarianism, especially their similar mistreatment of minority populations, rendered Holocaust stories an effective teaching tool.[44] Such accounts also proved popular with the baby boomer generation seeking to contemplate the enormity of this earlier time. In 1978, the American miniseries *Holocaust* attracted more than one hundred million viewers.[45] A few years later, the commercial appeal of literature-to-film adaptations like *Sophie's Choice* reaffirmed the empathetic American commitment to remembering.

Perhaps the best known example of this is Steven Spielberg's film *Schindler's List*. Its story tells of a Nazi factory owner who came to reject German racial laws and save Jewish lives. *Schindler's List* is not squarely a World War II film. It does not index the American wartime experience at all. However, Spielberg's messaging stirred domestic audiences because it situated Holocaust lessons within the Christian redemptive metanarrative. Commemorating Oskar Schindler as the archetypical sinner turned savior provided nontraditional audiences, those with no personal ties to the story, with a familiar bridge to memory.[46] At the time of its release, the head of Walt Disney film studios remarked that the picture will "end up being more than a movie . . . it will affect how people on this planet act and think."[47] Indeed, *Schindler's List* creators had clear pedagogical ambitions. During his acceptance speech for the film's best-picture honor, Spielberg implored educators, "please teach this [Holocaust] in your schools."[48] He made the film available for free school screenings.[49] Corporate entities like the Ford Motor Company also took up the cause. In 1997, they sponsored *Schindler's List* for free airing on network television. Combined with the opening of the United States Holocaust Memorial Museum, which followed shortly after the picture's debut, President Carter's earlier vision about Americans welcoming the Holocaust into public memory appeared to have taken form.

It was a timely development. The surge in mid-1990s Holocaust awareness came about at approximately the same moment in which the generation for whom the destruction remained a personal memory was starting to disappear. This transition from lived, personal recollections to culturally imagined representations captured the weight of Spielberg's pleas. Absent the survivor's authority, students, educators, and artists must now assume all responsibility for remembrance.[50] The growing centrality of mediated accounts, however, also unintentionally focuses scrutiny on what and how educators are teaching. It raises the issue of how prepared current students are to receive the legacy. Some students may decide that their "emotional plate" is too full for someone else's tragedy from the past, while others may reject the requirement to participate in a social ritual to which they find no personal connection or which may even appear to usurp their own victimhood or marginalization.[51] At the other end of the spectrum, we also note the existence of students who are poised and ready to "suffer," as a socially conditioned expectation and a personal proclivity.[52] One thing seems clear. Now may be the time to rethink how we teach our students. Bringing into the classroom new literature, absent Aristotelian catharsis, can complement traditional empathy-arousing techniques and provide students with the tools they need to form intellectual connections.

Part Two: Modeling Distance in American Holocaust Pedagogy

In 1986, during his Nobel Peace Prize acceptance speech, Elie Wiesel implored people to "take sides" against social persecution. "Silence," he observed, "encourages the tormentor, never the tormented."⁵³ Twenty-first-century American classroom educators have widely accepted Wiesel's challenge. Most teachers generally agree that the primary goal of Holocaust lessons is promoting empathetic sensibilities and prosocial behaviors that will motivate their students not to become bystanders to (or even perpetrators of) genocide. At times, like with the Whitwell, Tennessee, "paper clips" project,⁵⁴ the approach is successful, and nontraditional learners embrace the memory. By representing European Jewish suffering as an emotionally universal lesson—the byproduct of racism and silence—Whitwell's middle schoolers (and their community) made Holocaust stories usable in their own lives. Representing the victims' deaths via piles of paper clips offered a scalable model for contemplating the losses. Bringing an authentic German cattle car to rest on their school grounds expanded the topography of the genocide.⁵⁵ Embracing the curriculum also charted multidimensional memory in the sense that remembering European Jewish victimization enabled community members to confront localized tales of African Americans' persecutions.⁵⁶

Such holistic learning illustrates how later generations can join bygone traumas to their own social environments. As Jeffrey Alexander explains, "We redeem tragedy by experiencing it, but despite this redemption, we do not get over it. Rather, to achieve redemption we are compelled to dramatize and redramatize, experience and reexperience the archetypal trauma. We pity the victims of the trauma, identifying and sympathizing with their horrible fate."⁵⁷ Alexander's analysis provides a rationale for why middle schoolers with limited attachments to the memory might have committed to remembering. Less well understood is how this tendency—embracing *pathos*-centric narratives as a value in and of itself—influences the type of knowledge that students ultimately form.⁵⁸ We recommend confronting the idea that we know very little about real learning outcomes of Holocaust education. Some experts actually conclude that studying the subject yields "dubious long-term benefits."⁵⁹ We are especially concerned that contemporary American adolescents and young adults are primed to experience appropriative empathy by virtue of their immersion in a culture that values and promotes emotional entertainment for personal benefit. That these learners prove eager to internalize gritty Holocaust accounts does not mean they are forming any useful knowledge, however, and may instead be primarily satisfying a narcissistic impulse.⁶⁰

American educators have also occasionally rendered murky experiential encounters. In 2009, a Las Vegas high school disciplined one of its teachers for encouraging students to question the scope of Jewish losses.[61] In 2013, an Albany, New York, teacher likewise faced discipline after asking learners to write an essay supporting the Nazis' Holocaust perspective.[62] Even in regions with visible Jewish communities, like New York City, instructors at the Ethical Culture Fieldston School taught sixth graders that the swastika denoted varying cultural messages.[63] Redirecting the swastika's meaning toward its benign rather than genocidal connotations points to a larger destabilizing of canon. And this is not just an American phenomenon. The annual Iranian Holocaust Cartoon festival,[64] or the unwillingness of Dutch Muslim students to study Anne Frank,[65] points to contests about remembering, or forgetting. As Gavriel Rosenfeld explains in *Hi Hitler!*, this contest will define twenty-first century Holocaust commemoration. Like it or not, rejecting Jewish pleas for empathy is no longer entirely taboo. The Third Reich (and its crimes) is no longer reflexively depicted as sinister, and in cultural postmemory it may even present as comical or fun.[66]

In this protean environment, we are wondering if something that we are terming "distance" might disrupt emotional involvement and instead direct students to the harder tasks of educational inquiry. Distancing techniques point out to students the subtle workings of cultural sentimentalism. They might specifically pique nontraditional students' interest, those skeptical of Holocaust texts as the definitive word on suffering, because, as Young observes, the educative focus shifts from achieving a collective emotional end to gleaning narrower insights about unique experiences.[67] We are suggesting two distancing techniques: shifting learners' focus to studying formal literary techniques and the choice of texts that carve out space for readers' contemplation by undermining affective empathy.

How might this pedagogy look? Take, for example, an approach that compares a classical Holocaust narrative, Elie Wiesel's *Night*,[68] to a lesser known and taught text, Imre Kertész's *Fatelessness*.[69] Both authors gained wide recognition through their Holocaust literature: Wiesel became the Nobel Peace Prize winner, and Kertész became the Nobel Prize winner for literature. Wiesel's work is universally recognized as canonical. Kertész's text was translated into its best English adaptation in 2004, shortly after his 2002 Nobel Prize award, but is largely unknown in the United

States. Comparing such literature is useful because, as Hungerford notes, it trains attention on the variations possible in Holocaust storytelling.[70] Be it the prior text of Dante's *Divine Comedy* before reading Primo Levi's chapter "The Canto of Ulysses," or, in our case, the prior text of *Night* next to *Fatelessness*, the comparative process directs student attention toward interrogating narrative technique and away from the affect that these techniques might create.[71] Even if teachers cannot assign both Wiesel and Kertész, there exists a need to think about how such an approach could work.

One easily accessible point of analysis and comparison is the narrator. A focus on the narrator, of a single text or two compared, will require students to disengage from the effect of the narrative to understand the goals of each author and the techniques used to achieve them. Both texts employ a first-person narrator. In the case of *Night*, this narrative voice is the implied author, Wiesel, the survivor. Standard pedagogy finds American educators inserting the text in their courses as if it were testimony.[72] In fact, numerous educators recommend *Night* precisely because it is perceived as being historically accurate, short, and possessing of an "approachable" narrative voice.[73] What may be ignored in this approach are the fictional techniques that mark the text as memoir. First and foremost, *Night* is a text of witness. What kind of witness? One in which readers are invited to see for themselves the horror as Wiesel narrates it. In his important work on secondary witness, Weissman explores the American drive to "feel the horror" experientially as a means of understanding the Holocaust and to hedge against forgetting.[74]

There are, according to Rothberg, two approaches to Holocaust representation toward which writers gravitate: the realist or the antirealist.[75] Wiesel's narrative is antirealist insofar as the narrative gesture throughout *Night* is one of "you cannot know," echoing already Wiesel's own position that the Holocaust is a sacred, unknowable caesura of human history; only the survivor can truly grasp its meaning. Thus, for his readers to witness what, according to Wiesel himself, they cannot understand, Wiesel makes uses of literary fictional techniques, the most readily recognizable being his use of prophetic figures and symbolism, but also dialogic strategies such as free indirect discourse.[76] We agree with Hammond that literary modernism developed the processes needed to bring readers closer to another person's thoughts and feelings. Such methods put forward what she calls "cognitive alignment" as character, narrator, and reader briefly overlap."[77] Helping students note the differences between testimony and memoir as genre would certainly lead to questions about the choices the author Wiesel made in an historical moment when testimony itself was rare, and few audiences for Holocaust witness yet existed.[78] It may also lead to an exploration of the genre used by survivors of other catastrophes.

So successful has *Night* become that educators can be lulled into the expectation that the book will "do the work" of promoting empathy and, by extension, prosocial behavior.[79] Consequently, instruction is often narrowly focused on reader identification with the protagonist. A useful distancing technique would be instead to direct attention to the narrator as narrator, that is, to ask how Wiesel created a narrator that invites cowitnessing of the reader. Deconstructing the literary technique will reveal that Wiesel's narrative voice is in fact the adult Eliezer, who knows far more about the historical situation than the child Eliezer could possibly know. Such a narrator can attribute thoughts to his childhood self, add factual information, and comment on the narrated scene. Hernandez, in describing his approach to teaching *Night* to middle schoolers, suggests that the intervening years between narrative voice and adolescent protagonist are less important.[80] But even middle schoolers could be directed to see the interplay of the implied author (Wiesel), the adult narrator, and the child protagonist and could be guided to ask why Wiesel chose such techniques. Nontraditional students especially may appreciate searching for "clues" to when/how authors' techniques prod their compassion. Educators can very easily direct student attention to narrator interjections, for example, as sites of emotional production, but also as points at which Wiesel's narrator insists that moral and spiritual questions be pondered.[81] Finally, *Night's* emotional poignancy is enacted not only through identification with young Eliezer, but also in part through situational empathy. Such empathy functions through recognition of one's own prior experience (and associated feelings) in the story of another.[82] How situational empathy functions through literary technique is a further topic teachers could address with students.

The focus on the narrator in *Night* will prepare students for a critical reading of *Fatelessness* because it is precisely the narrative perspective that provides an entirely different co-witnessing function. At nearly three hundred pages, *Fatelessness* does not compete with *Night* for brevity. But, similar to *Night*, its first-person narrator, fifteen-year-old Gyuri, is an adolescent boy. Also like *Night*, the historical contours of the story follow Kertesz's own biography: deportation from Hungary, transport to

Auschwitz and then Buchenwald, and a return to his native Budapest. Unlike *Night*, however, Kertesz's text is identified in the peritext as a novel. Does the choice of fiction over memoir undermine the authenticity that many educators and students seek when approaching the Holocaust? Yes and no. The consonant first-person narration of *Fatelessness*, the voice of a fifteen-year-old, and its mimetic reproduction of everyday life through embodied subjectivity signal a certain authenticity. However, the reader's expectations of a memoir qua *Night* are quickly undermined. This narrator is not reflecting on past events; rather, he is narrating events as they occur, as the opening line makes clear, "I didn't go to school today."[83] From this perspective, the fifteen-year-old narrator does not know what the reader already knows, namely, that the daily events he lives through will become known as the Holocaust. This technique obviates an authoritative narrative voice anticipating the catastrophe to come. Unlike in *Night*, no adult perspective instructs readers as to where to direct their considerations. Rather, Kertesz positions his readers as distanced observers watching Gyuri work his way down a winding path toward an end the readers already know.[84] Whereas Wiesel's omniscient narrator keeps the reader within the narrative, Kertesz's text forces the reader into the position of authorial audience; that is, Kertesz's use of irony requires the reader to read the text from the outside looking in.

Readers who engage *Fatelessness* are often particularly intrigued by the propensity of the text to undermine their expectations of Holocaust canon.[85] Kertész uses the standard tropes (roundups, deportation, selection, dehumanization), but their unpacking is atypical because the events are observed through the filter of the narrator's ignorance. For example, Gyuri likens the death camp selection process to a friendly competition with his buddies to see who "makes the team."[86] He describes the atmosphere at the Buchenwald railway station as "friendly." Such incongruity between Gyuri's perceptions and concentration camp realities exasperates readers' expectations. However, it is precisely this incongruity that can prompt substantive classroom discussions not only about Kertesz's intentions, but also about the nature of our daily experiences. *Fatelessness* does not entirely deny readers' emotional needs. In the Zeitz subcamp, Gyuri, now a *Muselmann* and near death, has an understanding of his experiences that finally corresponds to Holocaust realities. This is the point in the narrative when the readers' needs for familiar testimony are met. From his anger and raw survivalist language, Kertész permits sympathy, which earlier in the novel proved elusive. But even in these potentially empathic scenes, Kertész insists on impudence. "I would like to live a little bit longer in this beautiful concentration camp," Gyuri declares.[87] Here the potential irony of the word "beautiful" applied to a concentration camp is mitigated by the reader's recognition that Gyuri understands his predicament, and life is indeed preferable to death.

This is how readers come to recognize that, although it is unorthodox, *Fatelessness* is not a farce. What Kertész uniquely brings to consideration of the Holocaust—and Holocaust literature—is his attempt to understand and explain how civilized human beings can become involved with genocide. Through the eyes of a fifteen-year-old, we see the mundane steps of everyday life. We come to recognize how seemingly innocuous, gradual daily steps pave a path to catastrophe.[88] And who is to blame? Gyuri casts a wide net, irreverently pointing fingers at victims, himself included, declaring that humankind collectively played a role in facilitating the program of murder.[89] While awkward and unsatisfying, such judgments reflect new types of learning opportunities for new types of student learners. It is a sophistication born of readers' cognitively engaging difficult narratives without the aid of collective compassion. Recovering more of what Walter Reich has termed these "unwelcome narratives,"[90] stories devoid of closure, forgiveness, or hope have a transformative potential in the classroom, helping people with no necessary Holocaust ties to recognize how their choices ultimately may render them bystanders, rescuers, perpetrators, or victims.

Conclusion: Challenges of Distance and Empathy in American Holocaust Pedagogy

In May 2014, a Holocaust denial scandal erupted in Rialto, California. Local journalists published stories describing an essay assignment given to the community's middle schoolers.[91] The learning prompt was troubling. It asked the twelve-year-old respondents, "Do you believe claims that the Holocaust was an actual event, or is it a propaganda tool used for political and monetary gain?"[92] Some two thousand students submitted essays. Several dozen affirmed the assertion that the Nazis' war on Jews was imagined. Because this essay was designed as the capstone to the school's Anne Frank literary unit, onlookers were puzzled as to how these students had gleaned the exact opposite messages from those conveyed in the familiar adaptation of her diary. As Rialto's community is overwhelmingly composed of citizens with no ties to this history, reflecting what we have termed nontraditional witnesses, some Jewish leaders voiced concerns that the memory was in danger of being lost.[93]

The denialist essays proved to be only part of the problem. Equally worrying was the fact that the district's language arts teachers awarded some of these essays top scores, presumably because the focus of the teachers' rubric was on writing skills, not content. One student wrote, "With the evidence I have seen, it was obvious that the Holocaust was a hoax and I wouldn't know why anyone would think otherwise." Another learner exclaimed, "Six million Jews died in 'gas chambers.' Like seriously 'gas chambers,' do they even exist?! Not real!"[94] Further inflaming the emerging scandal was evidence that Rialto teachers had unwittingly sanctioned some of this denialism. In what was depicted as an effort to foster "critical thinking," faculty members disseminated literature downloaded from white supremacist websites that assailed Anne's diary as fake.[95] For those students who may have already been ambivalent about the story's historical significance, the denialist arguments, unchallenged by their teachers, could have presented an alternative truth taken from authority.

Such goings-on are more than just anecdotal. They partially reflect the incommensurable demands on teachers to meet multiple learning outcomes, making it possible for them to lose sight of important priorities. Furthermore, the long-standing prominence of Holocaust history in American culture may have unwittingly left in some teachers an expectation that the mere exposure to victims' accounts is enough to promote compassion and learning. This may no longer be the case. We have attempted to explain how this traditional empathetic expectation can undermine Holocaust education. It overlooks how contemporary American culture, with its emphasis on the production of emotional entertainment, provides a backdrop against which students have learned to consume Holocaust stories for their personal enjoyment. This may be why, after visiting Anne Frank's Amsterdam memorial in 2013, Canadian pop star Justin Bieber characterized her as a "great girl."[96] Younger people report higher levels of emotional thrill seeking and empathetic sadness (e.g., "I like being moved to tears," "I like being overwhelmed with emotion") than adults, which impacts their Holocaust learning.[97] In this sense, taking the emotional literary "plunge" may signal not so much learners' desires to internalize aspects of European Jewish suffering as their self-directed efforts to soothe their own egotistical needs. Unless educators are prepared to explain to their classes that "enjoying" Holocaust literature is not the same as studying it, students may walk away from their curriculum work with no discernable prosocial outcome.[98]

We can help remedy this gap by analyzing the exclusive use of particular narrative types, specifically those most likely to produce affect, as authoritative texts. To this canon we can begin adding stories that carve out distance, which are more likely to enjoin cognitive empathy, a powerful form of critical thinking. Such texts are particularly useful for students who have little Holocaust awareness. Texts such as *Fatelessness* are much more likely to facilitate the types of critical thinking skills that Rialto teachers, and other teachers facing the same challenges, hoped to engender. Of course, no reason exists that nontraditional learners cannot also form emotional bonds to Holocaust tales. As Rialto students read *Night* as part of their relearning about the Holocaust, one teacher reported "not a dry eye" in his classroom.[99] However, "seeing with" is not equal to "seeing the same thing" because our cultural horizons of experience and expectation impact our reception and memory. Moreover, as Sharon Holland reminds us, each generation must "enter into a history that is literally not their own."[100] With regard to Holocaust remembrances, the universalist traditions that have brought people along since the 1960s—teaching based on calls for compassion—now appear susceptible. Temporal and physical distance, changes in target audiences, and the reality that ours is a world scarred by repeated instances of mass murder collectively increase potential gaps between the victims' suffering and its memorialization.[101]

These sorts of fissures do not necessarily index Holocaust rejection so much as they point out the limits of rooting genocide lessons in purely emotional ways. As Peter Novick observes in "The American National Narrative of the Holocaust: There Isn't Any," the Nazis' war on Jews is not really an American memory. Its high visibility in the United States, he concludes, is a "byproduct—to some extent an unintended byproduct—of American Jews' heightened concern with its remembrance."[102] Novick's analysis hints at the existence of additional fault lines in the commemorative landscape such as those that cropped up in Rialto, which in turn raise questions about teaching the discipline moving forward. Just because postwar non-Jewish Americans have joined their Jewish neighbors in deploring the Holocaust does not simultaneously signal its permanent dialogic truth.[103] Some people may have venerated Holocaust accounts at the expense of confronting more localized tales of persecution perhaps involving violence against African Americans or Native Americans. Others may have seen in the legacy a metaphor for repentance, forgiveness, and ultimately closure. Complacently vague banalities about the imperative to "never forget," while common in public discourse and pedagogy, are not analogous to remembering.[104] As cultural and literary producers continue to reconstitute the legacy's meaning and representation in sometimes shocking and unorthodox ways,[105] classroom educators and their students confront the shared challenge of ensuring that the Holocaust is remembered at all. Such observations highlight a subtler truth. It ultimately matters less if Americans dutifully honor victims' memories than it does that this guardianship affirms the idea that combating genocide bolsters the nations' values. Absent this commitment, ritualized remembrances may only end up highlighting, first, Americans' continued failure to stamp out the practice and, second, the limits of teaching literature as a method for reaching this end.

Notes

1. Zev Garber and Bruce Zuckerman, "Why Do We Call the Holocaust "The Holocaust?": An Inquiry Into the Psychology of Labels," *Modern Judaism* 9, no. 1 (1989): 202; Leon Jick, "The Holocaust: Its Use and Abuse Within the American Public," *Yad Vashem Studies* 14 (1981): 303–18.

2. Ronald Grigor Suny, *"They Can Live in the Desert but Nowhere Else": A History of the Armenian Genocide* (Princeton: Princeton University Press, 2015).

3. Richard Breitman, *The Architect of Genocide: Himmler and the Final Solution* (New York: Knopf, 1991), 41; Kevork Bardakjian, *Hitler and the Armenian Genocide* (Cambridge: Zoryan Institute), 1985, 1. Significant debate surrounds the question of whether or not Adolf Hitler ever uttered this statement. In a written correspondence with the co-author (Demsky), historical consultant Peter Black noted that Hitler rarely mentioned the Armenians in either his writings or ramblings. Moreover, the harsh language associated with the popular quote appears only in a questioned version of the speech that was provided to Louis P. Lochner, the chief of the Associated Press Bureau in Berlin, by a "German youth leader." While uncertainty about the Lochner version surfaced immediately, the rendition has nevertheless taken hold in both popular and academic memory. Peter Black, email message to co-author, June 29, 2016.

4. Peter Novick, *The Holocaust in American Life* (Boston: Houghton Mifflin, 1999), 85.

5. For more on Americanization, see Sarah Pinnock, "Atrocity and Ambiguity: Recent Developments in Christian Holocaust Responses," *Journal of the American Academy of Religion* 75, no. 3 (2007): 516; Pól Dochartaigh, "Americanizing the Holocaust: The Case of *Jakob the Liar*," *Modern Language Review* 101, no. 2 (2006): 459.

6. Henryk Broder, "We Invented the Holocaust!," *Transition* 89 (2001): 74.

7. As quoted in James Young, "America's Holocaust: Memory and Politics of Identity," in *The Americanization of the Holocaust*, ed. Hilene Flanzbaum (Baltimore: Johns Hopkins University Press, 1999), 72–73.

8. Emerging during the late 1960s and visible in current literature is the claim that Christian American anti-Semitism across society and government produced a de facto "abandonment" of European Jewry. While some prominent Holocaust scholars have tried repositioning this finding, noting President Franklin Roosevelt's many "humanitarian" impulses, our point is simply that the US government was not close to the genocide issue when it was happening. For American wartime anti-Semitism, see Joseph Bendersky, *The Jewish Threat: Antisemitic Politics of the US Army* (New York: Basic Books, 2000), 300; Suzanne Brown-Fleming, "The Worst Enemies of a Better Germany": Postwar Antisemitism among Catholic Clergy and US Occupation Forces," *Holocaust and Genocide Studies* 18, no. 3 (2004): 379–401; David Wyman, *The Abandonment of the Jews: America and the Holocaust, 1941–1945* (New York: Pantheon Books, 1984), 14. For analysis of philo-Semitism in wartime American society reaching into the White House, see Richard Breitman and Allan Lichtman, *FDR and the Jews* (Cambridge, Massachusetts: The Belknap Press of Harvard University Press, 2013), 59, 116, 273; Joseph Bendersky, "Dissension in the Face of the Holocaust: The 1941 American Debate over Antisemitism," *Holocaust and Genocide Studies* 24, no. 1 (2010): 89–92; William Rubenstein and Hilary Rubinstein, *Philosemitism: Admiration and Support in the English-speaking World for Jews* (New York: St. Martin's Press, 1999), 191.

9. David MacDonald, "First Nations, Residential Schools, and the Americanization of the Holocaust: Rewriting Indigenous History in the United States and Canada," *Canadian Journal of Political Science* 40, no. 4 (2007): 997.

10. In 1902, Secretary of State John Hay received a petition from American Jewish leaders concerned with Czarist pogroms. His sentiments were fulsome. "In the future when students of history come to peruse this document," Hay exclaimed, "they will wonder how the petitioners, moved to profound indignation by intolerable wrongs perpetrated on the innocent and helpless, could have expressed themselves in a language so earnest and eloquent . . . It is a valuable addition to public literature, and it will be sacredly cherished among the treasures of the Department." Despite the approbations, nothing was done. As quoted in Stephen Whitfield, "The Jewish Vote," *Virginia Quarterly Review* 61 (1986): 9.

11. Edward Tabor Linenthal, *Preserving Memory: The Struggle to Create America's Holocaust Museum* (New York: Viking, 1995), 63.

12. "Facts and Figures," United States Holocaust Memorial Museum, February 1 2016, https://www.ushmm.org/information/press/press-kits/united-states-holocaust-memorial-museum-press-kit.

13. Erica Lehrer, "Shoah-business, Holocaust Culture, and the Repair of the World in Post-Jewish Poland: A Quest for Ethnography, Empathy, and the Ethnic Self after Genocide," Ph.D. diss., University of Michigan, 2005, 31; Norman Finkelstein, *The Holocaust Industry: Reflection on the Exploitation of Jewish Suffering* (New York: Verso, 2000), 108; Phillip Lopate, *Portrait of My Body* (New York: Anchor Books, 1996), 91–93; Tim Cole, *Selling the Holocaust: From Auschwitz to Schindler: How History Is Bought, Packaged, and Sold* (New York: Routledge, 1991), 81.

14. Alison Landsberg, "America, the Holocaust, and the Mass Culture of Memory: Toward a Radical Politics of Empathy," *New German Critique* 71 (1997): 63–66.

15. "Laughter at Film Brings Spielberg Visit," *New York Times*, April 13, 1994, http://www.nytimes.com/1994/04/13/us/laughter-at-film-brings-spielberg-visit.html.

16. *Seinfeld*, episodes 82 and 83, "The Raincoats," directed by Tom Cherones, written by Larry David and Jerry Seinfeld, featuring Jerry Seinfeld, aired April 28, 1994, on NBC.

17. Rachel Feldhay Brenner, "Holocaust Culture In Perspective: Evading the Holocaust Story and Its Legacy of Responsibility," *Dapim* 26, no. 1 (2012): 125.

18. Phillip Roth, *Portnoy's Complaint* (New York: Random House, 1969), 75.

19. Zayin B'Ayin, "Crossfit Is Dumb. Crossfit at a Holocaust Memorial Is Even Dumber," *Heeb*, August 10, 2015, http://heebmagazine.com/crossfit-is-dumb-crossfit-at-a-holocaust-memorial-is-even-dumber/55314.

20. Ronald Bayor, *Neighbors in Conflict: The Irish, Germans, Jews, and Italians of New York City, 1929–1941* (Baltimore: Johns Hopkins University Press, 1978), 106–7; Ira Katznelson, "Strangers No Longer: Jews and Postwar American Political Culture," in Deborah Dash Moore and S. Ilan Troen, eds., *Divergent Jewish Cultures: Israel and America* (New Haven: Yale University Press, 2001), 304–18.

21. Yosefa Loshitzky, introduction to *Spielberg's Holocaust: Critical Perspectives on Schindler's List*, ed. Yosefa Loshitzky (Bloomington: Indiana University Press, 1997), 4.

22. Ruth Klüger, *Still Alive: A Holocaust Girlhood Remembered* (New York: Feminist Press at the City University of New York, 2001), 123.

23. Ibid., 38.

24. Tova Reich, *My Holocaust: A Novel* (New York: Harper and Collins, 2007).

25. David Margolick, "Happy Campers," *New York Times*, May 27, 2007, http://www.nytimes.com/2007/05/27/books/review/Margolick-t.html?_r=0.

26. See Rider for a typology of Holocaust texts in terms of their generation of affect. N. Ann Rider, "The Perils of Empathy: Holocaust Narratives, Cognitive Studies and the Politics of Sentiments," *Holocaust Studies* 19, no. 3 (2013): 43–72.

27. Laura Jockusch, *Collect and Record!: Jewish Holocaust Documentation in Early Postwar Europe* (New York: Oxford University Press, 2012), 194; Roni Stauber, *Laying the Foundations for Holocaust Research: The Impact of the Historian Philip Friedman* (Jerusalem: Yad Vashem, 2009); Joseph Lichten, "Phillip Friedman—Founder of Holocaust Historiography," *Polish Review* 27, nos. 3/4 (1982): 216.

28. As quoted in Boaz Cohen, "Jews, Jewish Studies and Holocaust Historiography," in *Writing the Holocaust*, ed. Jean-Marc Dreyfus and Daniel Langton (New York: Bloomsbury Academic, 2011), 101.

29. Raul Hilberg, *The Destruction of the European Jews* (Chicago: Quadrangle Books, 1961), 666.

30. Daniel Torday, *The Last Flight of Poxl West: A Novel* (New York: St. Martin's Press, 2015), 180.

31. Hannah Arendt, *Eichmann in Jerusalem: A Report on the Banality of Evil* (New York: Viking Press, 1963), 253–55. See also A. Dirk Moses, "Das römische Gespräch in a New Key: Hannah Arendt, Genocide, and the Defense of Republican Civilization," *Journal of Modern History* 85, no. 4 (2013): 877; Charles Turner, "The Motivating Text: Assigning Hannah Arendt's *Eichmann in Jerusalem*," *PS: Political Science and Politics* 38, no. 1 (2005): 68.

32. For the phrase as a call to arms, see Meir Kahane, *Never Again!: A Program for Survival* (Los Angeles: Nash Publishing, 1971).

33. Nina Fischer, *Memory Work: The Second Generation* (Basingstoke: Palgrave Macmillan 2015), 106; Thomas Fallace, "The Origins of Holocaust Education in American Public Schools," *Holocaust and Genocide Studies* 20, no. 1 (2006): 80; Alan Berger, "The Holocaust, Second-Generation Witness, and the Voluntary Covenant in American Judaism," *Religion and American Culture* 5, no. 1 (1995): 23–47.

34. Harriet Parmet, *The Terror of Our Days: Four American Poets Respond to the Holocaust* (Bethlehem, PA: Lehigh University Press, 2001), 20.

35. Gale Swiontkowski, *Imagining Incest: Sexton, Plath, Rich, and Olds on Life with Daddy* (Selinsgrove, PA: Susquehanna University Press, 2003), 145.

36. Ted Hughes, ed., *Sylvia Plath: The Collected Poems* (New York: Harper Perennial Modern Classics, 2008), 222.

37. As quoted in Katie Roiphe, ""Daddy" Is Mommy," *Slate Magazine*, February 11, 2013, http://www.slate.com/articles/double_x/roiphe/2013/02/sylvia_plath_s_poem_daddy_is_about_her_mother.html.

38. For Plath's Holocaust appropriations, see Jacqueline Rose, *The Haunting of Sylvia Plath* (Cambridge, MA: Harvard University Press, 1992), 205–38.

39. Howard Caygill, "Lyric Poetry Before Auschwitz," in *Adorno and Literature*, ed. David Cunningham and Nigel Mapp (New York: Continuum, 2006), 70.

40. Jeffrey Shandler, *While America Watches: Televising the Holocaust* (New York: Oxford University Press, 1999), 23.

41. The Twilight Zone, episode 4, "He's Alive," written by Rod Serling, directed by Stuart Rosenberg, featuring Dennis Hopper et al., aired January 4, 1963, on CBS.

42. Jeffrey Shandler, *While America Watches: Televising the Holocaust* (New York: Oxford University Press, 1999), 140.

43. Serling, *He's Alive*.

44. Michael Rothberg, *Multidirectional Memory: Remembering the Holocaust in the Age of Decolonization* (Stanford: Stanford University Press, 2009), 117; John Elsom, *Cold War Theatre* (New York: Routledge, 1992), 31.

45. Lawrence Baron, "The Armenian-Jewish Connection: The Influence of Holocaust Cinema on Feature Films about the Armenian Genocide," in *The Holocaust: Memories and History*, ed. Victoria Khiterer, Ryan Barrick, and David Misral (Newcastle upon Tyne: Cambridge Scholars Publishing, 2014), 295; Emiliano Perra, "Narratives of Innocence and Victimhood: The Reception of the Miniseries *Holocaust* in Italy," *Holocaust and Genocide Studies* 22, no. 3 (2008): 414; Jeffrey Shandler, "Schindler's Discourse: America Discusses the Holocaust and Its Mediation, from NBC's Miniseries to Spielberg's Film," in Loshitzky, *Spielberg's Holocaust*, 1997, 154.

46. Henry Gonshak, *Hollywood and the Holocaust* (New York: Roman and Littlefield, 2015), 201–2.

47. As quoted in Alvin Rosenfeld, *The End of the Holocaust* (Bloomington: Indiana University Press, 2011), 82.

48. Steven Spielberg, "Acceptance Speech," 66th Annual Academy Awards, Dorothy Chandler Pavilion, United States, March 21, 1994), http://aaspeechesdb.oscars.org/link/066-16/.

49. Bryan Alexander, "Spielberg Takes Horrors of the Holocaust into Classrooms," *USA Today*, March 3, 2013, http://www.usatoday.com/story/life/movies/2013/03/03/steven-spielberg-holocaust-shoah/1957625/.

50. Lynn Rapaport, "Hollywood's Holocaust: *Schindler's List* and the Construction of Memory," *Film & History* 32, no. 1 (2002): 55–65.

51. Diana Dumitru, "The Use and Abuse of the Holocaust: Historiography and Politics in Moldova," *Holocaust and Genocide Studies* 22, no. 1 (2010): 56; Elena Ivanova, "Ukrainian High School Students' Understanding of the Holocaust," *Holocaust and Genocide Studies* 18, no. 3 (2004): 402–20.

52. Rider, "Perils," 53.

53. Elie Wiesel, "Acceptance Speech," Nobel Prize Awards Ceremony, Oslo Grand Hotel, Norway, December 10, 1986, https://www.nobelprize.org/nobel_prizes/peace/laureates/1986/wiesel-acceptance_en.html.

54. Peter Schroeder and Dagmar Schroeder-Hildebrand, *Six Million Paper Clips: The Making of a Children's Holocaust Memorial* (Minneapolis: Kar-Ben Publishing, 2004).

55. Tim Cole, *Holocaust Landscapes* (London: Bloomsbury Continuum, 2016), 5–6; Allan Cooper, *The Geography of Genocide* (Lanham: University Press of America, 2009), 8; Andrew Charlesworth, "The Topography of Genocide," in *The Historiography of the Holocaust*, ed. Dan Stone (Houndsmills: Palgrave, 2004), 221–22.

56. Rothberg, *Multidirectional*, 2, 120. For a thematically related study, see Maxim Silverman, *Palimpsestic Memory: The Holocaust and Colonialism in French and Francophone Fiction and Film* (New York: Berghahn Books, 2013), 74.

57. As quoted in Jeffrey Alexander, "On the Social Construction of Moral Universals," in Jeffrey Alexander et al., *Cultural Trauma and Collective Identity* (Berkeley: University of California Press, 2004), 227.

58. As Keen has argued in numerous venues, the case for altruism arising from novel reading itself is unproven. Suzanne Keen, *Empathy and the Novel* (Oxford: Oxford University Press, 2007), vii.

59. Michael Gray, *Contemporary Debates in Holocaust Education* (Houndsmills: Palgrave Macmillan, 2014), 35. Of course, we do have much anecdotal information, such as that movingly portrayed by Dutton. But several things are clear: we do not have systematic, empirical research that tells us unquestionably about the outcomes of Holocaust education. And, second, an entire Holocaust unit, with historical and sociocultural information, is necessary to reach the outcomes we seek. Our concern is with the Holocaust lesson that is positioned into the curriculum only via empathy-arousing literature. Beth Dutton, "Tapping the Sensibilities of Teens," in *Teaching Holocaust Literature*, ed. Samuel Totten (Needham Heights: Pearson, 2001), 177–96.

60. Nancy Eisenberg and Natalie Eggum, "Empathic Responding: Sympathy and Personal Distress," in *The Social Neuroscience of Empathy*, ed. Jean Decety and William Ickes (Cambridge, MA: Massachusetts Institute of Technology Press, 2009), 71.

61. Emily Richmond, "Teacher's Holocaust Remarks Spur Probe," *Las Vegas Sun*, December 29, 2009, http://lasvegassun.com/news/2009/dec/29/teachers-holocaust-remarks-spur-probe/.

62. Jesse McKinley, "Students Told to Take Viewpoint of the Nazis," *New York Times*, April 12, 2013, http://www.nytimes.com/2013/04/13/nyregion/albany-teacher-gives-pro-nazi-writing-assignment.html.

63. Tayla Zax, "Fieldston School Under Fire Over Middle School Swastika Incident," *Forward*, December 11. 2015, http://forward.com/news/breaking-news/326792/fieldston-under-fire-over-swastika-incident/.

64. Ishaan Tharoor, "Iran Revs Up for Its Latest Holocaust Cartoon Contest," *Washington Post*, May 12, 2016, https://www.washingtonpost.com/news/worldviews/wp/2016/05/12/iran-revs-up-for-its-latest-holocaust-cartoon-contest/.

65. Annemarike Stremmelaar, "Anne Frank Speaks Turkish: Retelling the Story of the Holocaust in the Netherlands," Conference paper, Millersville University 34th Conference on the Holocaust and Genocide, Millersville, PA, April 6, 2016; Abigal Esman, "On Anniversary of Anne Frank's Death, No Let-Up in Attacks On Europe's Jews," *Algemeiner* (blog), March 31, 2015 (11:25 a.m.), http://www.algemeiner.com/2015/03/31/on-anniversary-of-anne-franks-death-no-let-up-in-attacks-on-europes-jews/#. For a story of a Muslim learner embracing Anne's legacy, see Rosa Doherty, "Muslim Student Wins Anne Frank Poetry Prize," *Jewish Chronicle*, October 19, 2015, http://www.thejc.com/news/uk-news/147626/muslim-student-wins-anne-frank-poetry-prize.

66. Gavriel Rosenfeld, *Hi Hitler!: How the Nazi Past Is Being Normalized in Contemporary Culture* (Cambridge: Cambridge University Press, 2015), 6. For a recent literary example of contemporary observers having "fun" with Hitler and his memory, see Timur Vermes, *Er ist wieder da: der Roman* (Eichborn-Verlag, 2012).

67. James Young, *Writing and Rewriting the Holocaust: Narrative and the Consequences of Interpretation* (Bloomington: Indiana University Press, 1988), 10.

68. Elie Wiesel, *Night* (New York: Bantam, 1986).

69. Imre Kertész, *Fatelessness*, trans. Tim Wilkinson (New York: Random House, 2004).

70. Amy Hungerford, "Teaching Fiction, Teaching the Holocaust," in *Teaching the Representation of the Holocaust*, ed. Marianne Hirsch and Irene Kacandes (New York: Modern Language Association, 2004), 180–90.

71. Schaneman advocates such comparisons but addresses the fears of diminution of the content when the focus is on literary technique. We contend that the content is not undermined, only the total focus on affect. Judith Clark Schaneman, "Teaching *La Nuit* in Comparative Contexts," in *Approaches to Teaching Wiesel's Night*, ed. Alan Rosen (New York: Modern Language Association, 2007), 59–68. Horváth also suggests a comparison of the two texts, but confines her analysis to the common historical experience of Wiesel and Kertész among the last Hungarian transports. Rita Horváth, "Wiesel and Kertész: *Night* in the Context of Hungarian Holocaust Literature," in Rosen, *Approaches*, 69–75.

72. We don't share Totten's conjecture that *Night* is most frequently taught as a novel, though this would be a mistake as well. Our concern here is that teaching *Night* as testimony would ignore its literary qualities, which are necessary to understand *Night's* impact. See "Entering the 'Night' of the Holocaust," in *Teaching Holocaust Literature*, ed. Samuel Totten (Boston: Allyn and Bacon, 2001), 215–42.

73. Carol Danks, "Using the Literature of Elie Wiesel and Selected Poetry to Teach the Holocaust in the Secondary School History Classroom," *Social Studies* 87, no. 3 (1996): 101.

74. Gary Weissman, *Fantasies of Witnessing: Postwar Efforts to Experience the Holocaust* (Ithaca: Cornell University Press, 2004), 20.

75. Michael Rothberg, *Traumatic Realism: The Demands of Holocaust Representation* (Minneapolis: University of Minnesota Press, 2000), 107–8.

76. For these and other examples, see Susanne Klingenstein, "*Night's* Literary Art: A Close Reading of Chapter 1," in Rosen, 76–82.

77. Meghan Hammond, *Empathy and the Psychology of Literary Modernism* (Edinburgh: Edinburgh University Press, 2014), 24.

78. Wiesel was cognizant of his role in pioneering a new literary form. "If the Greeks invented tragedy," he wrote, "the Romans the epistle, and the Renaissance the sonnet, our generation invented a new literature, that of testimony." As quoted in introduction to *Jewish American Holocaust Literature: Representation in the Postmodern World*, ed. Alan Berger and Gloria Cronin (Albany: State University of New York Press, 2004), 2.

79. And this is the crux of the problem. As Culbertson has noted, the popularity of Anne Frank has led to the book's ubiquity in the classroom in various annotated versions. And yet it is perhaps the least likely narrative to help students understand the Holocaust. Elaine Culbertson, "The Diary of Anne Frank: Why I Don't Teach It," in Totten, *Teaching*, 63–69.

80. Alexander Hernandez, "Telling the Tale: Sharing Elie Wiesel's *Night* with Middle School Readers," *English Journal* 91, no. 2 (2001): 59.

81. Most educators' writing on teaching *Night* focuses on these most important aspects of the text. Eisenstein more than others recognizes the text's capacity to engage critical thinking by undermining the certitude of our understanding of the world. Paul Eisenstein, "*Night* and Critical Thinking," in Rosen, *Approaches*, 107–14.

82. Keen, *Empathy*, 80; Patrick Colm Hogan, *The Mind and Its Stories: Narrative Universals and Human Emotion* (Cambridge: Cambridge University Press, 2003), 142.

83. Kertész, *Fatelessness*, 3.

84. J. Hillis Miller, "Imre Kertész's *Fatelessness*: Fiction as Testimony," in *After Testimony: the Ethics and Aesthetics of Holocaust Narrative for the Future*, ed. Jakob Lothe, Susan Rubin Suleiman and James Phelan (Columbus: Ohio State University Press, 2012), 32–33.

85. Julia Karolle, "Imre Kertész's *Fatelessness* as Historical Fiction," in *Imre Kertész and Holocaust Literature*, ed. Louise Vasvári and Steven Totosy de Zepetnek (West Lafayette, IN: Purdue University Press, 2005), 91–92.

86. Kertész, *Fatelessness*, 86.

87. Ibid., 189.

88. Imre Kertész, "Eureka! The 2002 Nobel Lecture," *World Literature Today* (April–June 2003): 6.

89. Sarah Cohen, "Imre Kertész, Jewishness in Hungary, and the Choice of Identity," in Vasvári and Totosy de Zepetnek, *Imre*, 26–27.

90. Walter Reich, "Unwelcome Narratives: Listening to Suppressed Themes in American Holocaust Testimonies," *Poetics Today* 27, no. 2 (2006): 466.

91. Beau Yarbrough, "Holocaust Denied by Students in Rialto School Assignment," *San Bernardino Sun*, July 11, 2014, http://www.sbsun.com/social-affairs/20140711/exclusive-holocaust-denied-by-students-in-rialto-school-assignment#disqus_thread.

92. Beau Yarbrough, "Rialto Unified Defends Writing Assignment on Confirming or Denying Holocaust," *San Bernardino Sun*, May 4, 2014, http://www.sbsun.com/social-affairs/20140504/exclusive-rialto-unified-defends-writing-assignment-on-confirming-or-denying-holocaust.

93. Beau Yarbrough, "Angry Public Blasts Rialto School Board for Holocaust Assignment," *San Bernardino Sun*, May 7, 2014, http://www.sbsun.com/social-affairs/20140507/angry-public-blasts-rialto-school-board-for-holocaust-assignment.

94. Yarbrough, "Holocaust Denied."

95. Yarbrough, "Rialto Unified."

96. Matt Weinstock, "Anne Frank, Belieber?" *New Yorker*, April 17, 2013, www.newyorker.com/books/page-turner/anne-frank-belieber.

97. For a related story, see Anne Bartsch, "Emotional Gratification in Entertainment Experience," *Media Psychology* 15, no. 3 (2012): 285.

98. Gary Weissman, "Questioning Key Texts: A Pedagogical Approach to Teaching Elie Wiesel's *Night*," in Hirsch and Kacandes, *Teaching*, 333.

99. Beau Yarbrough, "Rialto Unified Teachers on Second Holocaust Assignment: There Wasn't a Dry Eye in the Room," *San Bernardino Sun*, December 11, 2014, http://www.sbsun.com/social-affairs/20141211/rialto-unified-teachers-on-second-holocaust-assignment-there-wasnt-a-dry-eye-in-the-room.

100. Sharon Holland, *The Erotic Life of Racism* (Durham: Duke University Press, 2012), 20.

101. Judith Butler, *Frames of War: When Is Life Grievable?* (London: Verso, 2009), 24.

102. As quoted in Peter Novick, "The American National Narrative of the Holocaust: There Isn't Any," *New German Critique* 90 (2003): 32.

103. Jeff Jacoby, "'Never Forget,' the World Said of the Holocaust. But the World Is Forgetting," *Boston Globe*, May 1, 2016, https://www.bostonglobe.com/opinion/2016/04/30/never-forget-world-said-holocaust-but-world-forgetting/59cUqLNFxylkW7BDuRPgNK/story.html.

104. Alan Mintz, *Popular Culture and the Shaping of Holocaust Memory in America* (Seattle: University of Washington Press, 2001), 174.

105. Jeffrey Demsky, "Searching for Humor in Dehumanization: American Situational Comedies, the Internet, and the Globalization of Holocaust Paro-

dies," in *Analysing Language & Humor in Online Discourse*, ed. Rotimi Taiwo, Akinola Odebunmi, and Akin Adetunji (Hershey, PA: IGI Publishing, 2016), 1–19; Liat Steir-Livny, "Holocaust Humor, Satire, and Parody on Israeli Television," *Jewish Film and New Media* 3, no. 2 (2015): 202; Lee Behlman, "The Escapist: Fantasy, Folklore, and the Pleasures of the Comic Book in Recent Jewish American Holocaust Fiction," *Shofar* 22, no. 3 (2004): 56–71.

13

Teaching Jewish American Literature in a Spanish Context

Gustavo Sánchez Canales

I

Eurydice (the Spanish branch "Eurydice España REDIE"—*red española de información sobre Educación*) is a network that supports European cooperation within the framework of lifelong learning and provides information on education systems and policies in thirty-seven countries—the twenty-eight member-states of the European Union,[1] Bosnia and Herzegovina, the former Yugoslav Republic of Macedonia, Iceland, Liechtenstein, Montenegro, Norway, Serbia, Switzerland, and Turkey. The general introduction of the well-known report *Teaching Reading in Europe: Contexts, Policies and Practices* published by the Education, Audiovisual and Culture Executive Agency begins:

> The written word is present everywhere and therefore reading is a fundamental skill which is increasingly needed in almost every sphere of life. A *wide range of reading skills, including digital reading, are essential for an individual's personal and social fulfilment,* for taking an informed and active part in society and exercising full rights of citizenship. Furthermore, *these skills are essential for entering and advancing in the labor market.*

> *Those with inadequate reading skills have their life chances limited in today's society.* In essence, acquiring the ability to read well is a basic requirement for the social and economic demands of 21st century society. (7; emphasis added)

This statement, which addresses the significance of reading competence, focuses on two key issues. First, it points out that if an individual does not master this skill, his or her personal development will be severely curtailed (see, among others, Carter and Long, *Teaching Literature* 16–19); and, second, a lack of command will hinder his or her access to the labor market (consult, e.g., Sánchez Canales, "Competencia lectora" 11–12). In the section titled "Scope," reading competence or skill "is defined as the comprehensive aptitude to understand, use, and reflect on written language forms in order to achieve personal and social fulfilment" (7). While the 2011 European Commission report underscores the importance of developing good reading skills, it fails to take up a major reading-related issue that teachers should be attentive to in their classes: reading is/as a pleasurable activity. To my mind, motivating students to read should be a priority. However, this priority should not come at the expense of academic rigor. Undoubtedly, combining these two goals is a most challenging yet stimulating and eventually rewarding task. In fact, this is what I did for years when I taught Jewish-American authors at the Universidad Complutense de Madrid (hereafter UCM). In the Faculty of Philology at this university, as well as at other Spanish universities with English studies departments, there are courses devoted not only to US canonical literature but also to ethnic literatures, literature of minorities, and literature of the Diaspora. In the case of the UCM, teaching Jewish-American authors is an effective way to address a number of competences included in courses such as "Ficción Contemporánea en los Estados Unidos"[2] and "Literatura de Etnicidad en los Estados Unidos: Literatura Afronorteamericana y de la Diáspora."[3] Section III, which pays special attention to Mary Antin, Abraham Cahan, Saul Bellow, Philip Roth, and Chaim Potok, focuses on the benefits of exposing university students to literature in terms of competences to be acquired as specified in these two courses.

II

Although it seems obvious that students will benefit from better literature classes if teachers succeed in presenting reading as a pleasurable activity, the ways to carry it out are not so clear. In *How to Read and Why* (2000), Harold Bloom claims that "[r]eading well is one of the great pleasures that solitude can afford you, because it is, at least in my experience, the most healing of pleasures" (19). In Bloom's claim, there are two key words that should not be overlooked: "solitude" and "healing." To be sure, reading is an inherently solitary task because, as Bloom explains, "finally you are alone, going on without further meditation" (19). There is the other component pertaining to reading, the supposed cathartic, "healing" effect that it provokes. What does Bloom imply by "healing"? Reading in this context might be thought of as therapeutic because it is a soul-searching task that leads the mind to return "to its needs for beauty, truth, and insight" and ultimately helps human beings to come to terms with themselves (*Where Shall Wisdom* 1). At the outset of *Where Shall Wisdom Be Found?* (2004), Bloom says, "I have only three criteria for what I go on reading and teaching: aesthetic splendor, intellectual power, wisdom" (1). Bloom's "three criteria" not only contribute to better "individual's personal and social fulfilment," as specified in the general introduction of *Teaching Reading in Europe*, but they are also essential to developing a good reading competence. This skill is one of the key elements of the European Union's competence-based approach. What is more, developing students' reading competence has been a priority since the implementation of the so-called Bologna declaration initiated in a number of European universities in the academic year 2010–2011. First, by virtue of the signature of the Bologna declaration by ministers of education from twenty-nine European countries in 1999, and, second, thanks to the adoption of the Budapest-Vienna Declaration in 2010, the European Commission aimed to create what is known as the European Higher Education Area (EHEA) (Espacio Europeo de Educación Superior, or EEES in Spanish). The commission's main goals have been, among others, the promotion of mobility and employability of European citizens and a shift from a teacher-centered to a student-centered approach in education through the development of students' competences. (Throughout this ten-plus-year process, universities have undoubtedly played a major role in the betterment of a European cultural area.)

As explained previously, "competence(s)" is a fundamental concept in current European education policies. The European Commission, which has been working with EU countries for years, aims to improve "key competences"—"knowledge, skills, and attitudes that will help learners find personal fulfilment and, later in life, find work and take part in society."[4] These include not only traditional skills such as math and science, foreign languages, and literacy but also "horizontal skills" such as learning to learn, cultural awareness, and creativity. In terms of "horizontal skills," a "key competence" is "cultural awareness." Chapter 5 of *The Common European Framework of Reference for Language: Learning, Teaching and Assessment* (2001), "The user/learner's competences," devotes considerable attention to "cultural awareness." It explicitly says that "[k]nowledge, awareness and understanding of the relation—similarities and distinctive differences—between the 'world of origin' and the 'world of the target community' produce an intercultural awareness."[5] The importance of "cultural awareness" includes, for example, literary analysis of texts in English; and modernist and postmodernist movements such as feminism, psychoanalysis, cultural studies, and multiculturalism.

In the next section, I attempt to demonstrate not only that teaching works of Jewish-American novelists such as Antin, Cahan, Bellow, Roth, and Potok, to give just a few examples, is highly recommended if the competence of cultural awareness is to be acquired, but also the relevance of Jewish-American fiction[6] as a way to teach competence-based literature in Spain as an epitome of the European educational model.

III

If we look at the syllabus of the course "Literatura de Etnicidad en los Estados Unidos,"[7] we can see that the so-called attitudinal competence focuses on linguistic, literary, and cultural aspects. The "attitudinal competence" is crucial because it helps students build up knowledge from a cognitive, behavioral, and affective perspective. In terms of the "specific competence," the aim is to enable students to make sound judgments from an aesthetic, historical, and literary standpoint. Without a doubt, Mary Antin's *Promised Land* (1912) and Abraham Cahan's *The Rise of David Levinsky* (1917), among others, are ideal novels to work on these competences.

A first element that Mary Antin's *The Promised Land* and Abraham Cahan's *Rise of David Levinsky* share is that, although Yiddish was the authors' primary language, they chose English as their vehicle of expression, allowing them to more effectively voice their immigrant experience. In linguistic terms, Antin's and Cahan's English brought about a new variety of American English infused with Yiddish syntax, inflections, and words. (This is a trait also studied in Jewish-American writers of the next generation, such as Bernard Malamud,[8] who, unlike Antin and Cahan, was born on American soil.)

In "The Heritage," chapter 20 of *The Promised Land*, linguistic assimilation proves the importance of education—especially of literacy and English-language education—as the surest way to climb up the career ladder. Antin writes:

> *Having traced the way an immigrant child may take from the ship through the public schools, passed on from hand to hand by the ready teachers;* through free libraries and lecture halls, inspired by every occasion of civic consciousness; *dragging through the slums the weight of private disadvantage, but heartened for the effort by public opportunity;* welcomed at a hundred open doors of instruction, initiated with pomp and splendor and flags unfurled; seeking, in American minds, the American way, and finding it in the thoughts of the noble,—*striving against the odds of foreign birth and poverty, and winning, through the use of abundant opportunity, a place as enviable as that of any native child,—having traced the footsteps of the young immigrant almost to the college gate*, the rest of the course may be left to the imagination. Let us say that from the Latin School on I lived very much as my American schoolmates lived, having overcome my foreign idiosyncrasies, and the rest of my outward adventures you may read in any volume of American feminine statistics. (*The Promised Land* 359–60; emphasis added)

Without a doubt, Antin's keen interest in education epitomizes the Jews' devotion to learning as the way to ensure success in the New World.

For its part, *The Rise of David Levinsky* is a largely autobiographical novel whose protagonist, while rejecting orthodoxy, somehow regards it as a buttress to the authentic Jewish experience. I have chosen some passages where the narrator expresses a certain attachment to his life in Russia. For example, chapter 7 included in "Book XIV, Episodes of a Lonely Life" begins "Am I happy?" (*Rise of David Levinsky* 525). A few lines below, the reader perceives that in spite of the protagonist's success in the Promised Land, he misses in a way the old times when he felt more attuned to his fellow countrymen. Part of his unhappiness is likely to stem from his feeling that

[t]he gloomiest past is dearer than the brightest present. In my case there seems to be a special reason for feeling this way. *My sense of triumph is coupled with a brooding sense of emptiness and insignificance*, of my lack of anything like a great, deep interest. (526; emphasis added)

I know bachelors who are thoroughly reconciled to their solitude and even enjoy it. I am not. No, I am not happy. (526)

Most of the people at my hotel are German-American Jews. I know other Jews of this class. I contribute to their charity institutions. *Though an atheist, I belong to one of their synagogues.* (528; emphasis added)

. . . *I often long for a heart-to-heart talk with some of the people of my birthplace.* I have tried to revive my old friendships with some of them, but they are mostly poor and my prosperity stands between us in many ways." (528–29; emphasis added)

Like Antin's protagonist, Cahan's David seeks fortune in the New World. Unlike her, his way to climb up the career ladder is not through education but through hard work. The passages above show that David succeeds in making his fortune, but the cost is deep self-alienation.

To my mind, approaching these two novels from a biographical standpoint is very effective because it allows us to place "an emphasis on the parallels between the trajectories of fiction and the trajectories of an individual life" (Showalter, *Teaching Literature* 89). In effect, an obvious advantage of using this approach is that it helps to establish parallels between the writer's fiction and life. This is not only a valuable resource to develop the "attitudinal competence" pointed out above, but it also engages individuals in lifelong reading, a major goal set by the already cited *Teaching Reading in Europe: Contexts, Policies and Practices*.

A second circumstance accounts for the suitability of introducing autobiographical writing such as Antin's and Cahan's in a Spanish university context: during the 1950s and 1960s, millions of Spanish people emigrated to more prosperous European countries (e.g., Germany and Switzerland) and South American countries like Argentina and Brazil. A significant number of the students exposed to this kind of texts have grandparents who knew the hardships of emigrating. Consequently, engaging students through references to their grandparents' own experiences is easier and more effective. More recently—two decades or so ago—the once outward movement was reversed, and Spain became a destination for millions of immigrants. No wonder then that nowadays it is very likely to have in the same classroom students not only from other European countries (e.g. Bulgaria, Poland, Romania, and Russia) but also from Asia (mainly from China) and from South America (including, but not limited to, countries like Argentina, Brazil, Chile, Colombia, Ecuador, Mexico, Peru, and Venezuela). A large number of students, who typically prefer the novel and/or the short story over poetry and/or drama, are happy to find that "[a]s teachers of literature in the twenty-first century, we are most likely to be teaching the novel" (Showalter, *Teaching Literature* 88).[9]

While first-generation Jewish-American narratives such as Mary Antin's *Promised Land* and Abraham Cahan's *Rise of David Levinsky* are ideal for working on linguistic, historical, cultural, and literary aspects, introducing a novel such as Saul Bellow's *Dangling Man* (1944) is advisable for exploring two major themes (e.g. World War II and alienation) addressed by Jewish-American fiction writers of the next generation, such as Norman Mailer, Bernard Malamud, Philip Roth, and Bellow. (Because World War II is cross-curricular in English studies, it is an excellent topic for introducing these novelists' works as part of a number of course syllabi.)

In reference to the novelists above, Malcolm Bradbury explains that "one can see the transformation of the older tradition of Jewish-American writing. Now the theme was no longer the immigrant victim struggling for place and recognition in the New World," as was the case with Antin and Cahan—alongside Anzia Yezierska's *Hungry Hearts* (1920) and *Bread Givers* (1925) and Henry Roth's *Call It Sleep* (1934), among many others—but "rather that of the Jew as modern victim forced by history into existential self-definition, a definition that was not solely religious, political, or ethnic" (Bradbury, *Modern American Novel* 165). Malcolm Bradbury adds that many wartime and postwar Jewish-American novels

> became complex explorations of the individual's place as beneficiary or exile in the contemporary world, and are largely conducted as metaphysical enquiries, speculations on the predicament of disoriented modern man in a world of urban anonymity, behavioural indifference, and the totalitarian massing of social force. Humanism was the aim, but it was hard to forge in the face of disjunctive modern experience. (165)

I find that Bradbury's explanation fits Bellow's *Dangling Man* and *The Victim* (1947) perfectly well. Clearly influenced by European existentialist writers such as Jean-Paul Sartre and Albert Camus, Bellow's first two novels depict marginal characters—Joseph and Asa Leventhal, respectively—who find it difficult to fit into society.[10] In *Dangling Man*, Joseph is waiting to be abducted, and he "dangles" in the meantime. He is trapped between civilian and military life, and consequently he feels at a loss. Like Antoine Roquetin in Sartre's *La Nausée* (1938) and Raymond Meursault in Albert Camus' *L'Étranger* (1942), Joseph feels paralyzed and confused. At the outset of the novel, the city's hustle and bustle contrast with the protagonist's passivity:

> I have begun to notice that the more active the rest of the world becomes, the more slowly I move, and that my solitude increases in the same proportion as its racket and frenzy. . . . I grow rooted to my chair. It is a real, a bodily feeling. I will not even try to rise. It may be that I could get up and walk around the room or even go to the store, but to make the effort would put me in a disagreeable state. (*Dangling Man* 13)

There is, however, a huge difference between the Jewish-American novelist and his French counterparts. While Sartre's and Camus's respective heroes have resignedly accepted their fates, the Bellovian character struggles to overcome the agonizing situation he has been going through until he eventually comes to terms with himself. When Bradbury says that "[h]umanism was the aim," what he means is that in Bellow's (fictional) world there is room for freedom and therefore for hope.[11] When Joseph is called up in the end, his final cry, "Long live regimentation," paradoxically brings about his liberation because he ceases to be a dangling man (191). When Asa Leventhal asks, "Who runs things?" at the novel's end, one may think, from an existentialist perspective, that God does, or perhaps nobody does, or who knows whether it is "man himself" (*The Victim* 264). Ada Aharoni explains that

> Asa is not the driver of his symbolic "train" of life, but he can choose the "stations" he wants to alight at. The possibility of choosing the right "station" or values or orientations in life, is also symbolically rendered in *The Victim*, having missed a stop there is no return; the dark train of life continues on its way. (Aharoni, "Bellow and Existentialism" 47)

In reference to *Dangling Man* and *The Victim*, Peter Hyland thinks that "[t]he essential bleakness that the two books share can be accounted for in part by the fact that they were under the immediate shadow of World War II" and that they "reflect a more general unease about the insecurity and fragmentation of modern urban life" (Hyland, *Saul Bellow* 15–16). In spite of the grim era the United States of the mid-1940s had been going through as depicted in both novels, Bellow firmly believes in the individual's ability to get ahead because he or she is free. In a 1963 interview where Bellow's fiction up to that time is defined as having "a single, dominant theme, it is this one of freedom," Bruce Cook reproduces a most significant claim made by the novelist during his interview:

> Our period has been created by revolutions of all kinds—political, scientific, industrial. And now we have been freed by law from slavery in many of its historical, objective forms. The next move is up to us. Each of us has to find *an inner law by which he can live*. Without this, objective freedom only destroys us. So the question that really interests me is the question of spiritual freedom in the individual—the power to endure our own humanity. (Cook, "Saul Bellow" 17–18; emphasis added)

To my mind, the "inner law by which he can live" echoes what Augie March calls "the axial lines" in Bellow's 1953 eponymous novel (*Adventures* 454–55). "Spiritual freedom" and "humanity" are at the core of Bellow's fiction[12] and are the two major themes covered in the other Universidad Complutense course presented here called "Literatura de los Estados Unidos desde 1950."

While it is timely to approach Mary Antin's and Abraham Cahan's fiction in "Literatura de Etnicidad en los Estados Unidos" from a biographical stance, for a course such as "Ficción Contemporánea en los Estados Unidos," it is very appropriate to analyze the literary texts introduced in class in terms of intertextuality, facilitating the acquisition of the "general competence."[13]

Bellow's *The Dean's December* (1982), which explores the themes of freedom and the defense of the human being, is an in-depth reflection on romantic poetry.[14] In large part because of the countless references Bellow makes to Blake, Shelley, and Yeats, among others, this novel is the perfect text to approach Jewish-American literature from an intertextual standpoint.

A claim such as "the burden of Romantic poetry is absolute freedom" (Bloom, *Ringers in the Tower* 39) is subscribed to by Albert Corde, the protagonist of *The Dean's December*. Corde, a former journalist and currently the dean of an unnamed university, is a good reader of the romantic poets. Just like them, he denounces social injustice and inequalities that are annihilating the modern individual. To give an example, at one point of the novel Corde describes the Chicago of his time as "Cain's city built with murder," an explicit reference to the third line of Blake's poem "Then She Bore Pale Desire" (c. 1777).[15] Chicago embodies for Corde (and Bellow) what Babylon embodied for William Blake: war, lust, scientific determinism—in a word, anything that entails decadence and the human being's degeneration.[16] In Allan Chavkin's explanation, "[f]or Code, Chicago has degenerated into a kind of Babylon where science, religion, and sex are distorted" (Chavkin, "*The Dean's December*" 23). Apart from Blake's "Cain's city built with murder," Corde also quotes "An old, mad, blind, despised, and dying king," which comes from P. B. Shelley's "Sonnet: England in 1819" (1839). The line points not only to the tyrannical king George III but also to the tyrannical system that Corde sees in his own country, whose society is, like that of the England denounced by Shelley, divided by rulers who "neither see, nor feel, nor know."[17]

In one of his *Harper's* articles, Corde uses the phrase "those dying generations"—the third line of W. B. Yeats's "Sailing to Byzantium" included in his 1928 *The Tower*—to summarize the atmosphere of decadence the dean perceives around him. While the Irish poet feels hopeless about the fate of civilization, Corde feels in despair about what he calls the "underclass," a group of impoverished black people who live in detoxification centers, prisons, and slums. Corde blames the Chicago politicians for the unbearable situation created in his city. Like the romantics, the Bellovian character needs to escape the city and return to a more natural environment to come to terms with himself.

Curiously, Philip Roth also resorts to a line of Yeats's "Sailing to Byzantium" to reflect on the theme of decadence. Roth deals specifically with the problems of becoming an old person and trying to feel alive even when he is growing into "a dying animal":

Consume my heart away; sick with desire
And fastened to a dying animal
It knows not what it is. ("Sailing to Byzantium" 21–23;
  The Dying Animal 102)

Yeats believed that to escape his mortal condition, it was imperative to leave the "country for old men" (i.e., his fatherland, Ireland) and travel to Byzantium, his embodiment of the cornerstone of European civilization, a place where sages can become the "singing-masters of my soul" (20). Roth's alter ego, David Kepesh, is an elderly teacher of literature who is having a love affair with a woman half his age named Consuela Castillo. About halfway through the story, Kepesh tells his lover that "if you turn this to sixty, the beats will be seconds" (*The Dying Animal* 102).[18] The scene where this line appears deals with the classic maxim "tempus fugit."[19]

The above are just a few examples of how integrating Jewish-American fiction into a general course on US literature in the Spanish curriculum is not only possible but also imperative for at least two reasons: (1) the quality of the wide variety of writers studied in this chapter is well established; and (2) the novels and short stories of authors like Saul Bellow and Philip Roth, to give just two examples, work very well in literature classes. In the case of Bellow and Roth, the fact that their fiction is full of literary references facilitates a comparative analysis, and thus students of literature within a Spanish context are exposed not only to Jewish-American writing but also to other writers about whom they had read little or nothing during their university studies. This kind of approach fosters a study of the themes, background, and other elements in works by both the aforementioned Jewish-American writers and those alluded to in texts analyzed in the classroom. Elaine Showalter provides a good suggestion for what can be done when a teacher approaches a postmodern novel like the ones pointed out above:

> I organize the texts thematically, as well as chronologically, in terms of dystopias, female gothics, fairy tales, reimaginings, magical realism, postcolonialism, metafictions; and theoretically, in terms of defamiliarization, intertextuality, breaking the frame, hybridity, and hyperreality. All of these can be made part of the technique of the course as well, incorporated into lectures, and made available for student discussion. (Showalter, *Teaching Literature* 96)

In *Teaching Literature*, Showalter alludes to "the complex interactions of region, race, gender, class, and narrative technique" (88). Chaim Potok's reference of "core-to-core culture confrontation"[20] is an excellent choice to address the issue of race and the concept of "the other"[21] through Jewish-American fiction in a Spanish context.[22]

As Potok explains, "core-to-core culture confrontation" typically occurs when someone is located at the heart of his or her own culture, knows that culture, constructs the world through the value system of that culture, and then encounters core elements from another culture. This is the case with two characters of his novel *The Chosen*: Danny Saunders, placed at the heart of Hasidism, encounters an element from the canon of Western culture—the psychoanalytic theories of Sigmund Freud. Reuven Malter, a Modern Orthodox Jew, comes into contact with Danny's Hasidic world. Until their mutual understanding eventually leads to their mutual acceptance, the Malters/Saunders confrontation somehow reveals the existing clash between the individual and his or her tradition.[23] Potok's interest focuses on the premise that we are born and brought up in a reduced world—family, neighborhood, community, town, city, and country. At the same time, we are exposed to influences from beyond that little world. Typically, these influences are at odds with those values we have been—and are still being—taught in our own world. We are bound to experience a clash of values or—to use Potok's term—a "core-to-core culture confrontation" because influences come to our ideas from the core, that is, from the heart of that outside, alien world. It is then that a person finds his or her inherited values confronting those of the mainstream culture. The fanatic, who is a zealous guardian of faith, fails to assimilate part of those outside values into his or her own tradition (Potok, *The Chosen* 147).[24]

I would like to borrow Elaine Showalter's phrase "teaching as a spiritual journey" to summarize how "student-centered" classes are regarded nowadays *(Teaching Literature* 34–35). At one point in her explanation, Showalter says that, according to professional educational specialist Parker J. Palmer, it is essential to create

> a "learning space" characterized by "openness, boundaries, and an air of hospitality." Most important is the hospitality which does not "make learning painless" but rather makes possible the painful things "without which no learning can occur—things like exposing ignorance, testing tentative hypotheses, challenging false or partial information, and mutual criticism of thought." (Showalter, *Teaching Literature* 34)

I think this explanation somehow connects with Harold Bloom's three criteria—"aesthetic splendor, intellectual power, wisdom" (*Where Shall Wisdom* 1). Additionally, teachers should engage their students by trying to avoid lecturing. As Showalter recalls, Professor Martin Bickman "came to the conclusion that lecturing is an active form of thinking *for the teacher*, but a passive form for the listener" (49; emphasis in original). In "Teaching Jewish Literature in the South," Erin G. Carlston gives a perfect example of how his students may be placed at the center of the teaching/learning process. At one point of the interview, he explains how his classes benefit thanks to some of his students' Jewish background.

> *It's especially helpful to me to have the more religiously knowledgeable students*, because that's my weakest area. I'm okay on basic theology, but don't know much about liturgy and have almost no Hebrew. When religious ritual comes up in our readings, I may not even recognize it, let alone know how to talk about it. *I lean heavily on my students there and have been lucky that I've always had enough of them who were able to translate Hebrew, explain textual references*, and so on. ("Teaching Jewish Literature" 195; emphasis added)

It is crucial to make a change in focus—whenever possible "student centered" rather than "teacher centered," as in Carlston's case—and to place more emphasis on Jewish-American fiction, as in my case. Reading and analyzing novelists like Antin, Cahan, Bellow, Roth, and Potok, among others, offers an excellent opportunity to explore major literary issues such as the Jewish immigrant experience and Jewish-American identity. Additionally, because almost two decades have passed since the beginning of the twenty-first century, it is probably good to try to come up with an answer for a question like the one Victoria Aarons raises in the introduction to *Third-Generation Holocaust Narratives: Memory in Memoir and Fiction* (2016): "Are we finding *something else*, something new in the literature in the decades surrounding the new millennium?" (xi). Considering that that volume explores the fiction of writers with no firsthand experience of the Holocaust, it is no wonder that these "narratives of collision and collusion . . . are works that make imperative the ethical demands inherent in reading well, in engaging in the shared experience of reading responsibly" (xv). It is clear to me that providing university students with a comprehensive understanding of Jewish-American literature from cultural, historical, literary, and aesthetic perspectives will be to the advantage of their learning not only in a Spanish context but also on a European scale.

Notes

1. The years when the member-states joined the European Union are given parenthetically: Austria (1995), Belgium (1958), Bulgaria (2007), Croatia (2013), Cyprus (2004), Czech Republic (2004), Denmark (1973), Estonia (2004), Finland (1995), France (1958), Germany (1958), Greece (1981), Hungary (2004), Ireland (1973), Italy (1958), Latvia (2004), Lithuania (2004), Luxembourg (1958), Malta (2004), The Netherlands (1958), Poland (2004), Portugal (1986), Romania (2007), Slovakia (2004), Slovenia (2004), Spain (1986), Sweden (1995), and the UK (1973). The UK will withdraw from the European Union in March 2019 following the Brexit referendum held in June 2016.

2. Syllabus for "Ficción Contemporánea en los Estados Unidos," https://www.ucm.es/estudios/grado-estudiosingleses-plan-802224.

3. Syllabus for "Literatura de la Etnicidad en los Estados Unidos: Literatura Afronorteamericana y de la Diáspora," https://www.ucm.es/estudios/grado-estudiosingleses-plan-802232.

4. For further information, see http://ec.europa.eu/education/policy/school/competences_en.

5. *Common European Framework of Reference for Languages: Learning, Teaching, Assessment* (Cambridge, UK: Press Syndicate of the University of Cambridge, 2001), 103, http://www.coe.int/t/dg4/linguistic/Source/Framework_EN.pdf.

6. For an analysis of Jewish-American writing as a genre, see Cappell, *American Talmud*.

7. See link in note 3.

8. For an in-depth study of Malamud's fiction, consult, for example, Avery, *The Magic Worlds*; and Aarons and Sánchez Canales, *Bernard Malamud: A Centennial Tribute*, which compiles essays from France, Germany, Greece, Spain, and the United States.

9. Interestingly, after an undergraduate seminar named "Jewish Identity and Performance in the U.S." taught by the authors at Princeton in fall 2010, Dolan and Wolf shows how effective using performance may be as a pedagogical tool for Jewish studies. One of the interesting aspects is that they combined textual analysis and improvised performances: "While our class frequently looked closely at texts and discussed passages from plays and critical essays, we often organized the class around both planned and spontaneous performance. In this way, the students' embodiment was an ever-present feature of the seminar" ("Performing Jewishness" 203). What they refer to as "performative tasks" led their students to what they call "to inhabit Jewishness" (205). Extrapolating this experience to a Spanish context is a most appropriate way to work on "attitudinal competence," among others.

10. For an extended study of the theme of existentialism in Bellow's early works, see, for example, Aharoni and Sánchez Canales, "Alienation and Marginality."

11. For an extended analysis of the theme of humanism in Saul Bellow's fiction, see, among others, Clayton.

12. For an in-depth study of themes such as identity formation, existentialism, and the place of the United States in a globalizing world in Bellow's fiction, see Aarons, *Cambridge Companion*.

13. See note 2.

14. For an extended analysis of this theme, see, among others, Chavkin, "The Dean's December" and "Bellow and English Romanticism"; and Sánchez Canales, "Romantic Spirit."

15. See Sánchez Canales, "Influence of Romantic Poetry," 144.

16. For a detailed study of the impact of the city on the Bellovian character, see Aarons, "Special Issue."

17. For an extended analysis of Shelley's poetry, see, for example, Leighton, McNiece and Weisman. For a study of the presence of Shelley's poetry in Bellow's *The Dean's December*, see Sánchez Canales, "Romantic Spirit," 115ff.

18. For a study of the Kepesh-Consuela relationship, see Safer, "*The Dying Animal*," in *Mocking*.

19. For a more extended analysis of the presence of Yeats's "Sailing to Byzantium" in Roth's *Dying Animal*, consult, for instance, Trendel, "Master and Pupil"; and Sánchez Canales, "European Literary Tradition."

20. For an extended study of Chaim Potok's concept "core-to-core (culture) confrontation," see, for example, Potok, "Martin Buber"; Walden, "Potok's Asher Lev,"; and Sánchez Canales, "Significance."

21. See Goffman, *Imagining Each Other* for a book-length study of Jewish-Black relations from a literary point of view.

22. For an in-depth analysis of Potok's works, consult Walden, *Chaim Potok* and *Conversations*.

23. See, for instance, Purcell's "Potok's Fathers and Sons," where through the theme of the father-son relationship he explores the values of Chaim Potok's Jewish background in *The Chosen*; also consult Potok, "Martin Buber," 45ff, in which he analyzes Martin Buber's well-known "I-It" and "I-Thou" relationships, whose influence is, to my mind, perceived in Potok's 1967 novel. For a study of the presence of Buber's "I-It" and "I-Thou" relationships in *The Chosen*, see Sánchez Canales, "Significance."

24. Potok explains the concept of "core-to-core confrontation" in Chavkin's "A MELUS Interview" in more detail.

References

Aarons, Victoria, ed. *The Cambridge Companion to Saul Bellow*. Cambridge: Cambridge University Press, 2017.

———. "Special Issue on Saul Bellow's Urban Landscapes." *Saul Bellow Journal* 26, nos. 1–2 (2013).
———. *Third-Generation Holocaust Narratives: Memory in Memoir and Fiction*. Lanham, MD: Lexington Books, 2016.
Aarons, Victoria, and Sánchez Canales, Gustavo. *Bernard Malamud: A Centennial Tribute*. Detroit, IL: Wayne State University Press, 2016.
Aharoni, Ada. "Bellow and Existentialism." *Saul Bellow Journal* 2, no. 2 (1983): 42–54.
Alonso Gallo, Laura, and Domínguez Miguela, Antonia, eds. *Evolving Origins: Transplanting Cultures: Literary Legacies of the New Americans*. Huelva, Spain: Universidad de Huelva, 2002.
Antin, Mary. *The Promised Land*. Boston: Houghton Mifflin, 1912.
Avery, Evelyn, ed. *The Magic Worlds of Bernard Malamud*. Albany: State University of New York Press, 2001.
Bellow, Saul. *The Adventures of Augie March*. 1953. Reprint, London: Penguin Books, 1984.
———. *Dangling Man*. 1944. Reprint, London: Penguin Books, 1988.
———. *The Dean's December*. London: Penguin Books, 1982.
———. *The Victim*. 1947. Reprint, London: Penguin Books, 1988.
Blake, William. *The Complete Poetry and Prose of William Blake*. Rev. ed. Edited by David E. Erdman. Berkeley: University of California Press, 1982.
Bloom, Harold. *How to Read and Why*. New York: Touchstone/Simon and Schuster, 2000.
———. *The Ringers in the Tower: Studies in Romantic Tradition*. Chicago: University of Chicago Press, 1971.
———. *Where Shall Wisdom Be Found?* New York: Riverhead Books, 2004.
Bradbury, Malcolm. *The Modern American Novel*. 2nd ed. Oxford: Oxford University Press, 1992.
Cahan, Abraham. *The Rise of David Levinsky*. 1917. Reprint, New York: Harper Torchbooks, 1960.
Cappell, Ezra. *American Talmud: The Cultural Work of Jewish American Fiction*. Albany: State University of New York Press, 2007.
Carter, Ronald, and Michael T. Long. *Teaching Literature*. New York: Longman, 1991.
Chavkin, Allan. "Bellow and English Romanticism." *Studies in the Literary Imagination* 17, no. 2 (1984): 7–18.
———. "*The Dean's December* and Blake's *The Ghost of Abel*." *Saul Bellow Journal* 13, no. 1 (1995): 22–26.
Chavkin, Laura. "A MELUS Interview: Chaim Potok." *MELUS* 24, no. 2 (1999): 147–57.
Clayton, John J. *Saul Bellow: In Defense of Man*. 2nd ed. Bloomington: Indiana University Press, 1979.

Cook, Bruce. "Saul Bellow: A Mood of Protest." In Cronin and Siegel, *Conversations*, 6–18.
Cronin, Gloria L., and Ben Siegel, eds. *Conversations with Saul Bellow*. Jackson: University Press of Mississippi, 1994.
Dolan, Jill, and Stacy Wolf. "Performing Jewishness In and Out of the Classroom." *MELUS* 37, no. 2 (summer 2012): 201–15.
Eurydice. *Teaching Reading in Europe: Contexts, Policies and Practices*. Brussels: Education, Audiovisual and Culture Executive Agency, 2011. http://eacea.ec.europa.eu/education/eurydice.
Goffman, Ethan. *Imagining Each Other: Blacks and Jews in Contemporary American Literature*. Albany: State University of New York Press, 2000.
Hyland, Peter. *Saul Bellow*. London: Macmillan, 1992.
Leighton, Angela. *Shelley and the Sublime: An Interpretation of the Major Poems*. Cambridge: Cambridge University Press, 1984.
McNiece, Gerald. *Shelley and the Revolutionary Idea*. Ann Arbor, MI: U.M.I., 1989.
Morton, Timothy, ed. *The Cambridge Companion to Shelley*. Cambridge: Cambridge University Press, 2006.
Núñez Cortés, Juan A., ed. *Lectura y literatura en Educación Primaria*. Madrid: CEU Ediciones, 2015.
Potok, Chaim. *The Chosen*. 1967. Reprint, New York: Ballantine Books, 1982.
———. "Martin Buber and the Jews." *Commentary* 41, no. 3 (1966): 43–49.
Purcell, William F. "Potok's Fathers and Sons." *Studies in American Literature* 26 (1989): 75–92.
Roth, Philip. *The Dying Animal*. Boston: Houghton Mifflin, 2001.
Safer, Elaine B. *Mocking the Age: The Later Novels of Philip Roth*. Albany: State University of New York Press, 2012.
Sánchez Canales, Gustavo. "Alienation and Marginality in Saul Bellow's Early Novels." In Alonso Gallo and Domínguez Miguela, *Evolving Origins*, 177–88.
———. "La competencia lectora como factor clave en el desarrollo de la persona." In Núñez Cortés, *Lectura*. 11–17.
———. "European Literary Tradition in Roth's Kepesh Trilogy." In Sánchez Canales & Aarons, *History*. http://docs.lib.purdue.edu/cgi/viewcontent.cgi?article=2404&context=clcweb.
———. "'Recover the world that is buried under the debris of false description': The Influence of Romantic Poetry on Saul Bellow's *Dean's December*." *Partial Answers: Journal of Literature and the History of Ideas* 14, no. 1 (January 2016): 141–58.
———. "The Romantic Spirit in Saul Bellow's The *Dean's December*." *Estudios Ingleses de la Universidad Complutense* 11 (2003): 111–22. http://revistas.ucm.es/index.php/EIUC/article/view/EIUC0303110111A.

———. "The Significance of Martin Buber's Philosophy of Dialogue and Suffering in the Overcoming of 'Core-to-core Confrontation' in Chaim Potok's *The Chosen*." *Estudios Ingleses de la Universidad Complutense* 18 (2010): 53–65. http://revistas.ucm.es/index.php/EIUC/article/view/EIUC1010110053A/7629.

Sánchez Canales, Gustavo, and Aarons, Victoria. *History, Memory, and the Making of Character in Roth's Fiction* (A Thematic Issue). *CLCWeb: Comparative Literature and Culture* 16, no. 2 (2014). http://docs.lib.purdue.edu/clcweb.

Showalter, Elaine. *Teaching Literature*. Malden, MA: Blackwell Publishing, 2003.

Trendel, Aristi. "Master and Pupil in Philip Roth's *The Dying Animal*." *Philip Roth Studies* 3, no. 1 (2007): 56–65.

Walden, Daniel, ed. *Chaim Potok: Confronting Modernity Through the Lens of Tradition*. University Park: Pennsylvania State University Press, 2013.

———. *Conversations with Chaim Potok*. Jackson: University Press of Mississippi, 2001.

———. "Potok's *Asher Lev*: Orthodoxy and Art: The Core-to-Core Paradox." *Studies in American Jewish Literature* 29 (2010): 148–53.

———. "Chaim Potok: A Zwischenmensch ("between-person") Adrift in the Cultures." *Studies in American Jewish Literature* 4 (1985): 19–25.

Weisman, Karen. "The Lyricist." In Morton, *The Cambridge Companion*, 45–64.

Yeats, W. B. "Sailing to Byzantium." In *Selected Poetry*, edited by A. Norman Jeffares, 104–5. London: Macmillan, 1990.

14

Teaching William Styron's *Sophie's Choice*
Understanding the Holocaust

Zygmunt Mazur

This chapter examines some approaches to teaching a classic of American literature, William Styron's 1979 novel *Sophie's Choice*, as a text that enables students to arrive at a better understanding of some of the key issues related to anti-Semitism and the Holocaust. My experience, which I draw on in this chapter, is that of teaching this novel to graduate university students majoring in English in the United States and in Poland.

Sophie's Choice, Styron's ambitious attempt at tackling the topic of the Holocaust, was a considerable literary and critical success. Commercially it fared equally well, remaining a best seller for a long time and eventually becoming firmly established as a classic of American literature. However, the acclaim it met with was by no means unanimous; to the contrary, *Sophie's Choice* has been the target of some very extensive and harsh criticism, both in scholarly articles and in initial reviews in popular magazines and newspapers. This last point is of major importance in the teaching of *Sophie's Choice* in literature classes, and, in my opinion, it is a major asset. The fact that the novel raised so many controversies makes it possible to juxtapose critical texts that offer contradictory views on the same features of the novel, thus encouraging students to engage intellectually with the viewpoints presented and making it possible for them to gain a deeper understanding of both the text and the crucial concepts relevant to the controversies Styron's novel provokes.

One such controversy that is well represented in the body of criticism on *Sophie's Choice* concerns the issue of misrepresentation of the Holocaust. Critics have suggested that the novel promotes a universalizing view of evil, mostly (but not only) because its main character is non-Jewish. Styron's choice of a Polish Catholic woman as the heroine of the story has been one of the most significant accusations leveled at Styron by, among others, Alvin Rosenfeld,[1] Cynthia Ozick,[2] and D. G. Myers,[3] who claimed that Styron was intentionally trying to de-Judaize the Holocaust. The basis for this criticism is what has come to be known as the "uniqueness thesis," the idea that "the Holocaust is so much unlike anything else in human history that it warrants 'classification' as a unique event."[4] Myers argues that "Styron's novel about a Polish Catholic woman who survived Auschwitz only to die tragically in America puts under interrogation the claim that the Holocaust was a uniquely Jewish catastrophe. . . . Styron does not merely dissent from the orthodoxy of the "uniqueness thesis" (as it has come to be known); he delivers an elenchus, a strong rereading of the Holocaust which goes beyond challenging the predominant view to reverse it."[5] Reading Myers's essay and contrasting it with Styron's own "A Wheel of Evil Come Full Circle,"[6] in which he explains his point of view and understanding of the Holocaust, offers a good starting point for an in-class discussion of this topic. The choice of a Polish Catholic woman for his central character is the result of Styron's ideas about the universality of evil. Evil is everywhere, and the equivalent of the Holocaust could happen to other ethnic groups in specific circumstances. As Styron said in an interview, Auschwitz is the culmination "of the titanic and sinister forces at work in history and in modern life that threaten all men, not only Jews."[7] The specific perception of the Holocaust in *Sophie's Choice* is thus connected to Styron's belief in the universality of evil. This belief, in turn, results in a deeply pessimistic vision of the world in general,[8] despite the deep compassion that Styron (and his narrator, Stingo) seems to have for all "the beaten and butchered and betrayed and martyred children of the earth."[9]

This universalizing view of evil is augmented in the novel in a number of different ways. One of the motifs that feeds into this vision of the world is the recurrent comparison of the Nazi regime and concentration camps with the system of slavery in the American South. The analogy is often made explicitly and directly, such as in the narrator's commentaries. Sometimes such comparisons are made in passing, at other times they are implied, and in some instances the conversations between the characters invite the making of such comparisons by the readers, as in the case of the story of Bobby Weed, which is mentioned when Nathan brings up the topic of Nazi concentration camps for the first time. He tells Stingo that "in the *concentration camps* the brutes in charge would not have stooped to *that* bestiality" (73). By "*that* bestiality" is meant the vengeance exacted by the crowd on a sixteen-year-old black boy who ogled and maybe molested a simpleton girl, Lula. Her father and the crowd lynched him, and while he was still alive his genitals were cut off and put into his mouth and then a letter "L" was branded on his chest with a blowtorch. According to Nathan, who seems to be attempting to make Stingo feel guilty, "the South today has abdicated any right to connection with the human race" (71), and every Southerner is responsible for the tragic death of Bobby Weed and should be held accountable. This mention is just one of many such parallels in which a comparison between the Nazis and the white oppressors of African Americans is invited.

Another feature of the novel that can be usefully exploited in the teaching context is the fact that the story central to the novel, Sophie's experience at the Auschwitz concentration camp, is not told directly; it becomes accessible to the reader through a number of narrative layers and temporal shifts, and, most importantly, it is mediated through a secondhand account by Stingo. The story in the novel does not unfold in chronological order; it is told on three major temporal planes with frequent changes between them. The narrator is the middle-aged Stingo, an established novelist writing in the 1970s about his experiences as a young man in 1947. Sophie's prewar and wartime experiences several years earlier form the third temporal level of the story.

Stingo's situation parallels that of the reader, who (especially when we think of today's university students) has not had direct experience of concentration camps. The reader finds out from Stingo only whatever Sophie was willing to tell him, and the reader has to face the possibility that Stingo, who at times seems naive and ignorant, may be unable to understand some of the clues given by Sophie. Moreover, the reader cannot be entirely convinced of Stingo's reliability as a narrator. Such a way of organizing the narrative means that the reader is following someone else's gradual path to knowing and understanding what happened. More than a story about Auschwitz, the novel becomes a story about Stingo's finding out about Auschwitz.

This indirect way of telling Sophie's story serves yet another role: that of drawing the reader into a reading experience that inevitably must become painful and disturbing. The reader, like Stingo, is unfamiliar with Sophie's story and most likely unwilling to find out about the horrors of Auschwitz. Richard Law makes the excellent point that "because of its literally almost unspeakable subject, the manner of the unfolding of the tale is an exercise in overcoming, or putting to sleep, reader resistance."[10] Accordingly, at first, Stingo's interest in Sophie is related to her physical attractiveness. Later it develops into a fascination, and, in parallel, the reader is also gradually drawn into Sophie's story. This slow process of getting the reader interested in the secret of Sophie begins with the description of her physical appearance as first perceived by Stingo:

> While it was a beautiful body, with all the right prominences, curves, continuities and symmetries, there was something a little strange about it—nothing visibly missing and not so much deficient as reassembled. And that was precisely it, I could see. The odd quality proclaimed itself through the skin. It possessed the sickish plasticity (at the back of her arms it was especially noticeable) of one who has suffered severe emaciation and whose flesh is even now in the last stages of being restored. Also I felt that underneath that healthy suntan there lingered the sallowness of a body not wholly rescued from a terrible crisis. (51)

Through the eyes of Stingo, Styron gradually builds a psychological portrayal of Sophie's struggle with the memory of pain and grief. He comes to understand at some point that Sophie's almost masochistic relationship with the schizophrenic Nathan is a desperate attempt to suppress her own excruciating pain and guilt by allowing more pain to be inflicted on her. There is a gradual buildup of doom, a premonition of disaster, which Stingo feels very early on in the story of his acquaintance with Sophie. The sense that she is unwell in body and spirit, as indicated by the sallowness of her skin, is strengthened by the nostalgic music playing at that revealing moment, the First Symphony of Brahms. Stingo notes "the lordly and tragic French horn mingling in my head with the flute's antiphonal, piercing birdcall to fill my spirit with a sadness and nostalgia almost more intense than any I had felt before" (52). Sophie, after a falling-out with Nathan, is literally "drowning in her sorrow"; her weeping is inconsolable; she is a vessel containing incredible grief and "this raw devastating woe" (52). Stingo feels that such despair cannot have been inspired only by her lover. He has a dream that night, a nightmare, and when he wakes up "with a start just before dawn, in the dead silence of that hour, with a pounding heart and an icy chill," he understands that Sophie is doomed (53).

The fact that Stingo comes to understand Sophie gradually, switching his attention—if with some difficulty—from her physical attractiveness and his fantasies about making love to her to who she is and to her past experience, underscores the contrast, which permeates the entire novel, between the unspeakable horrors of concentration camps and the trifle, at times utterly ridiculous, preoccupations of Stingo with his sexual exploits.

Propelled by his interest in Sophie, Stingo sets out on a journey of discovery, trying to learn as much as possible about the Holocaust and anti-Semitism. This process also involves his having to question his own beliefs and expectations concerning Jews and revising some of his initial assumptions. Naturally, because of its subject matter, *Sophie's Choice* contains representations of various kinds of anti-Semitism. There are the "deadly" varieties—most importantly, the Nazi version of anti-Semitism, which is likely to be well-known (as a phenomenon thoroughly studied and described at length in accounts of the history of the Third Reich) and thus the least controversial.[11] There is the Polish version of anti-Semitism, as represented, most obviously, by Sophie's father, Zbigniew Biegański, the author of a treatise suggesting mass extermination of the Jews; and the elusive anti-Semitism of Sophie herself, which is hard to pin down, as it is not clear to what extent Sophie ever voices her real beliefs.[12] Stingo's story, however, draws attention to a much less obvious, and much less defined, issue of the stereotyping and prejudice related to Jews in the United States.

The young Stingo comes to Brooklyn, the most Jewish of New York City's five boroughs, from Virginia. The 515 pages of the novel reveal, first of all, that he—like many people in the world—is a repository of all kinds of stereotypes and generalizations about the Jews: their language, culture, and religious practices. He recalls that, as a small boy, he was ignorant of the connection between Judaism and Christianity. However, as a Bible student, he was familiar with the Old Testament stories about the Hebrew people and their history, especially with the Book of Leviticus. What he imagined Jewish life to be like was based mostly on impressions he had from reading Scripture, as well as on his familiarity with frequent stereotypes about Jews in popular culture and certain expressions commonly heard in the English language. Thus, trying to imagine what happened in a synagogue, he came up with the following vision:

> My childish fancy suggested that they blew a shofar, whose rude untamed notes echoed through a place of abiding gloom where there was a rotting old Ark and a pile of scrolls. Bent kosher women, faces covered, wore hair shirts and loudly sobbed. No stirring hymns were sung, only monotonous chants in which there was repeated with harsh insistency a word sounding like "adenoids." Spectral and bony phylacteries flapped through the murk like prehistoric birds, and everywhere were the rabbis in skullcaps moaning in a guttural tongue as they went about their savage rites—circumcising goats, burning oxen, disemboweling newborn lambs. (163)

Stingo imagines Jewish rites as mysterious, gloomy, sinister, incomprehensible, and inscrutable. Stingo, in his childhood, "was not mystified by Jews themselves" (162), for in his Southern town they were assimilated; they were "merchants, doctors, lawyers, a spectrum of bourgeois achievement" (162), and he deeply admired some of them. However, he suspected that at some point during the day they must be undergoing a disturbing transformation:

> But I saw how Jews seemed to acquire another self or being. It was out of the glare of daylight and the bustle of business, when Jews disappeared into their domestic quarantine and the seclusion of their sinister and Asiatic worship—with its cloudy suspicion of incense and rams' horns and sacrificial offerings, tambourines and veiled women, lugubrious anthems and keening banshee wails in a dead language—that the trouble began for an eleven-year-old Presbyterian. (162)

This and many similar passages in the novel have a comic undertone, satirizing the typical young American Protestant who has no actual experience of Judaism and only a set of vague, ridiculous ideas. This somewhat humorous approach is perhaps best illustrated in the story of

Stingo's first visit to the Lapidus family home, in which the narrator (Stingo's older self) exploits the comic potential of the juxtaposition between the young Stingo's expectations and reality. Waiting for his tryst with Leslie, Stingo realizes that he has never visited a Jewish household before. He searches his mind and recalls a synagogue, "the homely yellow-brick temple housing the Congregation Rodef Sholem" (162), in his hometown and what it symbolized to him in his childhood: "the silent and shuttered synagogue with its frowning cast-iron portals and intaglio star of David seemed in its intimidating quietude to represent for me all that was isolate, mysterious and even supernatural about Jews and Jewry and their smoky, cabalistic religion" (162). Having no other experiences, Stingo associates the house "as with a synagogue—. . . with gloom and darkness" (163). On a rational level, he knows that "the Lapidus family must be light years away from the slums as well as from the shtetl" (163), but "such is an enduring power of prejudice and preconception" (163) that he nevertheless imagines a house of "dim, even funereal oppressiveness," with "shadowy rooms paneled in mission oak." He expects that "on one table would be the menorah, its candles in orderly array but unlit, while nearby on another table would be the Torah, or perhaps the Talmud, opened to a page which had just undergone pious scrutiny by the elder Lapidus" (163). Echoing yet another stereotype, he imagines that, "although scrupulously clean, the dwelling would be musty and unventilated, allowing the odor of frying gefilte fish to waft from the kitchen" (163). He expects "the mother pathetically overweight in the manner of Jewish mothers, bashful, diffident, mostly silent" (164) and the father able to talk about his trade only and speaking with a heavy Yiddish accent.

Much to his astonishment, the Lapidus house is like nothing he expected it to be. It is so "stunningly swank" that he initially passes by it several times, not taking in the possibility that he may be at the right address. When the door opens to this very modern structure, "a gracefully restored Greek revival brownstone" (164), in another ironic twist, he is greeted by a black maid from North Carolina. Seated in an opulent living room, he experiences a cultural shock, being "totally unprepared for such affluence the likes of which my provincial eyes had glimpsed in the pages of *The New Yorker* and in movies but never actually beheld" (165). Leslie's parents impress Stingo with their learning, excellent manners, and sophistication; the anecdote continues further in this vein. The final irony and the strongest clash between Stingo's preconceived ideas and the reality come at the end of the Leslie episode. Stingo is elated at the prospect of having sex with "a remarkably beautiful, sexually liberated, twenty-two-year-old Jewish Madonna" (120). He feels intoxicated at the prospect of "the crazy bliss of fornication with a hot-skinned, eager-bellied Jewish girl with fathomless eyes and magnificent apricot-and-ocher suntanned legs that all but promised to squeeze the life out of me . . ." (120). He begins to obsess about having sex with Leslie, always in the context of her Jewishness: "I was conscious that the principle of the attraction of opposites was very much in effect. Jew and *goy* in magnetic gravitation" (125). Partly misled by Leslie's apparent willingness to engage in sexual activity, partly by the things he hears about young Jewish women from other people, he assumes that Jewish girls are different from girls in the South: "This Jewish dryad has more sensuality in one of her expressive thumbs than all the locked-up virgins I ever knew in Va. & N.C. put together" (128). The final joke is that Leslie turns out to be as resistant to Stingo's attempts at initiating sexual intercourse as any of the women he had approached in the South.

Another useful approach to the teaching of *Sophie's Choice* is to follow Stingo's path as he seeks to deepen his understanding of anti-Semitism and the Holocaust. Stingo's encounters and conversations with Sophie and her remarks about Auschwitz prompt him to ask questions about the causes and origin of death camps and their meaning. He also undertakes some research and consults several recognized authorities on the subject matter in question. One of them is the critic George Steiner, author of a collection of essays, *Language and Silence*, who writes about time relation. Stingo becomes acutely aware that on April 1, 1943, when Sophie arrived in Auschwitz, falling into "the slow hands of the living damnation" (217), he was gorging himself on bananas in Raleigh, North Carolina, trying to meet the weight requirements for enlistment in the Navy. On that day, like almost all Americans, he had no idea about Auschwitz or Treblinka. He had not even heard about the extermination of European Jews or the death camps. For Americans, the focus was on the Japanese, who, having overrun the Pacific, were perceived as a more genuine threat to the United States. Steiner (and Stingo along with him) asks the question: "Are there, as science fiction and Gnostic speculation imply, different species of time in the world, 'good time' and enveloping folds of inhuman time, in which men fall into the slow hands of the living damnation?" (210–11). Steiner introduces two orders of time: "This notion of different orders of time simultaneous but in no effective analogy or communication, may be necessary to the rest of us, who were not there, who lived as if on another planet" (217). Stingo does not accept Steiner's conclusion that silence is the answer in the face of the unspeakable; he believes that, as an artist, he should at least make an attempt at understanding. The process of understanding involves the recognition of Sophie's position and her plight and getting at the meaning of the death camps.

Underlying this process are several books about the Holocaust to which the narrator refers—by authors such as Elie Wiesel, Hannah Arendt, and George Steiner—but one book in particular, *The Cunning of History* by Richard L. Rubenstein, seems to inform the foundations of the whole novel. A closer look at the "masterful little book" (235), as Stingo calls it, reveals a great deal about the ideological design of *Sophie's Choice* and is thus an important clue to the meaning of the novel.

Richard Lowell Rubenstein is a New York City–born rabbi and theologian who, with the publication of *After Auschwitz*,[13] began a public debate on the religious meaning of the Holocaust. *The Cunning of History* was published in 1975 and has become one of the most influential studies of mass death and contemporary civilization. Styron wrote an introduction to the book in 1978 in which he expressed his admiration for it and called it a revelation, full of "startling" and "prophetic" insights.[14] He even speaks of the "effect of keen illumination" on "the most compelling theme in history"—"that of the catastrophic propensity on the part of human beings to attempt to dominate one another."[15]

Rubenstein observes that the Holocaust was "a thoroughly modern exercise in total domination that could only have been carried out by an advanced political community with a highly trained, tightly disciplined police and civil service bureaucracy."[16] It was unique because "it was the first attempt by a modern, legally constituted government to pursue a policy of bureaucratically organized genocide both within and beyond its own frontiers."[17] While Rubenstein claims that the Holocaust is unique, he emphasizes that it must be considered in the context of the "unprecedented magnitude of violence" that characterized the twentieth century,[18] which involved the death of about one hundred million people slaughtered as a direct outcome of the political and military activity of the world's superpowers.

Even more importantly, Rubenstein sees the Holocaust as a natural outcome of the political, religious, moral, and demographic trends that had been taking place in Western civilization for some time. A key factor in this process is the rise of the importance of bureaucracy. Rubenstein uses Max Weber's observations on the nature and functions of modern bureaucracy:

> In order to understand how the moral barrier was crossed that made massacre in the millions possible, it is necessary to consider the importance of bureaucracy in modern political and social organization . . . Its specific nature which is welcomed by capitalism develops the more perfectly the more bureaucracy is "dehumanized," the more completely it succeeds in eliminating from official business love, hatred, and all purely personal, irrational and emotional elements which escape calculation.[19]

According to Rubinstein, Auschwitz was made possible by the efficient German bureaucracy and the terror apparatus of the SS that ensured control all the way through the process:

> At Auschwitz, the Germans revealed new potentialities in the human ability to dominate, enslave and exterminate. They also revealed new areas in which capitalist enterprise might profitably and even respectably be employed. The camps were thus far more of a permanent threat to the human future than they would have been had they functioned solely as an exercise in mass killing. An execution center can only manufacture corpses; a society of total domination creates a world of the living dead that can serve as a prototype of a future social order, especially in a world confronted by catastrophic crises and ever-increasing, massive population redundancy.[20]

As for religion, Rubenstein believes that "before the twentieth century, the Christian religious tradition was both the source of much traditional anti-Jewish hostility and an effective barrier against the final murderous step."[21] Typical Christian stereotypes about the Jews go back to Martin Luther and the pan-German anti-Semites of the nineteenth century, with the Nazis needing to add very little to that large inheritance: "In every instance, the Jew was depicted as an enemy within the gates, a criminal and a kind of plague or species of vermin."[22] When traditional religious and moral restraints were finally removed in the twentieth century, people could go far beyond the scope of the mass murders that had previously occurred in the history of Western civilization.

The fundamental values of Western culture are "derived from a religious tradition that insists on the dichotomous division of mankind into the elect and the reprobate"; there is "no escape from the self-defeating ethos of exclusivism and intolerance."[23] Therefore, according to Rubenstein, the society of total domination originates in the Bible—this is the "night side of religion."[24] In Rubenstein's words:

> Without that [religious] tradition, or at least the ethos it engendered, it is likely that neither fully rationalized bureaucracy nor the death camps would have developed. Nor can we ignore the biblical roots of the hideous Nazi caricature of the Chosen People doctrine, the claim that pure-blooded Germans are a *Herrenvolk*, a master race destined to rule, enslave or exterminate non-Germans.[25]

In *Sophie's Choice*, Styron takes advantage not only of the general ideas provided by Rubenstein, but also of all kinds of details that allow him to design and structure both the plot of the novel, the names of his characters, and the general background, all of which reflect a close connection between Styron's perception of Auschwitz and Rubenstein's study. Like Styron's novel, Rubenstein's writing also features a parallel between slavery and the Nazi system of mass extermination. What Styron finds strikingly accurate in Rubenstein's reflections is the dual function of Auschwitz: "a depot for mass murder but also a vast enclave dedicated to the practice of slavery" (235). The concentration and death camps were "in reality new forms of human society," a society of "total domination" that is seen as having grown directly out of the slavery introduced by the ancient Romans and continued in the Western Hemisphere, including in the United States.

As a new form of slavery, concentration camps were based on the "absolute expendability of human life" (235). This concept of expendability, which is much emphasized in *Sophie's Choice*, is explained in detail by Rubenstein in the first chapter of *The Cunning of History*. He sees World War I as an important step in the emergence of this concept on a hitherto unprecedented scale. In World War I, both the French and the German governments were determined to win battles regardless of the human losses. At the Battle of Verdun, General von

Falkenhayn, the German commander, attempted to slaughter the French soldiers; his "strategy was biological."[26] Almost half a million French soldiers died, and with the German casualties approximately matching this number, some one million men died in a battle that lasted almost nine months and did not move the front lines in a significant way. Both the German and French leaders were prepared to sacrifice a large number of their people to win the war, and they were not alone in their determination. The British command may have been even more careless in their attitudes, which is a point that Rubenstein illustrates with the Battle of the Somme. General Sir Douglas Haig, attempting to break through the enemy lines, sacrificed the lives of 410,000 British soldiers to advance six miles in five months. When 500,000 Germans and 190,000 French are added to the total number of casualties, then the Battle of the Somme becomes probably the most insane carnage in the world's history. The French, British, and German leaders must have arrived at the same conclusion: the lives of their young soldiers were expendable. As Rubenstein puts it: "This was a giant step towards the death camps of World War II."[27]

Rubenstein concludes by stating that death camps are a logical outcome of the evolution of Western civilization, grounded as it is in the foundations of the Judeo-Christian tradition. The humanistic values inherent in that tradition were defeated by rational, secularized, modern economic and political structures. "Civilization is an organic process,"[28] says Rubenstein "It means slavery, wars, exploitation, and death camps. It also means medical hygiene, elevated religious ideals, beautiful art, and exquisite music."[29] This very pessimistic conclusion—that savagery is part of our civilization and cruelty will always be around—feeds into the essentially very dark vision of the world presented in Styron's novel. It explains why Sophie "hates all religion."

Perhaps the most memorable comment by Rubenstein is the one implying that interpreting the Holocaust as "unique" would actually be seeing it in an unduly optimistic way. This is how Styron sums it up in his introduction to Rubenstein's book:

> Rubenstein is forcing us to reinterpret the meaning of Auschwitz—especially, although not exclusively, from the standpoint of its existence as part of a continuum of slavery that has been engrafted for centuries onto the very body of Western civilization. Therefore, in the process of destroying

the myth and the preconception, he is making us see that the encampment of death and suffering may have been more horrible than we had ever imagined. It was slavery in its ultimate embodiment. He is making us understand that the etiology of Auschwitz—to some a diabolical, perhaps freakish excrescence, which vanished from the face of the earth with the destruction of the crematoria in 1945—is actually embedded deeply in a cultural tradition that stretches back to the Middle Passage from the coast of Africa, and beyond, to the enforced servitude in ancient Greece and Rome.[30]

Sophie's Choice is a book that made both Poles and Jews extremely unhappy with the portrayal of Jewish and Polish characters in the novel, respectively.[31] While some of the criticism that *Sophie's Choice* has attracted over the years is certainly justified, I have found the novel very useful in introducing both Polish and American students to the complex and difficult issues of the Holocaust and anti-Semitism. It is possible to discuss *Sophie's* Choice as an imaginative work of fiction and point out it its strengths and weaknesses while at the same time learning about the ideology of anti-Semitism and mass extermination. The novel allows for the contextualization of anti-Semitism by providing literary representations of various types of anti-Semitic belief. Finally, considering the novel in light of some important background texts, such as Rubenstein's *The Cunning of History*, allows for an appreciation of the importance of a certain vision of the history and nature of humankind for the novel's overall design.

Notes

1. Alvin H. Rosenfeld, "The Holocaust According to William Styron," *Midstream* 25, no. 10 (1979).
2. Cynthia Ozick, "A Liberal's Auschwitz," *Confrontation* 10 (1975).
3. D. G. Myers, "Jews Without Memory: 'Sophie's Choice' and the Ideology of Liberal Anti-Judaism," *American Literary History* 13, no. 3 (2001).
4. Nigel Pleasants, "The Question of the Holocaust's Uniqueness: Was It Something More Than or Different from Genocide?," *Journal of Applied Philosophy* 33, no. 3 (2016): 297.
5. Myers, "Jews Without Memory," 500.

6. William Styron, "A Wheel of Evil Come Full Circle: The Making of *Sophie's Choice*," *The Sewanee Review* 105, no. 3 (1997).

7. Sue Vice, *Holocaust Fiction* (London: Routledge, 2000), ft. 12.

8. This tendency to see the dark side of humankind as dominant, and the emergence of evil as inevitable, has in Styron criticism been discussed in the context of the Southern Gothic tradition in American literature (see, e.g. John Gardner, "A Novel of Evil," *New York Times*, May 1979).

9. William Styron, *Sophie's Choice* (New York: Random House, 1979). In subsequent references to *Sophie's Choice*, page numbers are given in parentheses.

10. Richard G. Law, "The Reach of Fiction: Narrative Technique in Styron's *Sophie's Choice*," *The Southern Literary Journal* 23, no. 1 (1990): 48–49.

11. An important aspect of Nazi anti-Semitism is its Christian dimension, which is insightfully discussed by Michel Lackey in "The Theology of Nazi Anti-Semitism in William Styron's *Sophie's Choice*," *Lit: Literature Interpretation Theory* 22, no. 4 (2011), and "Nazi Children, Christian Anti-Semitism, and the New Atheist in William Styron's *Sophie's Choice*," MFS *Modern Fiction Studies* 60, no. 1 (2014).

12. The characters of both Professor Biegański and Sophie have inspired commentaries by Polish academics and reviewers, who generally found them unconvincing for reasons related to the issue of representation. See Jerzy R. Krzyżanowski, "What's Wrong with *Sophie's Choice*?" *Polish American Studies* 40, no. 1 (1983); Thomas J. Napierkowski, "*Sophie's Choice*: The Other Holocaust, Revisited, Revised and Renewed," *Polish American Studies* 40, no. 1 (1983): 73–87; Joanna Rostropowicz-Clark, "Review of *Sophie's Choice* by William Styron," *The Polish Review* 25, no. 2 (1980). Contemporary reviews of *Sophie's Choice*, especially written by people with firsthand experience of life in wartime and occupied Poland, emphasized the various ways in which both Sophie and her father were not typical; for example, for a woman of Sophie's upbringing and social position it would have been unthinkable to undress on a beach in public view (Rostropowicz-Clark, "Review of *Sophie's Choice*"). In the case of Biegański, his being an anti-Semite was conceived as more likely than his being such an ardent Germanophile that his daughter was first taught to speak in German, then Polish; such extreme cases of Germanophilia have not been known to any of those who remembered the prewar Jagiellonian University circles and who expressed their opinion on *Sophie's Choice* (see the discussion in Andrea Bernard and Elżbieta Oleksy, "*Sophie's Choice*: The Depiction of Poles in the American Popular Imagination," in *Images of Central Europe in Travelogues and Fiction by North American Writers*, ed. Waldemar Zacharasiewicz (Tübingen: Stauffenburg Verlag, 1995).

13. Richard L. Rubenstein, *After Auschwitz: Radical Theology and Contemporary Judaism* (Indianapolis: Bobbs-Merrill, 1966).

14. William Styron, "Introduction," in *The Cunning of History: The Holocaust and the American Future*, by Richard L. Rubenstein (New York: Harper, 1987), vii.

15. Styron, "Introduction," vii.
16. Richard L. Rubenstein, *The Cunning of History: The Holocaust and the American Future* (New York: Harper, 1987), 4.
17. Ibid., 7.
18. Ibid.
19. Ibid., 22.
20. Ibid., 96.
21. Ibid., 5.
22. Ibid., 6.
23. Ibid., 93.
24. Ibid., 92.
25. Ibid., 92–93.
26. Ibid., 8.
27. Ibid.
28. Ibid., 92.
29. Ibid.
30. Styron, "Introduction," x.
31. See, e.g., Barbara Foley, "Fact, Fiction, Fascism: Testimony and Mimesis in Holocaust Narratives," *Comparative Literature* 34, no. 4 (1982), for an example.

References

Bernard, Andrea, and Elżbieta Oleksy. "*Sophie's Choice*: The Depiction of Poles in the American Popular Imagination." In *Images of Central Europe in Travelogues and Fiction by North American Writers*, edited by Waldemar Zacharasiewicz, 261–68. Tübingen: Stauffenburg Verlag, 1995.

Foley, Barbara. "Fact, Fiction, Fascism: Testimony and Mimesis in Holocaust Narratives." *Comparative Literature* 34, no. 4 (1982): 330–60.

Gardner, John. "A Novel of Evil." *The New York Times Review of Books*, May 1979.

Krzyżanowski, Jerzy R. "What's Wrong with *Sophie's Choice*?" *Polish American Studies* 40, no. 1 (1983): 64–72.

Lackey, Michael. "The Theology of Nazi Anti-Semitism in William Styron's *Sophie's Choice*." *Lit: Literature Interpretation Theory* 22, no. 4 (2011): 277–300. doi:10.1080/10436928.2011.622697. http://www.tandfonline.com/doi/abs/10.1080/10436928.2011.622697.

———. "Nazi Children, Christian Anti-Semitism, and the New Atheist in William Styron's *Sophie's Choice*." *MFS Modern Fiction Studies* 60, no. 1 (2014): 138–64. doi:10.1353/mfs.2014.0007. http://muse.jhu.edu/content/crossref/journals/modern_fiction_studies/v060/60.1.lackey.html.

Myers, D. G. "Jews Without Memory: '*Sophie's Choice*' and the Ideology of Liberal Anti-Judaism." *American Literary History* 13, no. 3 (2001): 499–529. http://www.jstor.org/stable/3054558.

Napierkowski, Thomas J. "*Sophie's Choice*: The Other Holocaust, Revisited, Revised and Renewed." *Polish American Studies* 40, no. 1 (1983): 73–87.

Ozick, Cynthia. "A Liberal's Auschwitz." *Confrontation* 10 (1975): 125–29.

Pleasants, Nigel. "The Question of the Holocaust's Uniqueness: Was It Something More Than or Different From Genocide?" *Journal of Applied Philosophy* 33, no. 3 (2016): 297–310. doi:10.1111/japp.12113.

Rosenfeld, Alvin H. "The Holocaust According to William Styron." *Midstream* 25, no. 10 (1979): 43–49.

Rostropowicz-Clark, Joanna. "Review of *Sophie's Choice* by William Styron." *The Polish Review* 25, no. 2 (1980): 97–100.

Rubenstein, Richard L. *After Auschwitz: Radical Theology and Contemporary Judaism*. Indianapolis: Bobbs-Merrill, 1966.

———. *The Cunning of History: The Holocaust and the American Future*. New York: Harper, 1987.

Styron, William. *Sophie's Choice*. New York: Random House, 1979.

———. "Introduction." In *The Cunning of History: The Holocaust and the American Future*, vii–xv. New York: Harper, 1987.

———. "A Wheel of Evil Come Full Circle: The Making of *Sophie's Choice*." *The Sewanee Review* 105, no. 3 (1997): 395–400.

Vice, Sue. *Holocaust Fiction*. London: Routledge, 2000.

15

"A novel that dare not speak its name"
Biographical Approaches to Saul Bellow

Judie Newman

When Roland Barthes described biography as "a novel that dare not speak its name," he drew attention to the primacy of narrative in biographies, and thus to their essential fictionality.[1] How do we use biography in studying Jewish-American writing? What constraints (legal, psychological, operational) complicate the biographical undertaking? Which biographies engage the student most fully? Saul Bellow provides an instructive case study with biographies varying in their degrees of idealization or denigration, including the family memoir (Greg Bellow, *Saul Bellow's Heart*), the fan letter (Ann Weinstein, *Me and My (Tor) Mentor Saul Bellow*), the hatchet job (Harriet Wasserman, *Handsome Is: Adventures with Saul Bellow*), a comprehensive, unauthorized academic biography (James Atlas, *Bellow*), and the first volume of a second, authorized academic biography (Zachary Leader, *The Life of Saul Bellow: To Fame and Fortune, 1915–64*). In addition, faced with lack of cooperation, Ruth Miller turned from the man to the literary works in *Saul Bellow: A Biography of the Imagination*, while Mark Harris (*Saul Bellow: Drumlin Woodchuck*) transformed his failure to become Bellow's biographer into a self-deprecating memoir. Eight biographical works and more to come. With the exception perhaps of Harris and Weinstein, it has to be acknowledged from the start that the image that emerges is not a flattering one. Atlas's account of Bellow's relentless pursuit of women from early in his first marriage, not to mention his prickliness and vengefulness, prompted some hostile reviews. Both Wasserman and Greg Bellow portray Bellow as a master of evasion, endlessly shilly-shallying and avoiding potentially angry reactions by using others as intermediaries. Moreover, there is little debate over his evolution from radical, bohemian Trotskyist to a moral conservative whose later views on race and women lost him readers. Though his family loved him, none of his other biographers ended up liking him very much. Ruth Miller shuts the lid on this complicated, slippery man with a particularly resounding clang. Describing him as complex and difficult to pin down, she closes:

> I know that for Bellow there is only one box to which he will consign himself, into which he will helplessly fit. He has no way to evade that measured space.[2]

Nevertheless, there is universal agreement that Bellow is one of the greatest writers of his age. Should the reader therefore simply draw a line between the author and the man, and decide that biography has little to offer?

That is, of course, also a question frequently asked of literary biography per se. As D. H. Lawrence said, "Never trust the artist. Trust the tale."[3] Even if we do not go to the lengths of following Roland Barthes and declaring the author dead, the general tendency of high modernism, beginning with Wimsatt and Beardsley's attack on the intentional and affective fallacies, is to maintain a separation between the living individual and the mind that creates.[4] Even if we do accept that biography can shed light on the work, there remain limitations. Biography demands funds—to travel, carry out interviews, visit archives, reproduce photographs, and write. In this respect, the personal memoir (Greg Bellow, Wasserman, Weinstein) has a head start on the commissioned literary work. Access to archives may also pose problems, depending on the degree of cooperation of the subject, the executors, or the lawyers. According to Atlas, Ruth Miller had full access to the Regenstein Library Archives and enjoyed long interviews with Bellow, who urged his publishers to allow her to quote without charge from his work and sent her copies of important letters. She had known him and his first wife socially and met him intermittently over some forty years. She also showed him a draft. Once the book had been typeset, however, Bellow changed his mind and eventually denied her permission to quote from his letters or papers, enlisting legal support.[5] Though James Atlas was in no way "authorized," he had full access, and by the time Bellow could get cold feet, it was too late to rescind his permission. Atlas keeps a firm and stylish grasp on the narrative, combining scholarship with considerable intellectual verve, across a highly readable book of 700 pages. As Michael Benton notes, "authorized" lives throw up their own challenges: "privileged access to all the documents . . . offers a temptation to prolixity that is hard to resist."[6] Indeed, Zachary Leader appears at times to be drowning in a flood of source material and gets his subject born only some fifty pages into the account. Gregory Bellow was refused access to his father's papers in the Regenstein Library by the Andrew Wylie Literary Agency (the agents for Bellow and now for his estate) but found it in some respects a creative benefit.[7] As a boy he had resented the closed study door and the silence imposed on him as his father wrote, but in writing the memoir he adopted his father's routine and found a new connection with parts of his father's life, which he had previously found intimidating. It is worth reminding ourselves here that Bellow lived from 1915 to 2005, a long life and a gregarious one, with five wives, four children (the first in 1944, the last in 1999), siblings, school friends whom he knew all his life, a variety of publishers, four literary agents, many changes of location, and a tendency to attract worshipful disciples. The paper trail is a long one. Benjamin Taylor's edition of Bellow's letters, despite its 600 pages, included only 708 letters, about two-fifths of Bellow's surviving output. Though often offering a real sense of Bellow's life—his enduring friendships, generosity as a reader and critic, and willingness to serve on literary committees—there are no letters to his first or his fourth wife. No life can be recaptured in its totality; selection, emphasis, and the need to maintain a narrative arc will shape it. As a result, any biography will have to leave things out.

If our first question is whether biography assists at all and our second is what has been left out, our third inevitably concerns the biographer's own raison d'être. Laying aside the financial imperative, there remain other motivations. The biographer may immerse him- or herself in the subject's life as a way of indirectly examining his or her own, as was the case of André Maurois writing about Shelley. Greg Bellow's memoir reflects on his own identity as a son as well as on his neglectful father and produces an affecting meditation on fathers and sons, a genre with a fine pedigree, which begins with Edmund Gosse's *Father and Son* (1907). Biographers may suggest some sort of "mythic parity" between themselves and their subject, or at least aggrandize themselves by association. The biographer may also be protectionist. Thomas Hardy wrote his own life (which he credited to his wife); James Joyce rewrote Herbert Gorman's biography; and many works suffer from what Edmund Gosse called the "widow factor," as in the example of Mary Shelley, presenting her husband as a paragon of virtue.[8] The "warts and all" biography has its defenders. Humphrey Carpenter argued (apropos of Britten) that the murkier areas of an artist's life may often be at the center of the creative personality.[9] By contrast, the daily rituals of a writer's life are almost always extremely boring. Bellow wrote every day, all morning, behind a closed door, and apart from the fact that he wrapped a towel around his neck and listened to Mozart, there is almost nothing interesting to say about those hours.

Or is there? The answer may be to move away from the man toward an understanding of the social processes through which Bellow's works emerged: the textual material, social supports on offer, and intellectual biography. In short, scholars need to move their attention from the big fish to the stream in which it swims. Textual biography—the genetic study of the writing itself—is an often overlooked aspect of the life-writing of authors.[10] Daniel Fuchs's study of the manuscripts, while not at all a biography, chronicles the stops and starts of Bellow's novels from *The Adventures of Augie March* to *Humboldt's Gift*, quoting in detail from the manuscripts. Once there is better access to these (now much augmented in volume and not yet fully organized) textual biography will become a major priority for scholars. Bellow abandoned countless works, including of course his last unfinished novel, set in New Guinea. But the published works were also in constant flux. Bellow rarely made notes or a plan, writing his way into the story and revising over and over again, sometimes as much as twenty times for parts of *Herzog*. The "ideas" letters were a very late development in *Herzog*, which began as a vengeful account of Bellow's cuckolding by his best friend but moved toward redemption and reconciliation at the close. Early versions of *The Adventures of Augie March* had a much more serious political theme, with Augie as a member of a movement involving socialism in industry and land redistribution; other versions offer a serious defense of the idea that all love is adultery and that everyone's deeper consciousness is outlaw. Some works are strongly influenced by other people; the manuscript of

Mr. Sammler's Planet is annotated in part by Edward Shils. There are some 6,000 pages of material on *Humboldt's Gift,* and in early drafts Citrine is married to an old-fashioned socialist who represents the dignity of the common life, a fact that somewhat undermines the association made by some readers between the character of Denise and Bellow's third wife, Susan Glassman. Characters often appear in many different guises, a useful reminder that despite the claims that certain characters are based on Bellow's wives or friends (for example, Allan Bloom as Ravelstein) they are fundamentally creations of the imagination.

As well as allowing literary biographers to give an account of the activity of writing itself, a textual archive offers information on the material, legal, and market conditions that influenced it. Publishers' archives promise a rich biographical resource in Bellow's case, given that he moved fairly frequently between them. Rather than consider the writer as standing alone, it is useful to consider him as at the center of a cluster of agents, editors, publishers, publisher's readers, and audience. Copyright law, permissions, contracts, paratextual elements, correspondence about anthologies, film rights, and foreign translations—all contribute to the life of the text. Arguably, literary biography can be refreshed by the development of the history of the book as a field of study, offering a way to make manifest the conditions of a book's making.[11] Texts may originate in the writer's mind, but they emerge through a social process involving other people. On the whole, Bellow's biographers say very little about the process of publication, contracts, legal issues, copyright, cover designs, blurbs, translators, foreign reception, or spin-offs.

A useful exception is Harriet Wassermann's memoir. Agents are something of the "elephant-in-the-room" in biographies of Bellow. His first agent, Maxim Lieber, was a card-carrying Communist who fled to Mexico in 1951 and then to Warsaw and was believed to be a covert agent of the Soviet Union.[12] Henry Volkening of the Russell and Volkening agency was the second, followed by Wasserman and then Andrew Wylie. In this respect, the awkwardness of the two-volume chronological biography makes itself evident. Presumably Leader will consider Wasserman in more detail in the second volume covering the period after 1964, when she was most active, but in the first volume she scarcely features at all. In a footnote, Leader describes Wasserman as working in Volkening's office as an assistant until his health declined in the early 1970s and she became Bellow's sole agent.[13] In the main text, he does not mention that she wrote a memoir or that she ran her own literary agency to which

Bellow moved. A footnote gives the publication details of Wasserman's book.[14] By contrast, James Atlas, who interviewed Wasserman, describes her as Bellow's one mainstay, in contact with him on a daily basis over some twenty years, at times perhaps envisaging herself rather too much as his sole defender, but nonetheless the woman who accompanied him to the Nobel Prize ceremony, agreed to act as Allan Bloom's literary agent purely because he was Bellow's friend, shopped for Bellow, took him to the dentist, and dispatched his preferred razor blades to Spain.[15] The end of this relationship makes for painful reading. In 1996, the *New York Times* announced that after twenty-five years Bellow was leaving Wasserman to sign up with the Wylie agency. According to Atlas, Bellow kept denying that he was planning to change agents and, when challenged, cast himself as the deserted person.[16] Wasserman's book is an odd mixture of adoration and ambivalence and has the look of a work that may have been much abbreviated textually (it offers episodes rather than a complete account). The photographs at the end, however, speak for themselves, illustrating her presence in Bellow's life and his standing in hers—at the close, he is wittily juxtaposed photographically with Buster Keaton. Wasserman had functioned, in Bellow's description, as "coach, manager, and trainer" for a quarter of a century and considered him a man of genius, moral vision, and high art.[17] She also describes him as a man who could be snappy and vain and pocketed royalties that should have gone through the office.[18] He was very demanding: a seven-hour phone call dictated changes to the proofs. The volume is highly informative regarding changes of publishers (Vanguard, Viking, Harper and Row, Morrow, John Lehmann, Weidenfeld, Secker and Warburg) and writing habits. Wasserman was Bellow's first reader from *Humboldt's Gift* onward; she knew his fellow writers, friends, and family; and she portrays a man of surprising domesticity, a keen gardener who made blueberry jam, scoured pots, and vacuumed. She makes some telling observations. Bellow was five foot seven, but most of his protagonists are six feet tall. For Wasserman he revised too much, and in the case of *The Dean's December*, the novel's immediacy and elasticity were sacrificed.[19] She auctioned the sale of the manuscripts of *Mr. Sammler's Planet* (galleys and proofs) in 1988 for $60,000 and was instrumental in the publication of *A Theft*, the first time a major American literary figure had chosen to be published originally in paperback. Wasserman also spells out financial details of which the ordinary reader would normally be ignorant, particularly the economics of Bellow's backlist and foreign rights. According to Wasserman, Andrew Wylie had originally approached her with an offer to buy the backlist and foreign rights. Foreign rights are usually negotiated for limited periods, so that on expiration all Bellow contracts for old and new titles would have become Wylie contracts.[20] According to her, the Wylie agency had been in touch with Bellow for months before she became aware of it.[21] A week after she was negotiating a contract for him with Viking Penguin for his collected short stories, a lawyer told her that she was to remain his primary agent "under Wylie's supervision," an offer she indignantly rejected.[22] She was then informed that Bellow was going to Wylie. Wasserman dissolved the agency in 2007; its papers—rich in material on Bellow—are held at Duke University Library and span the years 1948 to 1993, mostly after 1974. Those prior to 1974 concern her clients when she was at Russell and Volkening, who moved with her to her own agency, including Bellow. The importance of the role of the literary agent cannot be underestimated. Andrew Wylie continues as agent for the Bellow estate, was the agent for James Atlas when he wrote his biography, and is warmly saluted by Leader at the head of his "Acknowledgments" as first suggesting that he write Bellow's biography and as a staunch supporter of this book throughout.[23] In Europe, Barley Allison functioned as Bellow's agent and played a significant role in his career, and he left Weidenfeld to follow her to Secker and Warburg when she started her own imprint.

Biography is often a work of demystification. For Mark Greif, the real secret of Bellow's success, and perhaps that of Jewish-American writing, may be that it coincided with a period that believed that the fate of the novel was in some way an indication of the health of its society.[24] A constant theme of the early reviews concerns Bellow's achievement in redeeming the form of the novel and the ways in which his characters represent the modern condition.[25] After Herzog, however, this changes, and his characters come to be seen as oddballs and cranks. To some extent, the disillusionment of biographers may be traced to the way in which Bellow had previously been exalted as a savior figure, the defender of humanism and the individual in an age of standardization, underlining the moral importance of fiction. Greg Bellow notes the awe felt by Brent Staples, a young black man who wrote an essay about his desire to confront Bellow and his inability to do so.[26] For Greg, this was an illustration of how Bellow's public persona had taken on a mythical quality, drawing disciples who were interested in him because he was famous or because he seemed to represent a higher form of wisdom. Similarly,

Mark Harris begins his biography by describing various people who were obsessed with Bellow and exaggerated their knowledge of him.[27] Ann Weinstein saw him not just as a great writer but also as a great life instructor and mentor and felt that she had internalized his philosophy of life.[28] Ruth Miller's biography describes how Bellow was pestered by letters asking for advice or assistance.[29]

Biography needs to consider the established literary persona, the man made by the various people involved in his emergence, but also to mark a distance from it, to allow the reader to see the writer as he was before he became fixed in the public mind. While the subtitle of Leader's biography (*To Fame and Fortune*) appears to conflate those two concepts, chapter 7 of Greg Bellow's memoir is titled "Fame and Misfortune: 1963 to 1976," introducing the period in which his father became "Saul Bellow the famous author."[30] Greg had been raised by a frugal mother and a father who had no steady income until Greg was eighteen, and he was decidedly taken aback by the opulence of his father's later lifestyle. His parents had encouraged independence, appreciation of art and culture, contempt for ostentation, support for organized labor, and respect for people of all races. His account gives the reader intimate access to "Young Saul," the Bellow who wrote the masterpieces *The Victim*, *The Adventures of Augie March*, *Seize the Day*, *Henderson the Rain King*, *Herzog*, and *Humboldt's Gift*, as opposed to the later, less popular books. "Old Saul" may be more familiar to today's reader in the shape of a public persona associated with neoconservative views and Allan Bloom. Greg also reminds us of the importance of the Jewish immigrant background (a fine, even-handed account of Bellow's ancestry and family) but primarily underlines the extent to which young Jews of Bellow's generation were part of socially conscious movements, especially left-wing groups. Harriet Wasserman was one woman on whom Bellow depended, but she followed in the footsteps of four more: Anita and Sonia Goshkin, his first wife and mother-in-law, plus the Goshkin aunts. While Anita worked, the Goshkins, notably Sonia, a fervent believer in socialism, supported Bellow in their home for nine months of uninterrupted writing, getting his career off to a flying start. Anita and Saul had met as Trotskyists involved in the radical journal *Soapbox*. They did not keep kosher, observe religious practices or demand that Greg attend Hebrew school or have a bar mitzvah, and sent him to a progressive, mixed-race school. As a young father, Bellow apparently was emotionally accessible and able to laugh at himself—more a rebellious, irreverent son than an autocratic patriarch. Greg reminds the reader to question the image of the writer fixed in the public mind. After 1976, he had boycotted all public events held in honor of his father to avoid substituting a literary persona for the father he loved. When Bellow died, his lawyer contacted the media before he contacted the family. Greg learned the news from his car radio. His memoir emphasizes that the funeral and memorials were for the public man. No family member was invited to speak at the funeral. The title of the introduction, "Awakened By a Grave Robbery," conveys his feeling that literary "sons" and "daughters" (he mentions Martin Amis and Ruth Wisse) had replaced the real ones.[31] At the memorials in New York and Boston, no family members were included. When Greg asked to speak at the memorial at the University of Chicago, the request was placed in the hands of the Wylie agency, and five minutes were found.[32] For Greg, a moment of sorrow appeared to have been turned into a marketing opportunity.[33] Perhaps what is most valuable about his memoir is the way in which it distances itself from the public persona of the writer and restores a sense of the changing human being before he was cast in stone as a great writer. Fame brought burdens—as Bellow himself well understood. As his son argues, *Humboldt's Gift* provides an astute meditation on fame and the meaning of culture. Von Humboldt Fleischer, a distinguished poet, cuts himself off from American society and goes insane. Charlie Citrine, his biographer, is smothered by people who want to rub shoulders with cultural heroes at cocktail parties and risks seduction by the people they both began by despising, wealthy philistines with no real commitment to art. In "Him with His Foot in His Mouth," Shawmut has to listen to a socialite, dripping with diamonds, explaining how the great philanthropic foundations divide up their patronage of the different fields of art. When she tells him she is writing her memoirs, his social mask slips and he jibes, "Will you use a typewriter or an adding machine?"[34] This was a joke that Bellow himself originally made.[35] The scene explicitly dramatizes the subordination of the arts to the world of finance.[36]

The "culture wars" of the 1970s were particularly difficult for Bellow, who lined up on what was seen as the conservative side of the argument. His son ascribes this political change partly to disillusionment with his previous optimism, fed by a Utopian socialist ideology about the betterment of mankind, which crumbled in the face of the Holocaust and the triumph of various totalitarian regimes, disillusionment that the Marxist ideas in which he had placed so much faith had become a rationale for murderous totalitarian dictatorships, and disappointment in the failure of art to transform the world into a less materialistic place.[37]

Urban decay in Chicago also contributed to his bitterness, additionally fueled by anti-Semitic statements by elected black officials. Where *The Victim* carried the moral that we are all our brothers' keepers, Bellow later appeared to lose faith in collective action and human solidarity. In the past he had been a writer who brought great thinkers down to earth—with wickedly satirical skill (as in the letters in *Herzog*). But later his commitment to the canon positioned him with the great thinkers, changing "from a young man full of questions to an old man full of answers."[38] "Old Saul's" persona involved portraying himself as largely self-taught, tutored only by the great writers, and tended to ignore the support and constructive criticism of friends, family, and even visitors to the house, with whom he eagerly shared work in progress, reading excerpts aloud.[39]

Bellow did however reidentify with one social group. "Young Saul" had resisted the label of "Jewish writer," but after going to Israel in 1967 Bellow publicly embraced causes in support of Israel and badgered Greg unsuccessfully to force his son to attend Hebrew school and have a bar mitzvah. Before *The Adventures of Augie March*, the Jewish voice in American literature was scarcely heard except as a localized ethnic phenomenon. Yet that novel established Bellow as a major American author. He treated his Jewishness as something circumstantially attached to him, not as a quality essential to who he was. While always accepting his Jewishness, he didn't write as a Jew, for Jews, or on behalf of the Jewish community.[40] Nevertheless, Yiddish, which he spoke all his life, was very important to his writing style, as was his knowledge of the sacred books. James Wood has provided a cogent account of Bellow's lifelong study of the Hebrew Bible and the Christian New Testament, identifying biblical references throughout the works, and delineating his style as biblically English, with run-on sentences, semantic parallelisms, loose melodic compounds, and repetitions.[41] Bellow shared a house for a time with Ralph Ellison, with whom he also shared a loathing for literary taxonomy and the condescending classification of their work and selves according to their minority status. When presented with an award from the Anti-Defamation League, he remarked that in Israel he was often asked what sort of Jew he was and how he defined himself, the implication being that the life of a Jew in the Diaspora must be inauthentic. Bellow roundly condemned this idea.[42]

Greg Bellow wrote about the heart of a writer who was more often seen as all head, keenly intellectual. One thing that astonished Greg was that his father apparently saw no resemblance between the women in his novels and those in his life.[43] And yet, as Menand notes, today's belief that his biography was central to his novels was not at all current in his heyday. Reviews of *Herzog* emphasized the redemptive and transcendent power of the novel and treated it as a report on the human condition. Nobody referred to it as biographical. Identifying character with so-called "models" neglects what might be the most important biographical account of Bellow's writing: his intellectual biography. Julia Kristeva's definition of intertextuality, "Every text builds itself as a mosaic of quotation, every text is absorption and transformation of another text," has a particular resonance in the case of Bellow, who refers to a battery of different writers and thinkers throughout his work and draws on a wealth of different languages—Yiddish, Hebrew, Russian, French, English—all of them carrying in their individual words a freight of culture and history.[44] While none of Bellow's biographers offers a full-scale intellectual biography (limitations of space would make this an impossible task, even in a two-volume work), both Atlas and Leader provide extensive discussions of literary and intellectual influences, and Miller is particularly interesting on Bellow's engagement with anthroposophy. Novels are not individual, freestanding entities, appearing from nowhere like Adam in the Garden, but are made from other books and other languages. Just as the novels emerged from manuscript to print through a social process, just as they depended on familial or social support networks, so the intellectual biography depends on a whole group of writers and thinkers. Unusually too, in many cases the actual structure of Bellow's novels depended on this intellectual scaffolding. Dostoevsky's *Notes from Underground* provides much of the plot machinery for *Dangling Man*. *The Victim* borrows the plot partly from Dostoevsky's *The Eternal Husband*, partly from Otto Rank's *The Double*. Doubles are a constant feature of the fiction, from Leventhal and Albee through Dahfu and Henderson, Mosby and Lustgarten, Herzog and Gersbach, Citrine and Cantabile, Humboldt and Citrine, Benn and Kenneth, and Chick and Ravelstein. Herzog clutching his pistol and spying on Gersbach recalls Raskolnikov in *The Brothers Karamazov*. Even Augie's adventures with

Caligula depend on Dan and Jule Mannix's account of hunting with an eagle in Mexico.[45]

A useful companion to the student of Bellow's intellectual biography is the index to either of the two academic biographies, each of which provides accounts of important literary and intellectual influences. But the best friends to the student are the detailed studies by individual scholars of particular topics, often in succinct essayistic form. Importantly, Bellow's Jewish background also informs his intellectual biography. Three areas are particularly significant: his political evolution, his engagement with psychoanalytic thought, and the importance of his education in social anthropology. As Gloria Cronin and Lee Trepannier have suggested, Bellow's political thought was rooted in philosophical and religious concerns about alienation, spirituality, and the nature of modern civilization. In their *Political Companion* to Bellow, different essayists trace Bellow's evolution from Trotskyism to social democracy, his early politics of Jewish identification, disaffiliation and reaffiliation, gender politics in his works, the subversion of racism, the effect of the Holocaust, and the movement toward a culturally conservative position in opposition to multicultural politics and New Left social protest. (There is also an excellent annotated bibliography of essays on Bellow's politics, invaluable to the student.) One chapter offers a series of interviews with Bellow's three sons on "Our Father's Politics."[46] Given the age gaps between Greg (born 1944), Adam (born 1957), and Daniel (born 1964), their accounts open overlapping chronological windows into some six decades of Bellow's political thought. All three recount Bellow's steady loss of youthful idealism, growing cynicism, misogyny, racial anxiety, and fearfulness of urban violence. But they also see "neoconservative" as far too simplistic a description. Bellow found fellowship with the political right only in matters of high culture and the arts; his primary concerns were with the viability of civilization and culture in the United States, and he generally remained aloof from political issues. Adam describes Israel and the status of the Jews as central to his father's politics, particularly in the era when the fate of Soviet Jewry was a hot issue. Tellingly, when Adam asked his father what books to read in college, Bellow eschewed literary works and recommended biographies of the great figures of evil in the twentieth century: Hitler, Stalin, and Mao. Adam also discusses Bellow's later politics from an informed perspective. In his view, contemporary Americans are more homogenized than in his father's day, when the United States had strong regional cultures and accents, and different states were very different, a variety and diversity that his father prized.⁴⁷ Bellow himself described the United States of his adolescence as a more open society "before ethnic protectionism began."⁴⁸ Adam draws attention to the serious research carried out by Bellow, who immersed himself in the racial politics of Chicago, visiting housing projects, courts, jails, and hospitals.⁴⁹ He was a writer who did his political homework.

Bellow's engagement with psychological thought was also sustained and wide-ranging. Andrew M. Gordon delineates his love-hate affair with psychoanalysis, about which he was both intellectually sophisticated yet also derisive.⁵⁰ *The Last Analysis* constitutes a full-length parody of the analytic process, yet many of Bellow's protagonists appear to experience therapeutic catharsis, and some are also analyzed: Herzog, Citrine, and Henderson. Freud was at one point Bellow's bedtime reading.⁵¹ Yet all the psychoanalysts in his novels are comic characters, often caricatures. Bellow described comedy as a fundamental form of freedom. He argued that "Him With His Foot in His Mouth" was

> written on a theme, the legitimate irresponsibility of comedy. The life of Shawmut developed out of that. It's an interesting problem; things just pop out of your mouth. They come from comic inspiration, and that is one of the prominent forms of freedom.⁵²

"Him With His Foot in His Mouth" is essentially structured on a series of Freudian slips, which establish a critique of American society. Bellow collected Jewish jokes and was keenly aware of the ways in which Freud's Jewish identity informed his writings. Above all, he rejected any form of psychoanalytic orthodoxy or labeling. James Atlas argues that Bellow rejected Freud because he posed a threat to the independence of the artist.⁵³ Yet he underwent analysis four times himself, first in 1951 with Chester Raphael, a Reichian analyst. Reich, who was of Jewish parentage, had fled Europe in 1939 and was popular in the 1940s and 1950s, largely because he was seen as politically more radical than Freud. For some years Bellow regularly sat (stark naked) in a Reichian orgone box, acting out rage and terror by shouting and screaming. Dahfu puts Henderson through radical Reichian therapy in *Henderson the Rain King*. In 1958 he saw Paul Meehl, an eclectic therapist; in 1960 Albert Ellis, who had moved away from Freudian psychoanalysis toward cognitive-behavioral therapy; and in 1969 Heinz Kohut, the founder of self-psychology, which emphasizes the critical role of empathy in explaining human development.[54] (Greg Bellow's doctorate was on Kohut.) Although Gordon argues that Bellow's fiction moved away from psychoanalytic thought after 1964, *The Dean's December*, *More Die of Heartbreak*, and *A Theft* demonstrate a deepening engagement with the writings of Jung and a focus on women as a center of value, particularly in relation to the mother figure. *The Dean's December* establishes an entire community of loving women in Romania headed by the matriarch Valeria.[55] *A Theft* brings together the archetypal figures of maiden, mother, and crone in Lucy, Gina, and Clara.[56] *More Die of Heartbreak* follows Jung in emphasizing love as the conduit to higher ideals, placing the mythical figure of Psyche in contrast to modern psychology.[57]

Bellow's Jewish immigrant background and his early education in social anthropology are also intimately related.[58] He graduated from Northwestern in 1937 with honors in anthropology and sociology. One of his tutors was Melville J. Herskovits, whose studies of cattle cultures provided the material for *Henderson the Rain King*. Bellow described anthropology as linked to the cause of demystification in the cause of freedom:

> Anthropology students were the farthest out in the 1930s. They seemed to be preparing to criticise society from its roots. Radicalism was implied by the study of anthropology. . . . It indicated that human life was much broader than the present. It gave young Jews a greater sense of freedom from the surrounding restrictions.[59]

Many of the founders of the field were Jewish: Durkheim, Levy-Bruhl, Marcel Mauss, Boas, Sapir, and Lowie. Bellow's own choice of topic for research fieldwork was to investigate bands of Eskimos who were reported to have chosen to starve rather than eat foods that were under taboo. How much, he wondered, did people conform to culture, and at what point would the animal need to survive break through the restraints of custom and belief? Bellow suspected that so-called "primitive" peoples had the edge over the "civilized":

> I'm not at all certain now that civilized minds are more flexible and capable of grasping reality, or that they have livelier, more intelligent reactions to the threat of extinction. I have read

writers on the Holocaust who made the most grave criticisms of European Jewry, arguing that they doomed themselves by their unwillingness to surrender their comfortable ways, their property, their passive habits, their acceptance of bureaucracy, and were led to slaughter unresisting.[60]

Although Bellow does not endorse this latter, tendentious argument, the development of his thought—from Eskimo taboos to the Holocaust—suggests that questions of cultural change and adaptation had special relevance for him as a Jew. It is precisely this issue—obedience to custom versus adaptive plasticity—on which Henderson and the Arnewi part company. The Arnewi prefer their cows to die of thirst rather than drink water polluted by taboo frogs. Henderson blows up custom, frogs, and water source all together in a scene of wholesale destruction.

For Bellow, his immigrant status was also relevant to the choice of anthropology. Describing himself as "an exotic among other exotics," he pointed to the lack of stability available to the children of immigrants, who therefore needed to adapt as speedily as possible to their new environment. "The word for this was 'Americanization.' The masses that came from Europe in the great wave of immigration between 1870 and 1930 wanted to be as American as possible."[61] Bellow cited Augie March's desire for fraternity, for example, as common to adolescent Americans of immigrant background. Augie's refusal to be conditioned by a time and place, whether as the result of his Jewish background or his American present, was also shared by his creator. In juxtaposing these autobiographical statements with Bellow's comments on anthropology, a common thread can be discerned: a concern with the influence of, and the resistance to, environment, and with the degree to which human adaptation in customs and in culture is desirable or even possible. In the same interview, Bellow expressed his belief that the weakening of the older, traditional branches of civilization might open fresh opportunities, forcing an independent reassessment of what culture is. Later Bellow became identified with neoconservative scholars defending the classical canon of humanist and literary works rather than advancing the claims of those marginalized from culture as a result of race or gender. Arguably, however, Bellow had no quarrel with his supposed opponents; he had been writing about cultural change and culture wars from the start. Motifs from social anthropology provide structural pivots in the plots of *Seize the Day* (the trickster figure), *Henderson the Rain King* (East

African cattle cultures), *Humboldt's Gift* (gift exchange), "Mosby's Memoirs" (death customs), and "Cousins" (shamanism), among others. His last unfinished novel drew on D. Carleton Gajdusek's work on funerary cannibalism in New Guinea.[62] Bellow's intertextuality is creative, multifarious, and something of a challenge to most of his readers; his intellectual biography informs the style, structure, and content of his works.

As James Atlas noted, biography is itself a collective enterprise, assembled out of letters, interviews, journals, manuscripts, and the testimonies of friends, enemies, family, and disciples.[63] If Bellow's biography is indeed a novel that dare not speak its name, it is a novel with a large cast. And Bellow himself appears as very different characters over the course of the action: as son, father, husband, lover, playwright, novelist, essayist, thinker, political radical, conservative, analyst and analysed, Jew, and American. Biography opens the door to his character, but he remains resistant to easy definition.

Notes

1. Roland Barthes, "Réponses," *Tel Quel* 47 (1971): 89.
2. Ruth Miller, *Saul Bellow: A Biography of the Imagination* (New York: Saint Martin's, 1991), 339.
3. D. H. Lawrence, *Studies in Classic American Literature* (London: Secker, 1924), 9.
4. William K. Wimsatt and Monroe Beardsley, *The Verbal Icon* (Lexington: University of Kentucky Press 1954), 3–18.
5. James Atlas, *Bellow: A Biography* (New York: Random House, 2000), 557–58.
6. Michael Benton, *Literary Biography. An Introduction* (Chichester: Wiley-Blackwell, 2009), 172.
7. Greg Bellow, *Saul Bellow's Heart. A Son's Memoir* (London: Bloomsbury, 2013), 210.
8. John Batchelor, ed., *The Art of Literary Biography* (Oxford University Press, 1995), 214.
9. Batchelor, *The Art of Literary Biography*, 272.
10. Warwick Gould and Thomas F. Staley, eds., *Writing the Lives of Writers* (London: MacMillan, 1998), 175.
11. Gould and Staley, *Writing the Lives of Writers*, 187.
12. Benjamin Taylor, ed., *Saul Bellow. Letters* (New York: Viking, 2010), 35.

13. Zachary Leader, *The Life of Saul Bellow: To Fame and Fortune, 1915–1964* (New York: Alfred A. Knopf, 2015), 720 n.10.
14. Leader, *The Life of Saul Bellow*, 732 n.64.
15. Atlas, *Bellow: A Biography*, 414.
16. Atlas, *Bellow: A Biography*, 585.
17. Atlas, *Bellow: A Biography*, 585.
18. Harriet Wasserman, *Handsome Is: Adventures with Saul Bellow. A Memoir* (New York: Fromm, 1997), 167.
19. Wasserman, *Handsome Is*, 83.
20. Wasserman, *Handsome Is*, 182.
21. Wasserman, *Handsome Is*, 184.
22. Wasserman, *Handsome Is*, 190.
23. Leader, *The Life of Saul Bellow*, 654.
24. Mark Greif, *The Age of the Crisis of Man. Thought and Fiction in America, 1933–1973* (Princeton: Princeton University Press, 2015), 143–204.
25. Louis Menand, "Young Saul. The Subject of Bellow's Fiction," *New Yorker*, May 11, 2015, 71–77.
26. Greg Bellow, *Saul Bellow's Heart*, 123.
27. Mark Harris, *Saul Bellow Drumlin Woodchuck* (Athens: University of Georgia Press, 1980), 9–10.
28. Ann Cheroff Weinstein, *Me and My (Tor)Mentor: Saul Bellow. A Memoir of My Literary Love Affair* (New York: Universe, 2007), 18.
29. Miller, *Saul Bellow*, 261.
30. Greg Bellow, *Saul Bellow's Heart*, 115.
31. Greg Bellow, *Saul Bellow's Heart*, 2.
32. Greg Bellow, *Saul Bellow's Heart*, 216.
33. Greg Bellow, *Saul Bellow's Heart*, 216.
34. Saul Bellow, "Him with His Foot in His Mouth," in Bellow, *Him with His Foot in His Mouth and Other Stories* (London: Secker and Warburg, 1984), 28.
35. D. J. Brucker, "A Candid Talk with Saul Bellow," *New York Times Magazine*, April 15, 1984, 60.
36. Judie Newman, "Bellow and the Theory of Comedy," in "Faces in a Sea of Suffering: The Human Predicament in Saul Bellow's The Victim," ed. Victoria Aarons and Gustavo Sánchez Canales, *Partial Answers: Journal of Literature and History of Ideas* 14, no. 1 (January 2016): 159–73.
37. Greg Bellow, *Saul Bellow's Heart*, 140.
38. Greg Bellow, *Saul Bellow's Heart*, 156.
39. Greg Bellow, *Saul Bellow's Heart*, 180.
40. Miller, *Saul Bellow*, 43.
41. James Wood, "The Jewish King James Version: Saul Bellow—Not Exactly English But Biblically English," *Times Literary Supplement*, August 5, 2005, 12–13.

42. Saul Bellow, "I Took Myself as I Was . . . ,"*Anti-Defamation League Bulletin* 33 (December 1976): 3.
43. Greg Bellow, *Saul Bellow's Heart*, 174.
44. Julia Kristeva, *Semiotike, recherches pour une semanalyse* (Paris: Seuil, 1969), 149 (my translation).
45. Eusebio L. Rodrigues, "Augie March's Mexican Adventure," *Indian Journal of American Studies* 8, no. 2 (1978): 39–43.
46. Gloria L. Cronin, Gloria, "Our Father's Politics: Gregory, Adam and Daniel Bellow," in *A Political Companion to Saul Bellow*, ed. Gloria L. Cronin and Lee Trepannier (Lexington: University Press of Kentucky, 2013), 185–232.
47. Cronin, "Our Father's Politics," 206.
48. Leader, *Saul Bellow*, 135.
49. Cronin, "Our Father's Politics," 204.
50. Andrew M. Gordon, "Psychology and the Fiction of Saul Bellow," in *Critical Insights. Saul Bellow*, ed. Allan Chavkin (Pasadena: Salem Press, 2012), 33–52.
51. Daniel Fuchs, "Bellow and Freud," in *Saul Bellow in the 1980s*, ed. Gloria L. Cronin and L. H. Goldman (East Lansing: Michigan State University Press, 1989), 27.
52. Brucker, "A Candid Talk with Saul Bellow," 5.
53. Atlas, *Bellow: A Biography*, 295.
54. Atlas, *Bellow: A Biography*, 295.
55. Judie Newman, "Bellow and Nihilism: *The Dean's December*," in "The Philosophical Dimension of Saul Bellow's Novels," special issue, *Studies in the Literary Imagination* 17, no. 2 (1984): 111–22; Susan Rowland, "The Need for Alchemy in *The Dean's December*," *Saul Bellow Journal* 13, no. 2 (1995): 19–29.
56. Marianne M. Friedrich, *Character and Narration in the Short Fiction of Saul Bellow* (New York: Peter Lang, 1995).
57. Judie Newman, "From Psyche to *Psycho*: Saul Bellow and the Degradation of Love," *Saul Bellow Journal* 11, no. 1 (1992): 9–20.
58. Judie Newman, "Saul Bellow and Social Anthropology," in *Saul Bellow at Seventy-five: A Collection of Critical Essays*, ed. Gerhard Bach (Tubingen: Gunter Narr Verlag, 1991), 137–49.
59. Nina A. Steers, "'Successor' to Faulkner?: An Interview with Saul Bellow," *Show* 4 (September, 1964): 36.
60. Saul Bellow, *To Jerusalem and Back: A Personal Account* (New York: Viking, 1976), 130–31.
61. Rockwell Gray, Harry White, and Gerald Nemanic, "Interview With Saul Bellow," *TriQuarterly* 60 (1984): 21.
62. Leader, *Saul Bellow*, 207.
63. Atlas, *Bellow: A Biography*, 601.

References

Atlas, James. *Bellow: A Biography*. New York: Random House, 2000.
Barthes, Roland. "Réponses." *Tel Quel* 47 (1971): 89–107.
Batchelor, John, ed. *The Art of Literary Biography*. Oxford: Oxford University Press, 1995.
Bellow, Greg. *Saul Bellow's Heart. A Son's Memoir*. London: Bloomsbury, 2013.
Bellow, Saul. *To Jerusalem and Back: A Personal Account*. New York: Viking, 1976.
Bellow, Saul. "I Took Myself as I Was. . . ."*Anti-Defamation League Bulletin* 33 (December 1976): 3.
Bellow, Saul. "Him with His Foot in His Mouth." In *Him with His Foot in His Mouth and Other Stories*, by Saul Bellow, 3–62. London: Secker and Warburg, 1984.
Benton, Michael. *Literary Biography. An Introduction*. Chichester: Wiley-Blackwell, 2009.
Brucker, D. J. "A Candid Talk with Saul Bellow." *New York Times Magazine*, April 15, 1984, 52–62.
Cronin, Gloria L. "Our Father's Politics: Gregory, Adam and Daniel Bellow." In *A Political Companion to Saul Bellow*, edited by Gloria L. Cronin and Lee Trepannier, 185–232. Lexington: University Press of Kentucky, 2013.
Friedrich, Marianne M. *Character and Narration in the Short Fiction of Saul Bellow*. New York: Peter Lang, 1995.
Fuchs, Daniel. *Saul Bellow: Vision and Revision*. Durham: Duke University Press, 1984.
Fuchs, Daniel. "Bellow and Freud." In *Saul Bellow in the 1980s*, edited by Gloria L. Cronin and L. H. Goldman, 27–50. East Lansing: Michigan State University Press, 1989.
Gordon, Andrew M. "Psychology and the Fiction of Saul Bellow." In *Critical Insights. Saul Bellow*, edited by Allan Chavkin, 33–52. Pasadena: Salem Press, 2012.
Gould, Warwick, and Thomas F. Staley, eds. *Writing the Lives of Writers*. London: Macmillan, 1998.
Gray, Rockwell, Harry White, and Gerald Nemanic. "Interview With Saul Bellow." *TriQuarterly* 60 (1984): 12–34.
Greif, Mark. *The Age of the Crisis of Man. Thought and Fiction in America, 1933–1973*. Princeton: Princeton University Press, 2015.
Harris, Mark. *Saul Bellow Drumlin Woodchuck*. Athens: University of Georgia Press, 1980.
Kristeva, Julia. *Semiotike, recherches pour une semanalyse*. Paris: Seuil, 1969.
Lawrence, D. H. *Studies in Classic American Literature*. London: Secker, 1924.
Leader, Zachary. *The Life of Saul Bellow: To Fame and Fortune, 1915–1964*. New York: Alfred A. Knopf, 2015.

Menand, Louis. "Young Saul. The Subject of Bellow's Fiction." *New Yorker*, May 11, 2015. http://www.newyorker.com/magazine/2015/05/11/young-saul.

Miller, Ruth. *Saul Bellow: A Biography of the Imagination*. New York: Saint Martin's, 1991.

Newman, Judie. "Bellow and Nihilism: *The Dean's December*." In "The Philosophical Dimension of Saul Bellow's Novels." Special issue, *Studies in the Literary Imagination* 17, no. 2 (1984): 111–22.

Newman, Judie. "Saul Bellow and Social Anthropology." In *Saul Bellow at Seventy-five: A Collection of Critical Essays*, edited by Gerhard Bach, 137–49. Tübingen: Gunter Narr Verlag, 1991.

Newman, Judie. "From Psyche to *Psycho*: Saul Bellow and the Degradation of Love." *Saul Bellow Journal* 11, no. 1 (1992): 9–20.

Newman, Judie. "Bellow and the Theory of Comedy." In "Faces in a Sea of Suffering: The Human Predicament in Saul Bellow's The Victim," edited by Victoria Aarons and Gustavo Sánchez Canales. Special issue, *Partial Answers: Journal of Literature and History of Ideas* 14, no. 1 (2016): 159–73.

Rank, Otto. *The Double: A Psychoanalytic Study*. Translated and edited by Harry Tucker Jr. Chapel Hill: University of North Carolina Press, 1971.

Rodrigues, Eusebio L. "Augie March's Mexican Adventure." *Indian Journal of American Studies* 8, no. 2 (1978): 39–43.

Rowland, Susan. "The Need for Alchemy in *The Dean's December*." *Saul Bellow Journal* 13, no. 2 (1995): 19–29.

Steers, Nina A. "'Successor' to Faulkner?: An Interview with Saul Bellow." *Show* 4 (September 1964): 36–38.

Taylor, Benjamin, ed. *Saul Bellow. Letters*. New York: Viking, 2010.

Wasserman, Harriet. *Handsome Is: Adventures with Saul Bellow. A Memoir*. New York: Fromm, 1997.

Weinstein, Ann Cheroff. *Me and My (Tor)Mentor: Saul Bellow. A Memoir of my Literary Love Affair*. New York: Universe, 2007.

Wimsatt William K., and Monroe Beardsley. *The Verbal Icon*. Lexington: University of Kentucky Press, 1954.

Wood, James. "The Jewish King James Version: Saul Bellow—Not Exactly English But Biblically English." *Times Literary Supplement*, August 5, 2005, 12–13.

Contributors' Notes

Victoria Aarons holds the position of O.R. and Eva Mitchell Distinguished Professor of Literature at Trinity University, where she teaches courses on American Jewish and Holocaust literatures. She is the author of more than seventy scholarly articles and the author or editor of *A Measure of Memory: Storytelling and Identity in American Jewish Fiction* and *What Happened to Abraham: Reinventing the Covenant in American Jewish Fiction*, both recipients of the CHOICE Award for Outstanding Academic Book; *The New Diaspora: The Changing Landscape of American Jewish Fiction*; *Bernard Malamud: A Centennial Tribute*; *Third-Generation Holocaust Narratives: Memory in Memoir and Fiction*; *The Cambridge Companion to Saul Bellow*; *Third-Generation Holocaust Representation: Trauma, History, and Memory*, co-authored with Alan L. Berger; and the forthcoming collection *The New Jewish American Literary Studies* (Cambridge University Press, 2019). Aarons is one of three judges for the Edward Lewis Wallant Award, an annual award given to a rising American Jewish writer of fiction. Her work has appeared in a number of scholarly venues, and she is on the editorial board of several journals, including *Philip Roth Studies*, *Studies in American Jewish Literature*, and *Women in Judaism*.

Jeffrey Demsky is a tenured member of the San Bernardino Valley College faculty. His scholarship exists at the intersection of postwar American cultural history and Holocaust memory. His specific research focus is second- and third-generation literary and artistic representation. He has published numerous essays and peer-reviewed articles on these topics with academic presses in the United States, Canada, France, England, and Germany. In addition to his scholarly work, he has worked as a consultant with secondary schools, helping educators design and implement their Holocaust and genocide studies curriculum.

Hilene Flanzbaum is a critic and creative writer who has published work in the *Yale Journal of Criticism*, *Ploughshares*, *Tikkun*, *The Massachusetts Review*, and *ELH* (*English Literary History*) and *ALH* (*American Literary History*), among others. She is also the editor of *Jewish-American Literature—A Norton Anthology and the Americanization of the Holocaust*. She has been a fellow at the Institute of Advanced Holocaust Studies and holds the Allegra Stewart Chair in Modern Literature. Currently, she directs the MFA program in creative writing at Butler University.

Sandor Goodhart is professor of English and Jewish studies at Purdue University in the Department of English and director of the Religious Studies Program in the School of Interdisciplinary Studies at Purdue. He is the author of six books on literature, philosophy, and Jewish studies, including *Möbian Nights: Reading Literature and Darkness* (Bloomsbury, 2017); *The Prophetic Law: Essays in Judaism, Girardianism, Literary Studies, and the Ethical* (Michigan State University Press, 2014); *Sacrifice, Scripture, and Substitution: Readings in Ancient Judaism and Christianity* (Notre Dame University Press, 2011; co-edited with Ann Astell); *For René Girard: Essays in Friendship and Truth* (Michigan State University Press, 2009; co-edited with James Williams, Thomas Ryba, and Jørgen Jørgensen); *Reading Stephen Sondheim: A Collection of Critical Essays* (Garland, 2000); and *Sacrificing Commentary: Reading the End of Literature* (Johns Hopkins University Press, 1996). A seventh book, *Of Levinas and Shakespeare: "To See Another Thus"* (co-edited with Moshe Gold), appeared from Purdue University Press in 2018. He directed the Jewish Studies Program at Purdue (1997–2002), the Philosophy and Literature Program (2005), and the Classical Studies Program (2007–2011). He served as guest editor for a special issue of *Shofar* 26, no. 4 (summer 2008) on Emmanuel Levinas; as co-editor (with Monica Osborne) of a special issue of *Modern Fiction Studies*, 54, no. 1 (Spring 2008) on Emmanuel Levinas; and as editor of a special issue of *Religion, An International Journal* 37, no. 1 (March 2007) on René Girard. He is a founding board member of the North American Levinas Society, the former president of the Colloquium on Violence and Religion (2004–2007), and the author of more than one hundred essays.

Andrew M. Gordon, late professor emeritus of English at the University of Florida and vice president of the PsyArt Foundation, published *An American Dreamer: A Psychoanalytic Study of the Fiction of Norman Mailer*;

Empire of Dreams: The Science Fiction and Fantasy Films of Steven Spielberg; and, with Hernan Vera, *Screen Saviors: Hollywood Fictions of Whiteness*. With Peter Rudnytsky, he edited *Psychoanalyses/Feminisms*, and he published one hundred articles and fifty reviews on science fiction and fantasy film and on Jewish-American fiction, especially the novels of Saul Bellow and Philip Roth. Professor Gordon passed away during the final stages of the preparation of this volume, and we wish to recognize the significant contribution he made to the Jewish American & Holocaust Literature Symposium and also to the profession that he was devoted to for so many productive years.

Jessica Lang is associate professor of English and the Newman Director of the Wasserman Jewish Studies Center at Baruch College, City University of New York. Her scholarship focuses primarily on American, Jewish, and Holocaust literature. Her book *Textual Silence: Unreadability and the Holocaust* was published by Rutgers University Press in August 2017.

Phyllis Lassner, professor in the Crown Center for Jewish and Israel Studies, Gender Studies and the Cook Writing Program at Northwestern University, has published on interwar and wartime women writers, including two books on Elizabeth Bowen; *British Women Writers of World War II*; *Colonial Strangers*; and *Anglo-Jewish Women Writing the Holocaust*. She has also published essays on Holocaust representation in literature and film. Her most recent book is *Espionage and Exile: Fascism and Anti-Fascism in British Spy Fiction and Film*. She created and is editor of the Northwestern University Press Series "Cultural Expressions of World War II: Interwar Preludes, Responses, Memory." She holds the International Diamond Jubilee Fellowship at Southampton University, UK.

Dr. Holli Levitsky is the founder and director of the Jewish Studies Program and Professor of English at Loyola Marymount University in Los Angeles. Her research interests include post-war reception of the Holocaust, Jewish American and Holocaust Literatures, and Literature of Exile. She is co-editor of two volumes, *The Literature of Exile and Displacement: American Identity in a Time of Crisis* and *Summer Haven: The Catskills, the Holocaust and the Literary Imagination*, and a number of articles, essays, book chapters and reviews. Among other honors and awards, she has been an Advanced Holocaust Studies Fellow at the United State Holocaust Memorial Museum, a Fulbright Distinguished

Chair in American Literature in Poland, a Schusterman Fellow at the Summer Institute for Israel Studies, and the Florida International University Exile Studies Scholar-in-Residence. She is an affiliated professor at the University of Haifa in Haifa, Israel.

Zygmunt Mazur is associate professor of English and head of the American Literature, History and Culture Studies program at the Jagiellonian University, Poland. He is the author of *The Representation of History in Post-War American Fiction* and numerous articles on the twentieth-century American novel, and co-editor of four volumes of *The Legacy of the Holocaust*.

Sol Neely is an associate professor of English and philosophy at the University of Alaska Southeast. He completed his PhD in 2009 in the Philosophy and Literature program at Purdue University, where he co-founded the North American Levinas Society. His work lies at the intersections of postsecular phenomenology, cultural studies, existentialism, and critical theory, and he teaches courses that draw this work into pedagogies of social justice and repair. He has published in a variety of journals, including *Analecta Husserliana*, *Environmental Philosophy*, and *Screen Bodies*. In 2012, he founded the Flying University, a prison education program that brings university students inside the prison for collaborative study in philosophy, religious studies, and critical theory.

Judie Newman, OBE, is emeritus professor of American Studies at the University of Nottingham. She has published eleven books and some one hundred scholarly essays, including *Utopia and Terror in Contemporary American Fiction* (Routledge 2013); *Public Art, Memorials, and Atlantic Slavery* (with C.-M. Bernier, Routledge, 2009); and *Fictions of America: Narratives of Global Empire* (Routledge, 2007). Together with Celeste-Marie Bernier and Matthew Pethers, she has edited the *Edinburgh Companion to Nineteenth-Century American Letters and Letter-Writing* (Edinburgh University Press, 2016).

Monica Osborne is visiting assistant professor of Jewish Studies at Pepperdine University. She has written for *The New Republic*, *The Chronicle of Higher Education*, *The Jewish Journal of Los Angeles*, *Religion and Literature*, *Tikkun*, *Studies in American Jewish Literature*, *Shofar*, *Modern Fiction Studies*, MELUS, *The Jewish Daily Forward*, and various edited collections. She is also a co-editor (with Holli Levitsky and Stella Setka) of *Literature of Exile and Displacement: American Identity in a Time of Crisis*. Her work in Jewish literary and cultural studies addresses the ethics of representation, Midrash in a modern context, the Holocaust and other collective tragedies, American comedy, and the philosophy of Emmanuel Levinas. She is a co-founder of the North American Levinas Society. Her most recent book is *The Midrashic Impulse and the Contemporary Literary Response to Trauma* (Lexington Books, 2018).

Aimee Pozorski is professor of English and director of English graduate studies at Central Connecticut State University. She is author of *Roth and Trauma: The Problem of History in the Later Works* (2011) and *Falling After 9/11: Crisis in American Art and Literature* (2014). She has edited *Roth and Celebrity* (2012) and the *Critical Insights* edition of Philip Roth (2013); and co-edited, with David Gooblar, *Roth After 80: Philip Roth and the American Literary Imagination* (2016). She was president of the Philip Roth Society from 2009 to 2015. Her current research focuses on AIDS, trauma, and politics in contemporary American literature.

N. Ann Rider is chair of the Department of Languages, Literatures, and Linguistics program at Indiana State University and associate professor of German. She is an active member of the CANDLES Holocaust Museum and Education Center in Terre Haute, Indiana.

Gustavo Sánchez Canales teaches English at the Faculty of Teacher Training and Education at the Universidad Autónoma de Madrid, where he was vice dean for research and innovation (2014–2016). He served as vice dean for international relations between 2011 and 2013. From 1999 to 2010 he taught English and US literature at the Universidad Complutense de Madrid. His research focuses on contemporary Jewish-American Literature. He has published book chapters, articles and essays on Saul Bellow, Philip Roth, Bernard Malamud, Cynthia Ozick, Chaim Potok, Rebecca Goldstein, Allegra Goodman, and Michael Chabon, among others. He has co-edited with Victoria Aarons (Trinity, San Antonio, TX) a thematic volume on Philip Roth titled *History, Memory, and the Making of Character in Roth's Fiction* in *CLCWeb: Comparative Literature and Culture* 16, no. 2 (June 2014), http://docs.lib.purdue.edu/clcweb/vol16/iss2/. He has also co-edited with Victoria Aarons a forum titled "Saul Bellow as a Novelist of Ideas" in *Partial Answers* 14, no. 1

(January 2016), http://partialanswers.huji.ac.il/volumes.asp?id=27; and a monograph on Bernard Malamud titled *Bernard Malamud: A Centennial Tribute* (Detroit: Wayne State University Press, 2016), http://www.wsupress.wayne.edu/books/detail/bernard-malamud.

Naomi B. Sokoloff is professor of Near Eastern languages and civilization and professor of comparative literature at the University of Washington (Seattle), where she teaches modern Jewish literature, Hebrew, and Israeli culture. She is the author of *Imagining the Child in Modern Jewish Fiction* (1992) and of numerous articles on Israeli authors and American Jewish literature. She is co-editor of *Gender and Text in Modern Hebrew and Yiddish Literature* (1992); *Infant Tongues: The Voice of the Child in Literature* (1994); *Traditions and Transitions in Israel Studies* (2002); and *Boundaries of Jewish Identity* (2010). She edited a special issue of the journal *Shofar* (1998) on *Israel and America: Cross-Cultural Encounters and the Literary Imagination*. Her recent research focuses on the fiction of David Grossman and the evolution of Holocaust studies. A current project is a co-edited volume, *What We Talk About When We Talk About Hebrew (And What It Means to Americans)*.

Eric J. Sundquist is the Andrew W. Mellon Professor of the Humanities at Johns Hopkins University and the author or editor of twelve books, including *Writing in Witness: A Holocaust Reader* (2018) and *Strangers in the Land: Blacks, Jews, Post-Holocaust America* (2005), which received the Weinberg Judaic Studies Institute Book Award.

Index

Aarons, Victoria, 8–9, 55, 61, 69, 279, 321
absence/loss/silence. *See* silence/loss/absence
Ada, or Ardor: A Family Chronicle (Nabokov; 1969), 88–89
Adorno, Theodor, 12, 22, 184, 246
The Adventures of Augie March (Bellow; 1953), 275, 304, 308, 311–12, 315
African Americans and racism in America, 154, 219, 248, 256, 276, 287, 291, 310
After Auschwitz (Rubenstein; 1966), 293
AH (alternate history). *See* alternate Jewish histories
akedah (binding of Isaac), 34, 176–77
Alegri (Greek Jew), 21
Alexander, Jeffrey, 248
Allison, Barley, 307
Alter, Robert, 118n21
alternate Jewish histories, 9, 85–100
  Chabon and, 85–86, 87, 88, 90–91, 96–100
  genre, AH (alternate history) as, 85–90
  Jewish authors' interest in AH, 90–91, 100
  The Plot Against America (Roth; 2004), 9, 86, 88, 91, 92–96, 97–100
  Roth and, 85–86, 87, 88, 90–96, 97–100
  types of AH, 88–89
  The Yiddish Policemen's Union (Chabon; 2007), 9, 86, 88, 96–100
  Yossel, April 19, 1943 (Kubert; 2003), narrative and counternarrative in, 69–73
Altvater, Johanna, 32
American culture, memorialization of/desensitization to Holocaust in, 241–44, 253–56
American Literature Association, Jewish American and Holocaust literature subsection, 5
"The American National Narrative of the Holocaust: There Isn't Any" (Novick; 2003), 255
American Pastoral (Roth; 1998), 91–92, 99
American sign language (ASL) and Shema, 105–7, 112
Amis, Martin, 309
Anarchy and Justice: An Introduction to Levinas' Political Thought (Simmons; 2003), 141

327

Andrew Wylie Literary Agency, 303, 305, 306, 307, 309
angels, in Jewish tradition, 125–33
Anilewicz, Mordechai, 231
"An Animal to the Memory" (Bezmozgis; 2004), 228–32, 237, 238
Anne Frank
  The Diary of Anne Frank/Diary of a Young Girl, 183–85, 187, 191, 192, 209–11, 220–21n6, 221n11, 224, 229, 253, 254, 263n79
  Dutch Muslim students unwilling to study, 249
  Englander on (See "What We Talk About When We Talk About Anne Frank")
  Justin Bieber on, 254
Anne Frank, figuration, and the ethical imperative, 11–12, 183–200
  Broadway adaptation of diary, 187
  definitions of figuration, 188
  The Ghost Writer (Roth; 1979), 11–12, 91, 184, 185, 186, 188, 189–93, 197, 199
  Hope: A Tragedy (Auslander; 2012), 184, 185, 188, 193
  literary trope or figure, ambivalence about Anne Frank's evolution into, 184–88
  stories and ethics, relationship between, 189–90
  "What We Talk About When We Talk About Anne Frank" (Englander; 2011), 11–12, 184, 185, 188–91, 193–200
  "Who Owns Anne Frank?" (Ozick; 1997), 186–87, 189, 191, 193
"Anne Frank game," 188–89, 197–99, 206, 219
Anne Frank house, Amsterdam, 183, 221n11, 254
Anne Frank statue, Westermarkt, Amsterdam, 183
"Anne Frank Today Is a Syrian Girl" (Kristof; 2016), 221n11
Anne Frank Unbound: Media, Imagination, Memory (ed. Kirshenblatt-Gimblett and Sandler; 2012), 185–86
anomaly, AH due to, 88
Anti-Defamation League, 310–11
Antin, Mary, 3, 268, 270–73, 275, 279
anti-Semitism
  African American, 310
  in Bellow's *The Victim*, 82n6
  Christian, 257n8, 294–95, 298n11
  Holocaust education and, 208, 223, 246
  in Horn's *World to Come*, 120–21
  responding to current instances of, 154, 170
  Roth's *Plot Against America* and, 94–95, 99
  Rubenstein on, 294, 297
  sexual menace of Jew and, 28
  Sophie's Choice (Styron) and, 285, 289, 292, 294, 297, 298nn11–12
  third-generation writers and, 13, 223
Appelfeld, Aharon, 24
Arendt, Hannah, 245, 293
Armenian genocide, 241, 256n3
Arnold, Matthew, 146–47
ash, as Holocaust metaphor, 23–24, 25
ASL (American sign language) and Shema, 105–7, 112
Atlas, James, 301, 302–3, 306, 307, 311, 313, 316
Atta, Mohammed, 194, 195
attitudinal competence, 270, 272, 280n9

Index

Auschwitz
   Anne Frank and, 184, 192
   hidden child survivors and, 61, 62, 63
   in Kubert's *Yossel, April 19, 1943*, 73
   metaphors for Holocaust and, 21, 30, 31, 37, 38, 40
   nontraditional students, modeling empathy and distance for, 245, 246, 252
   Rubenstein on, 294–97
   in *Sophie's Choice* (Styron), 286, 287, 292, 295
   third-generation writers and, 227, 235, 237, 238
Auslander, Shalom, 184, 185, 188, 193

Babel, Isaac, 97
Babi Yar, 208
Back to the Future (film series), 88
"Back to the Garden: Jewish Hermeneutics, Biblical Reading, PaRDeS, and the Four-Fold Way" (Goodhart; 2014), 149, 153, 154–55
Bar Oni, Byrna, 38–39
Barth, John, 89
Barthes, Roland, 89, 301
Bartov, Omer, 26, 220n4
Bayor, Ronald, 243
The Bell Jar (Plath; 1963), 246
Bellow (Atlas; 2000), 301, 302–3, 306, 307, 311, 313, 316
Bellow, Adam, 312–13
Bellow, Daniel, 312
Bellow, Gregory, 301–4, 307–12, 314
Bellow, Saul, 3, 14, 82n6, 268, 270, 273–77, 279. *See also* biographical approaches to Saul Bellow
   The Adventures of Augie March (1953), 275, 304, 308, 311–12, 315

"Cousins" (1984), 316
Dangling Man (1944), 273–75, 311
The Dean's December (1982), 275–76, 306, 314
Henderson the Rain King (1959), 308, 313, 314, 315–16
Herzog (1964), 304, 307, 308, 310, 311, 313
"Him With His Foot in His Mouth" (1984), 309, 313
Humboldt's Gift (1975), 304, 305, 306, 308, 309, 316
More Die of Heartbreak (1987), 314
"Mosby's Memoirs" (1968), 316
Mr. Sammler's Planet (1970), 305, 306
A Theft (1989), 306, 314
The Victim (Bellow; 1947), 82n6, 274–75, 308, 310, 311
Belsen, 192, 245
Benton, Michael, 303
Berger, Alan L., 1, 15, 48
Berger, Thomas, 89
Bergman, Leoni Taffel, 61–63, 65
Bernasconi, Robert, 142
Bettelheim, Bruno, 36
Bezmozgis, David, 228–32, 237, 238
Bialik, Chaim Nachman, 35
Bickman, Martin, 279
Bieber, Justin, 254
biographical approaches to Saul Bellow, 14–15, 301–16
   Bellow (Atlas; 2000), 301, 302–3, 306, 307, 311, 313, 316
   Bellow's works, biography depicted in, 309
   different types of, 301–2
   Handsome Is: Adventures with Saul Bellow (Wasserman; 1997), 301, 302, 305–7
   indexes, using, 312
   intellectual biography, 311–12

biographical approaches to Saul Bellow *(continued)*
   Jewish identity of Bellow, 308, 310–11, 312, 314, 315
   The Life of Saul Bellow: To Fame and Fortune, 1915–64 (Leader; 2015), 301, 303, 305, 307, 308, 311
   literary persona, explication of, 307–9
   Me and My (Tor)Mentor (Weinstein; 2007), 301, 302, 308
   motivations of biographer, 303–4
   A Political Companion to Saul Bellow (ed. Cronin and Trepannier; 2013), 312
   political views of Bellow, 302, 308, 309–10, 312–13, 315
   psychological thought, Bellow's engagement with, 312, 313–14
   publishers' archives, agents, and agencies, 305–7
   Saul Bellow: A Biography of the Imagination (Miller; 1991), 301, 302–3, 308, 311
   Saul Bellow: Drumlin Woodchuck (Harris; 1980), 301, 308
   Saul Bellow: Letters (ed. Taylor; 2010), 303
   Saul Bellow's Heart (Gregory Bellow; 2013), 301–4, 307–9, 311
   social anthropology, Bellow's education in, 312, 314–16
   sources and access, 302–3
   textual biography, 304–5
Birkenau, 40
Black, Peter, 256n3
black Americans and racism in America, 154, 219, 248, 256, 276, 287, 291, 310

Black Lives Matter, 154, 219
black milk, 23–29, 35, 41
Blake, William, 275, 276
Blanchot, Maurice, 144, 146, 150
blood libel, 28
blood/racial purity, Nazi concern with, 27–29
Bloom, Allan, 305, 306, 308
Bloom, Harold, 269, 276, 278
Boas, Franz, 314
Bologna Declaration (1999), 269
Book of Blessings (Falk; 1996/1999), 108
The Book of Daniel (Doctorow; 1971), 89
Booth, Wayne, 122
Borowski, Tadeusz, 52, 61
The Boy in the Striped Pajamas (Boyne; 2006), 209
Bradbury, Malcolm, 273–74
Bread Givers (Yezierska; 1925), 273
Briggs, Deborah Plutzik, 16
Bring the Jubilee (Moore; 1955), 89
Britten, Benjamin, 304
Broder, Henryk, 242
The Brothers Karamazov (Dostoevsky; 1880), 311
Browning, Christopher, 31
Bruns, Gerald, 141, 146
Buber, Martin, 148
Buchenwald, 252
Budapest-Vienna Declaration (2010), 269
Bunyan, Paul, 113
The Butterfly Effect (film), 88

Cahan, Abraham, 3, 268, 270–73, 275, 279
Calisher, Hortense, 3
Call It Sleep (Henry Roth; 1934), 273
camp number tattoos, 110–11, 195–96, 209–10, 235, 236, 237

camp orchestras, 40
Camus, Albert, 274
Carasso, David, 105
Carlston, Erin G., 279
Carpenter, Humphrey, 304
Carter, Jimmy, 242, 247
Caruth, Cathy, 173, 189
Carver, Raymond, 194, 198, 205–7, 217
"Cathedral" (Carver; 1983), 194
Celan, Paul, 7, 23–27, 34, 35, 36
Chabad movement, 113
Chabon, Michael, 2, 9, 85–86, 87, 88, 90–91, 96–100
Chagall, Marc, 119–25, 129, 133, 135–36
Chandler, Raymond, 96
Chavkin, Allan, 276
chavruta, 15
Chełmno, 26, 34
children. *See* hidden child survivors; metaphor and the Holocaust; *specific entries at* Anne Frank
The Chosen (Potok; 1967), 277–78
Christian anti-Semitism, 257n8, 294–95, 298n11
Churchill, Winston, 89
"The City of Slaughter" (Bialik), 35
Cohen, Eliaz, 103, 109–10
Commandant of Auschwitz (Höss), 25
The Common European Framework of Reference for Language: Learning, Teaching and Assessment (2001), 270
The Confessions of Nat Turner (Styron; 1967), 89
A Connecticut Yankee in King Arthur's Court (Twain; 1889), 88
"Conversion of the Jews" (Roth; 1959), 229
Cook, Bruce, 275
Coover, Robert, 89

core-to-core culture confrontation, 277–78
The Counterlife (Roth; 1986), 87, 91, 95
"Cousins" (Bellow; 1984), 316
Critchley, Simon, 141
Cronin, Gloria L., 1, 15, 48, 312
Culbertson, Elaine, 263n78
The Cunning of History (Rubenstein; 1975), 293–97
Curiosities of Literature (D'Israeli; 1824), 87
Cyprys, Ruth, 37

Daddy (Plath; 1965), 245
Dangling Man (Bellow; 1944), 273–75, 311
Dante, *Divine Comedy*, 250
Dawidowicz, Lucy, 35
Days of Awe, 110
de Camp, L. Sprague, 88
The Dean's December (Bellow; 1982), 275–76, 306, 314
Defiance (film), 208
Delbo, Charlotte, 24, 33, 49, 52, 61
Demsky, Jeffrey, 13, 241, 321–22
The Deputy (Hochhuth; 1963), 25–26
Der Nister (Pinkhas Kohanovitch), 120–25, 129–30, 133, 135
derash, 154, 156
desensitization to Holocaust in American culture, 241–44, 253–56
The Destruction of European Jews (Hilberg; 1961), 245
Deuteronomy
  6:4, 104, 117n2
  6:4-9, 117n2
  11:13-21, 112, 117n2
"Diachrony and Representation" (Levinas; 1998), 143, 145, 151

The Diary of Anne Frank/Diary of a Young Girl, 183–85, 187, 191, 192, 209–11, 220–21n6, 221n11, 224, 229, 253, 254, 263n79. See also specific entries at Anne Frank
Dick, Philip K., 87, 88, 98
Dickstein, Morris, 5
The Difference Engine (Gibson and Sterling; 1991), 90, 98
Dinter, Artur, 28, 42n22
D'Israeli, Isaac, 87
distance and teaching the Holocaust, 244, 247–53, 255–56
Divine Comedy (Dante), 250
Doctorow, E. L., 85, 89, 96
Dolan, Jill, 280n9
Donat, Alexander, 37
Dostoevsky, Fyodor, 311
The Double (Rank; 1925), 311
Dreifus, Erika, 228, 229, 232–35, 237–38
Durkheim, Emile, 314
Dussel, Enrique, 142, 150
Dutton, Beth, 261n59
The Dying Animal (Roth; 2001), 276–77

Eaglestone, Robert, 228
"Earliest Memories: A Walk in the Park" (Bergman; 2013), 62–63
Education, Audiovisual and Culture Executive Agency, 267–68
Efrati, Shimon, 39
EHEA (European Higher Education Area), 269
Eichmann, Adolf, 245, 246
Eisenstadt, Oona, 153–54
El Maleh Rachamim, 230
Ellis, Albert, 313
Ellison, Ralph, 310
empathy and teaching the Holocaust, 244–49, 254–55, 261n59

Englander, Nathan, 2, 90, 220n2. See also "What We Talk About When We Talk About Anne Frank"
Epple, Ernest, 32
Eshel, Amir, 200
Esperanto, 99
The Eternal Husband (Dostoevsky; 1870), 311
Ethical Culture Fieldston School, New York City, 249
Ethics and Infinity (Levinas; 1985), 153
L'Étranger (Camus; 1942), 274
European Commission, 268, 269
European Higher Education Area (EHEA), 269
European Union (EU), 267, 269, 280n1
Eurydice (educational network), 267z
evil
  Radical Evil and the Scarcity of Hope: Postsecular Meditations (Matuštík; 2008), 161n14
  responsibility for resisting (See human responsibility)
  universalizing view of, in Styron's *Sophie's Choice*, 286–87, 298n8
"A Wheel of Evil Come Full Circle" (Styron; 1997), 286
Examined Life (documentary film), 158
Exodus 19:17, 174
expendability, concept of, 295–96
Extremely Loud and Incredibly Close (Foer; 2011), 195

Facing History and Ourselves project, 242
Falk, Marcia, 103, 108, 109
Falkenhayn, General von, 295–96
Fatelessness (Kertés; 2004), 13, 249–53, 255, 262n71

Father and Son (Gosse; 1907), 304
Fatherland (Harris; 1992), 90
FDR (Franklin Delano Roosevelt), 93, 96, 99, 257n8
Feldman, Ruth, 114
Felman, Shoshana, 225–26
Felstiner, John, 35, 36
Fink, Ida, 52, 60, 199
Finklestein, Norman, 208, 220n4
Fishbane, Michael, 141
"Five Problems in Levinas' View of Politics and the Sketch of a Solution to Them" (Critchley; 2004), 141
The Fixer (Malamud; 1966), 89
Flanzbaum, Hilene, 11, 12, 13, 205, 322
Foer, Jonathan Safran, 2, 90, 195
"For My Child" (Sutzkever), 34
Frank, Anne. *See specific entries at Anne Frank*
Freedom Writers (film), 210, 221n12
Freud, Sigmund, 208, 278, 313
Friedman, Bruce Jay, 222n21
Friedman, Philip, 244–45
"From Sacrificial Violence to Responsibility: The Education of Moses in Exodus 2-4" (Goodhart; 2014), 147, 159
"From Songs of Home" "A" and "B" (Pinhas-Cohen), 118n20
Fuchs, Daniel, 97, 304
Fugitive Pieces (Michaels; 1996), 139, 141, 142–43, 149, 157, 159, 160, 176, 177–79

Gabor, Octavian, 160n6
Gajdusek, D. Carleton, 316
Gans, Herbert J., 216
Gekhman, Lyusya, 38
gender issues
  midrash and, 168–69
  scholarly awareness of gendered Jewish American presence, 3
  Sheiber's drawing in *Soundless Roar* lacking gender definition, 55
  in Shema and Shema-related modern poetry, 104, 114–15, 116n1
Genesis
  1:2, 180n3
  22, 176
Geoffrey-Chateau, Louis-Napoleon, 87
George III (king of England), 276
German People's Health Through Blood and Soil (periodical), 28
The Ghost Writer (Roth; 1979), 11–12, 91, 184, 185, 186, 188, 189–93, 197, 199, 212
Gibson, William, 90
Glassman, Susan, 305
Goodhart, Sandor
  "Back to the Garden: Jewish Hermeneutics, Biblical Reading, PaRDeS, and the Four-Fold Way" (Goodhart; 2014), 149, 153, 154–55
  biographical information, 322
  "From Sacrificial Violence to Responsibility: The Education of Moses in Exodus 2-4" (Goodhart; 2014), 147, 159
  on Horn's *The World to Come*, 10, 119
  "'A Land That Devours Its Inhabitants': Midrashic Reading, Emmanuel Levinas, and Prophetic Exegesis" (Goodhart; 2008), 149, 150
  on literature and midrash, 11, 167–69, 174, 180
  on social justice and midrash, 140, 141, 143, 147–50, 152, 154–59, 160n6, 161n14, 162n39

Gordon, Andrew M., 9, 85, 313, 314, 323
Gorman, Herbert, 304
Goshkin, Anita and Sonia, 308
Gosse, Edmund, 304
graphic narratives, 69. See also *Yossel, April 19, 1943*
Gravity's Rainbow (Pynchon; 1973), 89
Greek, Levinas on translating Judaism into, 143, 148, 159
Greif, Mark, 307
Grese, Irma, 31
The Grey Zone (film), 208
Grimwood, Ken, 89
Grossman, David, 17
Grossman, Vassili, 30
Groundhog Day (film), 89
The Guns of the South (Turtledove; 1992), 90

Haig, General Sir Douglas, 296
haiku, Shema as, 105
Halfon, Eduardo, 227, 228, 229, 235–38
Hammett, Dashiell, 96
Hammond, Meghan, 250
Handsome Is: Adventures with Saul Bellow (Wasserman; 1997), 301, 302, 305–7
Hardy, Thomas, 304
Harris, Mark, 301, 308
Harris, Robert, 90
Hart-Green, Sharon, 112
Hartman, Geoffrey, 11, 141, 167, 171, 177–80
Harvey, Giles, 186
Hauptmann, Bruno, 100
Havel, Václav, 139, 140, 148, 157
Hawthorne, Nathaniel, 87
Hay, John, 257n10
"He who sees it says: this is it" (Pinhas-Cohen), 118n20

"Hear, O Lord" (Cohen; 2010), 109–10, 117n14, 118n20
Heeb (periodical), 243
Heidegger, Martin, 144
The Heiress (stage adaptation of James's *Washington Square*), 53
Hellekson, Karen, 88, 90
Hemingway, Ernest, 51, 205
Henderson the Rain King (Bellow; 1959), 308, 313, 314, 315–16
Hernandez, Alexander, 251
Herodotus, 87
Herskovits, Melville J., 314
Herzog (Bellow; 1964), 304, 307, 308, 310, 311, 313
Heyen, William, 245
Hi Hitler! How the Nazi Past Is Being Normalized in Contemporary Culture (Rosenfeld; 2015), 249
hidden child survivor narratives, 8, 47–65
  Bergman's stories in *Out of Chaos*, 61–63
  displacement and disorientation, sense of, 47–48, 57–58
  Jewish American identity and, 65
  memory in, 47–48, 49–52, 53, 59, 60–63, 65
  modernist aesthetics of, 50–52, 53, 54, 59, 63, 64, 66n9
  multilinguality and language struggles in, 49, 52, 53, 55, 60, 62, 65
  in *Out of Chaos* (ed. Fox), 48, 50, 52, 60–65
  "Rabbit" story in Scheiber's *Soundless Roar*, 57–60
  Scheiber's *Soundless Roar*, 48, 50, 52–60, 54 (illus.), 62
  Straus's stories in *Out of Chaos*, 63–65
  as testimony, 48–50, 52, 63

untitled poem and accompanying drawing in Scheiber's *Soundless Roar*, 54–56, 54 (illus.)
Hilberg, Raul, 245
Hill, Dara, 160n6
Hiller, Fanya, 25, 26
"Him With His Foot in His Mouth" (Bellow; 1984), 309, 313
Himmler, Heinrich, 28, 29–30
history. *See also* alternate Jewish histories
  amorality of, 139
  human content, restoring, 148
  Jewish American and Holocaust literatures, historical development of, 3–5
  Jewish relationship with, 85
  one-dimensional view of, 139, 140
  postmodern view of, 89
Hitler, Adolf, 27, 28, 94–95, 99, 100, 241, 246, 256n3, 312
Hochhuth, Rolf, 25–26
Hoffman, Bettina, 230
Hoffman, Emily, 194
Holland, Sharon, 255
Holocaust (TV miniseries), 246
Holocaust denial, 249, 253–54
The Holocaust in American Life (Novick; 1990), 208, 220n4
The Holocaust Industry: Reflections on the Exploitation of Jewish Suffering (Finklestein; 2000), 208, 220n4
Holocaust literature. *See* Jewish American and Holocaust literatures
Holocaust Museum, Washington, DC, 209, 221n13, 242, 247
Holocaust Reader (Dawidowicz; 1976), 35
Homer, 147
Hope: A Tragedy (Auslander; 2012), 184, 185, 188, 193

Hopper, Dennis, 246
Horn, Dara, 2, 124, 137n3. *See also World to Come*
Horowitz, Sara, 52
Horváth, Rita, 262n71
Höss, Rudolf, 25, 33
How Sweet It Is! (Rosenbaum; 2015), 16–17
How to Read and Why (Bloom; 2000), 269
Howe, Irving, 4
human responsibility (for resisting evil)
  "Anne Frank game" in "What We Talk About When We Talk About Anne Frank" (Englander; 2012), 188–89, 197–99, 206, 218–19
  midrash dealing with questions of, 169–71
  "When You're Excused, You're Excused" (Friedman; 2001), 222n21
The Human Stain (Roth; 2000), 92, 95, 100
Humboldt's Gift (Bellow; 1975), 304, 305, 306, 308, 309, 316
Hungerford, Amy, 250
Hungry Hearts (Yezierska; 1920), 273
Husserl, Edmund, 144
hybridity, 4, 65, 66n20, 194, 277
Hyland, Peter, 275

I Married a Communist (Roth; 1998), 95
Ickes, Harold, 99
If It Had Happened Otherwise (ed. Squire; 1931), 89
"If Lee Had Not Won the Battle of Gettysburg" (Churchill; 1930), 89
In the Image (Horn; 2002), 137n3

"In Those Nightmarish Days" (Zelkowicz; 1942/1976), 34–35
intellectual biography of Bellow, 311–13
intermarriage, 215
International Journal of Humanities and Cultural Studies (periodical), 186
intertextuality, 311
Iranian Holocaust Cartoon festival, 249
Iranian hostage crisis, 242
Israel
  Bellow's support for, 310, 312
  Eichmann trial and execution, 245, 246
  Palestinians and, 154, 216–18
  second Intifada, 110
  Shema and Israeli poetry, 109–13, 118n20
  in "What We Talk About When We Talk About Anne Frank" (Englander; 2012) on, 216–18
  Yom Kippur War, 217

Jabès, Edmond, 144–45, 151, 152, 178
Jacobs, Rita D., 183, 184
JAHLIT. See Jewish American and Holocaust literatures
James, Henry, 53
Janowska Camp, Lvov, 32
Jewish American and Holocaust Literature: Representation in the Postmodern World (ed. Berger and Cronin, 2004), 1, 15
Jewish American and Holocaust Literature Symposium, 5, 15–17, 223
Jewish American and Holocaust literatures, 1–17. *See also specific authors and works*
  alternate Jewish histories, 9, 85–100 (*See also* alternate Jewish histories)
  Anne Frank in (*See specific entries at* Anne Frank)
  biography and, 14–15, 301–16 (*See also* biographical approaches to Saul Bellow)
  hidden child survivors, 8, 47–65 (*See also* hidden child survivors)
  historical development of, 3–5
  history, Jewish relationship with, 85
  Howe's prediction of end of, 3–4
  memorialization of and desensitization to Holocaust in American culture, 241–44, 253–56
  metaphor, using, 7–8, 21–41 (*See also* metaphor and the Holocaust)
  Miami Beach in, 16–17
  midrash and, 10–11, 167–80 (*See also* midrash; social justice and midrash)
  new genres and forms, 2, 4
  for nontraditional students, 13, 241–56 (*See also* nontraditional 21st-century students, teaching the Holocaust to)
  performance, as pedagogical tool, 280n9
  reading and teaching practices, 2–3, 5–7, 10–15
  return to Holocaust as subject, 1–2, 5
  Shema and, 9–10, 103–16 (*See also* Shema)
  in Spanish context, 14, 267–79 (*See also* Spanish context, teaching Jewish American literature in)
  statistics on Jewish-American population, 222n17
  survivor testimony, coming end of, 2

Index 337

third-generation voices of, 2, 11, 12–13, 69, 223–38 (*See also* third-generation fiction, teaching the Holocaust through)
transnationalism of, 2, 4–5, 9–10, 13–14
Jewish Deaf Multimedia, 107
Joyce, James, 304
Jung, Karl, 314

Kafka, Franz, 91
Kahane, David, 32
Kakutani, Michiko, 193, 220n4
Kalaidjian, Walter, 188
Karl M. (former Wehrmacht soldier), 31
Katz, Claire, 141, 150, 153–54
Katznelson, Ira, 243
Kaufman, Andy, 127
Keaton, Buster, 306
Keen, Suzanne, 261n58
Kertés, Imre, 13, 249–53, 255, 262n71
Kirshenblatt-Gimblett, Barbara, 185–86
Kishinev pogrom (1903), 35
Klemperer, Victor, 27
Klüger, Ruth, 38, 244
Kohanovitch, Pinkhas (Der Nister), 120–25, 129–30, 133, 135
Kohut, Heinz, 313–14
Kolitz, Zvi, 81–82n4
Kosinski, Jerzy, 136–37
Krauss, Nicole, 2
Krell, Robert, 31, 47, 52
Kristallnacht, 100, 149, 231, 238
Kristeva, Julia, 311
Kristof, Nicholas, 221n11
Kube, Wilhelm, 32
Kubert, Joe. See *Yossel, April 19, 1943*
Küttner, Kurt, 32

LaCapra, Dominick, 225–26

LaGuardia, Fiorello, 95
Lamentations 4:7-8, 35–36
"'A Land That Devours Its Inhabitants': Midrashic Reading, Emmanuel Levinas, and Prophetic Exegesis" (Goodhart; 2008), 149, 150
Landsberg, Alison, 243
Lang, Jessica, 11, 12–13, 223, 323
Langer, Lawrence, 49, 63
language. *See also* metaphor and the Holocaust
  ASL (American sign language) and Shema, 105–7, 112
  breakdown of language and representational thinking in face of trauma, 172–73, 224–25
  hidden child survivor narratives, multilinguality and language struggles in, 49, 52, 53, 55, 60, 62, 65
  Yiddish language and culture, 3, 62, 65, 66n19, 97–99, 135, 270–71, 310
Language and Silence (Steiner; 1967), 292–93
Lanzmann, Claude, 220n3, 224–27, 229
Lassner, Phyllis, 8, 47, 323
The Last Flight of Poxl West (Torday; 2015), 245
Law, Richard, 288
Lawrence, D. H., 302
Leader, Zachary, 301, 303, 305, 307, 308, 311
Lebensborn initiative, 28
"Lebensraum" (Dreifus; 2011), 228, 234–35
Lehmann, Sophia, 201n13
Leigh, Robert Darby Jared, 106
Lemberg, Jennifer, 49, 52
Lengyel, Olga, 31, 38
Leone, Michael, 193

Lest Darkness Fall (de Camp; 1941), 88, 98
Levi, Primo, 21, 26, 39, 82–83n8, 103, 113–15, 208, 224, 229, 250
Levinas, Emmanuel
  Anarchy and Justice: An Introduction to Levinas' Political Thought (Simmons; 2003), 141
  "Diachrony and Representation" (1998), 143, 145, 151
  Ethics and Infinity (1985), 153
  "Five Problems in Levinas' View of Politics and the Sketch of a Solution to Them" (Critchley; 2004), 141
  Greek, translating Judaism into, 143, 148, 159
  "'A Land That Devours Its Inhabitants': Midrashic Reading, Emmanuel Levinas, and Prophetic Exegesis" (Goodhart; 2008), 149, 150
  NALS (North American Levinas Society), 141–42, 160–61n6, 161n9
  Nine Talmudic Readings (1990), 141, 159
  Otherwise Than Being (1981), 141, 144, 151
  political writings of, encountering midrash through, 141–42
  on relation of the ethical and the political, 153–54
  "A Religion for Adults" (1990), 151
  social justice and midrash through, 140, 141–46, 148–57, 159
  "The Temptation of Temptation" (1990), 146, 152, 173–74
  on "thou must" and "thou can," 170
  The Tin Drum (film), midrashic reading of, 169
  Totality and Infinity: An Essay on Interiority (1969), 141, 146
  "The Transcendence of Words" (1989), 145
  "Useless Suffering" (Levinas; 1998), 179
Levitsky, Holli, 1, 167, 323–24
Levy-Bruhl, Lucien, 314
Lieber, Maxim, 305
Life Is Beautiful (film), 208
The Life of Saul Bellow: To Fame and Fortune, 1915–64 (Leader; 2015), 301, 303, 305, 307, 308, 311
Limbo (film), 138n4
Lindbergh, Charles, 91–96, 99, 100
Lingis, Alfonso, 144
Literature in the Ashes of History (Caruth; 2013), 173
Little Big Man (Berger; 1964), 89
Livy, 87
Lochner, Louis P., 256n3
Łódź Ghetto, 30–31, 34, 37
Loshitzky, Yosefa, 244
loss/silence/absence. *See* silence/loss/absence
Lowie, Robert, 314
Ludwig, Katherine, 160n6
Lumet, Sidney, 171
Luther, Martin, 294

Maidanek camp, 37
Mailer, Norman, 273
Maimonides, 134, 138n7
Malamud, Bernard, 3, 89, 270, 273
The Man in the High Castle (Dick; 2015–17), 87, 88, 98
Mannix, Dan and Jule, 312
Mao Tse Tung, 312
Margarete, in Goethe's *Faust*, 23–24
maternal metaphors for the Holocaust, 21–27
Matuštík, Martin, 140, 143, 157, 161n14

Maurois, André, 303
MAUS (Spiegelman; 1986/1991), 69
Mauss, Marcel, 314
Mazur, Zygmunt, 14, 285, 324
Me and My (Tor)Mentor (Weinstein; 2007), 301, 302, 308
Meehl, Paul, 313
Mein Kampf (Hitler; 1925), 28
memorialization of and desensitization to Holocaust in American culture, 241–44, 253–56
memory
  Anne Frank in popular memory, 185
  forgetting of pre-natal schooling, in Horn's *World to Come*, 125, 128–31, 133
  in hidden child survivor narratives, 47–48, 49–52, 53, 59, 60–63, 65
  midrash and, 178–79
  midrashic reading and, 10
  morality of, 139
  multidimensional, 248
  prosthetic, 243
  in *Sophie's Choice* (Styron), 288
  third-generation narratives and, 11
  as trope of Jewish American and Holocaust literatures, 8, 17
Men Like Gods (Wells; 1923), 88
Menand, Louis, 311
messenger trope in Holocaust literature, 82n7
Messianism, 17, 85, 97, 100, 113, 133–34, 157
Metahistory (White; 1973), 89
metaphor and the Holocaust, 7–8, 21–41
  ash, 23–24, 25
  baby carriages, German appropriation of, 42–43
  biblical sources, 35–36
  black milk, 23–29, 35, 41

blood/racial purity, Nazi concern with, 27–29
  children, Nazi torture and killing of, 29–35
  Jewish reproduction, attacks on, 24–25, 30, 31, 33
  maternal metaphors, 21–27
  parental abandonment/mutual suicide/killing of children, 36–39
Metzner, Alfred, 31
mezuzah, 109
Miami Beach, in Jewish literature, 16–17
Michaels, Anne, 139, 141, 142–43, 149, 157, 159, 160, 176
midrash, 10–11, 167–80. *See also* social justice and midrash
  as both literature and commentary, 179–80
  defined, 150
  elasticity and fluidity of, 17
  human responsibility, dealing with questions of, 169–71
  literary studies and, 167–69
  memory and, 178–79
  Möbius strip metaphor for, 143, 147, 150, 155, 162n39, 180
  ontology of story, rediscovering, 140, 144, 146–48, 160
  as pedagogical tool, 159–60, 168
  on pre-natal schooling, in Horn's *The World to Come*, 120, 122, 123–25, 127–33, 135
  prison, teaching midrash and phenomenology in, 157–59
  silences and absences in text, preserving and responding to, 172–73, 175–79
  on "the world to come," 134
  trauma, applied to literature of, 167, 171–74
Midrash and Literature (Hartman; 1986), 180n6

"Midrash as Law and Literature" (Hartman; 2004), 167
midrashic impulse, 140, 142, 146, 148, 151, 168, 174
The Midrashic Impulse and the Contemporary Literary Response to Trauma (Osborne; 2018), 168
Miller, Ruth, 301, 302–3, 308, 311
Milowitz, Steven, 201n13
Mishkan Hanefesh (2015), 108
Mishkin, Marguerite, 62
Möbius strip metaphor for midrash, 143, 147, 150, 155, 162n39, 180
modernism, literary, 50–52, 53, 54, 59, 63, 64, 66n9, 240
Modernist Studies Association, 66n9
Moore, Deborah Dash, 17
Moore, Ward, 89
More Die of Heartbreak (Bellow; 1987), 314
"Mosby's Memoirs" (Bellow; 1968), 316
Moskowitz, Sarah, 48
Mr. Sammler's Planet (Bellow; 1970), 305, 306
multidimensional memory, 248
Multi-Directional Memory: Remembering the Holocaust in the Age of Decolonization (Rothberg; 2009), 211
multiple realities or multiverses, AH due to, 88–89
Muselmann, 252
My Holocaust (Reich; 2007), 244
Myers, D. G., 286

Nabokov, Vladimir, 88–89
NALS (North American Levinas Society), 141–42, 160–61n6, 161n9
Napoléon et la conquête du monde (Geoffrey-Chateau; 1836), 87
Narrative Ethics (Newton; 1995), 189
Natasha and Other Stories (Bezmozgis; 2004), 228, 229
La Nausée (Sartre; 1938), 274
Neely, Sol, 10, 139, 162n35, 324
Nemo, Philippe, 153, 154
New Critics, 54
The New Diaspora: The Changing Landscape of American Jewish Fiction (ed. Aarons, Patt, and Shechner; 2015), 5
New Guinea
  Bellow's last, unfinished work set in, 304, 316
  recitation of Shema in, 117n8
New York Times, 306
New Yorker (periodical), 186–87, 291
Newman, Judie, 14–15, 301, 324
Newton, Adam Zachary, 189
Nicholson-Weir, Rebecca, 160n6
Niddah (tractate), 122, 127–28, 132
Night (Wiesel; 1958), 13, 30, 82n7, 208, 209, 224, 249–52, 255, 262nn71–72, 263n81
9/11, 185, 194, 195, 200
Nine Talmudic Readings (Levinas; 1990), 141, 159
1984 (Orwell; 1948), 91
Ninth of Av (Tisha B'av), 36
Der Nister (Pinkhas Kohanovitch), 120–25, 129–30, 133, 135
Nobel Prizes, 247, 249, 306
Nomberg-Przytyk, Sara, 30
nontraditional 21st-century students, teaching the Holocaust to, 13, 241–56
  definition of nontraditional learners, 244
  distance, modeling, 244, 247–53, 255–56
  empathy, modeling, 244–49, 254–55, 261n59

Holocaust denial and, 249, 253–54
memorialization of and
desensitization to Holocaust
in American culture, 241–44,
253–56
North American Levinas Society
(NALS), 141–42, 160–61n6,
161n9
Notes from Underground (Dostoevsky;
1864), 311
Novick, Peter, 208, 220n4, 241–42,
255
number tattoos of camp survivors,
110–11, 195–96, 209–10, 235,
236, 237
Number the Stars (Lowry; 1989), 209
Numbers 15:37-41, 117n2
Nuremberg Laws (1935), 29
Nuremberg rally, 94–95
Nuremberg trials, 33–34
Nussbaum, Martha, 158

Olsen, Tillie, 3
Omer-Sherman, Ranen, 66n8
ontology of story, midrashic,
rediscovering, 140, 144, 146–48,
160
Orringer, Julie, 2
Orwell, George, 91
Osborne, Monica, 10–11, 140, 142,
151, 152, 160n6, 167, 324–25
Ostriker, Alicia Suskin, 168–69
Otherwise Than Being (Levinas;
1981), 141, 144, 151
Out of Chaos (ed. Fox; 2013), 48, 50,
52, 60–65
Ozick, Cynthia, 7, 22–23, 26, 30, 34,
35, 186–87, 189, 191, 193, 286

Pagis, Dan, 83n9
The Painted Bird (Kosinski; 1965),
136–37

Palestinian-Israeli conflict, 154,
216–18
Paley, Grace, 3
Palmer, Parker J., 278
paper clips project, Whitwell,
Tennessee, 248
Paradiso-Michau, Michael, 160n6
parallel worlds, AH due to, 88–89
PaRDeS, 149, 153, 154–57
Patrimony (Roth; 1991), 92
The Pawnbroker (film), 171, 173
The Pawnbroker (Wallant, novel;
1961), 3, 171, 209
performance, as pedagogical tool for
Jewish-American literature, 280n9
peshat, 154–56
phenomenology
of the face, 153–54, 155
midrashic approach to, 140,
142–48
prison, teaching midrash and
phenomenology in, 157–59
of sociality, 140, 143–44, 148, 152,
154–57
The Pianist (film), 208, 209
Pick, Hannah, 221n12
Piercy, Marge, 103, 108–9, 168, 180
Pinhas-Cohen, Hava, 103, 111–13,
118n20
Pinsker, Sanford, 184, 186, 193,
201n13
Pisar, Samuel, 39
Pius XII (pope), 25
Plath, Sylvia, 245–46
Plato, 147, 148, 159, 207
The Plot Against America (Roth;
2004), 9, 86, 88, 91, 92–96,
97–100
Plutzik, Hyam, 16
Plutzik, Jonathan, 16
"The Polish Boxer" (Halfon; 2012),
227, 228, 229, 235–38

Political Theory (periodical), 141
Portnoy's Complaint (Roth; 1969), 212, 243
postmodernism, 89, 90, 270, 277
Potok, Chaim, 14, 268, 270, 277–78, 279
Pound, Ezra, 51
Pozorski, Aimee, 11–12, 13, 183, 325
Prager, Brad, 70, 72, 74–75
pre-natal schooling, midrash on, in Horn's *The World to Come*, 120, 122, 123–25, 127–33
prison, teaching midrash and phenomenology in, 157–59
Promised Land (Antin; 1912), 270–73
prosthetic memory, 243
"P.'s Correspondence" (Hawthorne; 1845), 87–88
psychological thought, Bellow's engagement with, 312, 313–14
The Public Burning (Coover; 1977), 89
Pynchon, Thomas, 89

Quantum Leap (TV show), 87
"The Quiet American, or How to Be a Good Guest" (Dreifus; 2011), 228, 232–34, 237

Raba (in tractate *Shabbath*), 174
racial/blood purity, Nazi concern with, 27–29
racism in America, 154, 219, 248, 256, 276, 287, 291, 310
Radical Evil and the Scarcity of Hope: Postsecular Meditations (Matuštík; 2008), 161n14
Rank, Otto, 311
Raphael, Chester, 313
recursive AH, 89
Reich, Tova, 244
Reich, Walter, 253

Reichian analysis, 313
"A Religion for Adults" (Levinas; 1990), 151
remez, 154–57, 158
Renouvier, Charles, 88
Replay (Grimwood; 1986), 89
responsibility (for resisting evil). *See* human responsibility
Rider, N. Ann, 13, 241, 325
Riefenstahl, Leni, 95
The Ringers in the Tower: Studies in Romantic Tradition (Bloom; 1971), 276
The Rise and Fall of the Third Reich (Shirer; 1960), 30
The Rise of David Levinsky (Cahan; 1917), 270–73
Rittner, Carol Ann, 221n12
Roosevelt, Franklin Delano (FDR), 93, 96, 99, 257n8
"Rosa" (Ozick; 1983), 22–23
Rosenbaum, Thane, 16–17
Rosenberg case, 89
Rosenfeld, Alvin, 187, 228, 286
Rosenfeld, Gavriel, 87, 90, 249
Roth, Henry, 273
Roth, Philip
  alternate Jewish histories of, 9, 11–12, 85–86, 87, 88, 90–96, 97–100
  American Pastoral (1998), 91–92, 99
  on Anne Frank, figuration, and the ethical imperative, 11–12, 184, 185, 186, 188, 189–93
  "Conversion of the Jews" (1959), 229
  The Counterlife (1986), 87, 91, 95
  The Dying Animal (2001), 276–77
  Englander compared, 193–94
  The Ghost Writer (1979), 11–12, 91, 184, 185, 186, 188, 189–93, 197, 199, 212

as Holocaust novelist, 190
The Human Stain (2000), 92, 95, 100
I Married a Communist (1998), 95
Patrimony (1991), 92
The Plot Against America (2004), 9, 86, 88, 91, 92–96, 97–100
Portnoy's Complaint (1969), 212, 243
as second-generation Jewish American writer, 3, 273–77
Spanish context, taught in, 14, 268, 270, 273, 276–77, 279
Rothberg, Michael, 201n13, 211, 250
Rovner, Adam, 231–32
Royal, Derek Parker, 229
Rubenstein, Richard Lowell, 293–97
Rumkowski, Chaim, 34
Run Lola Run (film), 87
Russell and Volkening Agency, 305, 307

"Sailing to Byzantium" (Yeats; 1928), 276–77
Salanter, Israel, 150
Sánchez Canales, Gustavo, 14, 267, 325–26
Sandler, Jeffrey, 185–86
Sanhedrin (tractate), 134, 138n7
Sapir, Edward, 314
Sartre, Jean-Paul, 274
Saul Bellow: A Biography of the Imagination (Miller; 1991), 301, 302–3, 308, 311
Saul Bellow: Drumlin Woodchuck (Harris; 1980), 301, 308
Saul Bellow: Letters (ed. Taylor; 2010), 303
Saul Bellow's Heart (Gregory Bellow; 2013), 301–4, 307–9, 311
Sayers, Valerie, 90
Sayles, John, 138n4
Schaneman, Judith Clark, 262n71

Scheiber, Ava Kadishson, 48, 52–60, 62, 65
Schindler, Oskar, 246
Schindler's List (film), 208, 220n3, 243, 246–47
second Intifada, 110
second-generation Holocaust survivors, 69
second-generation Jewish-American writers, 273–77
Seinfeld (TV show), 243
Seize the Day (Bellow), 308, 315
Sekiewicz, Mieczyslaw, 31
self-psychology, 313–14
Selver-Urbach, Sara, 37
September 11, 2001, 185, 194, 195, 200
Serling, Rod, 246
"72 Years On: The Fictional Afterlife of Anne Frank" (Jacobs; 2016), 183, 184
sexual menace of Jews, Nazi concerns about, 28–29
Shabbath (tractate), 174
Shandler, Jeffrey, 246
"The Shawl" (Ozick, short story; 1980), 7, 22–24, 26, 27, 30, 34, 35, 36
The Shawl (Ozick, novella; 1989), 22–23, 171–72
Shelley, Mary, 304
Shelley, Percy Bysshe, 275, 276, 303, 304
"The Shelter" (Fink; 1983), 199
Shema, 9–10, 103–16
American Jewish poets and, 108–9
ASL (American sign language) and, 105–7, 112
biblical sources, 112, 117n2
defined, 103
gender issues and, 104, 114–15, 116n1

Shema (continued)
  as haiku, 105
  Israeli poetry and, 109–13, 118n20
  Levi's "Shema" (1958), 82–83n8, 113–15
  translating, 104–5
  Ve'ahavta, 106, 108, 109
  world literature, Jewish literature as, 9–10, 115–16
Shils, Edward, 305
Shirer, William, 30
Shoah (documentary film), 220n3, 224–27, 229
Showalter, Elaine, 272, 273, 277–79
Shulamith, in Song of Songs, 23–24, 27
Sidewise Award, 86
sign language, American (ASL), and Shema, 105–7, 112
silence/loss/absence
  hidden child survivors and, 41, 47, 48, 50, 52, 60
  in Kubert's Yossel, April 19, 1943, 79–81, 83n9
  midrash and, 150–52, 171–73, 175, 177, 179
  Shema and, 111, 112
  in Styron's Sophie's Choice, 289, 291, 293
  teaching nontraditional students how to read, 241, 247–48
  in third-generation Holocaust fiction, 223–27, 229, 233, 235, 236, 238
  as trope in Holocaust literature, 7, 22, 31, 39, 83n9
Simmons, William, 141, 142, 162n9
Simon Wiesenthal Center, 242–43
Sin Against Blood (Dinter; 1919), 28, 42n22
Singer, I. B., 3, 16
Slaughterhouse-Five (Vonnegut; 1969), 89

Sliders (TV show), 87
Sliding Doors (film), 87
Slipchenko, Lidia Maximovna, 32
"Smoke of Jewish Children" (Sutzkever; 1957), 33
Smolar, Hersh, 32
social anthropology, Bellow's education in, 312, 314–16
social justice and midrash, 10, 139–60
  from consciousness of seeing to consciousness turned hearing, 140, 145–46, 148, 152, 160
  intentionality to inspiration, moving from, 144–45, 148
  Levinas and, 140, 141–46, 148–57, 159
  ontology of story, rediscovering, 140, 144, 146–48, 160
  pedagogical foundations of, 159–60
  political writings of Levinas, encountering midrash through, 141–42
  prison, teaching midrash and phenomenology in, 157–59
  relation of the ethical and the political in Levinas's thought, 153–54
  sociality and midrash, 149–57
  translating midrash and postsecular phenomenology, 140, 142–48
sociality
  midrash and, 149–57
  phenomenology of, 140, 143–44, 148, 152, 154–57
sod, 154, 156–57
Sokoloff, Naomi, 9–10, 103, 326
Sollors, Werner, 215–16
Sonderkommandos, 39, 75–76
"Sonnet: England in 1819" (Shelley; 1839), 276
Sophie's Choice (film), 208, 246

Sophie's Choice (Styron, novel; 1979), 14, 285–97
  anti-Semitism in, 285, 289, 292, 294, 298nn11–12
  critical reception of, 285–86, 297, 298n12
  expendability, concept of, 295–96
  Holocaust, Stingo's efforts to learn about, 289, 292–93
  indirect, nonchronological telling of Sophie's story in, 287–89
  Judaism, Stingo's [mis]understanding of, 289–92
  Polish Catholicism of main character and universalizing view of evil in, 286–87, 298n8
  Rubenstein's *The Cunning of History* and, 293–97
  Southern Gothic tradition and, 298n9
The Sot Weed Factor (Barth; 1960), 89
Soundless Roar (Scheiber; 2002), 48, 50, 52–60, 54 (illus.), 62
Southern Gothic tradition in Styron's *Sophie's Choice*, 298n9
Spanish context, teaching Jewish American literature in, 14, 267–79
  attitudinal competence, fostering, 270, 272, 280n9
  core-to-core culture confrontation in teaching Potok, 277–78
  immigrant experience and first-generation narratives of Antin and Cahan, 270–73, 275
  reading competence skills and, 267–70
  student-centered learning, fostering, 278–79
  WWII and alienation through second-generation writers Bellow, Malamud, Roth, and Mailer, 273–77

Spiegelman, Art, 69
Spielberg, Steven, 220n3, 246, 247
Squire, John, 89
Stalin, Joseph, 53, 135, 312
Staples, Greg, 307
Steiner, George, 292–93
Sterling, Bruce, 90
Stern, Gerald, 245
Still Alive (Klüger; 2001), 244
Stoicea, Gabriela, 225
"Stories and Totalitarianism" (Havel; 1992), 139
Straus, Judith Levy, 63–65
Strawczynski, Oskar, 32
Streicher, Julius, 28–29
Strukova, Alexandra, 186
"Study for *Over Vitebsk*" (Chagall), in Horn's *World to Come*, 119–25, 129, 133, 135–36
Styron, William, 89. *See also* specific entries at *Sophie's Choice*
Sujo, Glenn, 53
Sundquist, Eric J., 7–8, 21, 326
Survival in Auschwitz (*Se questo e un uomo*; Levi, 1958), 21, 82–83n8, 113, 208, 209, 224, 250
survivor guilt, 71
Sutzkever, Abraham, 24, 33–34
Swann, Bryan, 114
Szmaglewska, Seweryna, 21

tattooed numbers (of camp survivors), 110–11, 195–96, 209–10, 235, 236, 237
Taylor, Benjamin, 303
Teaching Literature (Showalter; 2003), 272, 273, 277–79
Teaching Reading in Europe (Education, Audiovisual and Culture Executive Agency; 2011), 267–68, 269, 272
tefillin, 97, 107, 109, 111

"The Temptation of Temptation" (Levinas; 1990), 146, 152, 173–74
textual biography of Bellow, 304–5
A Theft (Bellow; 1989), 306, 314
"Then She Bore Pale Desire" (Blake; c. 1771), 276
Theresienstadt, 63
The Third Pillar: Essays in Judaic Studies (Hartman; 2011), 180n6
third-generation fiction, teaching the Holocaust through, 12–13, 223–38
  "An Animal to the Memory" (Bezmozgis; 2004), 228–32, 237, 238
  difficulties of contemporary teaching of Holocaust and, 223–29, 237–38
  "Lebensraum" (Dreifus; 2011), 228, 234–35
  "The Polish Boxer" (Halfon; 2012), 227, 228, 229, 235–38
  "The Quiet American, or How to Be a Good Guest" (Dreifus; 2011), 228, 232–34, 237
Third-Generation Holocaust Narratives: Memory in Memoir and Fiction (Aarons; 2016), 279
third-generation Holocaust survivors, 2, 11, 12–13, 69
Thirring, Hans, 149
This Must Be the Place (Winger; 2008), 195
Thomas, D. M., 208
tikkun olam, 140, 149
Time Cop (film/TV show), 87
time travel deviation and time-loop stories in AH, 88
The Tin Drum (film), 169
Tisha B'av (the Ninth of Av), 36
Tito, Josip Broz, 53

To the Golden Cities (Moore; 1996), 17
"Todesfuge" ("Deathfugue," Celan; 1948), 7, 23–27, 34, 36
Torday, Daniel, 245
Totality and Infinity: An Essay on Interiority (Levinas; 1969), 141, 146
Totten, Samuel, 262n72
"The Transcendence of Words" (Levinas; 1989), 145
transhistorical textual community, 118n21
"The Transit Camp" (Straus), 63–65
transnationalism of Jewish American and Holocaust literatures, 2, 4–5, 9–10, 13–14
Trauma: Explorations in Memory (ed. Caruth, 1995), 189
trauma studies/literature of trauma, 167, 171–74, 211
Treblinka, 30, 231
Trepannier, Lee, 312
Triumph of the Will (documentary film), 95
Trump, Donald, 96, 194
Turtledove, Harry, 90
Twain, Mark, 88
Twilight Zone (TV show), 246

Uchronie (Renouvier; 1857), 88
UCM (Universidad Complutense de Madrid), Jewish-American literature courses at, 268, 270, 275
Unclaimed Experience (Caruth; 1996), 189
uniqueness argument (for Holocaust), 211, 220n3, 221n7, 221n13, 223, 286, 293, 296–97
United Jewish Appeal, 215

universalizing view of evil, in Styron's *Sophie's Choice*, 286–87, 298n8
Universidad Complutense de Madrid (UCM), Jewish-American literature courses at, 268, 270, 275
USC Shoah IWitness collection, 242
"Useless Suffering" (Levinas), 179
ut pictura poesis, 136

Ve'ahavta, 106, 108, 109
Verdun, Battle of (WWI), 295–96
The Victim (Bellow; 1947), 82n6, 274–75, 308, 310, 311
Vietnam War, 120, 123, 242
Vilna decree (1941), 33
Volkening, Henry, 305
Vonnegut, Kurt, 89

Walden, Dan, 15
Wallant, Edward Lewis, 3, 171
Warsaw Ghetto, 38, 39
Warsaw Ghetto Uprising (1943), 30, 38, 231. See also *Yossel, April 19, 1943*
Washington Square (James; 1880), 53
Wasserman, Harriet, 301, 302, 305–7, 308
Watergate, 242
Weber, Max, 294
Weinstein, Ann, 301, 302, 308
Weissman, Gary, 250
Wells, H. G., 88
Westerbork Transit Camp, Netherlands, 63, 192
"What We Talk About When We Talk About Anne Frank" (Englander; 2011)
  "Anne Frank game" in, 188–89, 197–99, 206, 218–19
  Carver's influence on, 194, 205–7, 217
  figuration of Anne Frank and the ethical imperative in, 11–12, 184, 185, 188–91, 193–200
  on Israel, 216–18
  Jewish-American identity and, 205–7, 211–18, 222n17
  as 9/11 story, 185, 194, 195, 200
  Roth compared, 193–94, 212
  on secularism/Hasidism/Orthodoxy, 193, 207, 213–14, 218, 222n17
  talking about the Holocaust in, 195–97, 207–12
"What We Talk About When We Talk About Love" (Carver; 1981), 194, 205–7
"A Wheel of Evil Come Full Circle" (Styron; 1997), 286
"When You're Excused, You're Excused" (Friedman; 2001), 222n21
Where Shall Wisdom Be Found? (Bloom; 2004), 269, 278
White, Hayden, 89
The White Hotel (D. M. Thomas; 1981), 208
Whitwell, Tennessee paper clips project, 248
"Who Owns Anne Frank?" (Ozick; 1997), 186–87, 189, 191, 193
Wiesel, Elie
  on burning of children at Auschwitz, 30
  Night (1958), 13, 30, 82n7, 208, 209, 224, 249–52, 255, 262nn71–72, 263n81
  nontraditional students, teaching Holocaust literature to, 247–52, 263n78
  Styron consulting, 293

Wiesel, Elie *(continued)*
    third-generation Holocaust literature, teaching with, 224, 229
Wilhaus, Gustav and Heike, 32–33
The Williamsburg Trilogy (Fuchs; 1934/1936/1937), 97
Winchell, Walter, 95
Winer, Szalma, 26
Winger, Anna, 195
The Winter Vault (Michaels; 2009), 180n4
Wirth-Nesher, Hana, 66n19
Wisse, Ruth, 309
Wolf, Stacy, 280n9
Wolff-Zdzienicki, Kazimierz, 40
Wood, James, 310
Woolf, Virginia, 51
world literature, Jewish literature as, 9–10, 115–16
The World to Come (Horn; 2006), 10, 119–37
    Chagall's stolen painting in, 119–25, 129, 133, 135–36
    collapsing of world to come with pre-natal world, 122, 132–33, 134–35
    final chapter of, 123–25
    plot[s] of, 119–22
    pre-natal schooling, midrash on, 120, 122, 123–25, 127–33, 135
    preparation for final chapter, 125–27
    "world to come" in, 10, 122, 124, 126, 127, 132–37
World War I, 51, 57, 241, 295–96
"Written in Pencil in the Sealed Railway Car" (Pagis; 1970), 83n9

Wylie, Andrew, 303, 305, 306, 307, 309

Yeats, William Butler, 275, 276–77
Yezierska, Anzia, 3, 273
Yiddish language and culture, 3, 62, 65, 66n19, 97–99, 135, 270–71, 310
The Yiddish Policemen's Union (Chabon; 2007), 9, 86, 88, 96–100
Yom Kippur War, 217
Yossel, April 19, 1943 (Kubert, 2003), 8–9, 69–81
    anticipation of protagonist's death in, 79–80
    artist's perspective in, 73–79
    camps, secondhand witnessing of, 75–77
    narrative and counternarrative in, 69–73
    silence, final blackened page representing, 80–81
    superheroes in, 79, 80
    Warsaw Rebellion, depiction of, 78–80
"Yossel Rakovers Vendung Tsu G-ot" ("Yossel Rakover's Appeal to God;" Kolitz, 1946), 81–82n4
"You are Loneliness" (Pinhas-Cohen; 2003), 111–13
Young, James, 249

zachor, 17
Zeitz subcamp, Buchenwald, 252
Zelizer, Barbie, 56
Zelkowicz, Josef, 34–35
Zemel, Carol, 50, 51

www.ingramcontent.com/pod-product-compliance
Lightning Source LLC
Chambersburg PA
CBHW030127240426
43672CB00005B/47